Psychology Revival

Personality Structure and Measurement

Originally published in 1969, this book deals extensively with the description and measurement of personality.

Beginning with a statement of the principles of typological research in psychology, set against the background of general taxonomic principles in biology, the study discusses in detail results and generalisations from the Eysencks' previous work. The second part of the book describes several large-scale studies using personality questionnaires prepared by the authors, as well as the standard ones of Cattell and Guilford. There is a comparative study of the Eysenck, Cattell and Guilford inventories, which analyses the degree to which similar factors can be found in these three instruments and discusses areas of agreement and disagreement between the three authors. The third part deals with personality studies in children, and includes a chapter on personality structure in subnormal subjects. These studies are concerned with discovering the extent to which personality structure changes with increasing age, and to what extent it is possible to measure personality in younger children. They also examine sex differences in personality structure, and show quite marked differences between the sexes on a number of primary personality traits.

The results of the Eysencks' work in this field directed new light on the structure of personality and cast doubt on many widely accepted findings of the time.

Personality Structure and Measurement

Hans J. Eysenck and Sybil B.G. Eysenck

With the help of
A. Hendrickson, S. Rachman,
P.O. White, M.I. Soueif

Routledge
Taylor & Francis Group
LONDON AND NEW YORK

First published in 1969
by Routledge & Kegan Paul Ltd

This edition first published in 2013 by Routledge
27 Church Road, Hove, BN3 2FA

Simultaneously published in the USA and Canada
by Routledge
711 Third Avenue, New York, NY 10017

Routledge is an imprint of the Taylor & Francis Group, an informa business

Publisher's Note
The publisher has gone to great lengths to ensure the quality of this reprint but points out that some imperfections in the original copies may be apparent.

Disclaimer
The publisher has made every effort to trace copyright holders and welcomes correspondence from those they have been unable to contact.

A Library of Congress record exists under ISBN: 0710060483

ISBN: 978-0-415-84087-3 (hbk)
ISBN: 978-0-203-76680-4 (ebk)
ISBN: 978-0-415-84091-0 (pbk)

Personality Structure and Measurement

HANS J. EYSENCK

SYBIL B. G. EYSENCK

With the help of

A. HENDRICKSON S. RACHMAN

P. O. WHITE M. I. SOUEIF

ROUTLEDGE & KEGAN PAUL

LONDON AND HENLEY

First published 1969
by Routledge & Kegan Paul Limited
39 Store Street
London, WC1E 7DD and
Broadway House, Newtown Road
Henley-on-Thames
Oxon. RG9 1EN
Reprinted 1970
First published as a paperback 1977
Printed in Great Britain by
Western Printing Services Ltd, Bristol

ISBN 0 7100 6048 3 (c)
ISBN 0 7100 8661 X (p)

There is, of course, no logical way leading to the establishment of a theory, but only groping, constructive attempts controlled by careful considerations of factual knowledge.

A. EINSTEIN

To the Memory of Charles Spearman, F.R.S.,
who led the way

CONTENTS

EDITORS' INTRODUCTION

THIS book is intended to be complementary to *The Biological Basis of Personality* (Eysenck, 1967), which was written about the same time; the present volume deals extensively with the description and measurement of personality (as the title might have led the reader to anticipate), while the other one deals with the understanding and explanation of personality, along psychological and physiological lines. Description precedes explanation; were it not for the studies outlined in this book the other could not have been written. However, description without explanation suffers from excessive subjectivity; often, a choice has to be made between different equally acceptable systems of description, and the existence of an explanatory framework may be of considerable use in deciding between one approach and another. It is this mutual reliance of the facts and theories of the one book, and the results and methods of the other, which is intended by the term 'complementary'; each confirms and strengthens the other. It is this agreement between two rather different lines of work which suggests, more than anything else, that possibly we may be on the right track in our experiments and theories. Accidental agreements seldom show such long-lasting consistency of findings!

In essence, this book owes its being to two quite independent events. One of these is the availability of high-speed electronic computers; it is only in recent years that our Department has been in the position to plan the large-scale type of statistical analysis required for the purposes of this book. The other event was the arrival in the Department of two experts in statistics and computer programming, O. White and A. Hendrickson, who were capable of translating the needs of the psychologist into acceptable software. Most of this book is a memorial to their ability, zeal and determination; only those familiar at first hand with the distressing series of neurotic breakdowns suffered by the University of London's ATLAS computer will be able to realize the relevance of the third and last of these terms! We owe much to I.B.M. who allowed us to use their equipment for much reduced fees, and who made several allowance grants to students and staff members for free use of their installation; without this help, freely given, we would not have been able to carry out our programme.

Computers, as well as solving perennial problems, create others, and in one way this book may be regarded as a pioneering venture. Never hitherto have large multifactorial inventories and questionnaires been subjected to factor analysis item by item, and never has this been done to several inventories simultaneously. We have tried to investigate in considerable detail the relations between the systems of Cattell, Guilford and Eysenck, analysing the obtained relations between items and proceeding to primary and then higher order factors; this led to results in such quantity that when it came to writing up the account we were literally submerged under reams, bushels and bales of computer output. The task of sorting all this out, selecting the important and relevant parts, and preparing a manuscript which could pass for a book in the conventional sense took an incredible amount of time—not perhaps as much as had been saved by the use of the computer in the first place, but very nearly as much! At the back of our minds was the constant battle between the needs of the statistical expert, who needs so much detailed information that no possible selection can satisfy him, and the ordinary reader, who only wishes to see the results which have direct psychological significance. We have tried to compromise, as far as possible, and to produce a book which is capable of being read, and possibly even enjoyed, along the usual lines, without leaving the statistician frustrated and annoyed beyond all endurance; we are sure to have failed in this, but if so it has not been for lack of trying! Ultimately, our criterion has been that of psychological importance; those results which in our view contributed to psychological theory, or were relevant to theoretical discussions, were given in sufficient detail to justify our statements regarding the outcome, while intermediate stages of interest only in the most technical sense have been left out, or only mentioned cursorily.

We believe that our results are of importance both substantively and also from the point of view of psychometric theory and practice; naturally we have emphasized the former rather than the latter, and we hope that even the reader without expert knowledge of factor analysis will obtain a clear picture of our findings, even though he may have to take certain points on trust. We do not think that anything that so requires to be taken on trust is likely to be disputed by statisticians; a few points which are relatively novel, or little documented in the literature, are treated in a technical appendix.[1] The factors extracted from our various samples of men, women and children speak for themselves; if they were unable to do so no amount of interpretation would really be sufficient to convince the critical reader! In that sense the judgment of even the non-expert on psychometric minutiae is not likely to be wrong;

[1] We are indebted to H. F. Kaiser, S. Hunka and J. Bianchini for permission to print as an Appendix their unpublished paper 'Relating factors between studies based upon different individuals;' the methods suggested there played an important part in our analyses.

fortunately the answers to most of our questions were remarkably clear-cut, and do not depend on technical know-how or statistical leger-de-main.

Two main facts emerge with considerable clarity from all our analyses. The first is that the Cattell and Guilford primary factors are difficult or impossible to replicate, and are for the most part not invariant from one sex to the other; the Eysenck primary factors show the same tendency, but not to the same extent. The primary factors from one author are not very similar to those of the others. The second fact that emerges is that two higher-order factors, extraversion/introversion and neuroticism/stability, emerge from all three authors in almost identical form; they are invariant under change of sex and age. The conclusion drawn from these findings is that neither for research nor for practical application can we at the moment use the existing primary factor inventories, but that we are reasonably safe with the higher order factors E and N. This conclusion is perhaps not unexpected, but the decisive way in which the data supported both the lack of invariance of the primary factors and the remarkable invariance of the higher order factors was a welcome confirmation of theories previously advocated only with much hesitation (Eysenck, 1960e).

If the data from this book are taken together with the theories and findings of *The Biological Basis of Personality*, we may perhaps claim that at long last we have the beginnings of a proper taxonomy of human personality, as well as a link between this taxonomy and general psychological theory. Much further work will no doubt be required to put this view to the test, but the outlook is not discouraging.

H. J. EYSENCK
SYBIL B. G. EYSENCK

Institute of Psychiatry
(Maudsley Hospital)
University of London

PART ONE

Nature and History of Human Typology

By H. J. Eysenck

I

CLASSIFICATION IN SCIENCE

CLASSIFICATION is one of the classic methods of science and is fundamental in all fields of study. This is equally true in biology as in physics. Systems of classification are always at first simple, governed by common-sense appearances, and far removed from the complexities of later developments. Thus Thales, the first of the Greek philosophers to think about the constitution of the world and its elements, held the theory that everything was originally water, from which earth, air and living things were later separated out. Later on Anaximander and Anaximenes modified this hypothesis to include earth, air and fire as well as water as the main elements. These of course were mere pre-scientific guesses of little value in the actual development of chemistry and physics, but at least they served to pose a problem.

More fruitful was an approach which appears to have originated with the Chinese. In chemistry we are dealing with a fundamental duality which is exemplified by metals and non-metals; this we now know to be due to a shortage or excess of electrons. As Bernal (1957) has pointed out: 'There is evidence for tracing the first appreciation of this duality to the Chinese, who already in pre-historic times used red cinnabar as a magic substitute for life blood and had resolved it into its elements, sulphur and mercury. From these notions the Taoist sect developed a system of alchemy from which it is probable that first Indian and then Arabic alchemy was derived.' To these two opposites of sulphur and mercury a third element was added by Philipus Aureolus Theophrastus Bombastus von Hohenheim, who called himself Paracelsus to show his superiority to Celsus, the great doctor of antiquity. By adding the neutral *salt* he established the so-called *tria prima* as a foundation of his 'spagyric' art of chemistry.

Curious as these ancient methods of classification seem to us yet there is good modern justification for this spagyric system of mercury, sulphur and salt. We have here a reasonable prevision of three of the four sub-fields into which the general field of chemistry is now subdivided: that of the rare gases, where all electrons remain attached to atoms; that of metals, where there is an excess of electrons; that of nonmetals, where there is a lack of electrons; and that of salts, where exchanges have taken place between the metal and the nonmetal ions. Even the analogy from external appearance on which the spagyric art was originally based has now found an explanation in terms of quantum theory.

There are certain important lessons to be learned from this brief excursion into ancient chemical history. One of them is that progress in classification is ultimately dependent on, and in turn central to, general development of the science of which it forms a part. Another important idea is this. The principles of classification based on analogies from external appearance may incorporate very important insights without which the development of a science would be very much slower, although of course it is not suggested that we should rest content with arguments from external appearances. When we turn to the study of classification in the biological sciences we will encounter this point again.

The notion of classification always implies an idea about that which is being classified. Thus in chemistry it implies the very important notion of an element. Boyle gave the first precise definition: 'No body is a true principle or element . . . which is not perfectly homogeneous but is further resolvable into any number of distinct substances how small so ever.' This insight into the nature of elements unfortunately was unable to furnish him with techniques which could decide in any but a few cases whether a given substance was or was not an element; Boyle's criterion remained inapplicable for another hundred years. Finally of course Boyle's definition and the work of the next few centuries resulted in that great monument of classification, Mendeleev's periodic table of the elements, in 1869. This appeared a final step in classification for a time, but then came the discovery that the atom was not after all indivisible, and since then we have had a whole shower of long lived elementary particles and anti-particles, as well as resonances, isobars, and excited states—so much so that few except professional physicists can find their way about among the fermions and bosons, the leptons, baryons and mesons, the nucleons and hyperons and the neutrinos, neutrettos, muons, lambdas, sigmas, pions, kaons, and so on and so forth. Obviously another classification was required, and now that we have the theory of *unitary symmetry* known as SU(3) we have gone some way towards achieving a more satisfactory state, particularly since the discovery of the omego-minus particle has seemed to verify the principles on which the theory of unitary symmetry was based. Modern as all these recent advances may seem, many of them had been foreseen already by Newton, who had evolved a theory of the atom composed of shell within shell of parts held together successively more firmly. All these anticipations of future developments by Boyle and Newton were of little use in the development of chemistry because, as Bernal points out: 'In the seventeenth century chemistry was not yet in a state in which the corpuscular analysis could be applied. For that it needed the steady accumulation of new experimental facts that was to come in the next century. Chemistry, unlike physics, demands a multiplicity of experience and does not contain self-evident principles. Without principles it must remain an 'occult' science depending on real but inexplicable mysteries.'

This is an important limitation which applies to psychology just as much as it did to chemistry. The cry is often heard for a Newton to rescue us from the avalanche of facts, and to remedy the lack of self-evident principles in psychology. Yet even Newton, who worked at chemistry for much longer than at physics, did not in fact succeed in advancing that science to any particular degree. Both in the matter of classification and that of the creation of a genuine science of psychology we simply have to live within our means, and realize the bounds set by the nature of the material to the development of the laws we all would like to see develop.

2

PRINCIPLES OF NUMERICAL TAXONOMY

PSYCHOLOGISTS who work in the field of classification, whether that of normal or abnormal personality, seldom concern themselves with the history of classification in physics and chemistry. This may be explained in terms of the obvious differences between animate and inanimate matter. However, they also very rarely seem to show any interest in the history of biological classification or *taxonomy*, and this is rather more difficult to understand because most of the problems which occur in psychology have also been dealt with by biologists and botanists at various stages, and a knowledge of their experiences may be of considerable use in dealing with our own problems.

This is not to say that biological taxonomy has been an unqualified success, or has failed to develop problems of its own. Consider the following quotation from Singer (1959): 'We would stress the fact that, from the time of Linnaeus to our own, a weak point in biological science has been the absence of any quantitative meaning in our classificatory terms. What is a class, and does class A differ from class B as much as class C differs from class D? The question can be put for the other classificatory grades, such as order, family, genus and species. In no case can it be answered fully, and in most cases it cannot be answered at all . . . until some adequate reply can be given to such questions as these, our classificatory schemes can never be satisfactory or "natural". There can be little better than mnemonics—mere skeletons or frames on which we hang somewhat disconnected fragments of knowledge. Evolutionary doctrine, which has been at the back of all classificatory systems of the last century, has provided no real answer to these difficulties. Geology has given a fragmentary answer here and there. But to sketch the manner in which the various groups of living things arose is a very different thing from ascribing any quantitative value to those groups.'

Similarly, Sokal and Sneath (1963) in their classic book on *Principles of Numerical Taxonomy* have this to say: 'It is widely acknowledged that the science of taxonomy is one of the most neglected disciplines in biology. Although new developments are continually being made in techniques for studying living creatures, in finding new characters, in describing new organisms, and in revising the systematics of previously known organisms, little work has been directed towards the conceptual basis of classification—that is, taxonomy in the restricted sense of the theory of classification. Indeed, the taxonomy of today is but little advanced from that of a hundred, or even two hundred, years ago. Biologists have amassed a wealth of material, both of museum specimens and of new taxonomic characters, but they have had little success in improving their power of digesting this material. The practice of taxonomy has remained intuitive and commonly inarticulate, an art rather than a science.'

Sokal and Sneath give the following definition of classification: 'Classification is the ordering of organisms into groups (or sets) on the basis of their relationships, that is, of their associations by continuity, similarity, or both.' They go on to point out that there may be confusion over the term 'relationship'. As they say, 'This may imply relationship by ancestry, or it may simply indicate the overall similarity as judged by the characters of the organisms without any implication as to their relationship by ancestry.' The second of these meanings is the one which they prefer, and they give it the special name of 'phenetic relationship', using this term to indicate that relationship is judged from the phenotype of the organism and not from its phylogeny. In psychology too there is an important distinction corresponding to this, although the alternative to a phenetic relationship is not one based on ancestry but one based on genotypic consideration. We shall take up this point in some detail later on.

In setting up systems of classification we may follow one of two alternative routes which have been named by Sneath (1962) 'polythetic' and 'monothetic' (from *poly*: 'many', *mono*: 'one', *thetos*: 'arrangement'). As Sokal and Sneath point out: 'The ruling idea of monothetic groups is that they are formed by rigid and successive logical divisions so that the position of a unique set of features is both sufficient and necessary for membership in the group thus defined. They are called monothetic because the defining set of features is unique. Any monothetic system (such as that of Maccacaro, 1958, or in ecology that of Williams and Lambert, 1959) will always carry the risk of serious misclassification if we wish to make natural phenetic groups. This is because an organism which happens to be aberrant in the feature used to make the primary division will inevitably be removed to a category far from the required position, even if it is identical with its natural congeners in every other feature. The disadvantage of monothetic groups is that they do not yield "natural" taxa, except by lucky choice of the feature used for division. The advantage of monothetic groups is that keys and hierarchies are readily made.'

Sokal and Sneath go on to list the advantages of polythetic arrangements. Such arrangements, they say, 'place together organisms that have the greatest number of shared features, and no single feature is essential to group membership or is sufficient to make an organism a member of the group.' They credit Adamson (1727–1806) with the introduction of the polythetic type of system into biology. He rejected the *a priori* assumptions of the importance of different characters; he correctly realized that natural taxa are based on the concept of 'affinity'—which is measured by taking all characters into consideration—and that the taxa are separated from each other by means of correlated features.

The *analysis by phenetic relationship* which had become all but universal in biology received a set-back when *analysis by relation through ancestry* was reinstated after the publication of *The Origin of Species.* Suddenly Darwin's theory seemed to suggest the basis for the existence of natural systematic categories: their members were related because of descent from a common ancestor. Unfortunately, history has shown that this enthusiasm could only be short-lived; we cannot make use of phylogeny for classification since in the vast majority of cases phylogenies are unknown. Inviting as the argument from ancestry may appear, therefore, in its Darwinian guise, nevertheless it has to be rejected for reasons given in detail in books recently published by Hennig (1950), Remane (1956) and Simpson (1961), as well as in *Principles of Numerical Taxonomy* by Sokal and Sneath already quoted. The reasons for this rejection are very similar to those which in due course will cause us to reject principles of classification derived from Freudian psychoanalysis, and prefer those from a factor analytic approach. Freud's description of personality is in terms of anal, oral or other stage of infantile development; it presupposes knowledge which is not available, just as classification by phylogeny is inapplicable because of ignorance. (The same argument applies to Sheldon's derivation of body types from the three main germinal layers.) In both cases we are thrown back on our power of description and on such mathematical computations as we may find useful in giving quantitative assessments of similarities and differences between the observed characters.[1]

[1] An exciting recent development has led to the construction of phylogenetic trees by biochemists, who use quantitative estimates of variance between species as regards substances such as DNA and cytochrome *c*. Fitch and Margoliash (1967) have recently succeeded in constructing such a tree, based on data relating to the single gene that codes for cytochrome *c*, which was very similar to the 'classical' phylogenetic tree. The method is based essentially on the appropriate 'mutation distances' between two cytochromes, which is defined as the minimal number of component nucleotides that would need to be altered in order for the gene for one cytochrome to code for the other. This number is considered proportional to the

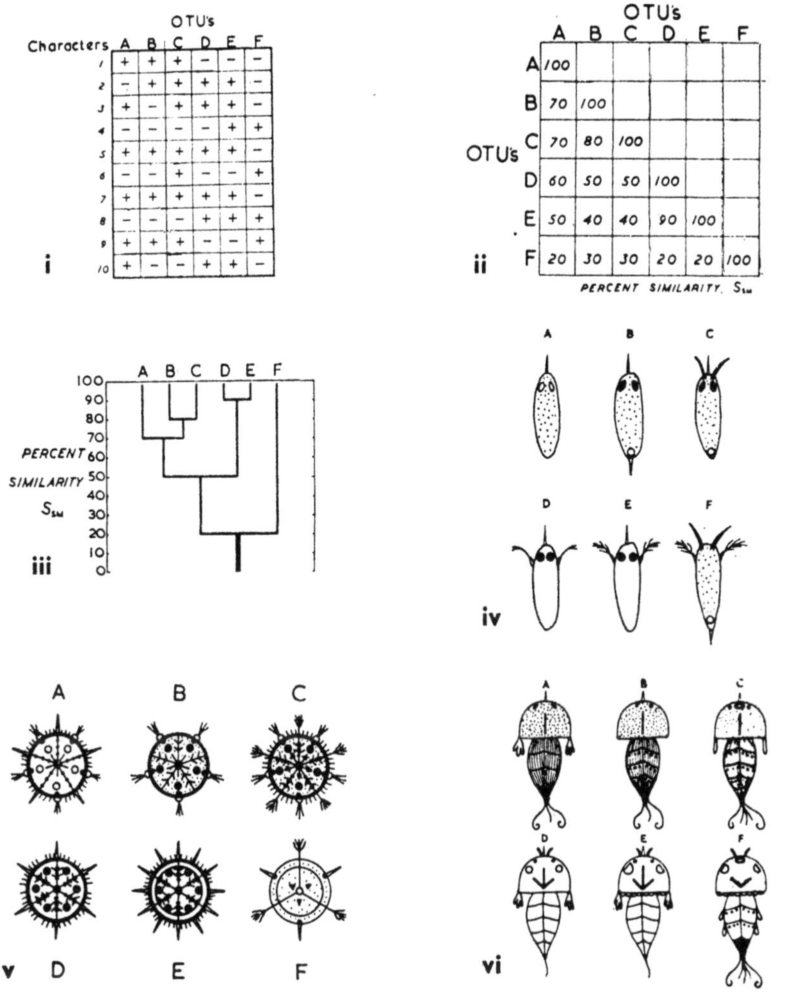

Characters	A	B	C	D	E	F
1	+	+	+	−	−	−
2	−	+	+	+	+	−
3	+	−	+	+	+	−
4	−	−	−	−	+	+
5	+	+	+	+	+	−
6	−	−	+	−	−	+
7	+	+	+	+	+	−
8	−	−	−	+	+	+
9	+	+	+	−	−	+
10	+	−	−	+	+	−

OTU's	A	B	C	D	E	F
A	100					
B	70	100				
C	70	80	100			
D	60	50	50	100		
E	50	40	40	90	100	
F	20	30	30	20	20	100

FIG. 2.1 An exercise in taxonomy using hypothetical organisms. (i) The character matrix used; (ii) the similarity matrix derived from (i) using simple matching coefficients. OTU stands for the operational taxonomic units; (iii) the dendrogram resulting from (ii); (iv) to (vi). Three different sets of 'artificial organisms' whose characters were allocated by scoring them as in (i), and whose overall similarities are consequently those shown in (ii) and (iii). The letters A to F identify the 'organisms' with the OTU's in (i) to (iii). In (iv) there are ten characters; in the other two there are twenty, but in the same proportions. Taken with permission from P. H. A. Sneath (1964).

How in fact does a biologist proceed? Sneath (1964) has set the procedures out according to the following four steps. (1) The organisms are chosen, and their characters are recorded in a table. (2) Each organism is compared with every other and their overall resemblance is estimated as indicated by all the characters. This yields a new table, a table of similarities. (3) The organisms are now sorted into groups on the basis of their mutual similarities. Like organisms are brought next to like, and separated from unlike, and these groups or *phenons* are taken to represent the 'natural' taxonomic groups whose relationships can be represented in numerical form. (4) The characters can now be re-examined to find those that are most constant within the groups that have emerged from the analysis. These can be used as diagnostic characters in keys for identifying specimens. Figure 2.1, taken from Sneath's article, shows this procedure. Hypothetical organisms are used, and the various steps involved are given in detail in the legend accompanying the figure.

Sokal and Sneath (1963) discuss in great detail the many theoretical problems that arise as well as the mathematical formulae useful in the estimation of taxonomic resemblances. Much of what they have to say is of great value and importance for psychology as well as for botany and zoology, although of course a number of problems are specific to each of these different sciences. However, we cannot in this book follow the general discussion of principles any further; having glanced at the methods, limitations and importance of classification and taxonomic principles in physics and biology we must next turn to the use which psychology has made of classificatory principles, particularly as expressed in the notion of typology.

---

number of mutations which have taken place in the descent from the apex of one cytochrome as compared with another. Thus it is claimed that this new method, which gives a quantitative measure of the event (mutation) which permits the evolution of new species, must give the most accurate of phylogenetic trees. In this way it may be possible to overcome the difficulties in the evolutionary method of classification by descent which we have noted above; it is reassuring that even when based only on a single gene the phylogenetic scheme is remarkably like that obtained by classical methods.

3

HISTORICAL DEVELOPMENT OF HUMAN TYPOLOGY

IF the task of classification in the physical sciences was the bringing of order into the various elements which make up inanimate matter, and if the task of taxonomy in the biological sciences was the bringing of order into the varied members of our flora and fauna, then the task of classification in psychology is surely that of bringing some order into the various activities practised by human beings. Already in the third century B.C. the Greek writer Theophrastus put the problem in his famous book *Characters* which he wrote in his ninety-ninth year: 'Why is it that while all Greece lies under the same sky and all the Greeks are educated alike, it has befallen us to have characters variously constituted?' He set himself the task of describing these various characters and he did so by taking a large number of traits and describing individuals in whom the particular trait had been developed to excess. Many writers since then have followed his example and a list of some of these is given in Roback's *Psychology of Character* (1931). Altogether the notion of describing behaviour in terms of certain hypothetical traits has been common to layman, literary artist and psychologist alike, and dictionaries abound with names of such traits which are used in everyday language.

Theophrastus does not in fact in his work answer the question he has put; he describes the variety of characters which can be observed in ancient Greece in terms of traits but he does not give us any theory as to why these characters should be so different. The causal or explanatory approach was also pioneered in Greece by Hippocrates, in his famous theory of the humours. As Roback makes clear, Hippocrates is concerned not so much with the description of personality but with the more scientific purpose of *explaining* differences in types. 'Hence the classification, to begin with, must be condensed and attached to some correlational scheme. In this way, Galen was able to assign a definite cause for each of the four outstanding types of individuals in the preponderance of so-called bodily humours. The sanguine person, always full of enthusiasm, was said to owe his temperament to the strength of the blood, the melancholic's sadness was supposed to be due to the overfunctioning of the black bile, the choleric irritability was attributed to the predominance of the yellow bile in the body, while the phlegmatic person's apparent slowness and apathy were traced to the influence of the phlegm.' Thus one approach leads to the description of a large number of traits; the other leads to an explanatory scheme for a small number of qualities on a physiological or biochemical basis.

These early ideas developed by Greek writers, thinkers and physicians already contain, if only in embryo, the three main notions which characterize modern work in personality In the first place, behaviour or conduct is to be described in terms of *traits* which characterize given individuals in varying degrees. In the second place, these traits cohere or correlate and define certain more fundamental and more all-embracing *types*. In the third place, these types are essentially based on *constitutional*, genetic or inborn factors, which are to be discovered in the physiological, neurological and biochemical structure of the individual. There is some evidence in Greek writings of the differentiation so important nowadays between *phenotype* and *genotype*, i.e. between behaviour as apparent in everyday life and conduct and the genetic basis for behaviour. This differentiation therefore leads to the important question of the degree to which environmental forces determine differences in personality and may thus affect the principles of classification derived essentially from phenotypic investigations. Admittedly all these points are embryonic and should not be stressed too much; there is always the danger that one tends to read into ancient documents modern ideas not properly contained in them. Nevertheless it can hardly be denied that all of these fundamental ideas are in fact contained in embryo in the early writings of the third and second centuries B.C.

There is no point here in tracing the history of the four temperaments throughout the medieval and Renaissance periods; we may perhaps take up their story in 1798 when Immanual Kant published his famous *Anthropologie*. Kant was not only Europe's foremost philosopher but also an accomplished scientist, and in this book he presents us with what is essentially a text-book of psychology. His chapter on temperament was widely read and accepted in Europe. His description of the four temperaments may therefore serve us as a kind of fundamental and basic theoretical position. This is how he describes the sanguine, melancholic, choleric and phlegmatic person.

'*The Sanguine Temperament*. The sanguine person is carefree and full of hope; attributes great importance to whatever he may be dealing with at the moment, but may have forgotten all about it the next. He means to keep his promises but fails to do so because he never considered deeply enough beforehand whether he would be able to keep them. He is good-natured enough to help others, but is a bad debtor and constantly asks for time to pay. He is very sociable, given to pranks, contented, doesn't take anything very seriously and has many, many friends. He is not vicious, but difficult to convert from his sins; he may repent, but this contrition (which never becomes a feeling of guilt) is soon forgotten. He is easily fatigued and bored by work, but is constantly engaged in mere games—these carry with them constant change, and persistence is not his forte.

The Melancholic Temperament. People tending towards melancholia attribute great importance to everything that concerns them. They discover everywhere cause for anxiety, and notice first of all the difficulties in a situation, in contradistinction to the sanguine person. They do not make promises easily, because they insist on keeping their word, and have to consider whether they will be able to do so. All this is so not because of moral considerations, but because interaction with others makes them worried, suspicious and thoughtful; it is for this reason that happiness escapes them.

The Choleric Temperament. He is said to be hot-headed, is quickly roused, but easily calmed down if his opponent gives in; he is annoyed without lasting hatred. Activity is quick, but not persistent. He is busy, but does not like to be in business, precisely because he is not persistent; he prefers to give orders, but does not want to be bothered with carrying them out. He loves open recognition, and wants to be publicly praised. He loves appearances, pomp and formality; he is full of pride and self-love. He is miserly; polite, but with ceremony; he suffers most through the refusal of others to fall in with his pretensions. In one word, the choleric temperament is the least happy, because it is most likely to call forth opposition to itself.

The Phlegmatic Temperament. Phlegma means lack of emotion, not laziness; it implies the tendency to be moved, neither quickly nor easily, but persistently. Such a person warms up slowly, but he retains the warmth longer. He acts on principle, not by instinct; his happy temperament may supply the lack of sagacity and wisdom. He is reasonable in his dealing with other people, and usually gets his way by persisting in objectives while appearing to give way to others.'

There are no compound temperaments, e.g. a sanguine-choleric; in all there are only these four temperaments, each of which is simple, and it is impossible to conceive of a human being which combines them in any way.

This view of the four temperaments as quite independent, separate and unrelated pigeon-holes, each presumably inherited as what we would now call a Mendelian dominant gene was clearly not in line with everyday observation, even if a great deal of allowance is made for differences between phenotype and genotype. Wundt (1903) put forward a rather different view. This is what he said: 'The ancient differentiation into four temperaments . . . arose from acute psychological observations of individual differences between people. . . . The fourfold division can be justified if we agree to postulate two principles in the individual reactivity of the affects: one of these refers to the *strength*, the other to the *speed of change* of a person's feelings. Cholerics and melancholics are inclined to strong affects, while sanguinics and phlegmatics are characterized by weak ones. A high rate of change is found in sanguinics and cholerics, a slow rate in melancholics and phlegmatics.

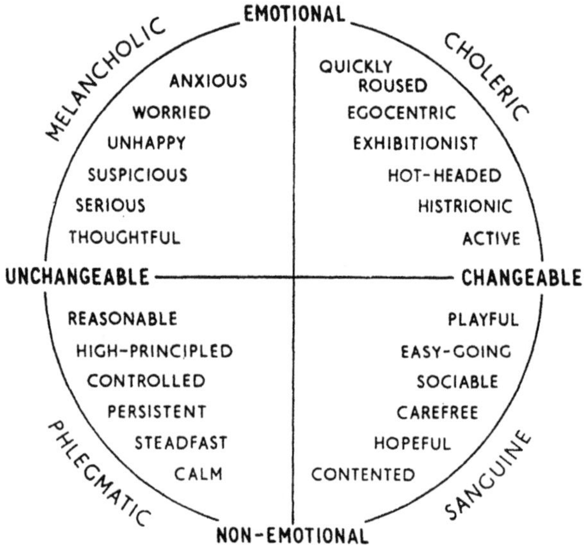

FIG. 3.1 Diagrammatic representation of the classical theory of the four temperaments as described by I. Kant and W. Wundt.

It is well known that the strong temperaments . . . are predestined towards the *Unluststimmungen*, while the weak ones show a happier ability to enjoy life. . . . The two quickly changeable temperaments . . . are more susceptible to the impressions of the present; their mobility makes them respond to each new idea. The two slower temperaments, on the other hand, are more concerned with the future; failing to respond to each chance impression, they take time to pursue their own ideas.'

Using the terms and descriptions of Kant and Wundt in combination we arrive at a theoretical picture of human personality rather like that given in Figure 3.1.[1] It will be seen that Wundt has shifted the emphasis

[1] Wundt is of course not the only psychologist to have attempted the conversion of the four temperaments into two dimensions. H. Ebbinghaus used the two

from a typology conceived as a *categorical system*, which only allocates people to one of four quadrants, to a quantitative, two-dimensional system in which people can occupy any position and any combination of positions on two major dimensions which he labels 'strong emotions' as opposed to 'weak emotions', and 'changeable' as opposed to 'unchangeable'. Within the Wundtian system we can adopt one or other of two

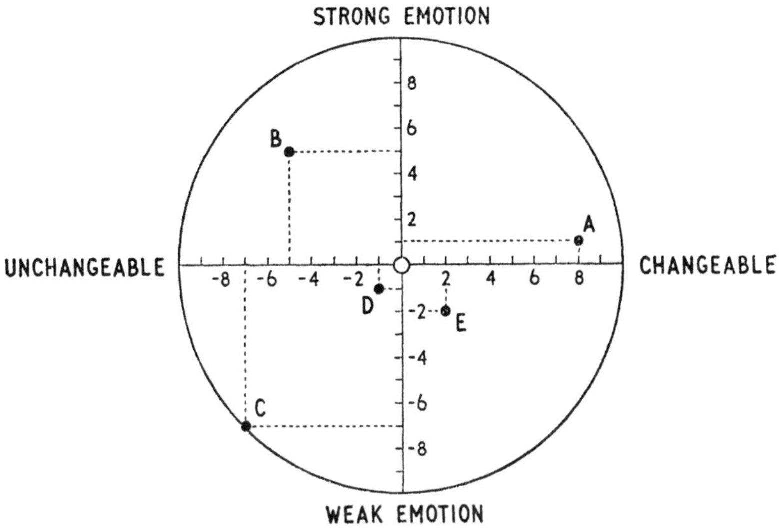

FIG. 3.2 Representation on Cartesian co-ordinates of five people showing different combinations of traits.

methods of allocating a given person to his appropriate space in this two-dimensional diagram. The first and most obvious one is through the use of Cartesian co-ordinates. We can subdivide our two dimensions into a number of equal steps starting perhaps with zero at the origin and making ten equal divisions to the circumference rather as shown in Figure 3.2. On this figure are also shown the positions of five people. 'A' is obviously highly changeable but almost average with respect to the strength of his emotion. 'B' is relatively unchangeable with fairly strong emotions. 'C' and 'D' would both be called phlegmatic as they fall into that particular quadrant but they differ strikingly in that the degree of both unchangeableness and weak emotionality shown by 'C' is very much in excess of that shown by 'D'. 'E' finally is somewhat changeable and endowed somewhat with weak emotions but does not

orthogonal factors optimism-pessimism and 'lebhaftes' vs. 'verhaltenes' Gefühlsleben. Rohracher (1965) states that already in 1911 W. Stern was able to describe 15 such attempts.

deviate very much from the completely average person, who would of course be at the origin. It will be seen that both 'C' and 'D' are phlegmatics whereas 'E' is sanguine yet in terms of their position in the diagram 'D' and 'E' are more alike than 'D' and 'C'. Thus the Wundtian scheme carried to its logical conclusion enables us to give a much more quantified picture of human typology and thus get away from the most unsatisfactory features of the Kantian scheme.

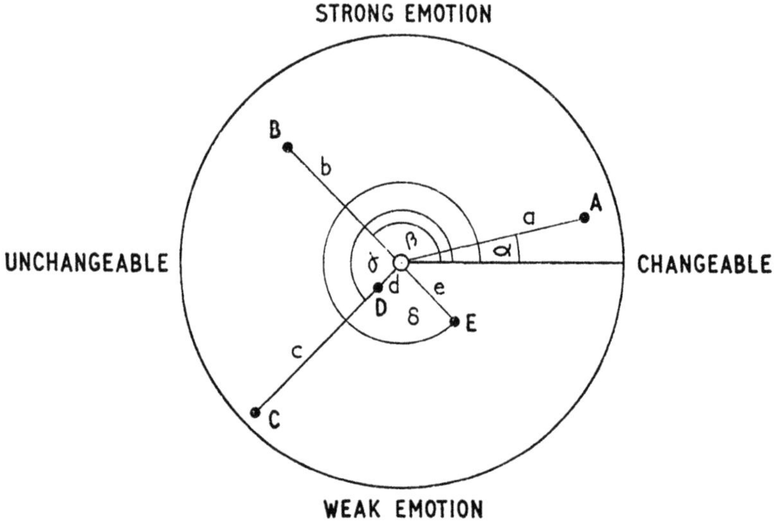

FIG. 3.3 Representation of the same five people as in preceding diagram, using polar co-ordinates instead of Cartesian co-ordinates.

An alternative method of representation is shown in Figure 3.3 which makes use of the system of polar co ordinates. Taking the line from the origin to extreme changeableness as its basis each point within the circle is joined to the origin by a line; thus A is joined to O by a; B by b, C by c, D by d, E by e. The length of this line is one of the two variables needed to specify exactly the position of each point, the other is the angle the line between the point and the origin forms with the base, i.e. angles alpha, beta, gamma and delta (the angle gamma is in common to points C and D). Mathematically of course polar co-ordinates and Cartesian co-ordinates are equivalent, but they both have their advantages and disadvantages. Psychologists have usually made use of Cartesian co-ordinates but the choice appears to have been made more on the basis of familiarity than of any particular superiority of this system. The system of polar co-ordinates has the obvious advantage that the angle always refers to a particular trait constellation within the diagram, whereas the length of the trace line always refers to the strength of expression of that particular set of traits. Thus both C and D have the same angle and therefore show the same temperamental predisposition, but as c is very much longer than d, C shows this constellation of traits much more clearly than does D.

There is thus no reason to believe that the notion of a *typology* presupposes a categorical system; both Jung and Kretschmer, who were probably the best known typologists of the inter-war period, postulated a *dimensional* rather than a *categorical* system. The widespread notion that typologies imply discontinuities, bimodal distributions, and the like, does not accurately represent the writings and views of modern typologists.

Most writers on the subject of personality come down in favour of either the categorical or the dimensional point of view without basing themselves on any experimental demonstration. This is probably unwise, and it should not be impossible to devise experimental and statistical means for verifying the one and falsifying the other hypothesis. Eysenck (1950) has tried to do this in terms of the method of *criterion analysis*, which relies on separate factor analyses of intercorrelations between tests administered to two or more criterion groups (say normals and psychotics), and the comparison of the factors emerging with a criterion column derived by serial correlation between the tests and the criterion. The results of this method have in every instance supported the doctrine of continuity, and failed to support the doctrine of categorization, even when the latter seemed most firmly entrenched, as in the case of psychosis (Eysenck, 1952b).

How was the typological system represented in Figure 3.1 originally arrived at? Essentially it owes its origin to unaided but fairly systematic observation, very much as did the Arab-Paracelsan spagyric system of mercury, sulphur and salt, which we have already encountered. With the development of quantum theory this general picture of physical reality in turn became quantitative; in the case of salt or ionic crystals the forces holding the whole crystal together, for instance, could be calculated in terms of known electrostatic potentials. Similarly in psychology also recent developments have made it possible to subject this system to a more searching quantitative type of enquiry than was possible at the time of Wundt.

What is it that is essentially being postulated by Hippocrates, Galen, Kant and Wundt? They appear to maintain that if we observe a large number of people and assess in some vaguely quantitative way their degree of impulsiveness, reasonableness, carefulness, optimism, sociability, persistence, changeableness, and so on, than it will be found that some combinations of these traits are more likely to appear in the same person than are other combinations of traits. The person who is active will also tend to be irritable, impulsive, histrionic and changeable; he will not be persistent, thorough, high principled, reasonable and steadfast. This of course is an empirical prediction, and it can be tested empirically provided we have a proper mathematical model which enables us to carry out the necessary calculations. Hippocrates and his successors relied essentially on subjective estimates of similarity, very much indeed as did the early systematists in biology. In the biological sciences it has certainly been found that these early observations tended to be very much along the right lines, and while later more quantitative work has in many cases improved the general picture, nevertheless in essence it has tended to support the major outlines of what had been found two or three hundred years previously (Sokal and Sneath, 1963). It will be our task to trace at least briefly the fate of this general theory when subjected to more modern methods of investigation.

Such investigations have been concerned essentially with improvements along two lines. (A) The measurement or rating of the traits themselves has been subject to a considerable degree of research, the main aim of which has been threefold. In the first place an attempt has been made to establish the reality or otherwise of the various traits postulated. In the second place an attempt has been made to measure these along some quantitative continuum, and in the third place an attempt has been made to establish the validity of the measurements which have been made. These points are discussed in considerable detail elsewhere (Eysenck, 1960e), and will not be dealt with exhaustively in this book. (B) The other great improvement has been through the perfection of mathematical indices of similarity such as the correlation coefficient, and the development of methods of analysing large numbers of correlation coefficients and transforming them into smaller numbers of more fundamental variables, dimensions or factors. Factor analysis of course is the outstanding method in this connection, and some familiarity with it is presupposed in the reader of the experiments described in this book (Lawley and Maxwell, 1963). Essentially however it may be said that the task which factor analysis sets itself is precisely analogous to that posited by the Wundtian scheme, i.e. to reduce the observed correlations between large numbers of traits, such as those printed on the outside circle in Figure 3.1, to a smaller number of more fundamental dimensions or factors such as those of emotionality and changeability. The very large amount of work done in this field has also been reviewed elsewhere (Eysenck, 1960e), and in briefly tracing the history of this particular scheme through the literature no effort has been made at completeness; we only have time to note the major figures and contributions.

4

THE BEGINNING OF THE MODERN PERIOD

KANT and Wundt had emphasized the descriptive function of typology. At the beginning of the modern period stand three writers who emphasized more the causal factors involved. The first, and probably the most important of these three, is the Austrian psychiatrist Otto Gross, whose two books on *Die Zerebrale Sekundaerfunktion* (1902), and *Ueber Psychopathologische Minderwertigkeiten* (1909), introduced the concepts of 'primary' and 'secondary' function. These concepts are basically physiological, although the physiology in question is, in part at least, mythological; the concepts refer respectively to the hypothetical activity of the brain cells during the production of any form of mental content, and to the hypothetical perseveration of the nervous processes involved in this production. Thus a nervous process that succeeds in rousing an idea in the mind is supposed to perseverate, although not at a conscious level, and to determine the subsequent associations formed by the mind.[1] Gross also postulated a correlation between the intensity of any experience and the tendency for that experience to persist secondarily and to determine the subsequent course of mental associations. Most intense and energy consuming in his view were highly affective and emotional experiences and ideas, and these would therefore be followed by a long secondary function during which the mental content would be influenced and in part determined by the perseverative effects of the primary function. There is of course an obvious similarity between the concept of 'secondary function' and that of 'refractory period'. Gross distinguishes two contrasted types which he labels 'deep-narrow' and 'shallow-broad'.

[1] Perseveration, as conceived by Gross, is similar in nature to the concept of 'consolidation' which has in recent years acquired excellent experimental support. A review of this work, and its application to personality differences, is given in Eysenck (1967).

In the deep-narrow type we find characteristically a primary function which is highly charged with emotion and loaded in affect, causing the expenditure of great nervous energy, and requiring a lengthy period of restitution during which the ideas involved in the primary function go on reverberating and perseverating (long secondary function). In the shallow-broad type on the other hand a much less intense primary function, necessitating the expenditure of comparatively little energy, is followed by a short period of restitution (short secondary function).

Certain personality characteristics follow from the 'type' hypothesis briefly described above. In the broad-shallow person the short secondary function enables a much greater frequency of primary functions to take place within a given time; this constant readiness for brief actions and reactions suggests a certain superficiality, a distractibility, as well as a prompt reaction to external events; it clearly aligns this type with Wundt's 'changeable' type. In the deep-narrow person the long perseverative secondary function makes the integration of different sets of what Gross calls 'themas' (sets of emotions, associations, determining, tendencies, complexes and sentiments centred around one idea which is the object of primary function), more difficult, and leads to a sejunctive (dissociated) type of personality. Dissociation leads to damming up of the available libido, to inhibition, and on the behavioural level to absorption in thought and social shyness. It is the basis for Wundt's 'unchangeable' type.

The physiological theories of Gross are of course quite outmoded and bear little relation to reality. However, if we substitute for his primary mental function the concept of the ascending reticular formation and the increase in the alertness or arousal of the cortex produced by this system, then we can see at once that his ideas are by no means as irrelevant to modern theorizing as they may at first seem to be (Eysenck, 1967). The functions of the activating reticular system are precisely those stressed by Gross, i.e. the arousal of the cortex and the facilitation of future activation of the cortex along the lines laid down by present stimulation of ideation. There is no need to insist on this comparison of course; as before we may here be in danger of reading into older writers ideas which they could not possibly have foreseen. However, the resemblances are striking enough to deserve at least passing mention.

The second writer to be mentioned in this section is C. G. Jung (1921), the Swiss psychiatrist and one-time follower of Freud. Basing himself on the work of many predecessors, Jung sees the main cause of typological differences in the extraverted or introverted tendency of the libido, i.e. in the tendency of the individual's instinctual energies to be directed mainly towards the outer world (objects), or towards his own inner mental states (subject). 'When we consider a person's life history we see that sometimes his fate is determined more by the objects which attract his interest while sometimes it is influenced rather by his own inner subjective states . . . quite generally one might characterize the introverted point of view by pointing to the constant subjection of the object and objective reality to the ego and the subjective psychological processes . . . according to the extraverted point of view, the subject is considered as inferior to the object; the importance of the subjective aspect is only secondary.'

It is somewhat hazardous to try and give descriptions of the behaviour of typical extraverts and introverts because Jung is concerned far more with attitudes, values, unconscious mental processes, and so on. Furthermore his account is complicated to an almost impossible extent by his insistence that people who are consciously extraverted may be unconsciously introverted and by the further insistence that these tendencies may find expression according to the four main mental functions. Jung regards extraversion and introversion as the two major attitudes or orientations of personality, but these find expression in the functions of *thinking*, *feeling*, *sensing*, and *intuiting*. Thinking and feeling are called *rational* functions because they make use of reason, judgement, abstraction and generalization. Sensation and intuition are considered to be *irrational* functions. Jung weaves a very complex web stressing the superiority of some functions, the auxiliary role played by others, and so forth. There is little point in recapitulating Jung's complete system as no modern psychologist has adopted it in its entirety and as in any case it seems difficult to apply in any rational manner.

However, making allowance for these complications and the obvious distortions which such neglect must introduce into his system, we may say that from Jung's accounts the extravert emerges as a person who values the outer world both in its material and its immaterial aspects (possessions, riches, power, prestige); he seeks for social approval and tends to conform to the mores of his society; he is sociable, makes friends easily and trusts other people. He shows outward physical activity, while the introvert's activity is mainly in the mental and intellectual sphere. He is changeable, likes new things, new people, new impressions. His emotions are easily aroused but never very deeply; he is relatively insensitive, impersonal, experimental, materialistic and tough-minded. He tends to be free from inhibitions, carefree and ascendant. The traits listed will perhaps suffice to show how closely Jung approximates to the Hippocrates-Galen-Kant-Wundt model and to the extension of it given by Gross. When in the rest of this book the terms *extraversion* and *introversion* are used it should always be borne in mind that they do not refer to the conceptions specifically introduced by Jung, but refer rather to the changeable-unchangeable dimension of Wundt, being perhaps more appropriate terms to use than the Wundtian ones, or the rather clumsy nomenclature introduced by Gross. In other words, just as we have been unable to follow Gross in his explanatory physiological conceptions, so we must refuse to take too seriously the technicalities of the Jungian system with its notion of libido, mental functions, and racial unconscious. It may seem unjust that we should take over terms from one author to characterize notions that may be characteristic of others, but it should be remembered that Jung did not in fact originate the terms extraversion and introversion; they had been in use in Europe for several hundred years before he popularized them, and there is no reason therefore why their use should remain sacrosanct.

Jung made one important addition to the ancient system of typology by linking his notions of extraversion and introversion with a distinction between the main neurotic disorders as given by Janet (1894, 1903). As is well known, Jung believed that the extravert in case of neurotic breakdown is predisposed to *hysteria*, the introvert to *psychasthenia*. 'It appears to me that much the most frequent disorder of the extraverted type is hysteria . . .' On the other hand, speaking of the introvert, he maintains that 'his typical neurotic disorder is psychasthenia, a disorder which is characterized on the one hand by marked sensitivity, on the other by great exhaustion and constant tiredness.' Nowadays we would probably refer to 'anxiety state' or 'reactive depression', phobia or obsessional state rather than to the obsolescent term psychasthenia. Eysenck (1947) suggested the term 'dysthymic' as a more modern equivalent to cover this syndrome of correlated affective disorders.

Jung never formally elaborated this part of his hypothesis but it can be seen that implicit in his scheme is a second dimension or factor additional to, and independent of, that of extraversion-introversion. This factor we may provisionally call emotionality or instability or neuroticism; it is identified as that particular quality which hysterics and psychoasthenics have in common as compared with normal persons. The independence of introversion and neuroticism is especially stressed by Jung: 'It is a mistake to believe that introversion is more or less the same as neurosis. As concepts the two have not the slightest connection with each other.' Thus if we wish to represent Jung's complete scheme in diagrammatic form then we require two orthogonal axes or dimensions very much as in Figure 3.1. Hysterics would then occupy the first quadrant, i.e. that labelled 'choleric', and psychasthenics or dysthymics would occupy the second quadrant, i.e. that labelled 'melancholics'. As given by Jung, this scheme of course is purely hypothetical, but there is some evidence from empirical studies to support it (Eysenck, 1947).

The third author to be mentioned in this section is Kretschmer (1948). He, too, took his prototypes from the psychiatric field, but unlike Jung he turned to the psychotic forms of disorder rather than the neurotic. Following Kraepelin and Bleuler he distinguished two main psychotic syndromes or groups of symptoms: the *schizophrenic* on the one hand, the *manic-depressive* or cyclic type of psychotic on the other. Unlike most other psychiatrists however Kretschmer considered these disorders not as in any way qualitatively different from normal mental states, but merely as the extremes of a continuum, as exaggerated forms of behaviour patterns characteristic of normal persons. This hypothesis may perhaps be illustrated in terms of Figure 4.1, showing the hypothetical distribution of the whole population in terms of a normal curve of distribution ranging from one extreme, schizophrenia, to the other, manic-depressive insanity. All persons left of the mean would be *schizothymics*, meaning by that merely that their personality make-up had in common certain elements which are grotesquely exaggerated in those psychotic patients whom we label schizophrenics, whereas those to the right of the mean would be *cyclothymics*, meaning by that that their personality make-up had in common certain elements which are grotesquely exaggerated in manic-depressive patients. Persons who are

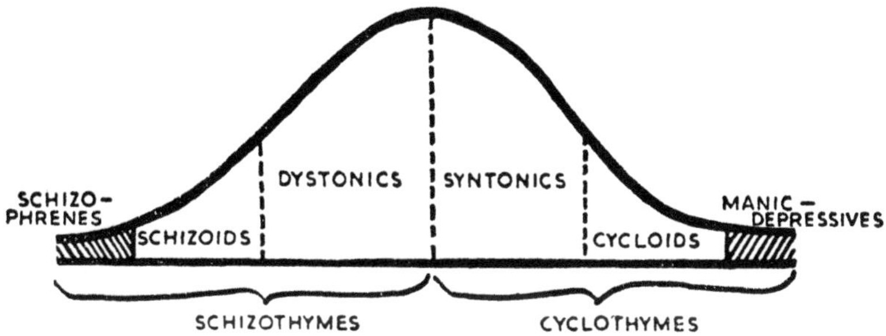

FIG. 4.1 Major dimension of personality according to Kretschmer. (Taken from Eysenck, 1960e.)

definitely abnormal but not yet psychotic, Kretschmer would call schizoid or cycloid respectively, according to the side on which they fell, whereas the large number of persons in the centre of the distribution he would call *syntonic* if they were on the cyclothymic side and *dystonic* if they were on the schizothymic side.

Kretschmer's description of the cyclothyme has certain similarities to the types already considered. Like the extravert, and the broad-shallow type, the cyclothyme is objective, realistic, sociable, optimistic, trustful, cooperative, and frank; he is also subject to mood changes without apparent cause. The schizothyme like the introvert and the narrow-deep type shows the opposite to these. Kretschmer's approach is more experimental than that of any of his predecessors and a review of some of the empirical studies carried out by him and his students has been presented by Eysenck (1950a). There is some independent evidence to show that his dimension coincides with that of extraversion-introversion. Shagass and Kerenyi (1958), for instance, have shown that patients suffering from manic-depressive insanity have low sedation thresholds, whereas reactive depressives, i.e. dysthymic neurotics, have high sedation thresholds, putting the latter at the introverted end, the former at the extraverted end. Similarly, Kretschmer has shown that schizothymes tend to be relatively narrow in body build, whereas cyclothymes are relatively broad; on the other hand there is much evidence, reviewed for instance by Rees (1960), to show that introverts also are lean, extraverts more broadly built. However, this whole question is still very much *sub judice* and it would be unreasonable at the moment to express any firm opinion on this point.[1]

The three authors we have considered have produced quite different conceptions regarding the causation of personality differences. Gross was very much concerned with the presumably inherited nature of the central nervous system. Jung was very much concerned with the direction taken by the person's libido; he admits both environmental and genetic factors. Thus he says (Jung, 1921) that 'every individual possesses both a mechanism of introversion and that of extraversion, and it is only the relative strength of the one as compared with the other which creates a type . . . external circumstances and inner dispositions frequently favour one mechanism and impede or restrict the other. This quite naturally leads to the dominance of one of the mechanisms.' Kretschmer clearly favours certain constitutional factors, as shown most clearly by his insistence on the close relationship between body-build and personality. In spite of a considerable amount of work done on all three theories, it cannot be said that the experimental evidence has been very favourable to any of them.

[1] In addition to his cyclothyme-schizothyme axis Kretschmer also requires a second, orthogonal axis contrasting normal and abnormal personalities. Unlike Jung, this second axis he postulates runs from normal to psychotic instead of neurotic. Neuroticism and psychoticism are orthogonal to each other (Eysenck, 1960a).

Kretschmer's main contribution has been his insistence on the constitutional basis of personality, and his demonstration of the relationship between body-build and temperaments. The constitutional nature of body-build has been documented by Vogel and Wendt (1956) and Verschuer (1952) in connection with extensive twin studies. Sheldon's contribution to this aspect of personality study falls in line with the rest (Eysenck, 1960e).

5

CORRELATIONAL STUDIES OF PERSONALITY

THE work of Gross, Jung, Kretschmer and others active around the same time did not add much material to the scientific description of personality; they still relied very much on intuition and argument rather than on measurement and calculation. The first to use these more modern approaches were two Dutch workers, G. Heymans and E. Wiersma (1909). They carried out a rating study in which some three thousand doctors in the Netherlands were asked each to pick one family and rate each member of it by a simple method of underlining or double underlining of a large number of traits. Four hundred doctors responded and sent in material on altogether 2,532 individuals. Heymans and Wiersma considered the replies in terms of a three-dimensional system which they had elaborated on the basis of relationships found in the analysis of biographic material derived from 110 historical persons about whom a great deal was known. These three principles were first of all *emotionality*, or emotional instability; secondly *activity* or general drive; and thirdly a primary function—secondary function factor, i.e. what we would now call extraversion-introversion. When the data were analysed statistically by Eysenck (1960) it was found that these three factors were not in fact independent. Emotionality is relatively orthogonal to the other two, but activity and extraversion are quite highly correlated, so that in the end their results seem to indicate that we need no more than *two* independent factors or dimensions to account for the data. These dimensions appear very similar to those postulated by Wundt, although now we may label them emotionality or neuroticism, and extraversion-introversion. Very detailed discussions and descriptions of the various types are given by Heymans and Wiersma, and some of these are reproduced by Eysenck (1960e). A perusal of these lists leaves little doubt about the meaningfulness of the identification of the types derived from this empirical study with those shown in Figure 3.1.

Somewhat later and quite uninfluenced by the Heymans-Wiersma study comes a whole set of correlational studies of questionnaires, mostly inspired by the success of the Woodworth personality data sheet, a measure of neuroticism worked out during the time of the First World War, and by the appearance of Jung's book on personality types. Attempts were made to use correlations between existing scales which were assumed to be separate measures of neuroticism, extraversion, ascendance, self-sufficiency, depression, and so forth, in order to discover either more parsimonious ways of arranging and scoring the tests or more fundamentally meaningful psychological variables. These efforts ended in almost complete failure. As Vernon (1938) has pointed out: 'The attempts to classify test items of symptoms logically into distinct groups has not, we must admit, been successful. On the one hand it is found that tests of presumably different traits intercorrelate very highly; on the other hand different tests of nominally the same trait . . . tend to give poor correlations with one another. It is doubtful then whether most of the traits at which the tests have been directed are unitary and discrete.'

This overlap between hypothetically different traits is most apparent in attempts to measure neuroticism and extraversion introversion. Vernon in the same publication quotes the results of 40 experiments showing that the average correlation between different introversion tests and the average correlation between introversion and psychoneurotic tendency tests are practically identical, namely +0·36. A further 18 experiments with the ascendance-submission test showed an average correlation of 0·30 between submissiveness and introversion, or psychoneurotic tendency. Tests of inferiority feelings also agreed quite closely with tests of introversion. Do these results argue against the value of theories such as those presented in Figure 3.1?

The answer to this problem may be provided in an excellent paper by Collier and Emch (1938), who showed that most questionnaire constructors have used Freud's conception of introversion rather than Jung's. Freud tends to identify introversion with incipient neuroticism. According to him: 'An introvert is not yet a neurotic but he finds himself in a labile condition; he must develop symptoms at the next dislocation of forces if he does not find other outlets of his pent-up libido' (1920). Jung's position already quoted is of course quite different; he believes in the complete independence of the two concepts. This conceptual identification of introversion and neuroticism, so common in much American work, rests on the misapprehension of Jung's theory and does not invalidate it in any way.

We may perhaps anticipate a point here which is to be made later because it is relevant to this problem. One of the traits most characteristic of extraversion is gregariousness or sociability; it follows that introverts tend to be socially withdrawn and shy. It has also often been observed, as for instance in the recent work of Russell Fraser (1947), that neurotics as compared to normals tend to be unsociable and withdrawn. If questionnaires of introversion-extraversion and of neuroticism make very much use of sociability questions, and this has been the practice of the period under consideration, then there is an almost built in tendency for introversion to correlate with neuroticism. However, Eysenck (1956b) has shown that there are in fact two kinds of social shyness, which are quite unrelated. The typical introvert does not value social participation very much but he can engage in social activity perfectly adequately and without any anxiety or fear. Neurotic social shyness, however, is quite different; here we have a tendency to wish to indulge in social activity but an active fear which prevents the person from doing so in case he might be snubbed, hurt, offended, etc. To put it slightly differently the introvert doesn't want to be with other people but doesn't mind if the need arises; the neurotic does want to be with other people but is afraid of joining them. By constructing questionnaires mixing up items measuring these two different kinds of sociability it is possible to get almost any kind of correlation between extraversion-introversion and neuroticism, and the failure of these early attempts to clarify the field are probably in large part due to this lack of realization of the complex constitution of sociability.

These early failures have had an almost traumatic effect on many psychologists, possibly because so many hopes had been invested in the feasibility of the questionnaire approach. The very terms extraversion and introversion were dropped from polite conversation in psychological circles and the existence of any such trait was considered as disproved. In fact of course it was the naïve assumptions underlying the tests and the lack of serious historical study characterizing their construction which were responsible for the failure of the researches to support the hypothesis; the theory of extraversion-introversion was not being properly tested and consequently the results cannot be used in evidence against it. What did become clear, however, was that the *a priori* construction of questionnaires and the naïve notion that because a questionnaire is given a particular label, therefore, it will measure this particular trait or type, had to be abandoned. It became clear that what was needed was a much more detailed approach in which very homogeneous questionnaires had to be constructed and intercorrelated in order to study the dimensionality of the whole field, and indeed it became necessary to go even further than that and intercorrelate individual items in order to achieve greater homogeneity in the measuring instruments. It is to this type of work that we must now turn.

6

FACTOR-ANALYTIC STUDIES OF PERSONALITY

THE honour of having carried out the first pioneering studies in this field goes to the London school, particularly to Charles Spearman (1927) who did so much to furnish psychology with a useable method of factor analysis. He was familiar with Gross's theory and with the work of Heymans and Wiersma, and at his suggestion Webb (1915) was the first to use the method of factor analysis in the non-intellectual field. He intercorrelated and factor analysed ratings made of students and schoolboys and discovered in this work a factor which he called (w), using the initial of the word 'will'; this he and later writers interpreted as the opposite of the factor of emotionality, i.e. a tendency not to over-react emotionally but to have a stable type of personality. Additional analyses of this material were carried out by Garnet (1918), McCloy (1936), Reyburn and Taylor (1939) and others and they all agreed that another factor rather similar to extraversion-introversion was contained in these data. Burt (1915), another member of the London school, also carried out a factor analytic study of 172 school children as well as another one on 329 adults and children, who were rated on eleven traits. He too claims the discovery of a general factor of emotionality, which he labelled 'e'. Later work by the same author (Burt, 1937, 1939, 1940) contains further support for this factor of emotionality, which he considers to be obverse of Webb's 'w', and for a factor of extraversion-introversion. Burt's most recent study (1948) also supports this two factor scheme.

Many other early studies from this school are mentioned in Eysenck (1960e) and on the whole they give convincing support to the reality of some such scheme as that depicted in Figure 3.1. The same may be said of a large body of independent work carried out with both ratings and self-ratings in the United States, in South Africa, in England and elsewhere, all of which has been reviewed in detail by Eysenck (1960e). Although at times identification of a given factor is difficult or tainted by obscurity, nevertheless on the whole the work reviewed there suggests that it is difficult to analyse any broadly based body of observations in the personality field without coming across two personality dimensions closely resembling emotionality or neuroticism on the one hand, and extraversion-introversion on the other.

Three workers have been particularly active in this field over many years, and as the main body of the empirical work discussed in this book relates to their efforts it is only fitting that in the rest of this chapter we shall be concerned primarily with their contributions. The first of these three writers is J. P. Guilford, who carried out most of his early work in collaboration with his wife, R. B. Guilford (1934, 1936, 1939). Recognizing the necessity of running correlations not between scores on clusters of items selected on *a priori* grounds but between individual items themselves, J. P. and R. B. Guilford administered in their first study 36 typical introversion-extraversion questions to 930 students, intercorrelated them and factor analysed the result. They obtained four factors tentatively identified as social introversion, emotional sensitiveness, impulsiveness and interest in self. In 1936 the analysis was repeated using more up to date methods of analysis and three main factors were found and identified. They labelled these S, for social shyness, E for emotional immaturity or emotional dependency; M for masculinity. A fourth factor they tentatively labelled R, 'the letter R standing for a word coined from the Greek "rhathymia", which means freedom from care.' A fifth factor, also difficult to interpret, seemed to emphasize the liking for thinking and tackling problems requiring thought, versus a liking for prompt overt action; this they label temporarily as factor T. These factors, it might be noted, were not independent. S and E for instance were intercorrelated to the extent of 0·46, and S and M to the extent of 0·40.

The factors R and T were investigated more fully in a later paper by the same authors (1939b). Nine factors were extracted from the intercorrelations between 30 items administered to 1,000 students. The first factor was one of depression (D); S, R and T were found again and an alertness factor (A) was also discovered. Some of the other factors were found not to be meaningful or easily interpretable. Two further factors were isolated in another paper appearing in the same year (1939a) in which 600 subjects were given a questionnaire of 24 items. One of these was factor N (nervousness or jumpiness), the other factor GE (general drive, characterized chiefly by pleasure in action).

This early work of the Guilfords has often been misinterpreted as doing away with the notion of extraversion and introversion as a descriptive factor in personality research. Thus Allport (1937) maintained 'that the Guilfords' factor analysis of items included in many tests for extraversion-introversion shows that quite independent clusters of responses may be involved.' This, however, is not true. In their 1939 paper for instance the Guilfords show that there are considerable correlations between factors D, S and T; these correlations range from 0·5 to 0·7. 'These relationships have distinct bearing on the question as to just what is introversion-extraversion. . . . It would seem that there is some basis for lumping together some characteristics bordering on seclusiveness with some implying a thinking person and still others that indicate depressed emotional tendencies and for calling the resultant picture the introvert. Because of the relationship between these three primary traits, it is easy to see how a more cursory inspection of personalities would lead to the conviction of a composite trait like introversion. The opposite composite of sociability, cheerfulness and lack of meditative thinking would of course be the extravert picture. . . . The use of the term 'introvert', as we have indicated, to represent the person who is simultaneously on the side of the shy, depressed and thinking for the dimension S, D and T would then seem to be justified by this statistical analysis.'

In more recent publications Guilford has isolated further factors which again are not independent of each other or of those isolated before; those added to his previous list are: C (for cycloid disposition or stability of emotional reactions as opposed to instability); A (ascendance-submission); I (inferiority feelings as opposed to self confidence); O (for objectivity as opposed to hypersensitiveness); Co (for co-operativeness); and Ag (for agreeableness as opposed to quarrelsomeness). Factor analyses done on the intercorrelations between scales by Lovell (1945) and North (1949) result in a fairly clear-cut picture which features mainly two very strong orthogonal factors identifiable as emotional stability versus emotional instability, and extraversion-introversion (Eysenck, 1960e, 184–188). The scales characterizing introversion are inactivity, inhibited disposition, submission and social shyness. Those characteristic of neuroticism or emotional instability are nervousness, hypersensitivity, depression, over-criticalness, quarrelsomeness and inferiority feelings. The results are to some extent vitiated by the fact that some items are scored for more than one factor, but it is doubtful whether this defect has resulted in any considerable misalignment of the factors or erroneous classification.

A study by Guilford and Zimmerman (1956) presents the latest and most extensive work of this school. They carried out a very large factor analysis embracing grouped items representative of the 13 factors originally hypothesized by Guilford. Intercorrelations were calculated for altogether 70 such small groups of items and the factor analysis revealed 13 factors either identical with those previously discovered, or at least similar to them. Guilford and Zimmerman give a brief description of these factors together with the letters by which they are to be known, and as these descriptions may make an understanding of our discussion easier it is here quoted in full.

Guilford's Main Personality Factors:

G. *General activity:* Energetic, rapid-moving, rapid-working person, who likes action and may sometimes be impulsive.

A. *Ascendance:* The person who upholds his rights and defends himself in face-to-face contacts; who does not mind being conspicuous, in fact may enjoy it; who through social initiative gravitates to positions of leadership; who is not fearful of social contacts; who is not inclined to keep his thoughts to himself. There is little to indicate that 'submission' accurately describes the negative pole, as was formerly believed.

M. *Masculinity vs. femininity:* Has masculine interests, vocational and avocational; not emotionally excitable or expressive; not easily aroused to fear or disgust; somewhat lacking in sympathy.

I. *Confidence vs. inferiority feelings:* Feels accepted by others, confident, and adequate; socially poised; satisfied with his lot; not self-centred.

N. *Calmness, composure vs. nervousness:* Calm and relaxed rather than nervous and jumpy; not restless, easily fatigued, or irritated; can concentrate on the matter at hand.

S. *Sociability:* Likes social activity and contacts, formal or informal; likes positions of social leadership; has social poise, not shy, bashful, or seclusive.

T. *Reflectiveness:* Given to meditative and reflective thinking; dreamer, philosophically inclined; has curiosity about and questioning attitude towards behaviour of self and others.

D. *Depression:* Emotionally and physically depressed rather than cheerful; given to worry and anxiety and to perseverating.

C_1. *Emotionality:* Emotions easily aroused and perseverating, yet shallow and childish; daydreamer. (Not identical with Factor C.)

R. *Restraint vs. rhathymia:* Self restrained and self controlled; serious minded rather than happy-go-lucky; not cheerfully irresponsible.

O. *Objectivity:* Takes an objective, realistic view of things; alert to his environment and can forget himself; not beset with suspicions.

Ag. *Agreeable:* Low-scoring individual is easily aroused to hostility; resists control by others; has contempt for others; and may be aroused to aggressive action. High-scoring person is friendly and compliant.

Co. *Co-operativeness, tolerance:* Low-scoring person is given to critical fault-finding generally; has little confidence or trust in others; self-centred and self pitying.

Guilford's work is of great originality and high value for anyone interested in this field; it is unfortunate that his results have often been misunderstood and misquoted. As pointed out before it is quite untrue to say that the finding of so many different traits contradicts in any way the possibility of the existence of a factor of extraversion-introversion. The traits themselves are not independent; they might be said to occupy the position on the outer ring in our Figure 3.1 which we have allocated there on purely descriptive and subjective grounds to the traits mentioned by Kant and the earlier workers. Guilford's work has been extremely important and influential in identifying a large number of these traits and demonstrating ways and means of isolating and measuring them. What he has not done and what he has not claimed to have done is to disprove the existence of such factors as emotionality and extraversion-introversion. If these exist they can be derived only from the observed intercorrelations between the primary traits which Guilford has done so much to isolate; the fairly high correlations existing between the primary traits demonstrate conclusively that higher order concepts such as extraversion and neuroticism are by no means ruled out. Possibly much of the misunderstanding that has arisen was due to the fact that Guilford himself has not shown much interest in the further analysis of these intercorrelations. This however should not preclude others from doing what he himself has failed to do.

The second worker to be singled out in this section is R. B. Cattell. In some ways he might perhaps be considered as a representative of the London school because it was from Spearman that he received his early training, and was stimulated in his interest in the development of factor analysis. However, since his removal to the United States his work has tended to grow away from the methods and beliefs of the London school and he is best regarded in his own right. Like Guilford he has carried out a very large number of factor analytic studies of questionnaires and has supplemented these by analyses of ratings. The results of both the rating and the questionnaire studies are surprisingly similar and he emerges finally with a list of primary personality factors which is reproduced below from the summary given by Eysenck (1960e).

Cattell's Main Personality Factors:

FACTOR A: *Cyclothymia vs. Schizothymia*

A+	A−
Easygoing	Obstructive, cantankerous
Adaptable (in habits)	Inflexible, 'rigid'
Warmhearted, attentive to people	Cool, indifferent
Frank, placid	Close-mouthed, secretive, anxious
Emotional, expressive	Reserved
Trustful, credulous	Suspicious, 'canny'
Impulsive, generous	Close, cautious
Co-operative, self-effacing	Hostile, egotistical
Subject to personal emotional appeals	Impersonal
Humorous	Dry, impassive

FACTOR B: *Intelligence*

B+	B−
Intelligent	Unintelligent
Thoughtful, cultured	Unreflective, boorish
Persevering, conscientious	Quitting, conscienceless
Smart, assertive	Dull, submissive

FACTOR C: *Ego strength vs. Neuroticism*

C+	C−
Emotionally stable	Emotional, dissatisfied
Free of neurotic symptoms	Showing a variety of neurotic symptoms
Not hypochondriacal	Hypochondriacal, plaintive
Realistic about life	Evasive, immature, autistic
Unworried	Worrying, anxious
Steadfast, self-controlled	Changeable
Calm, patient	Excitable, impatient
Persevering and thorough	Quitting, careless
Loyal, dependable	Undependable morally

FACTOR D: *Excitability vs. Insecurity*

D+	D−
Demanding, impatient	Emotionally mature
Attention-getting, exhibitionistic	Self-sufficient
Excitable, overactive	Deliberate
Prone to jealousy	Not easily jealous
Self-assertive, egotistical	Self-effacing
Nervous symptoms	Absence of nervous symptoms
Changeable, lacks persistence	Self-controlled
Untrustworthy	Conscientious

FACTOR E: *Dominance vs. Submissiveness*

E+	E−
Self-assertive, confident	Submissive, unsure
Boastful, conceited	Modest, retiring
Aggressive, pugnacious	Complaisant
Extrapunitive (in the sense introduced by Rosenzweig)	Impunitive, intropunitive
Vigorous, forceful	Meek, quiet
Wilful, egotistical	Obedient
Rather solemn or unhappy	Lighthearted, cheerful
Adventurous	Timid, retiring
Insensitive to social disapproval	Tactful, conventional
Unconventional	
Reserved	Frank, expressive

FACTOR F: *Surgency vs. Desurgency*

F+	F−
Cheerful, joyous	Depressed, pessimistic
Sociable, responsive	Seclusive, retiring
Energetic, rapid in movement	Subdued, languid
Humorous, witty	Dull, phlegmatic
Talkative	Taciturn, introspective
Placid, content	Worrying, anxious, unable to relax obsessional
Resourceful, original	Slow to accept a situation

FACTOR F: *Surgency vs. Desurgency* (*contd.*)

F+	F−
Adaptable	Bound by habit, rigid
Showing equanimity	Unstable mood level
Trustful, sympathetic, open	Suspicious, brooding, narrow

FACTOR G: *Superego strength*

G+	G−
Persevering, determined	Quitting, fickle
Responsible	Frivolous, immature
Insistently ordered	Relaxed, indolent
Conscientious	Unscrupulous
Attentive to people	Neglectful of social chores
Emotionally stable	Changeable

FACTOR H: *Parmia* (*Parasympathetic immunity*) *vs. Threctia* (*Threat reactivity*)

H+	H−
Adventurous, likes meeting people	Shy, timid, withdrawn
Shows strong interest in opposite sex	Little interest in opposite sex
Kindly, friendly	Hard, hostile
Frank	Secretive
Impulsive (but no inner tension)	Inhibited, conscientious
Likes to 'get into the swim'	Recoils from life
Self-confident	Lacking confidence
Carefree	Careful, considerate

FACTOR I: *Premsia vs. Harria*

I+	I−
Demanding, impatient	Emotionally mature
Dependent, immature	Independent-minded
Kindly, gentle	Hard
Aesthetically fastidious	Lacking artistic feeling
Introspective, imaginative	Unaffected by 'fancies'
Intuitive, sensitively imaginative	Practical, logical
Gregarious, attention-seeking	Self-sufficient
Frivolous	Responsible
Hypochondriacal	Free from hypochondria

FACTOR J: *Coasthenia* (*Thinking Neurasthenia*) *vs. Zeppia*

J+	J−
Acts individualistically	Goes with group
Passively, pedantically obstructs	Co-operative in enterprises
Slow to make up his mind	Decisive in thinking
Inactive, meek, quiet	Active, assertive
Neurasthenically, neurotically fatigued	Vigorous
Self-sufficient	Attention-getting
Evaluates intellectually	Evaluates by common standards
Personal, peculiar interests	Common 'wide' interests

FACTOR K: *Comention vs. Abcultion*

K+	K−
Intellectual interests, analytical	Unreflective, narrow
Polished, poised, composed	Awkward, socially clumsy
Unshakable	Easily socially embarrassed
Independent-minded	Going with the crowd
Conscientious, idealistic	Lacking sense of any social duty
Aesthetic and musical tastes	Lacking aesthetic interests
Introspective, sensitive	Crude

FACTOR L: *Protension (Paranoid trend) vs. Inner Relaxation*

L+	L−
Suspicious	Trustful
Jealous	Understanding
Self-sufficient, withdrawn	Composed, socially at home

FACTOR M: *Autia vs. Praxernia*

M+	M−
Unconventional, eccentric	Conventional
Aesthetically fastidious	Uninterested in art
Sensitively imaginative	Practical and logical
'A law unto himself', undependable	Conscientious
Placid, complacent, absorbed	Worrying, anxious, alert
Occasional hysterical emotional upsets	Poised, tough control
Intellectual, cultured interests	Narrower interests

FACTOR N: *Shrewdness vs. Naïvety*

N+	N−
Polished, socially skilful	Socially clumsy, awkward
Exact mind	Vague and sentimental mind
Cool, aloof	Company-seeking
Aesthetically fastidious	Lacking independence of taste
Insightful regarding self	Lacking self insight
Insightful regarding others	Naïve

FACTOR O: *Guilt proneness vs. Confidence*

O+	O−
Worrying	Self-confident
Lonely	Self-sufficient
Suspicious	Accepting
Sensitive	Tough
Discouraged	Spirited

Cattell warns that 'although no more than 15 L data (i.e. data derived from life situations) factors can be announced after several years of systematic research, based on the broad 'personality sphere', of common, real life, criterion behaviour, the student should not assume that this list is practically exhaustive. Doubtless some areas of behaviour are yet to be found not previously included in the personality sphere. . . . An estimate allowing for attenuation suggests that the present 15 factors account for about two thirds of the personality sphere variance.'

Cattell's fifteen factors too are not independent, and the intercorrelations in turn require to be submitted to factor analytic studies. These have recently been undertaken by Cattell (1957) and their publication, as he points out, 'yields two very striking findings—the general integration factor, and the introversion/extraversion factor.' It would appear therefore that Cattell's studies line up with the others reviewed in this chapter to define the same two fundamental dimensions of personality we have encountered so often. *Extraversion* is defined in terms of the following primary factors given here together with their factor loadings on extraversion: F (surgency): +0·70; M (autia): +0·54; E (dominance): +0·54; A (cyclothymia): +0·38; H (parmia): +0·17. The main primary factors defining *neuroticism* are: C (ego strength): −0·50; L (protension): −0·47; E (dominance: −0·32; H (parmia): −0·20. (It should be noted that Cattell prefers to call this factor 'anxiety versus integration or adjustment', to preserve uniformity we shall continue to call it neuroticism.)

Extraversion-introversion, or exvia-invia as Cattell prefers to call it, and neuroticism, or anxiety as Cattell prefers to call it, are labelled Q1 and Q2 in his system. In addition he has two further second-order factors, labelled Q3 and Q4. Q3 he calls 'Pathemia', or emotional immaturity vs. corticalertia, while Q4 is called 'Promethean will vs. religious resignation or subduedness.'

This is a very brief introduction to Cattell's work which is much more extensive than is suggested in these brief references. As in the case of Guilford we will later on in this book have occasion to grapple with many of his other findings and ideas. Here our intention is merely to present a brief introduction to them and put them into their historical perspective.

The third writer to be mentioned in this connection is the present author, who may be said to have continued the work of Spearman and Burt and to have carried on the spirit of the London school. His first factorial study (Eysenck, 1947) obtained ratings on 39 items from 700 neurotics in an army neurosis unit and submitted these intercorrelations to a factor analysis. The first two factors obtained are shown in Figure 6.1. The first factor, characterized by items such as badly organized personality, abnormal before illness, little energy, narrow interests, abnormality in parents, etc., is clearly one of emotional instability or neuroticism; the second factor opposes the introvert to the extravert group of traits, thus giving in combination with the first factor a typical picture on the one hand of the hysteric (conversion symptoms, sex anomalies unskilled, hysterical attitude, degraded work history, low I.Q., narrow interests, little energy) and on the other of the dysthymic (anxiety, depression, obsessional traits, apathy, irritability, somatic anxiety, tremor and effort intolerance). As far as they go these results tend to support the theories of Janet and Jung. Eysenck also attempted to verify another hypothesis, namely that the distributions of people on these two factors were continuous and similar to a normal curve rather

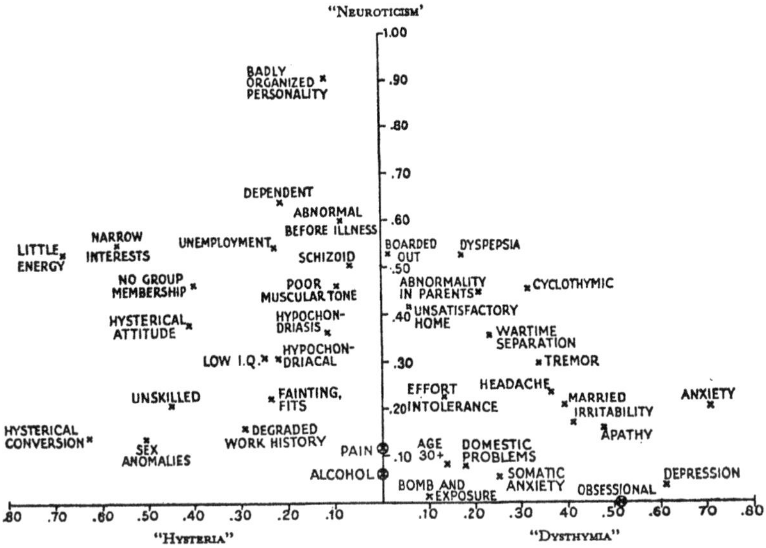

FIG. 6.1 Diagrammatic representation of the results of a factor analytic study of neurotic patients. (Taken from Eysenck, 1947.)

than bimodal. Distributions were plotted for 1,000 male and 1,000 female neurotics by a weighted combination of ratings for the various traits which go to make up these two factors. Distributions for both factors are closely similar to the normal curve of distribution, a result which is in good agreement with a similar demonstration by Burt on normal subjects (1940).

Eysenck's later work (1956, 1959; Eysenck and Eysenck, 1964) has been concerned with the development of personality questionnaires along factorial lines, particularly the Maudsley Medical Questionnaire (MMQ), the Maudsley Personality Inventory (MPI) and the Eysenck Personality Inventory (EPI). The development of these instruments is treated in more detail later on and is therefore only mentioned here. Another feature of his work has been the search for external criterion groups already apparent in the first study (1947) mentioned above. The choice of hysterics which was made on the basis of the Janet-Jung hypothesis was later on found to be only partly justified; responses of hysterics to questionnaires do show them to be more extraverted than

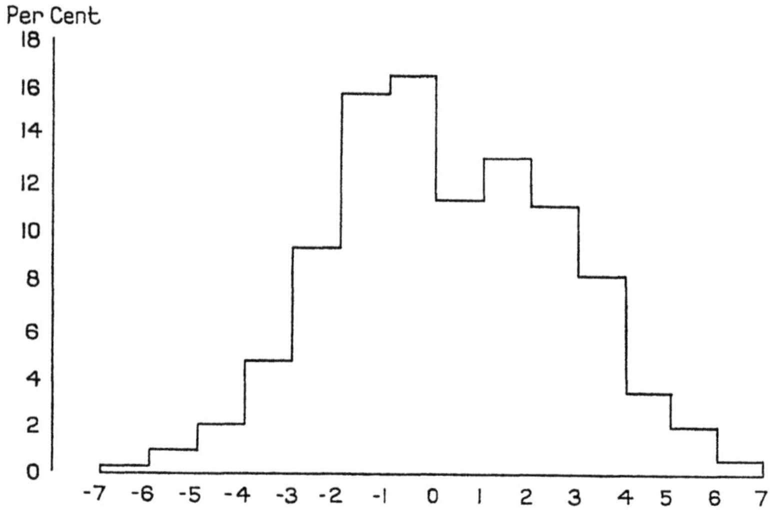

FIG. 6.2a Distribution of neuroticism in 1,000 soldiers. (Taken from Eysenck, 1947.)

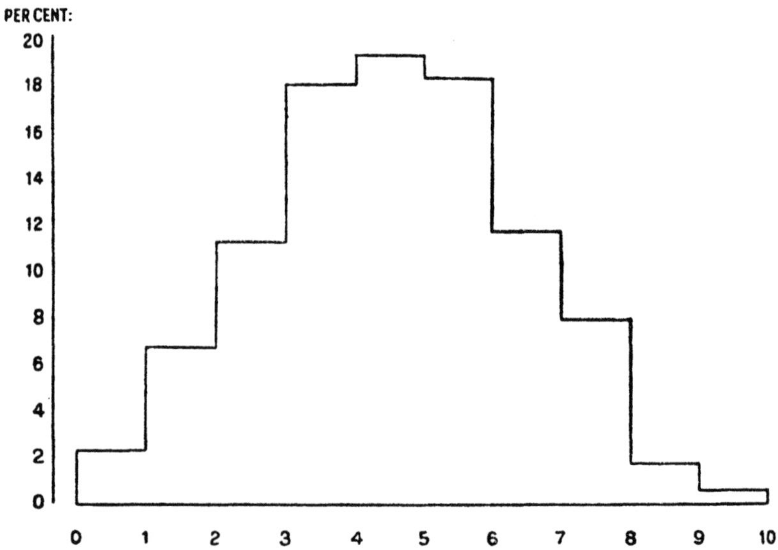

FIG. 6.2b Distribution of extraversion/introversion in 1,000 soldiers. (Taken from Eysenck, 1947.)

dysthymics, but on the whole not significantly more extraverted than normal controls (see Figure 6.3). Furthermore it has been found by several authors that there are differences in questionnaire responses between conversion hysterics and hysterics whose classification is based mainly on their possession of what is called 'hysterical personality', the latter having more extraverted scores than the former and also higher scores on neuroticism (Ingham and Robinson, 1964). On objective tests of personality, however, Eysenck and Claridge (1962) have shown that hysterics do differ from normal controls in a direction opposite to that

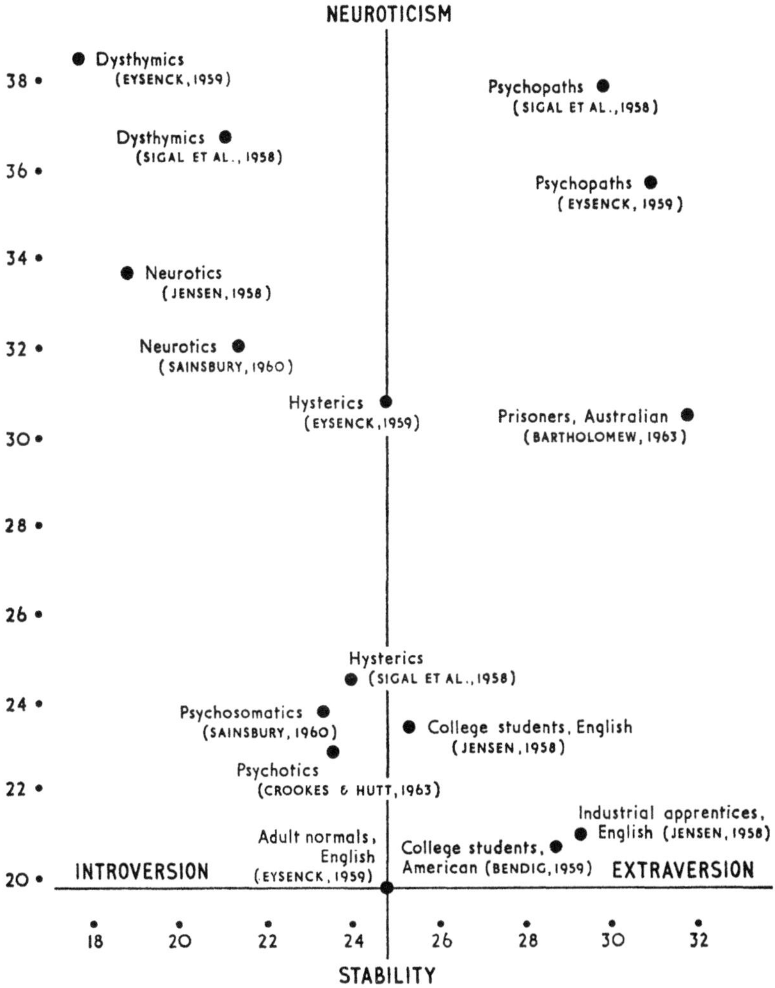

FIG. 6.3 Scores on the M.P.I. of various neurotic and convict groups, as related to normal control groups, psychotics and psychosomatics.

in which dysthymics differ from normal controls, so that the possibility arises that the contradiction to the Janet-Jung hypothesis may be an artefact of certain features of the questionnaires used. However that may be, the search was continued for other criterion groups of extraversion, and it was found that psychopaths ('moral imbeciles') were more suitable than hysterics, having nearly always extraversion scores which distinguishes them reliably from normal controls in the extraverted direction, as well as having high neuroticism scores (Hildebrand, 1958). This suggested the possibility that criminals whose conduct in many ways resembles that of psychopaths might also resemble that group in having high scores on neuroticism and extraversion, i.e. belonging to the choleric quadrant, and recent work by Eysenck (1964b) has shown that this is indeed so. Figure 6.3 shows the results of several studies which have been done with questionnaires and this diagram may serve to give a condensed summary of studies relevant to the various hypotheses.

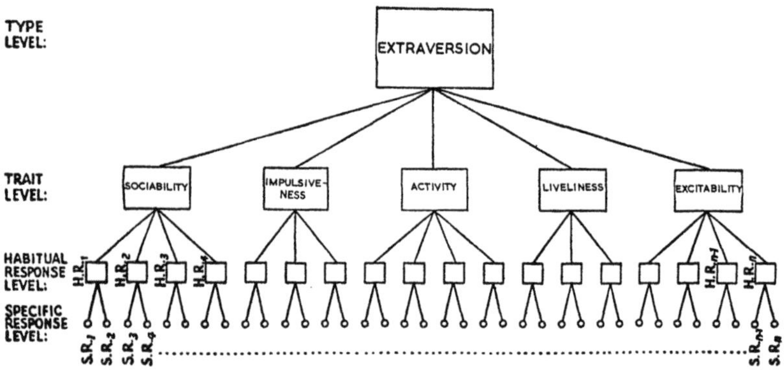

FIG. 6.4 Hierarchical system of personality description. (Taken with modifications from Eysenck, 1947.)

There are certain differences between Eysenck's approach (1947) and those of Guilford and Cattell which can best be discussed in relation to the descriptive model of personality first put forward by Eysenck in 1947. This model is illustrated in Figure 6.4. It will be seen that we are dealing there with four levels of behaviour organization. At the lowest level we have specific responses SR_1, SR_2, SR_3 . . . SR_n. These are acts such as responses to an experimental test or to experiences in everyday life which are observed once and may or may not be characteristic of the individual.

At the second level we have what are called habitual responses, HR_1 HR_2, HR_3 . . . HR_n. These are specific responses which can recur under similar circumstances, i.e. if the test is repeated a similar response is given, or if the life situation recurs the individual reacts in a similar fashion. This is the lowest level of organization; roughly speaking, the amount of organization present here can be measured in terms of reliability coefficients, i.e. in terms of the probability that in repetition of a situation behaviour will be consistent.

At the third level we have organizations of habitual acts into traits, $T_1, T_2, T_3 \ldots T_n$. These traits such as accuracy, irritability, persistence, rigidity, etc., are theoretical constructs based on observed intercorrelation between a number of different habitual responses; in the language of the factor analyst they may be conceived of as group factors or primary factors.

At the fourth level we have the organization of traits into a general type; in our example the introvert. This organization also is based on observed correlations, this time on correlations between the various traits, which between them make up the type under discussion. Thus in our example, sociability, impulsiveness, jocularity, carefreeness and various other traits would form a constellation of traits intercorrelating amongst themselves and giving rise to a higher order construct, the type. It will be noted that these four levels of personality organization correspond closely to the four types of factor distinguished by analysts; error factors, specific factors, group factors and general factors. An habitual response is merely a specific response divested of its error component, and made into a specific factor; a trait is a system of specific responses divested of its error and specific variance; a type is a system of specific responses which has lost its error, specific and group factor variance.

It will be clear that Guilford and Cattell, like most American writers, have concentrated very much on the *trait level* and have only incidentally and somewhat belatedly paid attention to the implications of the correlations actually observed between these traits. Eysenck, conversely, has been particularly interested in the *type level* and has paid scant attention until recently to primary factors themselves. Some misunderstandings arose at the beginning from the fact that in their early work Cattell and Guilford both used rotation into simple structure with retention of orthogonality; in this way they precluded the possibility of higher order factors and emerged with an analysis of personality exclusively into independent traits. Thus there was an apparent contradiction between Eysenck, discovering in his analyses very broad type factors of neuroticism and extraversion, and Cattell and Guilford apparently discovering no such type factors but rather a multiplicity of independent primary factors. Thurstone's advocacy of oblique factors and higher order factors has brought these two sides very much closer together, rather along the lines of the diagram shown in Figure 6.4. Both sides now recognize explicitly the descriptive value of primary traits as well as the existence of type factors such as neuroticism and extraversion. What is still in dispute is the usefulness (practical, theoretical and heuristic) of higher order factors as opposed to lower order traits. Peterson (1965) has recently reviewed the controversy, and arrived at the conclusion that 'available evidence now suggests that the most dependable dimensions drawn from conventional factor analyses of ratings and questionnaires are simple, familiar dimensions of broad semantic scope. It also appears that most of the initially obscure, apparently more precise, more narrowly defined factors many investigators claim to have revealed are either trivial, artifactual, capricious, or all three.' Peterson's conclusions, which are well in accord with Eysenck's suggestions (1947, 1957) are based on an examination of descriptive efficiency, sufficiency of factor extraction, factor invariance, and validity; we will return to this evidence again in the final chapter. (CF. also Linn, 1965; Bendig, 1962; and Becker, 1960.)

In our survey of factor analyses of questionnaires we have concentrated on the Cattell, Guilford and Eysenck ones primarily because it is these with which we will be concerned in later parts of this book. Furthermore, Eysenck (1960e) has surveyed in considerable detail the literature relating to other questionnaires and factor analytic studies, and there was no intention of repeating this work here. However, to indicate the fact that results can be generalized to other questionnaires we may perhaps single out three studies which have appeared since the publication of *The Structure of Human Personality* and which concern widely used methods of personality assessment. The first of these studies was carried out by Kassebaum, Couch and Slater (1959) and concerns the factorial dimensions of the MMPI. The authors state that a preliminary goal of their research 'was to achieve a clarification of the dimensions of the MMPI in more general terms than the clinical emphasis of the test has heretofore allowed. For this purpose we included 19 nonclinical scales in our analysis in addition to the original 13 clinical and validity scales. The selection of these scales was based upon our interest in predicting certain aspects of interpersonal behaviour and this concern determines the domain of scales to be analysed.' The 32 scales used are listed below.

L—Lie; F—Validity; K—Ego functioning; Hs—Hypochondriasis; D—Depression; Hy—Hysteria; Pd—Psychopathic Deviate; Mf—Masculine-feminine interest; Pa—Paranoia; Pt—Psychasthenia; Sc—Schizophrenia; Ma—Hypomania; Si—Social Introversion; Es—Barron's ego strength scale—predicts responses to psychotherapy; Ie—Gough's intellectual efficiency scale—a 'non-intellectual intelligence test'; Lp—Oettel's leadership scale; Ai—Gough's 'achievement via independence' —predicts academic achievement in introductory psychology courses; Sy—Gough's sociability scale; Ac—Gough's 'achievement via conformance'—predicts academic achievement in high school; Re—Social responsibility scale; Do—Dominance scale; Pr—Gough's prejudice scale; St—Gough's status scale; Im—Impulsivity; Sp—Social presence; Fm—Hecht's feminine masochism scale; Rp—McClelland's role-playing ability scale; R—Welsh's factorial scale of 'repression, denial'; A—Welsh's factorial scale of 'anxiety'; Dp—Navran's dependency scale; To—Tolerance scale; O-I—Originality potential.

The test was administered to 160 Harvard College Freshmen and the 32 scales were intercorrelated, and the matrix factor analysed by means of the complete centroid method of Thurstone. Three factors were extracted and the matrix was then rotated to simple orthogonal structure. The rotated factor loadings are given in the Table below.

TABLE 6.1

Main factors extracted from the MMPI. Taken with permission from Kassebaum, Couch and Slater (1959)

Rotated factor loadings

Item	I	II	III	h^2
1 L	−0·18	0·40	0·12	0·21
2 F	0·65	0·02	−0·21	0·47
3 K	−0·71	0·07	0·24	0·57
4 Hs	0·55	−0·01	0·34	0·42
5 D	0·65	0·40	0·28	0·66
6 Hy	0·04	−0·03	0·57	0·33
7 Pd	0·71	−0·20	0·09	0·55
8 Mf	0·48	0·10	0·35	0·36
9 Pa	0·34	0·06	0·30	0·21
10 Pt	0·91	0·00	0·16	0·85
11 Sc	0·89	−0·11	0·00	0·80
12 Ma	0·48	−0·63	−0·09	0·64
13 Si	0·69	0·58	−0·15	0·84
14 Es	−0·73	−0·23	−0·21	0·63
15 Ie	−0·72	−0·12	0·14	0·55
16 Lp	−0·85	−0·26	0·09	0·80
17 Ai	−0·36	0·17	0·39	0·31
18 Sy	−0·56	−0·55	0·16	0·64
19 Ac	−0·63	0·28	0·10	0·49
20 Re	−0·53	0·46	0·14	0·51
21 Do	−0·50	−0·20	0·01	0·29
22 Pr	0·71	−0·14	−0·35	0·65
23 St	−0·49	−0·42	0·14	0·44
24 Im	0·59	−0·56	−0·01	0·66
25 Sp	−0·71	−0·44	0·11	0·71
26 Fm	0·55	0·37	0·36	0·57
27 Rp	−0·68	−0·15	0·20	0·52
28 R	−0·10	0·69	−0·05	0·49
29 A	0·88	0·02	0·03	0·78
30 Dp	0·85	0·02	0·14	0·74
31 To	−0·80	0·19	0·35	0·80
32 OI	−0·32	0·28	−0·03	0·18
$Ea^2 =$	12·62	3·38	1·66	$\Sigma h^2 =$ 17·66

The authors interpret their factors as follows. They say that in Table 6.1 'the main elements in the interpretation of Factor I are readily apparent. High saturations may be noted with regard to Pt, Sc, and Welsh's A (Anxiety), thus providing a close match with previous studies. High negative loadings are contributed by Lp (Leadership), To (Tolerance), Es (Ego-Strength), and Ie (Intellectual Efficiency). We have defined this factor as a dimension of *Ego Weakness vs. Ego Strength.* Factor I accounts for 39 per cent of the total variance and 72 per cent of the common factor variance.

Factor II exhibits high positive loadings on Welsh's R (Repression), Re (Social Responsibility) and Si (Social Introversion) and negative loadings on Ma and Sy (Sociability). The nature of this bi-polarity suggested as interpretation of this factor in terms of *Introversion-Extraversion.* Factor II accounts for 10 per cent of the total variance and 19 per cent of the common factor variance.

The most important loading on Factor III is Hy, which has low saturations on I and II. None of the remaining loadings is of sufficient size or purity to be of substantial aid in the interpretation of the factor. It is worthy of note that the factor has loadings on all three members of the 'neurotic triad', and is thus very similar to the so-called 'neurotic factor' of some of the early studies. Other loadings, however, such as the positive loadings on To (Tolerance) and Ai (Achievement via independence) and the negative loading on Pr (Prejudice), suggest that the factor may be absorbing nonpathological elements from the clinical scales—an illustration of the hazards of factor interpretations based on clinical scales alone. We do not feel that a clear interpretation of this factor is possible at present, but have tentatively called it *Tender-Minded Sensitivity.* Because of its small size (it accounts for only 5 per cent of the total variance and 9 per cent of the common factor variance) and doubtful interpretation, Factor III was not included in the further analyses which are discussed below.

Kassebaum, Couch and Slater have added one further step to their analysis which essentially amounts to extracting what they call 'fusion factors', and which effectively means that they rotate the whole structure through an angle of 45° and pass the new 'fusion factors' through the centres of the four quadrants. The resulting factors and factor fusions are shown in Figure 6.5, which agree reasonably closely with previous results from studies of the MMPI.

It is not suggested that this study, or indeed any other of those mentioned, is definitive and *proves* the two-dimensional theory of personality description which underlies so much of the work reported here. All we are entitled to say is that the results are in line with the theory and can be predicted from it. Analyses using fewer scales, particularly those restricting themselves to the pathological scales, have found and will continue to find different patterns of factor structure, but it is perhaps reasonable to suggest that this is so because of the arbitrary restrictions imposed on their selection of scales. Kassebaum, Couch and Slater conclude that 'we should like to suggest the hypothesis that an orthogonal solution of a factor analysis of any personality inventory or battery of trait ratings of sufficient size and complexity, and drawn from a normal population, will produce a structure in which all eight 45° vectors of the two largest factors will be essentially similar to those we have identified. We feel that deviations from this structure are due only to peculiarities of samples, insufficiently 'covered' domains and the use of oblique solutions.' With this statement we are in full agreement.

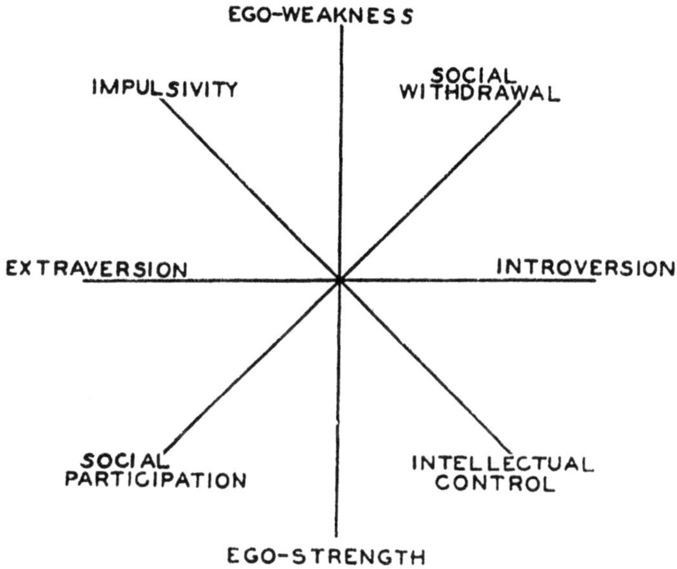

FIG. 6.5 Major dimensions of personality as identified by factor analysis of MMPI scales. (Taken with permission from Kassebaum, Couch and Slater, 1959.)

Interpretations and factor namings are of course subject to many errors and it would have been interesting to have some external criteria for the similarity of the Kassebaum factors and those of Eysenck, Cattell and Guilford. A study along these lines was undertaken by Corah (1964). He replicated the Kassebaum study but used a rather smaller number of MMPI scales which were known to have high loadings on the two factors. Having obtained results essentially identical with those of Kassebaum he then worked out a scheme for obtaining factor scores on extraversion and neuroticism as defined by the MMPI scales.

'MMPI records were obtained for 251 subjects from 9 different groups: 2 "normal" groups, 1 of 38 college students from Washington University, and 1 of 72 psychiatric aids and attendants; 5 outpatient neurotic groups consisting of 9 phobic reactions, 20 obsessive compulsives, 16 depressives, 22 hysterics and 39 anxiety neurotics; 2 inpatient groups with a primary diagnosis of sociopathic personality consisting of 24 patients with a subclassification of antisocial reactions and 11 with no subclassification ("sociopaths"). . . . Classifications were made on the basis of hospital staff diagnoses.'

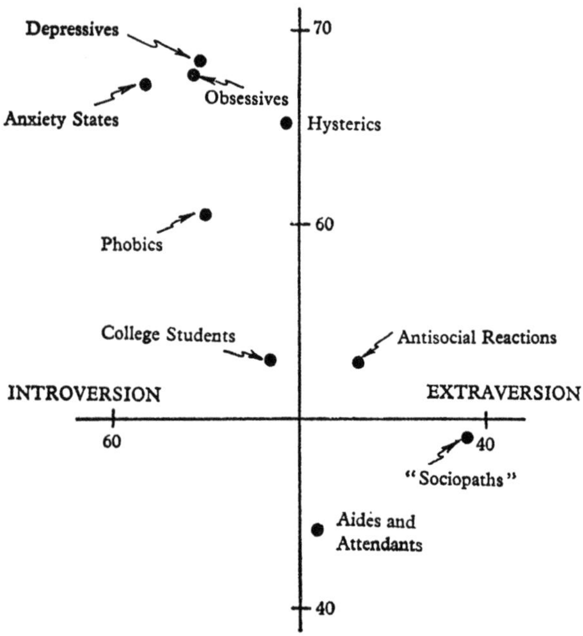

FIG. 6.6 Position of various groups on two main personality dimensions as diagnosed by the MMPI. (Taken with permission from Corah, 1964.)

The results of the analysis are shown in Figure 6.6. All of the patient groups except the 'sociopaths' were found to differ significantly from the normals on the neuroticism factor. None of the neurotic groups differed significantly from each other but they differed significantly from the sociopathic group. 'This first factor would seem to be reasonably well identified with the trait of neuroticism (N).'

'The scores on Factor II significantly differentiated the dysthymic group (Obsessives, depressives, anxiety neurotics and phobics) from the hysterics, the dysthymics from the normals, the normals from the sociopaths, and the hysterics from the sociopaths. None of the differences among the dysthymic groups or between the sociopathic groups was significant. The results with the scores for the second factor appear, for the most part, to meet Eysenck's criterion for a bipolar trait of introversion/extraversion (I-E).'

Corah next carried out another study by selecting from a group of 128 outpatient neurotics 25 extreme extraverts and 25 extreme introverts, on the basis of their I-E factor scores. 'The mean N factor scores of the groups were 68·88 for the extraverts and 71·32 for the introverts. The difference was not significant. The mean I-E scores were 41·84 for the extraverts and 70·72 for the introverts.' The hypothesis to be tested was one advanced by Eysenck (1960e) who had put forward the view that extraverted neurotics would be characterized primarily by somatic manifestations of anxiety, while introverted neurotics would be characterized by cognitive manifestations of anxiety.

The symptoms of all the patients were rated independently and blindly as to whether they indicated somatic or cognitive anxiety. 'Somatic symptoms included autonomic complaints, somatic complaints, motor activity and acting out. Cognitive symptoms included feelings of tension, fears, depression, anxious mood, insomnia, "bad" dreams and nervousness.' A 'proportion of somatic anxiety' score was obtained for each patient by subtracting the number of cognitive symptoms from the number of somatic symptoms and dividing by the total number of symptoms. The mean scores were 0·5152 for the extraverts, and 0·2809 for the introverts. 'The difference is significant beyond the 0·001 level.'

Further support for the contention that the second factor represented I-E was obtained by testing the hypothesis that the diagnoses of the two groups of patients would fall into the respective categories of dysthymic neurotics and hysteric psychopathic neurotics. Diagnoses were combined according to Eysenck's criteria into two groups—introverted neurotics and extraverted neurotics. This resulted in a 2×2 contingency table which gave a chi square of 11·68 ($p < 0·001$). 'The results of this research appear to substantiate the assumption that the MMPI factor dimensions studied are N and I-E.'

We next turn to an analysis of Gough's (1957) California Psychological Inventory which consists of 18 scales most of which have been derived by item analysis against such socially relevant criteria as social status, sex, intelligence, ratings of dominance, etc. Correlation matrices of the 18 C.P.I. scales reported in the Manual (Gough, 1957) for 4,098 males and 3,572 females were separately factor analysed by the principal components method with communalities estimated as the squared multiple correlation of each scale with all other scales (Nichols and Schnell, 1963). Three factors were retained from each analysis, and these were then rotated analytically to orthogonal simple structure according to the normalized varimax criterion. The factors obtained from the male and female matrices are very similar. 'The first two factors had high loadings on several scales while the third factor had a high loading only of flexibility, a scale which was not constructed by criterion keying. It was therefore decided to obtain factor scales only for the first two factors since these account for most of the common variance among the criterion keyed scales. In order to obtain factor scores which were relatively independent, high loading scales were selected to represent each factor so that positive and negative loadings on other factors tended to cancel each other. The scales chosen to represent each factor and the loadings are shown in Table 6.2.'

TABLE 6.2

Factors extracted from intercorrelations between the scales of Gough's California Psychological Inventory. Taken with permission from Nichols and Schnell (1963)

Factor loadings

	Factor I		Factor II		Factor III	
CPI scales	M	F	M	F	M	F
Factor I						
Sense of well-being	0·70	0·78	0·23	0·25	0·07	−0·02
Responsibility	0·68	0·67	0·10	0·18	−0·10	−0·14
Socialization	0·58	0·55	−0·04	0·02	−0·25	−0·33
Self-control	0·83	0·87	−0·26	−0·24	0·05	−0·15
Tolerance	0·71	0·74	0·20	0·32	0·34	0·22
Good impression	0·77	0·75	−0·05	0·05	0·06	−0·13
Achievement via conformance	0·79	0·75	0·19	0·23	−0·09	−0·25
Factor II						
Dominance	0·28	0·23	0·63	0·74	−0·18	−0·11
Sociability	0·22	0·31	0·78	0·79	−0·14	−0·06
Social presence	0·00	0·10	0·71	0·73	0·27	0·36
Self-acceptance	−0·08	−0·06	0·74	0·77	−0·14	0·04

As the authors themselves point out, Factor I appears to be the obverse of the numerous neuroticism and emotionality factors in the literature, whereas Factor II is clearly an extraversion one. They themselves suggest alternative names for these factors but there is little advantage perhaps in adding to an already overburdened nomenclature. Further evidence for this identification comes from a large number of correlations reported by them between factor scores on these factors and various other scales such as the MMPI, the Guilford scales, and so forth. There appears to be little doubt in the Gough personality inventory as in all the others we have surveyed there is impressive evidence for the presence of our two main dimensions of personality.

7

THE BIOLOGICAL BASIS OF PERSONALITY

EYSENCK has been particularly concerned with the question of the degree to which personality features are due to hereditary factors (Eysenck and Prell, 1951; Eysenck, 1956a). In the most recent study using items from the Eysenck questionnaires, Shields (1962) tested fraternal twins brought up together, identical twins brought up together and identical twins brought up in separation, and succeeded in showing not only that identical twins were much more alike with respect to extraversion and neuroticism than were fraternal twins, but also that identical twins brought up in separation were, if anything, more alike than were identical twins brought up together. On the basis of these and other studies Eysenck has come to the conclusion that a large proportion, possibly as much as three quarters of the total variance for differences between individuals with respect to extraversion and neuroticism, is due to hereditary factors. Support for this conclusion is found in the work of Lienert and Reisse (1961), Cattell *et al.* (1955), Gottesman (1963), Wilde (1964) and others.[1]

Eysenck has also been very concerned with making more specific the implications of causation contained in these findings. On the assumption that heredity can only influence bodily structures and not mental functioning, except in so far as mental functioning and behaviour are themselves determined by the physiological, neurological and hormonal constitution of the individual, he has suggested that there must be certain cortico-visceral factors at the basis of neurotic and criminal behaviour, i.e. of the factors of emotionality and of extraversion-introversion, and that it is the task of the psychologist and the physiologist to discover

[1] A review of the methods and results on which their conclusion is based is given in Eysenck (1967), which also contains a discussion of arguments, criticisms and other technical issues raised in this connection.

just what these are. As regards the factor of emotionality or neuroticism Eysenck (1960e) has suggested that the search is almost certainly a very circumscribed one as there seems to be little doubt that emotionality is closely related to the activity of the autonomic system, and more particularly the sympathetic branch. A review of this literature has been given by Eysenck (1960e) and more recently by Duffy (1962). These suggest that it is probably not so much the strength of the sympathetic reaction to novel, disturbing and painful stimuli which characterizes the emotionally labile person, but rather the *persistence* of such arousal. Furthermore the work of Lacey, Malmo and others suggests the existence of what is called *autonomic response specificity*, i.e. individuals tend to respond to stress with the activation of specific parts of the sympathetic system, regardless of the type of stimulation received, rather than responding with all parts of the sympathetic simultaneously. Unfortunately, much of the work in this field has not been of a very high quality, and there are many technical defects which are only too obvious. In spite of this the identification of the lability of the autonomic system with emotional instability is almost certainly along the right lines, and the extensive animal work carried out on emotionality in rats and its inheritance by Eysenck and Broadhurst (1964) very much supports such an interpretation. A full discussion of the most recent form of this theory, and the evidence on which it is based, is available in Eysenck (1967).

As regards extraversion and introversion Eysenck has made use of certain suggestions in the work of Pavlov, who maintained that cortical events could best be interpreted in terms of the concepts of excitation and inhibition, and who himself made a number of attempts to link these notions with psychiatric behaviour disorders (Gray, 1964). Eysenck proposed the formal hypothesis that 'introverted people are characterized by strong excitatory and weak inhibitory potentials, whereas extraverted people are characterized by weak excitatory and strong inhibitory potentials' (Eysenck, 1957). The terms excitation and inhibition in this formulation may be interpreted in two ways. A weak interpretation may be made using them in a purely descriptive psychological sense as hypothetical variables. Thus in this sense 'excitation' would mean simply facilitation of cortical events underlying perceptual, learning and motor movement phenomena, whereas 'inhibition' would refer to the depression of these phenomena. This is a very rough and ready description which even at the psychological level can be refined, as for instance by Clark Hull who used concepts such as reactive inhibition in a perfectly well defined manner, or by Köhler who elaborated the laws of perceptual inhibition or 'satiation' in considerable detail.

To test a theory of this kind is relatively simple. We can make detailed predictions in terms of specific tests and then correlate test scores of groups of subjects with a well established measure of extraversion/introversion. Thus we may predict that introverts should form conditioned responses better than extraverts, and as shown in Figure 7.1 this is indeed so (Eysenck, 1965). In an eyeblink conditioning experiment 35 subjects with high introversion scores were compared with 35 subjects with high extraversion scores on the M.P.I. and it will be seen that the scores of the former are at all points higher than those of the latter.

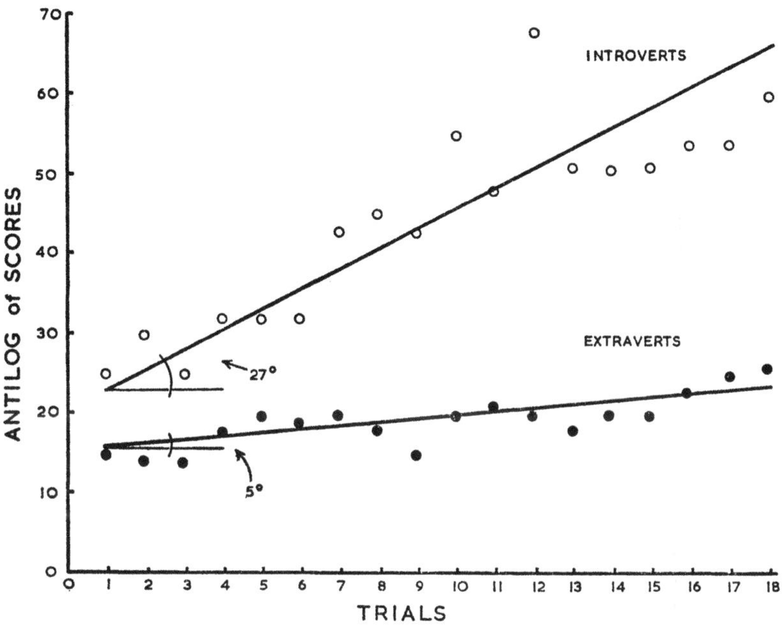

FIG. 7.1 Eyeblink conditioning scores (antilogs) of introverted and extraverted subjects. The original scores were taken from the work of Franks. (cf. Eysenck, 1965.)

Similar results have been found with galvanic skin response conditioning and verbal conditioning experiments (Eysenck, 1965b). The literature on this type of experiment is too large to even attempt to summarize at this point. Just for the sake of illustration it may be mentioned that in accordance with prediction introverts show better performance on vigilance tests, have longer after images, preserve visual fixation better, show less satiation, i.e. have weaker figural after effects, have greater tolerance for sensory deprivation but less tolerance for physical pain, and show better performance when a measure is made of their critical flicker fusion thresholds. There are about 50 separate predictions of this type which have been made and verified and there seems to be little doubt that in its weak form at least this law of excitation/inhibition is on the whole supported by the experimental evidence (Eysenck, 1957; 1960c; 1964b).

In its strong form the law of excitation/inhibition has been linked by Eysenck with the notion of the ascending reticular formation (Eysenck, 1963a, b; 1965a). Malmo (1959) and others have recently put forward the hypothesis of a continuum of cortical arousal which is attained in response to corticopetal impulses derived from lower centres. The continuum extending from deep sleep at the low arousal end to 'excited' states at the high arousal end is a function of the amount of cortical bombardment by the ascending reticular activating system, such that the greater the cortical bombardment, the higher the activation. As is well known, impulses transmitted through the long classical pathways appear in the main to be concerned with the carriage of detailed sensory and executive information; on the other hand impulses travelling through and elaborated within the reticular formation appear to be concerned with facilitatory or suppressor factors capable of modulating the transmission of impulses through other centres including reflex centres, to relay stations related to the long classical pathways and the cortical integrating mechanisms. It may be that the locus of the facilitatory and inhibitory cortical tendencies we have referred to in the weak statement of the law of excitation and inhibition may thus be found in the activating and synchronizing parts of the reticular formation respectively. Eysenck (1965a) has therefore reformulated the law as follows: 'Introverts are characterized by a reticular formation the activating part of which has a relatively low threshold of arousal, while the recruiting part of it has a relatively high threshold of arousal; conversely, extraverts are characterized by their possession of a reticular formation whose activating part has a high threshold of arousal and whose recruiting (synchronizing) part has a low threshold of arousal. Under identical conditions, therefore, cortical arousal will be more marked in introverts, cortical inhibition in extraverts.' (There are certain obvious similarities between this formulation and that of Gross to which attention has already been drawn in connection with the discussion of Gross's theories.) It is not of course suggested by Eysenck that the ascending reticular formation acts in isolation from the cortex or the autonomic systems; as is well known the action of the reticular formation on the cortex is supplemented by stimulation of the reticular formation by cortical impulses, and similarly it is known that autonomic stimulation affects the reticular formation both directly and through hormonal influences. Nevertheless as a first approximation and as a possible guide to further experimentation in this very complex field, the strong form of the law may perhaps be regarded as providing us at least with a statement definite enough to be capable of experimental support or disproof. A full discussion of the theory and the evidence concerning it is given in Eysenck (1967).

Support from the physiological side has come from several sources. The most obvious place in which to look for relevant evidence is of course the EEG. It is well known that states of fatigue and lowered alertness are accompanied by marked alpha rhythm, whereas states of cortical arousal are marked by desynchronization. Direct electrical stimulation of the activating and recruiting parts of the reticular formation respectively has been shown to destroy or facilitate the occurrence and amplitude of alpha rhythms respectively, and if the theory in question is in any way along the right lines, one would expect that under identical testing conditions extraverts would have greater amplitude of alpha rhythms. Savage (1964) studied alpha amplitude during 24 10-sec. artefact free periods, 10 secs after eyes closed, taking his reading from two electrodes on the occipital areas placements 18 and 20. The data were analysed by a low frequency analyser using amplitudes of alpha between 8 and 13 cycles per second. 10 introverted subjects were compared with 10 extraverted subjects, selected on the basis of their M.P.I. scores. The former had a mean amplitude of 29, the latter of 81, a difference which was significant at the 1 per cent level. Evidence from this study then seems to be in good agreement with the theory. Other supporting EEG studies are reviewed in Eysenck (1967).

The second proof derives from the study of evoked potentials. These are not normally visible in the usual EEG derived from scalp electrodes as they are obscured by 'spontaneous' brain rhythms. In order to record evoked potentials from the human scalp Shagass and Schwartz (1963) followed Dawson in applying the principle of averaging, thus cancelling out the background EEG rhythms and adding up the timelocked potentials. In this type of recording the primary potential begins with relative negativity in the active electrode which is maximum about 20 msec. after the stimulus. The negative component is followed by a positive component which reaches its peak from 2 to 10 msecs. after the maximum negativity. It is possible to measure the recovery cycle of evoked responses by administering paired stimuli, separated by varying intervals. The relative size of the second response compared to the first then indicates the extent to which responsiveness has been recovered after a given interval. Greater cortical excitation would be expected to lead to quicker recovery and it would follow from Eysenck's theory that recovery would be greater for introverts. Shagass and Schwartz reported data for 34 introverted neurotics and 36 extraverted neurotics using ratios to represent amount of maximum recovery after 20 msecs.; unity (1·0) indicates full recovery. The mean for the introverts was 1·25 that for the extraverts 0·81; the difference was significant at the 1 per cent level. This study too then supports the neuıophysiological interpretation of Eysenck's postulate.

A third proof relates to critical flicker fusion thresholds. A more efficient cortex, one in a high state of excitation, would be expected to show a higher threshold, consequently we would predict that introverts would have higher thresholds than extraverts. There is some evidence from the work of Lindsley (1957) to indicate that in animals stimulation of the ascending reticular activating system improves the efficiency of discriminating closely contiguous signals, and the work of Shagass and Schwartz just mentioned would also seem to support this. There are now several independent studies to show that critical flicker fusion thresholds are in fact higher for introverts although the evidence is far from conclusive (Eysenck, 1967). Here also therefore the evidence is in agreement with the hypothesis.

A fourth proof may be derived from the work of Grey Walter and his associates (1964) on the 'expectancy wave', a physiological measure of association derived from EEG waves taken from the pre-frontal areas. It appears that these 'expectancy waves' occur and can easily be observed in normal and neurotic subjects, but are very difficult to produce or observe in psychopathic subjects. Much remains to be learned, of course, of the precise nature and significance of these waves, and it is to be hoped that more quantitative relationships will be established with extraversion in normal, random samples of the population; until this is done the work along these lines can only be regarded as marginal support for our theory.

A fifth proof of Eysenck's postulate is related to the great volume of evidence which indicates that CNS stimulant drugs have introverting effects on a great variety of experimental tests, whereas CNS depressant drugs have an extraverting effect; a lengthy review of the evidence has been given elsewhere (Eysenck, 1963a) and will not be recapitulated here. On the whole the experimental evidence is in favour of the hypothesis; tests which differentiate extraverted and introverted subjects almost invariably respond to stimulant and depressant drugs in the predicted direction. Of particular interest in this connection has been the work of Shagass and many others on the sedation threshold, i.e. the amount of depressant drug required to produce a given reaction which may be formally identified in terms of changing EEG patterns, sleep, or performance decrement on behavioural tests. Eysenck's hypothesis would predict that extraverts already in a higher state of inhibition than introverts would have lower thresholds, i.e. require less depressant drug to reach the threshold point; introverts, on the other hand, should have very high thresholds, i.e. require a considerable amount of the drug. About a dozen empirical studies are now available to support this prediction in considerable detail; results from one such study are given in Figure 7.2.

Eysenck has indicated certain ways in which these individual differences in excitation and inhibition may be instrumental in mediating the behavioural phenomena specified as neurosis and criminal behaviour. He argues that neurotic symptoms such as phobias, anxieties, obses-

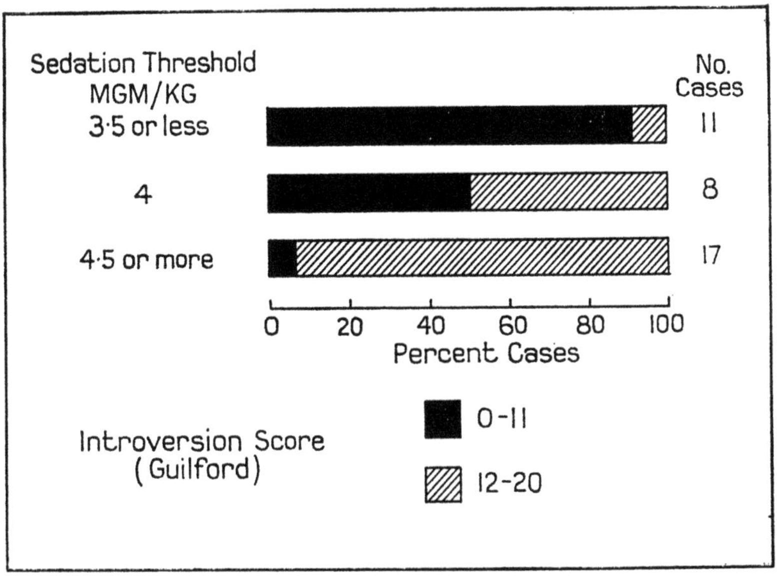

FIG. 7.2a Sedation thresholds of subjects high or low respectively on introversion. (Taken with permission from Shagass and Schwartz, 1963.)

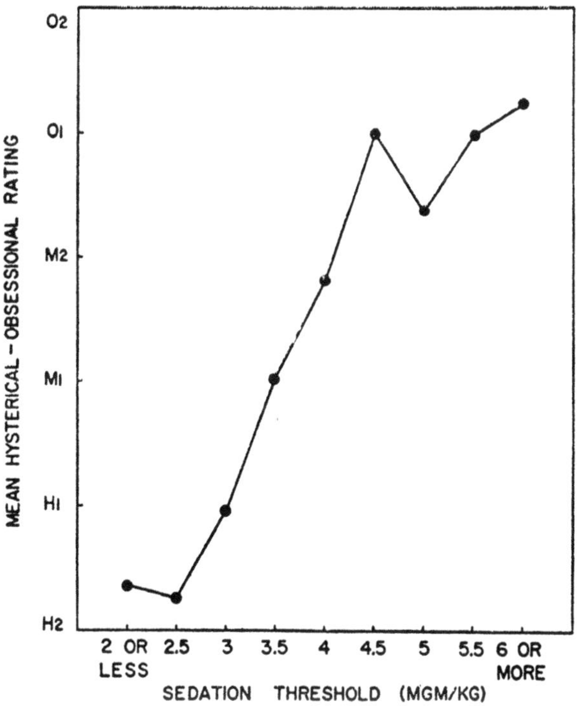

FIG. 7.2b Relationship between hysterical or obsessional personality and mean sedation threshold. (Taken with permission from Shagass and Schwartz, 1963.)

sional and compulsive behaviour patterns, reactive depressions and so forth, are essentially conditioned autonomic responses, or skeletal reactions made as a consequence of such conditioned autonomic responses. This conception of neurosis is of course quite different from the psychoanalytic and has lead to an entirely different system of treatment which has been called 'behaviour therapy' (Eysenck, 1960b, 1964a; Eysenck and Rachman, 1965). According to this way of thinking, if neurotic disorders are essentially conditioned autonomic responses then treatment should consist essentially in a process of extinction or deconditioning, or, as in the work of Wolpe (1958), of conditioning alternative responses. The success which behaviour therapy has had in its application suggests that this way of looking at neurosis may not be entirely valueless. Criminal behaviour conversely is accounted for in terms of a failure to elaborate those conditioned responses which underlie what in popular parlance is frequently called 'conscience' (Eysenck, 1964b). Mowrer (1950) has shown in some detail how the disciplinary activities of parents, school teachers and the child's peers may act as unconditioned stimuli to produce sympathetic autonomic reactions to the undesirable asocial type of behaviour which society requires to be stamped out. On Eysenck's theory unstable extraverts, who condition poorly, would therefore be predisposed towards criminal behaviour, while unstable introverts, who condition well, would be predisposed towards neurotic behaviour. The introvert, we might say, conditions *too* well, and hence a strong autonomic reaction to experiences inevitably encountered in the course of his life tends to become linked to conditioned stimuli which for the normal person would remain neutral; hence the build-up of symptomatology in such a person. The extravert, on the other hand, does not condition well enough and fails to form the conditioned responses which underlie social behaviour. In both cases a person of strong and lasting emotional responses makes matters worse by exacerbating the autonomic reactions which are being conditioned in the introvert, and by acting as a drive towards anti-social behaviour in the extravert. The argument from individual differences in conditionability is only one link between the law of excitation and inhibition on the one hand, and neurosis and crime on the other; Eysenck has suggested several other such links but it would take us too far afield in this book to enter into a detailed discussion of these.

There are certain interesting parallels between personality classification and biological taxonomy. Analysis by phenetic relationship corresponds to factorial analysis, as summarized elsewhere; analysis by relation through ancestry, i.e. the use of phylogeny for classification, corresponds to our use of physiological factors as a basis for causal analysis. The main difference between biology and psychology is to be found in this: analysis by relation through ancestry is not feasible in biology because in most cases phylogenies are unknown; analysis by reference to physiological and neurological factors in psychology is practicable and likely to lead to important experimental discoveries. In our view it is important to retain and strengthen the link between statistical-correlational types of study and physiological-experimental types of study, to the mutual support of both these lines of evidence.

The assertion that there is a genotypic basis for personality structure, and in particular for E and N, should not be taken to imply that any particular measure of E and N constitutes a genotypic assessment of personality. It is clear that the behaviour we take into account in identifying our dimensions of personality is phenotypic, and that genotypic inferences require rigorous and strict experimental and statistical methodologies before they are acceptable; it follows that both inventory results and experimental laboratory studies can only be regarded as phenotypic measurement which may approach some genotypic asymptote under favourable conditions, but which may also under unfavourable conditions deviate very grossly from successful assessment of the genotype. It seems likely that inventories are more likely to be imperfect measures of genotype than laboratory assessment, but there can be no question that any measurement we undertake is always of the phenotype, never of the genotype. This raises interesting questions of the influence of specified environmental modifications on E and N; unfortunately little is known in this field. Two sources in particular, however, have been studied to some degree, and results may be presented in this section. These two sources are (1) mental illness, and recovery therefrom, and (2) the influence of one's marital partner.

Coppen and Metcalfe (1965) administered the M.P.I. to thirty-nine patients just after admission to hospital and later when they were about to be discharged when all the patients were considered to be recovered or to be substantially improved. After consideration of their aetiology, the patients, all of whom were suffering from depressive illness, were subdivided into three groups of endogenous and reactive depression and a group of mixed aetiology. Changes in M.P.I. score are shown in Table 7.1, according to diagnosis; it will be seen that in spite of quite high test-retest correlations ($r = 0{\cdot}62$ for N and 0·80 for E) there are marked changes in score, particularly for N. Such changes are particularly marked for the endogenous patients, who show a decrease of 15 points after recovery, as compared with the reactive patients (7 points only) or the mixed patients (4 points only). This is in good accord with the hypothesis that psychoticism is a personality dimension orthogonal to neuroticism, and that a psychotic attack constitutes an environmental stress the emotional reaction to which results in grossly increased N scores; when the stress is removed, the N score returns to normal. The change in the neurotic and mixed groups is much less, although still notable. As Coppen and Metcalfe point out, 'even if the group of patients with reactive depression is considered separately, the mean N score for the group when recovered is just above the mean score for a normal population. . . . The present investigation certainly does not support the view that it would be possible to predict from their N scores those individuals who will develop a depressive illness of either an endogenous or a reactive aetiology.'

TABLE 7.1

Changes in M.P.I. scores of 39 patients from admission to discharge. Taken with permission from Coppen and Metcalfe (1965)

Changes in M.P.I. scores
(Patients grouped according to diagnosis)

	Reactive Depression		Endogenous Depression		Mixed Depression	
Number of patients	11		23		5	
Age range (years)	20–64		27–78		24–65	
Mean age (years)	45		52		50	
			Neuroticism score			
	Mean	S.D.	Mean	S.D.	Mean	S.D.
Clinical state:						
Depressed	30·6	14·1	30·8	10·8	28·4	8·7
Recovered	23·5	15·6	15·2	10·0	24·2	8·7
Level of significance of decrease	$p < 0{\cdot}001$		$p < 0{\cdot}001$			
			Extraversion score			
	Mean	S.D.	Mean	S.D.	Mean	S.D.
Clinical state:						
Depressed	20·1	7·3	16·3	8·7	15·8	4·4
Recovered	23·3	9·0	19·8	10·2	18·2	6·5
Level of significance of increase	0·10	$p < 0{\cdot}05$	$p < 0{\cdot}005$			

Coppen and Metcalfe retested 10 patients 3 to 11 months after discharge and found a continuation of the change noted on the occasion of the second test; the three successive scores for this group were: N—31·6, 18·7, and 13·2; E—16·0, 20·5, and 22·1. Thus the overall change for these patients was 18 points on N and 6 points on E.

It must of course be remembered that these are all patients who recovered. There is much evidence (Eysenck and Rachman, 1965) that probability and speed of recovery correlate with severity of neurosis, and probably with degree of neuroticism; it is possible that these recovered neurotics (our concern is of course only with the neurotic portion of the total group; the psychotic portion is not supposed to be predictable on the basis of the M.P.I.) were those who initially showed the lowest N scores. If non-recovered patients of the reactive type had been studied, and if M.P.I. scores had been available prior to breakdown, then a rather different outcome might have been expected. This expectation gains in plausibility when we consider the unexpectedly high correlation between N scores pre- and post-recovery; those who are highest on N remain so after recovery. Obviously efforts must be made to conduct predictive studies; it is not satisfactory to argue on the basis of post-recovery data in favour or against the possibility of predicting depressive breakdown.

Wretmark *et al.* (1961) also observed a decrease in N scores in endogenous depressives following recovery, as well as a slight (non-significant) increase in E. Bartholomew and Marley (1959) found little mean change in N or E score after 18 months, and correlations of 0·7 between first and second observation; they concluded from their observations that 'treatment and subsequent improvement in mental health do not greatly affect response to this personality questionnaire.' Knowles (1960) retested normal and neurotic groups after one year; he too found little change in mean score, and rather higher test-retest correlations. These studies bear out our suggestion that psychotic groups may show much greater changes over time, and with clinical improvement, than do neurotic groups. The most adequate study of the changes taking place in neurotics has been reported by Ingham (1966), who followed 119 neurotic patients over a three year period.

Personal interviews were conducted with each patient to assess his degree of improvement; this was recorded on a five-point scale, from 1 = worse to 5 = very much better. Ratings were obtained from the patient, from a relative, and from the interviewer. It was found that mean N scores of patients who had improved most had declined and were now virtually the same as those of a random sample. Mean N scores of patients who showed least clinical improvement were almost unchanged; they were substantially higher than those of the random sample on both occasions. Similarly findings were obtained for E scores, which increased with clinical improvement, but not in its absence. Ingham concludes 'that variations in N and E means between neurotic and normal samples probably arise from causes associated with the occurrence of the neurotic illness itself. Such variations are unlikely to reflect stable personality differences related to predisposition to neurosis.'

Ingham also found that 'the negative correlation between N and E in the neurotic sample (higher than that in the random sample and thus confirming previous findings), persisted after recovery in the most improved group. . . . The difference in correlations between neurotic and normal samples is, therefore, not likely to arise from causes associated with the occurrence of neurotic illness itself.'

Levinson and Meyer (1965), in a study of the effect of leucotomy by the technique of orbital undercutting, administered the M.P.I. to 29 patients before and after the operation; they also rated improvement on a five-point scale. They found a significant decrease in N and a significant increase in E; furthermore, the patients whose scores had changed most during the 9 months since the operation were those who had improved most according to the psychiatric rating.

It is somewhat difficult to draw far-reaching conclusions from these partly contradictory studies. Clearly we must take into account three separate factors. One is neuroticism, i.e. the genotypic lability of the emotional (autonomic) make-up of the person, which predisposes him/her to react to stress with neurotic/criminal behaviour; this we hope to measure, very imperfectly, with the M.P.I. neuroticism scale, at the phenotypic level. The second is neurosis, i.e. the result of neuroticism × stress; it seems clear that neurosis affects scores on the N scale, but whether this completely accounts for variation in N scores, and invalidates any claims for predictive usefulness of N scores in predicting neurotic breakdown and criminal behaviour may be doubted. Studies such as those of Burt (1965) show that ratings of N and E, even when done by teachers not trained in psychology, and using as subjects young schoolchildren, can predict with considerable accuracy neurotic breakdown and criminal behaviour some 35 years in the future; in interpreting the findings summarized on the preceding pages such direct evidence of the predictive accuracy of ratings and inventory responses should be borne in mind. (Other examples will be given elsewhere in this book, or are discussed in Eysenck, 1959.)

The third factor, viz. stress, has unfortunately not often been taken into account, or quantified; a recent study by Tauss (1964) is an exception to this rule. His sample was made up of a random selection of the Perth metropolitan population who were given a short version of the M.P.I. as a measure of neuroticism, as well as a questionnaire to assess neurotic symptoms (the Neurotic Manifestation Index). In addition a social stress score was obtained by the interviewers during hour-long interviews, scored on a composite conflict scale, made up of items such as religious, political, age, and educational differences between marriage partners, desire to change work, dissatisfaction with future prospects, and others. 'The sample was split on the median for neuroticism (Ne), and at the point of maximum discrimination for the neurotic manifestation index (NMI). Correlations were computed between the diagnosis of neurosis on the basis of NMI and the conflict scores, for both high and low Ne groups. For high Ne females, r = 0·30, while for low Ne females, r = 0·03. With males, the figures are 0·13 and 0·00, respectively. Combining both groups, there is a clear-cut and significant relationship between neurosis and conflict in the high Ne group, but none in the low Ne group. 'It is suggested that these findings support neuroticism as a predisposing factor, in the absence of which incidence of conflict situations will not tend to produce neurosis, while high neuroticism coupled with conflict would tend to produce neurotic symptoms. Both neuroticism and conflict might therefore be conceptualized as necessary but not sufficient conditions for the emergence of neurosis.' These conclusions agree well with the work of Symonds (1943), who found that 'the incidence of neurosis in different tactical duties varies directly with the amount of hazard encountered, as measured by the casualty rates.' From his data Slater (1944) calculated that the correlation between degree of predisposition and degree of stress in these breakdown cases was negative ($r = -0{\cdot}26$); thus the greater the degree of predisposition, the less stress was needed to provoke a neurotic reaction.

An interesting study demonstrating the interaction of predisposition and stress in determining N score has been reported by Kelvin *et al.* (1965). Test and retest data on the M.P.I. were available on 147 university students. As it proved, those who later on attended the Student Health Association with physical or psychological symptoms, or both, had higher N scores on admission to University; the means were 19·80 for non-attenders, 23·85 for attenders with physical symptoms only, and 27·03, 26·67 and 28·12 for those attending with different degrees of severity of mental symptoms. Thus the N score did in this case have some predictive validity. On retest the non-attenders' scores declined to 18·15 as did those of the physical symptom only students (to 21·10); those of the most maladjusted group rose to 36·12! We thus see an interaction between predisposition and breakdown in determining final N score; the same interaction comes out clearly in the following observation. When students are compared with respect to N scores on the basis of their success or failure at University, it is found that those who obtained a first-class degree had lower N scores on retest, while those who failed or dropped out had higher N scores. Thus clearly scores on N are affected by events happening to the person concerned, and are in no way to be regarded as genotypic indicators. (See also Savage, 1962, and Lucas *et al.*, 1964, for work on student success and failure as related to personality. Furneaux, 1962, has summarized his extensive findings in another brief but very relevant article.)

The other source of environmental effects on M.P.I. scores is documented in only one study (Kreitman, 1964), and the argument is based on inference only; yet it is mentioned here because of its intrinsic interest. M.P.I.s were given to neurotic and normal probands and their spouses, and the resulting correlations plotted in terms of the length of time the partners had been married. The results, based on 75 patients and 95 controls and their spouses, gave results which are shown in Figure 7.3. The patients' spouses had more physical and psychological symptoms than same-sex control subjects. Correlations between spouses were usually positive at significant levels in both groups, with the exception of extraversion. Length of marriage was reflected in a progressive increase in neuroticism among the patients' spouses when compared with controls; extraversion showed no such trend. Patients and their spouses had zero or non-significant correlations during the early years of marriage on introversion and neuroticism, while control subjects and their spouses showed highly significant positive correlations at the comparable period of marriage. As marriage progressed, patients and their spouses correlated increasingly highly on neuroticism, while in normal pairs the concordance fell progressively.

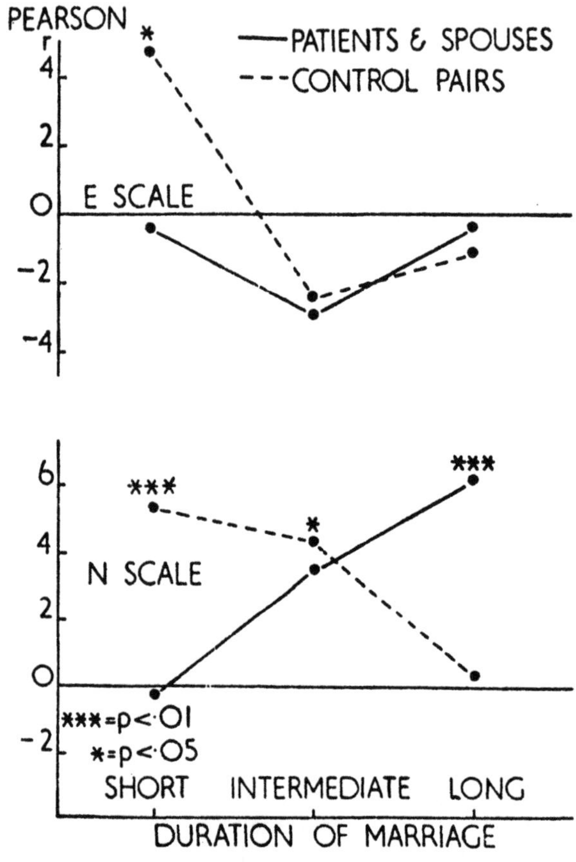

FIG. 7.3 Changes in personality resemblance of normal and neurotic responses over time for E and N. Quoted with permission from Kreitman (1964).

These figures are interesting, reflecting as they do a mixture of assortative mating and mutual influence; they are not as clear-cut as one might wish because of course the same pairs of spouses have not been followed through the years of marriage, and the selection of different pairs to exemplify different lengths of marriage is fraught with danger. However, as they stand the data suggest another source of environmental determination of M.P.I. scores which could with great advantage be studied further.

8

THE ORIGIN AND CONSTRUCTION OF THE M.P.I.

THE interest of Guilford and Cattell in *trait* as opposed to *type* factors resulted in the construction of numbers of multifactorial questionnaires which could not directly be used for the measurement of neuroticism and extraversion. In order to obtain questionnaire measures of these two factors for the investigation of the personality postulates discussed in the last section, Eysenck therefore found it necessary to try and construct inventories specially to fulfil this purpose. The first such inventory was

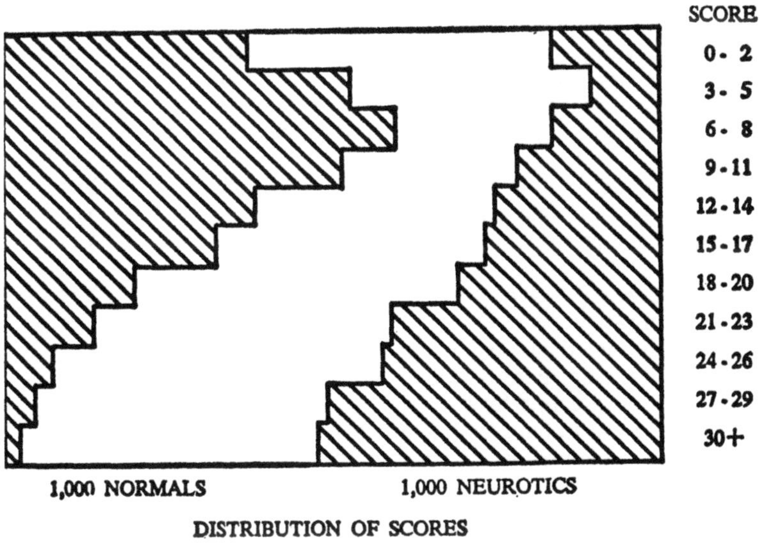

FIG. 8.1 Scores of normal and neurotic subjects respectively on the Maudsley Medical Questionnaire. (From Eysenck, 1952.)

the Maudsley Medical Questionnaire (Eysenck, 1952a), which is reprinted below. This was constructed to measure the personality trait of neuroticism and it succeeded in differentiating between normal and neurotic soldiers. Figure 8.1 shows the distribution of scores for these two groups; the scores of the neurotic group is roughly twice that of the normal group on the average, the respective means being 20·01 and 9·98. Also constructed was an 18-item lie scale which was frequently used in conjunction with the MMQ. Eysenck (1953) has shown some evidence for the validity of the lie scale by demonstrating that in a group of neurotic subjects the distribution of MMQ scores is bimodal, and that for those in the group having low MMQ scores the lie scores are significantly higher than in the other group. Item analyses were also carried out of the MMQ and some of the results have been reported in Eysenck (1952a, page 97).[1]

The Maudsley Medical Questionnaire

(1)	Do you have dizzy turns?	Yes	No
(2)	Do you get palpitations or thumping in your heart?	Yes	No
(3)	Did you ever have a nervous breakdown?	Yes	No
(4)	Have you ever been off work through sickness a good deal?	Yes	No
(5)	Did you often use to get 'stage fright' in your life?	Yes	No
(6)	Do you find it difficult to get into conversation with strangers?	Yes	No
(7)	Have you ever been troubled by a stammer or stutter?	Yes	No
(8)	Have you ever been made unconscious for two hours or more by an accident or blow?	Yes	No
(9)	Do you worry too long over humiliating experiences?	Yes	No
(10)	Do you consider yourself rather a nervous person?	Yes	No
(11)	Are your feelings easily hurt?	Yes	No
(12)	Do you usually keep in the background on social occasions?	Yes	No
(13)	Are you subject to attacks of shaking or trembling?	Yes	No
(14)	Are you an irritable person?	Yes	No
(15)	Do ideas run through your head so that you cannot sleep?	Yes	No
(16)	Do you worry over possible misfortunes?	Yes	No
(17)	Are you rather shy?	Yes	No
(18)	Do you sometimes feel happy, sometimes depressed, without any apparent reason?	Yes	No
(19)	Do you daydream a lot?	Yes	No
(20)	Do you seem to have less life about you than others?	Yes	No
(21)	Do you sometimes get a pain over your heart?	Yes	No
(22)	Do you have nightmares?	Yes	No
(23)	Do you worry about your health?	Yes	No

[1] The MMQ was never published in its English form, but a German translation was published and has been quite widely used in German-speaking countries.

(24)	Have you sometimes walked in your sleep?	Yes	No
(25)	Do you sweat a great deal without exercise?	Yes	No
(26)	Do you find it difficult to make friends?	Yes	No
(27)	Does your mind often wander badly, so that you lose track of what you are doing?	Yes	No
(28)	Are you touchy on various subjects?	Yes	No
(29)	Do you often feel disgruntled?	Yes	No
(30)	Do you often feel just miserable?	Yes	No
(31)	Do you often feel self-conscious in the presence of superiors?	Yes	No
(32)	Do you suffer from sleeplessness?	Yes	No
(33)	Did you ever get short of breath without having done heavy work?	Yes	No
(34)	Do you ever suffer from severe headaches?	Yes	No
(35)	Do you suffer from nerves?	Yes	No
(36)	Are you troubled by aches and pains?	Yes	No
(37)	Do you get nervous in places such as lifts, trains or tunnels?	Yes	No
(38)	Do you suffer from attacks of diarrhoea?	Yes	No
(39)	Do you lack self-confidence?	Yes	No
(40)	Are you troubled with feelings of inferiority?	Yes	No

The MMQ was found to be more suitable for neurotics than for normals, and when the time came for its revision the opportunity was taken also to carry out some research into the possibility of constructing a scale for the measurement of extraversion. In carrying out this research the factor analyses of Lovell and North of the Guilford questionnaires suggested that Guilford's C scale might be a good index of neuroticism, while his R scale might be a good index of extraversion. It might have been possible to use these scales as they stood instead of deriving a new set of measures, but there are various reasons why this was not considered suitable. There are certain weaknesses in the Guilford scales which makes them less useful than they might otherwise be for the measurement of neuroticism and extraversion.[1]

In the first place, the scales are long and repetitive. This, no doubt, increases split-half reliability but may not increase validity correspondingly. It also tends to put off intelligent subjects, who dislike being asked the same question in different guise, and it prolongs the time which can be allocated to the questionnaire part of an experiment unduly.

In the second place, little attention had been paid in the derivation of the scales to the possible importance of sex differences, i.e. to the

[1] The account that follows is copied in part from a paper by Eysenck (1956b). Having been published in an Italian journal, Rivista di Psicologia, this account is not easily obtainable by most students and as the empirical data contained in it are important for the development of the main theme of this book it seemed advisable to repeat its substance here.

possibility that an item which is a good predictor of a high score on the C or the R scale for men may not be a good predictor for women. We have observed considerable sex differences of this kind in our studies, and it seemed desirable to submit these accidental findings to a more definitive type of examination.

In the third place, it was our impression that some of the items included in the R scale correlated very little if at all with the total score on R, whereas items from other scales correlated quite highly with the total R score. Similarly, some C items did not appear to be correlated with C at all, whereas items from other scales actually had higher correlations with the C score than the majority of C items. It seemed desirable therefore to improve the validity of the R and C scales as possible measures of extraversion and neuroticism by carrying out an item analysis which would enable us to throw out poor items, and include items from scales other than R and C, provided that these items showed high relationships with either the R or the C score. (In all this, of course, a paramount consideration was that the zero correlations between the R and C scales, which had been empirically observed by several writers, should be preserved.)

In the fourth place, the scales are presented by Guilford as measures of unitary factors. Empirically it appeared that this hypothesis was not in fact always borne out, particularly in the case of the S (social shyness) scale. It appeared that some items were measures of an *introverted* type of social shyness, whereas others were measures of a *neurotic* type of social shyness, the total scale thus breaking up into two relatively unrelated parts. Again, a more definitive study of this point seemed desirable.

A questionnaire was prepared containing 261 items in all. Included in this were all the items from the Guilford scales S, D, C, R, G, and A. Also included were the items of the Maudsley Medical Questionnaire. This was included in order to obtain evidence on the relationship between neuroticism, as measured by this scale, and Guilford's C scale. It would have been desirable to have included items from other Guilford scales, but British subjects are very much less docile in their reactions to demands on the part of psychologists than are American students, and it proved very difficult indeed to find sufficient subjects to fill in even the relatively short questionnaire constructed in this fashion.

Our subjects were 200 men and 200 women, all British born, white, and over 18 years of age. The majority were in the 20–35 year age range, and most of them were upper middle, lower middle and skilled working class. Nearly all of them were urban, as testing was carried out only in London, Manchester, Bristol, Exeter, and other towns of similar size. Approximately half the subjects had had some kind of University education. The sample thus is by no means representative although certain points may be mentioned in connection with this. In the first place, our sample is probably more representative than samples on which questionnaires are usually standardized. In the second place, it is for practical purposes difficult to administer the *same* questionnaire to unskilled working class groups and to University students. Groups with low education fail to understand many of the questions in the Guilford scales, and if these are reworded in the kind of language spoken by lower working-class subjects, they are not acceptable to highly educated middle-class subjects. As this questionnaire is more likely to be employed with subjects having at least an average amount of education it seemed desirable to retain the original wording (except for one or two American terms which had to be changed as they would not be generally intelligible in Great Britain). Lastly, in our experience, the Guilford factors do not correlate appreciably with intelligence, education, age (up to 50), or sex,[1] so that a refined method of sampling taking these variables into account would, at the present stage of development, seem supererogatory.

Administration of the questionnaires was anonymous, but subjects were offered a chance to receive a detailed personality profile if they wanted this. The great majority did express a desire to have a personality profile, and, indeed, expressed a considerable degree of interest in the project and in the profile in particular. It is impossible to prove that the questionnaires were answered truthfully, but the combination of anonymity and the subjects' interest in finding out about themselves seems as potent a way of achieving relative sincerity as can be found at the present stage of development of psychological testing. Some time was spent with a few individuals who signed their names, and these interviews suggested strongly that no conscious efforts were made by these subjects to fake their scores.

TABLE 8.1

Intercorrelations of R, G, and A scales for men and women separately
In brackets Guilford's own values

	Males			Females		
	R	G	A	R	G	A
R	—	0·404	0·423	—	0·452	0·482
G	(0·56)	—	0·369	(0·56)	—	0·549
A	(0·52)	(0·44)	—	(0·52)	(0·44)	—

With respect to the intercorrelations of the various factors, we were particularly interested in two points. The first was the relationship between the three extraversion factors, i.e. R, G, and A. Table 8.1 shows separately the correlations between these three for males and females in our sample; given below the leading diagonal are the comparative

[1] This remark may seem to contradict what was said earlier about sex differences. This is not so. It is suggested that test *items* often have different factor loadings for men and women; scale *scores* are less likely to show such differences because different items compensate.

values obtained by Guilford. (These are put in brackets to indicate that they are taken from mixed sex groups.) By and large, the figures are all similar enough to suggest that the conclusions drawn from the American work are applicable to British populations also.

The correlation of these three variables with C is of some interest. Guilford has reported a correlation of 0·02 between C and R, a correlation of −0·19 between C and G and one of 0·31 between C and A. We summed scores on the R, G, and A factors and correlated this sum of the three extraversion scores with C. The resulting coefficients were −0·024 for the men, and +0·072 for the women; both of these are quite insignificant. It thus appears that here also results are essentially similar to Guilford's.

Our next step was to carry out an item analysis of all the 261 questions and their relationships with the C and R scores. This was done by taking the 100 men and 100 women with the highest C scores and comparing their replies on each question with those of the 100 men and 100 women having the lowest C scores. Similarly, the 100 men and 100 women having the highest R scores were compared with the 100 men and 100 women having the lowest R scores. The two sexes were kept separate throughout so that we have eight groups; high C males, high C females, low C males, low C females, high R males, high R females, low R males and low R females.

The statistic used to assess the relationship of answers to each of the questions with the R and C scales was chi square. It would have been more usual to have chosen some form of correlation coefficient such as phi, biserial, or tetrachoric, but there seemed to be little point in such a transformation. Our main interest lay in the significance of observed relationships, which can best be tested by means of chi square in any case, and as numbers of subjects are identical in the various groups, different values of chi square can be compared directly without being transformed into some semblance of a correlation.

We therefore end up with four series of figures, giving us the chi squares for all our 261 items with our two scales (R and C) for men and women separately. It is these figures on which we shall draw for most of the comparative studies made in the course of this paper.

Significance values of chi squared with the number of cases used here are 3·841 for the 5 per cent level, 5·412 for the 2 per cent level, and 6·635 for the 1 per cent level. Quite arbitrarily we have chosen as a standard of significance of chi square the value of 10 which is well in excess of the 0·1 per cent level of significance. Our reason for this choice was as follows. For each of our four groups (C male, C female, R male, R female) we have over 250 items, making a total of over 1,000 chi squares. By chance alone, 10 of these would be significant at the 1 per cent level (this is not quite accurate, of course, as the items are not independent, but it will serve to illustrate the point we are making). If we, therefore, use the 1 per cent level of significance we would be wrong in a sufficiently large number of cases to make our results less reliable than they ought to be. By taking a p value well in excess of the 0·1 per cent level we ensure as far as possible that of all the conclusions presented as reaching the level of significance none, or at most one, are at all likely to be reduced to insignificance on repetition of this study. Psychologists have traditionally accepted low levels of significance in most of their work, but the choice of a level of significance is arbitrary, and in the present type of work a higher level seems desirable. Fisher's distinction between errors of type one and errors of type two should be borne in mind in this connection. (Another point is important, although it does not affect our results to any considerable extent. Items in the R scale, because they contribute part of the total score, must be expected to have very slightly higher chi squares than all other items with the R scale. Similarly, items in the C scale must be expected to have slightly higher chi squares than all other items with the C scale. In view of the large number of items involved, the influence of this factor is probably negligible.)

A special analysis was undertaken of the S scale. It has already been pointed out that the S factor is highly correlated, both with introversion and with neuroticism. While this fact appears to be beyond dispute, there are certain alternative possibilities which deserve further investigation. One of these two possibilities is based on the factorial derivation of the S factor. If the items contributing to the total score in Guilford's S questionnaire are indeed univocal, as they should be in view of the fact that S is presented to us as a unitary trait, then not only should the total S score have high correlations with both introversion and neuroticism, but so should each single item in the scale, depending only on its factor saturation. In other words, if we plotted the correlations of all the items in the S scale against a good measure of introversion, such as the R scale, and a good measure of neuroticism, such as the C scale, then we would expect the items to be strung out in the form of an oval in the centre of the space generated by these two orthogonal factors or tests. This would seem to follow from the theory of factor analysis and from the method of test construction used by Guilford.

An alternative view, however, is indicated by a detailed study of social behaviour of people of known degrees of neuroticism and introversion. Such observation suggests that *introverted* social shyness is different in many ways from *neurotic* social shyness. To put the hypothesis suggested here in a nutshell, we might say that the introvert does not care for people, would rather be alone, but if need be can effectively take part in social situations, whereas the neurotic is anxious and afraid when confronted with social situations, seeks to avoid them in order to escape from this negative feeling, but frequently wishes that he could be more sociable. In other words, as pointed out before, the introvert does not *care* to be with other people; the neurotic is *afraid* of being with other people. If this hypothesis were true it seems likely that different items in the S scale would be chosen by introverts and neurotics respectively to express their non-sociable attitude. In the extreme case, i.e. where every item was indicative either of the neurotic or of the introvertive type of social shyness, but none of both, we would expect one set of items to have high correlations with a good measure of introversion, such as the R scale, but none with a good measure of neuroticism, such as the C scale, while another set of items would have high correlations with the C scale, but no, or very low, correlations with the R scale. We thus see that the factorial, and what we may perhaps call the clinical hypothesis, generate quite different expectations, and it will be of interest to see which of the two hypotheses is borne out in fact.[1]

All items of the S scale on which members of either sex produced a significant chi square with either the R or the C scale were tabulated (cf. Table 8.2). Even a casual look at the Tables will show that the clinical hypothesis is borne out and the factorial hypothesis refuted. For the men it is found that *none* of the items showing a significant relation with R shows a significant relation with C. Similarly, not one of the items showing a significant relation with C shows a significant relation with R. With the exception of one item the same is true for the women. It therefore appears that in the central part of the diagram where, according to the factorial theory, we would have expected all the items to lie, not a single item is found for the men and only one item out of over 50 for the women. This fact appears to furnish strong evidence against the factorial view and to support our hypothesis of the dual nature of sociability.

TABLE 8.2a

Items from the S scale significantly related to the R scale

	Chi-squared			
	R		C	
	M	F	M	F
Tendency to act quickly and confidently	45	24	1	0
Ability to have uninhibited fun at get-togethers	44	43	1	5
Liking to get together with others	40	22	0	0
Tendency to be over earnest	40	12	10	0
Self rating on vivaciousness	54	35	0	0
Self rating on sociability	32	31	4	0
Tendency to keep out of limelight at parties	52	30	0	0
Taking the lead in starting friendships	26	28	1	0
Preference for a quiet book over a formal social	8	26	0	0
Number of social outings	25	52	9	0

[1] It is of course quite possible that there is a *third* type of social shyness, linked with the personality dimension of *psychoticism*. Some people seem to actively dislike and hate other people, and this third variety of non-sociable behaviour may be linked with psychoticism. Research is going on at the moment in an attempt to study this point.

	Chi-squared			
	R		C	
	M	P	M	P
Worries about behaving out of place socially	23	8	6	6
Ability to get used to changes	24	13	0	4
Ability to 'be oneself' at get-togethers	22	22	7	2
Tendency to silence when with others	22	18	0	0
Enjoyment of parties	52	52	2	9
Limiting circle of friends	18	17	5	0
Preference for leadership	19	8	1	2
Mostly receiving rather than communicating ideas	7	19	1	0
Ability to get to know people	17	17	1	0
Problems in making firm relations with people	17	17	4	0
Fear of lecturing	4	17	3	0
Self rating on success at socials	5	16	5	8
Dislike of limelight at parties	12	15	6	0
Concern if deprived of many friends and acquaintances	14	15	1	2
Ease of reply to others	14	9	1	0
Unwillingness to take initiative at parties	13	8	0	1
Liking to get to know others	14	7	2	2
Unwillingness to have contact with superiors	13	9	6	7
Sociability	13	7	0	4
Bashfulness with the opposite sex	12	10	0	0
Ease of making up one's mind	10	5	7	6
Enjoyment of lecturing	6	10	6	1
Worry over feeling less good than others	2	17	14	28

TABLE 8.2b

Items from the S scale significantly related to the C scale

	Chi-squared			
	R		C	
	M	F	M	F
Loneliness	2	6	10	38
Undue nerves during crises	3	0	32	16
Worry over getting embarrassed easily	7	7	32	23
Worry over feeling less good than others	2	17	14	28
Embarrassment at meeting important people	5	5	23	10
Regrets over decisions in crises	0	3	14	23
Change of speed of thoughts	0	0	23	16
Feelings of derealization	0	0	16	24
Undue upset about embarrassing situations	17	9	4	19
Optimism	3	0	15	10
Social self confidence	3	5	12	2
Being troubled by bashfulness	3	2	7	12
Feeling uncomfortable when in company	2	7	19	12

NOTE: Items in this and the following Tables have been paraphrased to preserve copyright. The actual items used can be found in the relevant Guilford scales, or in the article by Eysenck (1956).

A glance at Table 8.2 will indicate to what extent our hypothesis regarding the precise nature of the difference between introvertive and neurotic sociability is borne out. The sociable extravert lets himself go and has a hilarious time, likes to mix socially, is a lively individual who does not take life seriously, is a good mixer who does not stay in the background on social occasions, who takes the initiative in making friends, has many social engagements, acts naturally at parties, adapts easily, and so forth. In other words, he is a person who enjoys social intercourse with people as opposed to the introvert who does not enjoy social intercourse with people. When we turn to the items indicative of neurotic social shyness we find the shy person troubled about being self-conscious, experiencing periods of loneliness, troubled with feelings of inferiority and self-conscious with superiors, worrying over humiliating experiences, and about being shy, ill at ease with other people, and not well poised in social contacts. In other words, we meet a kind of person who is troubled and worried over his social contacts, and would like to be more adequate in his dealing with other people, but whose emotional reactions seem to interfere with his social adjustment. The reader must judge for himself the adequacy of our theory regarding the nature of these two entirely separate aspects of social shyness. Our data are not sufficient to prove this hypothesis to be correct, of course, but merely furnish some preliminary support.

There are several hypotheses which may account for the difference of our results and those expected on the basis of Guilford's work. In the first place, Guilford's original work was done with American College students, our own work done with a more representative and older sample of British subjects; thus, age, education, and nationality in the two studies were markedly different. The fact that in our experiments norms on the Guilford scales for British groups of the kind used here are rather similar to those obtained by Guilford in the United States suggests, but does not prove, that this difference is unlikely to have been a decisive one.

Another possibility is that only some of the items of the S scale form part of the original factorial study; others were added later by Guilford to make the scale longer and more reliable. (Guilford has confirmed this point in a private communication.) It is possible that these additions, which were made on the basis of item analyses are responsible for the non-unitary nature of the resulting scale. This seems to the present writer a feasible hypothesis, and if true it suggests that all the Guilford scales would have to be investigated in order to weed out items added to the original pool of factorially pure questions in order to make the scales longer and more reliable.

An analysis similar to that reported in the preceding section was carried out on the items comprising the R and C scales, as well as on those comprising the Maudsley Medical Questionnaire. The results will not be presented in detail as they are of technical interest rather than being of general psychological importance, like the dual nature of sociability. We will first deal with results from the R and C scales.

In the first place, let us consider items scored for both R and C. Some of these items show significant relationships to both R and C, others to R but not to C, others yet to C but not to R, while yet a fourth group show no significant relationships to either R or C.

In the second place, items scored only for C mostly show significant relationships with C. Some also show significant relationships with R, some items show significant relationships with R only, but not with C, and several items show no significant relationship with either C or R.

In the third place, items scored only for R mostly show significant relationships with R. Some also show significant relationships with C, some items show significant relationships with C only, but not with R, and several items show no significant relationship with either R or C.

These findings re-enforce our belief that purification of the R and C scales by item analysis is desirable, and that a certain number of items in these scales are merely dead wood, and may in fact detract from the validity of the scales for which they are scored.

Similar findings were made in connection with the Maudsley Medical Questionnaire. One out of 40 items showed relationships only to the R but not to the C scale, and a number of items showed very low relationships with the C scale. As had been suspected, the item showing such low relationships tended to have very few endorsements. Of 80 chi square values (40 items for each sex), 35 were found in respect to items endorsed by over 20 per cent of subjects and 45 in items endorsed by fewer than 20 per cent of subjects. Of the former items 25 had high chi square values and 10 had low ones, whereas of the latter only 14 had high chi square values and 31 low ones. It would appear, therefore, that in part at least the unsatisfactory validity of the Maudsley Medical Questionnaire with normal groups may be due to the gross divergences from a 50/50 distribution of answers.

Twenty-nine items out of the 261 showed large differences in the number of 'Yes' answers between the two sexes, a large difference being arbitrarily defined as one of 30 or more points. The actual items involved and the number of men and women respectively answering 'Yes' to each are given in Table 8.3.

From these answers a fairly conventional and stereotyped picture of the two sexes emerges. According to their answer pattern men like to take the lead in group activities, are slow and deliberate in movement, overconscientious, inclined to stop and think things over before acting, frequently bored with people, tend to organize things on their own initiative, like to take on new and important responsibilities, speak out at meetings in order to oppose someone they think wrong, seek to avoid troublesome situations, and often take two steps at a time when climbing stairs.

TABLE 8.3

Items showing large sex differences in endorsement

	Endorsement	
	M	F
Leadership	79	46
Speed of movement	64	33
Liking to get to know others	149	180
Fear of lecturing	91	141
Tendency to be over perfectionist	127	87
Constant need for stimulation and bustle	49	118
Causeless depression	45	86
Non impulsiveness	166	128
Self rating on vivaciousness	72	111
Mood swings	57	95
Tendency to be over earnest	94	130
Mostly receiving rather than communicating ideas	76	116
Need for privacy of ideas	148	185
Sleeplessness through thoughts of recent events	30	77
Tendency to silence at meetings	62	105
Uninterested in others	75	33
Combatting shyness	56	93
Sociability	130	170
Mood dictated by that of companions	56	100
Worries about behaving out of place socially	104	141
Habit of taking large strides upstairs	169	118
Inability to dismiss unwanted tradesmen	47	91
Taking lead in making social or group arrangements	120	82
Unwillingness to take responsibility	77	139
Willingness to run or initiate a major concern	120	79
Arguing at meetings	126	82
Being considered vivacious	71	115
Need to keep out of possible fracas	134	104

Women are opposite to men on all these points; in addition they enjoy getting acquainted with most people, shrink from speaking in public, crave excitement, often feel 'just miserable' for no good reason at all, consider themselves as lively individuals, and are regarded as such by other people, sometimes feel happy and sometimes depressed without any apparent reason, tend to take life too seriously, be listeners rather than talkers in social conversation (!), like to have time to be alone with their thoughts, find it difficult to go to sleep at night because experiences of the day keep running through their head, keep their opinions to themselves during group discussions, have to fight against bashfulness, enjoy entertaining people, and are easily influenced in their mood by people around them. It embarrasses them a great deal to do or say the wrong thing in a social group. They find it difficult to get rid of salesmen, and, lastly, they would rather work for a good boss than for themselves.

It would be fascinating, though pointless, to discuss to what extent what our subjects say about themselves is in fact true. The fact that the women say that they prefer listening to talking may not be a reliable guide to objective fact, and altogether answers from both sexes may be to an unknown degree influenced by stereotypes and preconceptions. Our experiment was not designed to throw light on this point. Nor are we concerned with the eternal problem of causation, i.e. the question of whether observed differences are in any sense innate or are merely due to social pressure and the roles which society expects men and women to play. Our results are exclusively concerned with self reports, i.e. the way men and women in our society see themselves when answering questionnaires. Quite a different type of research would be required to answer the other questions raised in this context.

If the conceptions men and women have of themselves in relation to extraversion and neuroticism differ as much as is indicated in the figures presented above, then we should expect that considerable differences might also be found in the degree to which individual items measure extraversion and introversion for the two sexes respectively. This is a very important point because unless it is taken into account, this difference between the sexes will make the selection of items very much more difficult. Little appears to be known on this point, and a perusal of the literature does not suggest that sufficient attention has been paid to this problem.

Our first step in investigating this question consisted in determining the correlation between the chi square values of the 261 items between men and women. This correlation amounted to 0·803 for the C scale and 0·643 for the R scale. Both values are significant; both are significantly different from unity; and additionally they are significantly different from each other. It appears, then, that the meaning of our questions when regarded as measures of neuroticism or extraversion differs from sex to sex; that these differences are much more pronounced when we are concerned with the measurement of extraversion; and that in both cases positive steps have to be taken in the construction of a questionnaire to take these differences into account. This can be done in two ways. Either we can construct separate questionnaires for the two sexes, or we can use the same set of questions for both sexes, but take care in selecting the items to choose only those in which discrepancies are small or non-existent. If feasible, the second alternative is preferable, but enough items may not always be available, and in that case recourse must be had to the device of constructing separate questionnaires for men and women. Failure to use one or the other of these methods must seriously invalidate questionnaires constructed for the purpose of measuring extraversion or neuroticism, or indeed any personality trait in which sex differences of the kind discussed here can be demonstrated.

It may be of interest to have a look at the discordant items, i.e. items with large differences in the chi square values obtained by men and women respectively. Defining a large difference quite arbitrarily as one of 30 points, we find 14 such discordant items with respect to the C scale, and 12 such items with respect to the R scale. One item is common to both scales. Table 8.4 below lists the items concerned and the chi square values for men and women respectively.

TABLE 8.4a

Sex differences on R items

	Chi-squared	
	M	F
Judgement of self as happy-go-lucky	46	18
Tendency to keep out of limelight at parties	52	29
Acting on the spur of the moment (self rating)	4	46
Sensitivity to others who fault find	32	10
Tendency to be over earnest	40	12
Tendency to act quickly and confidently	45	24
Number of social outings	25	52
Unhappy about introspecting	34	3
Ability to get out of scrapes	0	26
Beginning tasks with eagerness	5	34
Willingness to be in sole charge	24	2
Hesitancy about speaking to a V.I.P.	28	8

TABLE 8.4b

Sex differences on C items

	Chi-squared	
	M	F
Worries over awful things that might occur	49	14
Mood swings	77	54
Acting on the spur of the moment (self rating)	39	10
Loneliness	10	38
Sensitivity to others who fault find	48	22
Tendency to quick and sometimes false judgements	46	23
Feeling fed up frequently	48	16
Fear of acting or lecturing	38	10
Need for privacy	24	48
Resentfulness when thwarted	55	24
Mood stability	42	20
Being quick tempered	35	9
Enjoying letting one's thoughts wander	44	15
Fear of facing up to things at critical moments	29	4

Bearing in mind that the fact of a particular item having a higher chi square for men than for women means that this item has more serious diagnostic implications for men than for women, we find that out of the 14 discordant C items, 12 have higher chi square values for men and only 2 have higher chi square values for women. Apparently, having periods of loneliness and seeking to be alone are both more diagnostic of neuroticism in women than in men. Conversely, worrying over possible misfortuntes, having ups and downs in mood, being impulsive, being depressed when criticized, jumping at conclusions, being disgruntled, having stage fright, being given to resentful thinking, not being in uniform spirits, being angry very quickly, day dreaming, and shrinking from meeting crises are much more indicative of emotional instability in men than in women. It almost appears as if to women, as long as they are extraverted enough, a certain amount of latitude is given in their display of emotionality. It is only when they show introvertive traits (periods of loneliness, seeking to be alone) that the prognosis becomes poor. One might think that where the stereotypes of male and female conduct differ, the fact that women come closer to the more neurotic stereotype of their own sex is in some sense taken as an ameliorative feature. If this hypothesis were correct we would expect a greater number of 'Yes' answers by men for those items in which women have a higher chi square, and a greater number of 'Yes' answers by women on items on which the men have higher chi squares. This, however, is by no means true. There are a few large differences in endorsement. The differences that are found are equal in both directions, and on both items in which women have higher chi squares they also have a larger number of 'Yes' answers. We cannot, therefore, account for the observed differences along these lines.

The same is true of the discordant R items. Apparently the following items are much more diagnostic of extraversion for men than for women: Being a carefree individual, not tending to keep in the background on social occasions, not being depressed when criticized, not taking life too seriously, being quick and sure in action, disliking to stop and analyse one's feelings, not liking to bear responsibilities alone, and not being reluctant to meet important people. Conversely, the answers to the following items are more significant of extraversion in women: Being impulsive, liking many social engagements, being good at bluffing when in difficulty, and starting new jobs with enthusiasm. The facts are there but they do not suggest any obvious hypothesis to the present writer.

On the basis of the considerations discussed in the preceding sections, and the factual results of the item analysis, two questionnaires were prepared in the hope that these might prove to be improved measures of extraversion-introversion and neuroticism, as compared with the R and C scales. Twenty-four items were selected to form the new neuroticism scale (to be called the N scale henceforth), and 24 items were selected to form the new extraversion-introversion scale (to be called the

E scale henceforth). Five spare items were added to the N scale, and seven spare items to the E scale in case one or the other of the chosen items might prove unsuitable, or in case it might later be desirable to lengthen the scales. For the purpose of computing split-half reliabilities each scale was divided into two parts: N_1, N_2, and E_1, and E_2, each consisting of twelve questions.

The principles governing the selection of questions were as follows: All items in the N scale should have significant relations with the C scale for both men and women, and insignificant relations with the R scale for both men and women. Items in the E scale, conversely, were chosen in such a way that all had significant relations with the R scale for both men and women, but not for the C scale. The actual chi square values, as well as the items selected and the scoring key, are given in Table 8.5, and it will be seen that the requirements are adequately met by these questions.

TABLE 8.5a

Neuroticism Scale

		Chi-squared			
N1:	Key	RM	RF	CM	CF
Moodiness	Y	5	1	54	44
Reveries of the unobtainable	Y	0	1	29	18
Tendency to brood over things that happened	Y	1	1	28	37
Causeless depression	Y	1	1	35	51
Indecisiveness	Y	1	0	30	27
Sleeplessness over troubles	Y	0	0	19	13
Mood swings	Y	0	0	64	61
Self blame	Y	3	0	25	25
Sensitive emotions	Y	2	2	27	20
Nervousness (self rating)	Y	0	1	25	13
Daydreams disturbing mental effort	Y	0	0	39	34
Loneliness	Y	2	0	10	38
N2:					
Mood swings	Y	0	0	77	54
Enjoying letting one's thoughts wander	Y	0	2	44	15
Frequently dwelling on past events	Y	1	1	18	25
Undue tiredness	Y	0	0	31	38
Regrets over decisions in crises	Y	0	3	14	23
Persistent thoughts causing sleeplessness	Y	0	0	42	30
Fluctuation of mood	Y	0	2	48	59
Worrying over persistent trivial idea	Y	1	0	16	25
Touchiness	Y	0	1	25	24
Feeling fed up frequently	Y	0	2	48	17
Inattention when talking to someone through day-dreaming	Y	0	2	30	39
Extreme fidgetiness	Y	0	5	11	28

TABLE 8.5b

Extraversion Scale

	Key	RM	Chi-squared RF	CM	CF
E1:					
Tendency to keep out of limelight at parties	N	52	29	0	0
Inhibitions about enjoying gay socials	N	28	20	1	0
Over carefulness	N	23	9	2	0
Liking to get together with others	Y	40	22	0	0
Limiting circle of friends	N	18	17	5	0
Tendency to act quickly and confidently	Y	45	24	1	0
Taking occupation too seriously	N	12	31	2	5
Number of social outings	Y	25	52	9	0
Preference for leadership	Y	19	8	1	2
Bashfulness with the opposite sex	N	12	10	1	1
Ease of reply to others	Y	14	9	1	0
Carefreeness (self rating)	Y	52	37	0	5
E2:					
Tendency to silence when with others	N	22	18	0	0
Ability to have uninhibited fun at get-togethers	Y	45	43	1	4
Enjoying occupation needing vigilance	N	13	6	1	0
Self rating on vivaciousness	Y	54	35	1	1
Concern if deprived of many friends and acquaintances	Y	14	15	1	2
Preference for work requiring speedy action	Y	10	24	4	3
Tendency to be easy going about work	Y	18	14	1	4
Being considered vivacious	Y	29	32	0	7
Taking the lead in starting friendships	Y	26	28	1	0
Fluency (self rating)	Y	39	24	1	1
Enjoying playing practical jokes	Y	28	17	2	4
Liking to do, rather than arrange to do, things	Y	21	16	0	5

TABLE 8.5c

Neuroticism Scale

	Key	RM	Chi-squared RF	CM	CF
N:					
Undue mood swings	Y	0	0	47	35
Inability to forget frustrating experiences	Y	2	6	44	29
Need for privacy	Y	4	0	24	48
Mood stability	Y	1	2	42	20
Feeling depersonalized	Y	0	0	27	11

Extraversion Scale

	Key	RM	Chi-squared RF	CM	CF
E:					
Judgement of self as happy-go-lucky	Y	46	18	7	2
Problems in making firm relations with people	N	17	17	4	0
Ability to get to know people	Y	17	17	1	0
Self rating on sociability	Y	32	31	4	0
Enjoyment of parties	Y	52	52	2	9
Liking to join in crowd enthusiasm	Y	17	10	0	3
Enjoying social side of life most	Y	12	14	2	1

Various other requirements were also borne in mind. Thus, an attempt was made to select only items where chi square values for men and women were not too dissimilar; where differences between the sexes were observed on one item another item was selected in such a way as to balance the disproportion. In this way it was hoped to obtain scales which could be used for both sexes equally. Another requirement was that items should not be mere duplicates of each other, slightly changed in wording, but should cover different aspects of neuroticism or of extraversion-introversion. Judgements here are, of course, subjective, although there is a partial check on their accuracy in the results of the correlational analysis to be described below.

The scoring of the two questionnaires is as follows: Any 'Yes answer' on the neuroticism scale is counted two points; any 'no' answer is counted 0 point; any '?' is counted one point. Similarly, on the extraversion scale, answers in conformity with the key are scored two points; answers contrary to the key are scored 0 point; '?' answers are scored one point. The highest possible score on either scale therefore is 48 points, the lowest is 0 points. The actual scores obtained by our 200 male and 200 female subjects are as follows: On the neuroticism scale the men have a mean score of 17·810 with a standard deviation of 11·321. The women have a mean score of 19·445±11·018. Men and women together have a mean score of 18·628±11·186. On the extraversion scale the mean for the men is 24·620±10·037, and the mean score for the women is 25·165±9·331. The total score for both sexes is 24·892±9·673. There are no significant differences between the sexes on either scale.

Split half reliability correlations, corrected for length, are as follows. On the neuroticism scale, $r = 0{\cdot}9013$ for men, 0·8658 for women, and 0·8839 for the two groups combined. On the extraversion scale, $r =$ 0·8468 for the men, 0·8173 for the women, and 0·8313 for the total sample. As regards the correlation between these two scales $r = -0{\cdot}1476$ for the men, −0·0364 for the women, and −0·0924 for the two sexes combined.

In view of the importance attaching to the independence of the two scales, and bearing in mind that cross validation is always desirable in analyses of this kind, the two scales were given to another male group of 200 subjects altogether. The mean scores of this group for neuroticism and extraversion respectively were 23·23±11·27 and 25·26±8·85. The correlation between the scales was −0·07. We thus end up with two scales which are virtually independent of each other, the very small negative correlation between them being equivalent to only about ½ per cent of the total variance.

As a check on the adequacy of the item analyses on which the selection of items was based a factor analysis was performed. The 48 items in the N and E scales were intercorrelated separately for men and women, using tetrachoric coefficients, and the resulting tables analysed by means of Thurstone's centroid method. Two factors were extracted from each of the two matrices, the residuals remaining after the extraction of these two factors being too small to warrant further analysis. Rotation was carried out according to the dictates of simple structure which, in this case, was relatively easy as the analysis disclosed two groups of items clustering closely around centroids which were orthogonal to each other. The results of the analysis are shown in Table 8.6.

TABLE 8.6

Factor saturations of men and women separately for the 48 items of the N and E scales

	Women		Men		
	I	II	I	II	h^2
1.	0·04	0·69	−0·04	0·75	0·5618
2.	0·03	0·72	−0·01	0·81	0·6625
3.	−0·12	0·59	−0·05	0·58	0·3449
4.	0·26	0·52	0·12	0·44	0·2122
5.	−0·03	0·49	0·10	0·59	0·3625
6.	−0·02	0·61	0·00	0·63	0·3973
7.	−0·05	0·72	−0·10	0·79	0·6425
8.	0·12	0·59	−0·04	0·67	0·4513
9.	0·05	0·71	−0·10	0·52	0·2788
10.	−0·08	0·65	−0·15	0·67	0·4736
11.	0·00	0·50	−0·13	0·57	0·3460
12.	−0·02	0·57	0·03	0·65	0·4181
13.	0·08	0·58	0·03	0·82	0·6673
14.	0·06	0·56	0·01	0·67	0·4537
15.	0·12	0·64	0·01	0·70	0·4925
16.	0·02	0·74	−0·06	0·83	0·6964
17.	−0·08	0·53	−0·01	0·54	0·2969
18.	0·08	0·65	0·11	0·45	0·2165
19.	0·17	0·43	0·23	0·55	0·3536
20.	0·08	0·58	−0·04	0·46	0·2180
21.	0·20	0·71	0·00	0·61	0·3706
22.	−0·09	0·65	−0·13	0·67	0·4597
23.	−0·03	0·59	−0·06	0·67	0·4517
24.	0·11	0·39	0·01	0·66	0·4349
25.	0·45	−0·30	0·51	−0·33	0·3681
26.	0·53	0·08	0·47	−0·10	0·2340
27.	0·22	0·07	0·29	−0·08	0·0925
28.	0·69	−0·15	0·80	−0·06	0·6370
29.	0·53	−0·16	0·70	−0·07	0·5013
30.	0·51	−0·04	0·58	−0·09	0·3425
31.	0·48	−0·29	0·38	−0·26	0·2152
32.	0·19	−0·09	0·38	−0·13	0·1521
33.	0·41	−0·06	0·41	−0·06	0·1754
34.	0·75	0·01	0·72	−0.02	0·5234
35.	0·45	0·17	0·57	0·11	0·3434
36.	0·23	0·00	0·31	−0·03	0·0986

TABLE 8.6 *(contd.)*

	Women			Men	
	I	II	I	II	h^2
37.	0·64	−0·09	0·40	−0·18	0·1933
38.	0·57	−0·01	0·63	−0·21	0·4450
39.	0·18	−0·37	0·29	−0·19	0·1181
40.	0·65	−0·16	0·87	−0·05	0·7540
41.	0·58	−0·08	0·67	0·03	0·4513
42.	0·66	0·10	0·59	0·12	0·3697
43.	0·78	−0·07	0·62	0·24	0·4381
44.	0·44	0·19	0·37	0·07	0·1429
45.	0·66	0·14	0·72	−0·15	0·5466
46.	0·48	0·29	0·47	0·12	0·2329
47.	0·66	0·08	0·57	0·24	0·3812
48.	0·73	0·03	0·70	−0·09	0·4964

It will be seen that our expectations are fulfilled. The neuroticism items cluster together; the extraversion items cluster together; and there appears to be no relationship between the two clusters. The cluster of neuroticism items is clearly more compact than the cluster of extraversion items; this fact, presumably, accounts for our observation of greater split-half reliability for the N scale than for the E scale. Some of the items are relatively poor measures of their respective factors, e.g.

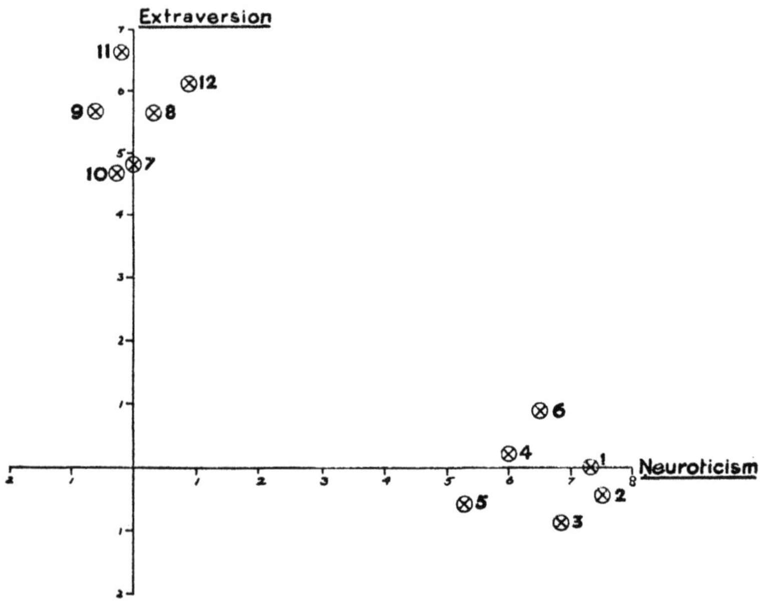

FIG. 8.2 Results of factor analysis of six extraversion and six neuroticism items constituting the short scale of the M.P.I. (From Eysenck, 1958.)

items 32 and 27 and 36 on the female side, and items 39 and 27 and 36 on the male side. Some items, such as 25 for both men and women, and 46 for women, have rather high loadings on the factor which they are not supposed to be measuring; as these loadings, however, appear to balance out on the whole it did not seem wise to disturb the balance of the test. In any case, it should be remembered that the correlations on which the analysis is based have standard errors of approximately 0·15, so that in a group of 2×48 items some considerable departures from the true values may be expected. On the whole the items selected emerge from the factor analysis reasonably well.

A short version of the M.P.I. was also prepared consisting of twelve of the most diagnostic questions; this version is given below (Eysenck, 1958). These questions were given to a quota sample of the population consisting of 1,600 men and women and their answers correlated with each other. Two factors were extracted and the position of the 12 items on these two factors is shown in Figure 8.2. It will be seen that a good approximation to simple structure is achieved and that all the items are in the predicted positions.

Short form of the M.P.I.

		Key
A.	Do you sometimes feel happy, sometimes depressed, without any apparent reason?	N
B.	Do you have frequent ups and downs in mood, either with or without apparent cause?	N
C.	Are you inclined to be moody?	N
D.	Does your mind often wander while you are trying to concentrate?	N
E.	Are you frequently 'lost in thought' even when supposed to be taking part in a conversation?	N
F.	Are you sometimes bubbling over with energy and sometimes very sluggish?	N
G.	Do you prefer action to planning for action?	E
H.	Are you happiest when you get involved in some project that calls for rapid action?	E
I.	Do you usually take the initiative in making new friends?	E
J.	Are you inclined to be quick and sure in your actions?	E
K.	Would you rate yourself as a lively individual?	E
L.	Would you be very unhappy if you were prevented from making numerous social contacts?	E

9

RESEARCH FINDINGS WITH THE M.P.I.

DETAILED reviews of research with the M.P.I. have been given by Jensen (1958, 1965), Knapp (1960), and others; here we will confine ourselves to certain general statements of the type of results which have been reported in the literature.[1] First of all we will note the results of work done in the English speaking countries, that is to say England, the United States, Canada and Australia; then we will go on to see to what extent these findings are duplicated in other countries like Italy, Japan, India and so on.

In the first place, then, it is found that normal subjects have mean neuroticism scores of 20 or so with a standard deviation of 11, and extraversion scores with a mean of 25 and a standard deviation of 10. N and E usually show a slight negative correlation, which rises in neurotic groups. Dysthymics have a neuroticism mean of between 30 and 40 and an extraversion mean of 20; psychopaths have a neuroticism mean of between 30 and 40 and an extraversion mean of 30. Criminals are very much like psychopaths again, with a neuroticism mean of between 30 and 40 and an extraversion mean of 30. Psychotics have neuroticism means considerably lower than neurotics, usually between 20 and 30, and extraversion means not notably different from the general population.[2] Hysterics have neuroticism means between 25 and 35 and extraversion means between 25 and 30. They are probably the most variable group of all possibly because of the fact that diagnoses of hysterical conversion and hysterical personality are often confounded; Ingham

[1] A detailed bibliography of references to studies using the M.P.I. is given in the sixth Buro's Mental Measurement Year Book, 1965. This also contains critical reviews of the test.

[2] Crookes and Hutt (1963) give some results which are typical of findings in this field; they are quoted in Table 9.1 below.

and Robinson (1964) have shown that this may cause confusion. Some typical research results are shown in Figure 6.2 which is an adaptation of Figure 1 from the American manual of the M.P.I.

TABLE 9.1

Mean neuroticism and extraversion scores

		N score		E score	
	N	M	SD	M	SD
Group					
Normals (Eysenck)	1,800	19·89	11·02	24·91	9·71
Schizophrenics	40	26·35	9·15	22·88	8·36
Affectives	40	19·80	11·23	24·25	9·84
Manics	20	14·60	9·21	28·80	7·66
Depressives	20	25·00	10·82	19·70	9·83
Total psychotics	80	23·08	10·70	23·56	9·10
Neurotics	60	31·35	10·11	—	—

In the studies which have produced these findings patients were carefully selected to give reasonably clear pictures of hysteria, dysthymia, psychosis and so forth. When this is done results are fairly congruent in showing the kind of distribution indicated in the Figure. It does not follow of course that similar results would be obtained when a random sample of patients is given the questionnaire and diagnosed psychiatrically. McGuire, Mowbray and Vallance (1963) for instance who carried out such a study came to the conclusion that 'this investigation of the Maudsley Personality Inventory in psychiatric patients showed that there was a considerable overlap in both neuroticism and extraversion scales for all diagnoses. The mean N score differentiated all our groups including psychotics from control patients, and the whole group was not significantly different on either N or E from a previously reported group of psychiatric outpatients . . . the M.P.I. . . . appears to have no value as a clinical tool.' (See also Caine and Hope, 1964.) Such a conclusion would appear to put the cart before the horse. McGuire and his colleagues appear to have started by accepting both the validity and the reliability of psychiatric diagnoses and to have used this as a criterion against which to measure the efficacy and usefulness of the M.P.I. This approach is quite contrary to that of Eysenck. As has often been shown, the reliability of psychiatric diagnosis is very poor (Eysenck, 1960a); so poor indeed that it is demonstrably impossible for any questionnaire or any test whatsoever, whether verbal or experimental, to give high correlations with it. To expect therefore that a test would give such correlations in a random sample of patients is somewhat naïve, and to attribute responsibility for the failure to do so to the questionnaire rather than to the unreliability of the psychiatric diagnoses made appears to be unjustified.

The writer would maintain that quite the opposite approach is wanted in this connection. If there is a failure of correlation between questionnaire and psychiatric ratings, then this is indicative of faults in the psychiatric ratings, both as regards validity and reliability, and it might further be suggested, not that the questionnaire has no value as a clinical tool, but rather that psychiatric diagnosis has no value as a clinical tool. The propriety of this argument becomes particularly apparent when we consider the question of whether psychiatric disorders can usefully be described in categorical terms, i.e. in terms of the notion of disease entities like hysteria, anxiety neurosis, reactive depressions, and so on, or whether it is more useful to regard these various symptoms as being distributed continuously along certain quantitative continua. The evidence reviewed by Eysenck (1960a, e), indicates rather strongly that the latter is a truer description of the facts and that the old categorical type of classification is merely a residue of medical habit inappropriately extended to the field of neurotic disorders. We would argue therefore that it is strictly speaking not permissible to talk about a categorical classification of psychopathy, say; what is true is that certain numbers of people are located in the first quadrant of our figure and that these tend to share certain extraverted and emotional characteristics. This sharing of certain characteristics has led the ancients to label these people as cholerics, just as it has led more modern writers to label them as psychopaths. It is however not true that this group of people is cut off from the rest of humanity in any absolute, categorical sense; exactly the contrary is true. Intermediate combinations of characteristics occur, shading over to the dysthymic on the introverted side and to the perfectly normal extravert along the other dimension. A given person's position is much better indicated either in terms of the Cartesian coordinates or polar coordinates of our two-dimensional Figure 3.1. It is true that when patients are selected as being particularly representative of diagnostic groupings like psychopathy, hysteria, anxiety states, and so on, then they do fall into predictable quadrants in our diagram, and in so far as that is true this fact helps us to build a bridge between research using psychiatric classification and research using the M.P.I. To admit that and to regard such results as mildly supporting the general personality theory developed here does not, however, amount to an admission that the psychiatric principles and methods of classification have any primacy. We would argue, not that the results validate the M.P.I., but rather that they validate to a small extent psychiatric principles of classification. This is an important point which has often been misunderstood and which is therefore made here at some length.

Of rather more interest, to our way of thinking, are studies which make use of psychiatric hypotheses, but without involving necessarily any psychiatric diagnosis. Consider the following case. On midday on Thursday, 7th October 1965 the Blackburn Medical Officer of Health received a phone call from the headmistress of a girls' secondary school.

In the earlier part of the morning a few of the girls in the school had complained of dizzy feelings, and some had fainted; later in the morning the number of faintings grew and assumed the proportions of an epidemic. Ambulances took 85 of the most severely affected girls to hospital; the rest were dismissed until the following Monday. Another epidemic broke out, and the school was dismissed for the remainder of the week. On the following Monday some 60 girls complained of some further symptoms, but none required hospitalization. Symptoms of the girls admitted to hospital were swooning, moaning, chattering of the

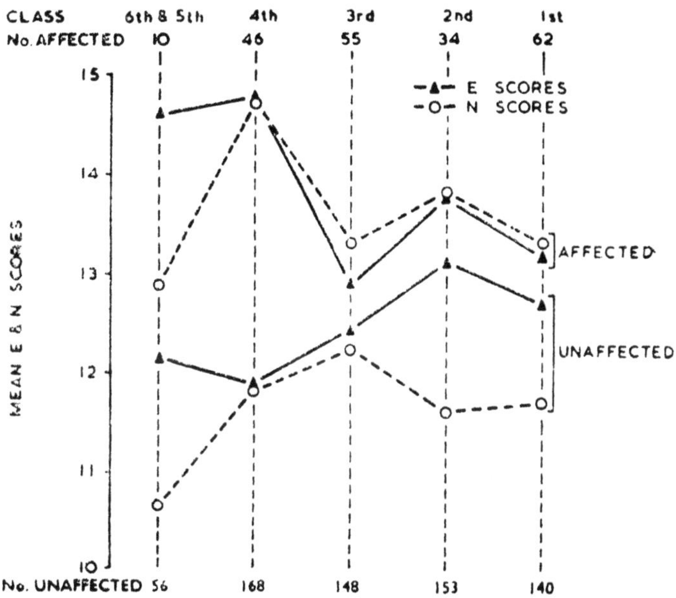

FIG. 9.1 E and N scores of affected and non-affected girls by school class attended. Quoted with permission from Moss and McEvedy (1966).

teeth, hyperpnoea, and tetany—all characteristic of a gross emotional upset. The psychiatric picture suggested an hysterical reaction; there was no evidence of pyrexia or any other physical cause. Moss and McEvedy (1966), who investigated this outbreak, stated a definite hypothesis to this effect, and deduced from the writer's general theory that the girls affected would be found predominantly extraverted and neurotic on the E and N scales of the E.P.I. Five hundred and thirty-five girls constituted the experimental population, of whom 519 were present and 141 affected on day 1; on day 5, 476 were present and 79 affected.

Figure 9.1 shows the E and N scores of the affected and the unaffected by class; it will be seen that throughout E and N scores of the affected are higher. The gap is rather narrow for the younger groups; this may be so because the E.P.I. is not a suitable test for young children. It is unfortunate that the Junior E.P.I. was not available at the time; it seems reasonable to assume that differences would have been emphasized had an appropriate inventory been administered. As the authors point out, 'the various age effects and the uneven incidence of the epidemic can be nullified if the E and N scores for each girl are totalled and each form is then ranged in descending order.' Figure 9.2 shows that when this is done the result is a slope showing a simple relation between form

FIG. 9.2 Percentage of girls affected as a function of their E+N scores. Quoted with permission from Moss and McEvedy (1966).

rank in E+N and involvement in the epidemic; 'nearly 40 per cent of the girls occupying the higher score places were affected, as against under a quarter in the mean position and under a fifth of those at the lower end of the ranking.' The whole episode is explained by Moss and McEvedy in terms of overbreathing due to emotional tension; a similar hypothesis may be applicable to another outbreak studied in another school by McEvedy *et al.* (1966); here too the affected girls showed higher N scores (but failed to show higher E scores).

This study shows a link between a psychiatric hypothesis (hysterics are prone to emotional epidemics) and a psychological theory (hysterics have high E and high N scores). Verification of the deduction (subjects high on E and N are prone to emotional epidemics) tends to support both the hypothesis and the theory, without any intermediate psychiatric diagnosis. Proof of this kind is probably more impressive and useful than any direct comparison of inventory scores with psychiatric diagnosis.

Research Findings with the M.P.I.

To revert to our discussion of the general characteristics of M.P.I. research results in the English speaking countries, we find that split half and Kuder-Richardson reliability coefficient for the neuroticism scale lie around 0·85 and for the extraversion scale around 0·80. Test-retest reliabilities are roughly of the same order as split-half reliabilities. On the whole it can hardly be denied that these reliabilities are reasonable for what is after all a relatively short questionnaire. Correlations between extraversion and neuroticism range around −0·20 but are significantly higher in groups with high neuroticism scores such as neurotics or criminals. We have already discussed some of the possible reasons for the emergence of this correlation (Eysenck, 1967).

Many correlations have been reported between the scales of the M.P.I. and various existing questionnaires such as the Cattell scales, the Taylor MAS, and so forth. The results have throughout been very much as one might have expected; thus the MAS and other measures of neuroticism such as those derived from the MMPI give high correlations with the N scale of the M.P.I.; the same is true of Cattell's anxiety scale and the Guilford D and C scales. The MAS has also a slight correlation with introversion while the Guilford R, G and A scales have quite high correlations with extraversion, as does the Cattell extraversion measure and the Si scale of the MMPI.

There are certain recurring age and sex correlations with personality in the data. Women tend to score more highly on the neuroticism scale than men, and men score more highly on the extraversion scale than women. Women, in other words, are more *dysthymic* (melancholic), men more *sanguine*. Scales measuring masculinity, such as the Guilford scale of that name, tend to find their place in the 'high E–low N' quadrant, as might be expected. As regards age, younger groups show more neuroticism and also more extraversion; in other words, youngsters are more psychopathic—immature—choleric, older people more phlegmatic. This finding will not be surprising to anyone familiar with the literature—or with life (Eysenck, 1958; Shaw and Hare, 1965). Social class does not appear to have very much effect on personality (or personality on social class), except that lower classes tend to have higher N scores (Eysenck, 1963c). (See also Child, 1966.) Urban dwellers are higher on N and on E, again not unexpectedly (Eysenck, 1963c). Young, male, lower-class urban groups are thus emerging as the most 'psychopathic' or choleric groups in terms of these sociological indices.

American students (N = 1064) have been found to have mean scores of N = 20·66±10·65 and E = 28·73±8·18 (Knapp, 1960). Canadian students (N = 1958) had scores of N = 23·64±9·87 and E = 27·93±9·33 (Hannah *et al.*, 1965). The Canadian study found males less neurotic ($p < 0{\cdot}001$) and more extraverted (N.S.); r_{NE} = 0·17.

Gutman (1966) tested 832 Canadian males and 587 females of different ages; her results are given in Table 9.2. Following Lynn's (1964) prediction, E scores decline with increasing age, but the overall correlation between E and age is very low ($r = -0{\cdot}069$), although statistically significant. N scores tended to decrease between young adulthood and middle age, and increase between middle age and senescence. Females were significantly higher on N than males (21·01 *v.* 19·23), a tendency shown at all age levels. On E, men were significantly higher than women only in the 40–49 age group; the overall scores were almost identical, with the men very slightly more extraverted (25·70 *v.* 25·14).

TABLE 9.2

Relation between age and personality. Taken with permission from Gutman (1966)

Age group	N	Extraversion		Neuroticism	
		Mean	s.d.	Mean	s.d.
17–25	726	25·81	8·80	21·40	9·40
30–39	213	25·60	8·92	16·66	10·11
40–49	225	25·29	8·69	17·78	9·73
50–59	55	24·09	8·87	19·85	10·50
60–69	50	26·38	6·68	19·20	10·34
70–79	102	23·39	8·49	21·53	10·44
80–94	48	23·63	7·87	20·92	10·11
Total	1,419				

Several studies have been carried out to investigate the relation between academic performance and personality (Furneaux, 1962; Bendig, 1960; Lucas *et al.*, 1965; Kelvin *et al.*, 1965; Kline, 1966; Savage, 1966; Estabrook and Sommer, 1966). The usual result has been to demonstrate that N (possibly by virtue of its drive properties) is positively correlated with achievement. On the other hand, E appears to be negatively correlated with achievement, possibly because addiction to sociable pursuits leaves less time for academic work. These findings are not invariable, but they seem to apply even to school achievement, and may be regarded as fairly well established. In addition, students as a whole would appear to be more dysthymic than non-students of similar age. Obviously, these findings must be viewed in the light of interaction between personality and intelligence, and in addition one must bear in mind the effects of personality on intelligence test scores (Eysenck, 1967). This whole area of study would probably repay concentrated further work.

We may now turn to a comparison of these data with results obtained in other countries where at first sight one might be at a loss to know whether or not personality questionnaires of this type would be applicable, and where there is no *a priori* evidence to suggest whether results would be similar or not. Consider experiments performed in Japan where Iwawaki, Sugiyama and Nanri brought out a Japanese version of the M.P.I. (1964). Table 9.3 gives the means and standard deviations of the various groups tested by them. It will be seen that the means and standard deviations for the N and E scales are not very different from these obtained in the English speaking countries. On the N scale the cadets and drivers have scores almost identical with the English and American norms, whereas the students, both in college and high schools, have somewhat higher scores. On the E scale on the other hand the college students have means very similar to the occidental ones whereas the cadets, drivers and the highschool students have somewhat higher means. Juvenile delinquents have elevated neuroticism scores and psychoneurotics even higher ones; the schizophrenics are if anything below the level of the normals. On the extraversion scale the delinquents score at a more extraverted level, the neurotics, who presumably are mainly dysthymic neurotics, at the most introverted level of all. Schizophrenics are not differentiated very much from the average. These results suggest that differences between Japanese and occidental scores are probably slight if they exist at all. No sex differences were observed for the two scales.

TABLE 9.3

Mean N and E scale values for Japanese groups. Taken with permission from Iwawaki et al. (1964)

Sample	N	N scale Means	N scale s.d.	E scale Means	E scale s.d.
Male college students	418	23·4	9·89	25·5	10·90
Female college students	433	24·3	10·11	26·3	10·36
Male high school students	147	22·0	9·33	28·4	9·65
Female high school students	84	22·1	9·66	29·3	9·76
Japanese cadets	408	19·7	9·83	28·9	10·51
Drivers	217	20·2	9·93	29·6	9·87
Juvenile delinquents	329	26·9	9·14	27·8	9·08
Psychoneurotics	45	30·9	10·19	21·4	11·69
Schizophrenics	100	19·2	12·24	26·3	10·09
Criminals (rape, violence, murder)	112	27·5	8·61	30·5	8·51

Correlations between N and E for the Japanese normal groups were low, ranging from −0·09 to −0·33, with a median r of −0·20. This correlation was much higher with the psychoneurotic group where it reached the level of $r = -0{\cdot}347$. The reliabilities of the scales were very much the same as we have noted already. For the N scale split-half reliabilities for college students averaged 0·86, whereas a test-retest correlation was found to be 0·82. For the E scale the split-half reliability was 0·90 the test-retest reliability 0·85.

Correlations with other questionnaires also were very similar as compared with results already reported. The Japanese version of the Taylor MAS correlated 0·74 with N and −0·45 with E on 176 Japanese cadets and 0·72 with N and −0·24 with E on 214 female Japanese college students. The score on Cattell's Anxiety scale correlated 0·70 with N and −0·35 with E on 125 Japanese cadets. Table 9.4 below shows the correlations of the M.P.I. scales with the Japanese version of the MMPI scales and the Guilford personality scales. Iwawaki *et al.* conclude that 'these data suggest that the Japanese version of the M.P.I. gives results very comparable to those obtained with the original version in England and the United States, and could be applicable to Japanese populations as a measure of these personality traits.'

TABLE 9.4

Correlations of M.P.I. scales and other inventories in Japanese sample. Taken with permission from Iwawaki et al. (1964)

Scale	Sample	N	Correlation	
			E-scale	N-scale
MMPI	Japanese cadets	177		
Hs			−0·304	0·518
D			−0·603	0·562
Hy			−0·269	0·554
Pd			−0·236	0·564
Mf			−0·285	0·354
Pa			−0·177	0·494
Pt			−0·426	0·656
Sc			−0·188	0·056
Ma			0·506	0·077
Si			−0·731	0·518
S (Social introversion)			−0·636	0·255
Guilford scores				
T (Thinking introversion)			−0·351	0·208
D (Depression)			−0·358	0·424
C (Cyclic tendency)			−0·216	0·546
R (Rhathymia)			0·370	−0·100
G (General activity)			0·484	−0·210
A (Ascendance) (reversed)			−0·658	0·344
I (Inferiority feelings)			−0·422	0·488
N (Nervousness)			−0·396	0·521
O (Lack of objectivity)			−0·204	0·524
Ag (Lack of agreeableness)			−0·247	0·087
Co (Lack of cooperativeness)			−0·175	0·391

Next let us turn to the work done with the Italian version of the M.P.I. published by Sibour, Amerio, and Jona (1963). They found mean scores for 360 male normals of 19·69±10·18 for the neuroticism scale, and 26·12±9·81 for the extraversion scale; for 236 normal female subjects the means were 18·27±9·63, and 24·39±9·03. There are no significant sex differences and the scores are very similar to the English and American ones.

A comparative study was carried out between 252 normal subjects, 55 reactive depressives and 35 hysterics. On the neuroticism scale the normals scored on the average 19·49±8·87, the depressives 35·59±4·34 and the hysterics 33·06±6·46. On the extraversion scale the normals had a mean score of 25·85±9·88, the depressives of 19·49±5·20, and the hysterics of 29·89±7·07. All the differences are similar to those observed previously in England and the United States and are fully significant.

The split-half reliability on 220 normal subjects was found to be 0·81 for neuroticism and 0·73 for extraversion; the test-retest reliability on 135 normal subjects was 0·67 for neuroticism and 0·82 for extraversion. Some of these values are somewhat lower than these noted so far but the groups on which they are calculated were not very large.

Sibour *et al.* also present some data on the relationship between the questionnaires and age. They find no correlation with neuroticism, but for extraversion there is a consistent decline from group 1 made up of 109 subjects below 25 years of age, through Group 2 made up of 59 subjects between 25 and 40 years, to Group 3, made up of 25 subjects older than 40 years. The means, for E are 27·28, 25·33, and 21·2. The differences between Groups 1 and 3 and Groups 2 and 3 are significant but of course the numbers are not really large enough to make the conclusion very definite. There also appears to be a correlation with education, again, confined to extraversion; two groups of 91 and 31 subjects characterized by average or superior education show higher extraversion scores than 71 elementary school subjects. Lastly Sibour *et al.* present a table giving an item analysis of the M.P.I. which shows considerable similarities to the factorial and item analysis studies carried out in England. Sibour *et al.* conclude that: 'L'adattamento italiano del M.P.I. ha dimonstrato, nella nostra esperienza, di rispondere alle caratteristishe che Eysenck si era proposto nella construzione di test a che si sono verificate nella edizione originale ingelese.'

A Swedish translation of the M.P.I. has been produced by Astrom and Olander (1960). They have standardized this on only a very small group of 43 normal subjects and find a mean for neuroticism of 17·90±7·15, and for extraversion 26·43±7·83. The test-retest reliabilities are 0·72 and 0·74 respectively, and the correlation between E and N is −0·02.

Astrom and Olander (1960) have also tested various clinical groups. By and large it may be said that all the abnormal groups have elevated scores on the neuroticism scale although the alcoholics do not score particularly highly. Psychopaths appear to have the highest N score. On the extraversion scale the most extraverted group are the normals, the most introverted the schizophrenics, endogenous depressives and dysthymics. Of the abnormal groups the hysterics are the most extraverted and are not in fact significantly differentiated from the normals. Psychopaths oddly enough go on the introverted side of the normals but it should be noted that they only number 11, which is not sufficiently large to draw any far-reaching conclusions. Also of course it should be noted that the normal group itself is very small. The results *in toto* suggest that on the whole the M.P.I. is applicable in Sweden and is likely to give similar results, but this conclusion is much less certain than that in relation to Japan or Italy, probably because the numbers used are so small.

A Spanish review of the M.P.I. has been used in Chile by A. C. Bolardos (1964) who applied it to 60 normal and 51 neurotic subjects, of whom 19 were diagnosed as hysterics and 32 as dysthymics. The mean neuroticism scores of the neurotic group was 34±8·5, that of the normal group was 17·2±8·0. The difference was significant at the 1 per cent level. Hysterics and dysthymics had neuroticism scores of 34·5 and 32·8 respectively, a difference which was not significant. On the extraversion scale it was found that hysterics had a score of 27·8, while dysthymics had a score of 17·9, a difference significant at the 1 per cent level. These results are very much in line again with those of the M.P.I. applied to English speaking groups.

Several investigations have been reported using a Hindi translation of the M.P.I. Jalota (1965) and Singh (1966) report reliabilities slightly lower than those given in the Manual, and correlations between the scales which are virtually zero. Singh found correlations between E and N of −0·14 and 0·07 for his criminal and non-criminal groups respectively, and corrected split-half reliabilities of 0·72 and 0·71 (N and E) for the latter; no figures are given for the former. Sinha (1966) and Rao (1966) give figures relating to occupational choice of extraverts and introverts, and personality scores of different professional student groups, respectively; many of these are significant. It is interesting to note that in India, Arts students are more extraverted than Science students (31 *v.* 27), with the former also having higher N scores (23 *v.* 19); this is the usual pattern in English-speaking countries too. Indian nurses, however, seem to be introverted; this sets them off from English-speaking ones, who are more frequently extraverted. On the whole Indian students seem to be more extraverted and more neurotic than English ones, and at least more neurotic than American ones.

A Panjabi version of the M.P.I. was prepared and administered by Jalota (1964) to 75 male and 75 female students at the Panjabi University of Chandigarh. The mean neuroticism score for the male and female groups combined was 23·2±10·0. For the extraversion scale the mean combined score was 27·8±6·2. There were no differences of any significance between males and females. The correlation between N and E was −0·22. The reliability of the N scale was 0·72, that of the E scale 0·53, when scores on the first half were compared with scores on the second half of the scale; these figures are somewhat lower than the comparative English ones, but it should be noted that Jalota did not use an odd-even reliability coefficient which would possibly have been higher than that of scores on the first being correlated with scores on the second half. (See also Das, 1961.)

In a series of studies from Poland, Choynowski (1966) has tested various groups of normals, neurotics and psychotics. Normal men and women have E scores very similar to English samples, but on N scores are characteristically higher by as much as ¾ S.D.; Choynowski attributes this to a greater willingness among Polish people to own up to neurotic-emotional traits—Poles are supposed to be a very emotional people! Neurotics have higher N and lower E scores, while schizophrenics have only slightly higher N scores and definitely lower E scores. Reliabilities are 0·87 for N and 0·86 for E (corrected); the correlation between E and N is −0·33, which is somewhat higher than in England. All in all, similarities outweigh differences in these studies too; the differences which remain may be due to inadequate sampling. Similar studies have been inaugurated by Choynowski in Czechoslovakia, but results are not yet complete; preliminary findings suggest that here too findings agree well with English experience.

Rafi (1965) used an Arabic form of the M.P.I. with a group of 160 young Lebanese normal adult males. He found a correlation of −0·14 between E and N, no correlation between either personality scale and various intelligence tests, and mean scores which 'show a striking similarity between the results of the present sample and those reported by Eysenck.'

The M.P.I. has also been translated into French (Choppy and Eysenck, 1960) and into German (Eysenck, 1959e, 1960d). Too little has been published in relation to the French version to enable us to come to any conclusion as to the similarities or differences to be found in that country.

In Germany, on the other hand, much use has been made of the MMQ and the M.P.I. (Eysenck, 1959e, 1960d), and one adapted form of the M.P.I. has been published by Brengelmann and Brengelmann (1960). Meyer and Golle (1966) and Warncke and Fahrenberg (1966) have conducted extensive item analyses and factor analyses of selected parts of the M.P.I., and have shown that the chosen items give rise to very similar factors in German, as well as to similar reliabilities and factor correlations. Experiments such as those of Dummer (1959, 1960, 1964), Michel (1960), and Fahrenberg (1966) demonstrate in addition that normals have scores not very different from English norms, while neurotic and psychosomatic groups have elevated N scores, as well as lower E scores than normals. Fahrenberg (1966) has constructed an inventory of functional somatic complaints, which he applied to 543 students, together with a version of the M.P.I. He found that female students were significantly more neurotic and less extraverted, a finding also in line with English experience; in addition he found correlations of 0·60 and 0·71 between his inventory and N (for men and women respectively). E and N in these two groups correlated −0·34 and −0·21, which is somewhat higher than might have been expected, but still within the boundaries set by English and American work.

Altogether we may conclude this section by noting that results from very different cultures appear to be strikingly congruent in many ways, and that it appears that the fundamental dimensions of personality measured by the M.P.I. are not confined to the English-speaking world or to Europe but can also be found in various oriental countries.

10

THE VALIDITY OF THE M.P.I.—NEGATIVE VALIDITY

THE notion of 'validity' is an interesting as well as an important one in psychology, and the misunderstandings attaching to it are legion. Textbooks often define it as the agreement between a test and some true measure of the property which the test is designed to measure, but of course it is only in trivial cases that such an outside criterion is in fact available. If we had a true measure of intelligence, or extraversion, or neuroticism, then we would hardly need to bother with less reliable and less valid tests of these properties; we would simply use the criterion itself. Thus we are obviously thrown back on other measures of validation and there is no agreement as to how precisely this should be done. This state of affairs is often contrasted unfavourably with that obtaining in physics where it is believed that the problem of validity hardly arises.

This, of course, is untrue, or at least it is untrue in relation to many physical properties which are perhaps less familiar to most psychologists than the obvious ones of time and space. Rheology in particular has thrown up a number of problems in measurement and definition which are very similar to those which occur in psychology and it is notable that physicists have been thrown back on to the use of factor analytic methods in efforts to overcome these problems. (Harper and Baron, 1948, 1951; Scott Blair, 1951; Harper, Kent, and Scott Blair, 1950.)

In geology too correlational and factor analytic methods are now being used. The application of factor analysis to geological data, as Merriam (1965) explains, 'has been almost entirely confined to determining the inter-relations of chemical, lithological, and biological constituents in recent and ancient sediments, thereby grouping sampled localities into similar areas; and in this way meaningful patterns are revealed. These patterns in turn are used to interpret the environmental history of the sedimentary unit in question. Such a study has been made of a thin (up to five feet thick), persistent, marine limestone—the Americus Limestone—in order to interpret the environment in which it was laid down by reconstructing the distribution of sediments on the sea floor in Early Permian time (about 250 million years ago). Rock specimens were sampled along an approximately 250 mile outcrop in eastern Kansas and Oklahoma. Quantitative information on their constituents was obtained by studying thin sections of the rocks and by chemical and spectrographic analyses. The raw data were first transformed to give each constituent approximately equal weight when comparing localities, then appropriate coefficients were computed for subsequent factor analysis. The factors extracted from the Americus Limestone data are plotted and major changes are indicated (labelled 'phases'), which are related to distribution of constituents determined from the original data. With this information, the depositional environment of the unit was re-created.' (A detailed description of these procedures is found in Harbaugh and Demirmen, 1964.)

In order to give the reader unfamiliar with physics some idea of the kind of problems that arise there and the similarity of these problems to those arising in psychology, we may perhaps choose as an example the measurement of 'hardness'. This is an elusive property that is really a combination of several properties; it has been found necessary to define it in terms of particular tests—so that in one sense one might apply in this physical domain the often quoted statements that 'intelligence is what intelligence tests measure'; in the revised version 'hardness is what hardness tests measure'.[1]

There are certain fundamental ideas underlying the concept of hardness. The concept is itself obviously derived from our experience with the fact that a given material can be drilled, sawn, indented or abraded with greater or lesser ease than another material. It is further intuitively obvious that the harder of two substances will scratch the other, will resist wear better, or suffer less damage when struck by a third material harder than either. As Mott has pointed out (1964) 'these concepts do not in fact involve a single physical property but various combinations

[1] For an exceptionally interesting account of the application of the principles of invariance to quasi-properties, such as 'firmness', which abound in rheology, see Scott Blair (1951a). Of particular interest is his suggestive section on the principles involved in factorial analysis and in the theory of quasi-properties (p. 13–15). The discussion by psychologists of the possibility of applying the principles and methods of physics to psychology have always suffered from the fact that adherents of both points of view seem to have had little acquaintance with modern physics; cursory references to Newton only conjure up a schoolboy's picture of physics long given up by serious workers in that field. There are many different principles and methods in physics, and the task of psychologists might perhaps be better defined as that of finding the appropriate analogues to his problems, rather than debating in the abstract the total applicability or lack of applicability of physicalistic theories.

of several properties. As a result there is more than one kind of hardness. For example abrasion hardness depends to a large extent on the properties of the surface so that the way the material was prepared and the effects of corrosion by the atmosphere can both be important. Scratch hardness involves a combination of plastic flow and fracture characteristics; here the shape of the scratching tool can also play an important part. Although plasticity, or lack of it, largely determines the indentation hardness, if the material is brittle it may crack or shatter. Thus lead and talc are both soft materials but for different reasons. Lead flows readily when indented; talc offers little resistance to fracture and crumbles easily. The range of properties loosely considered as hardness is so wide that it is impossible to arrive at a concise definition that includes every characteristic. Any precise definition of hardness depends on a particular measure of assessment.' We might thus say that hardness is a *type* concept based on the observed similarities between several *trait* concepts such as abrasion hardness, scratch hardness, indentation hardness and so forth. These relationships are by no means perfect and there is a loss in precision when a superordinate concept like hardness is invoked.

As is well known the first attempt to measure hardness was made in 1822 by the geologist F. Mohs who defined a scale of minerals on which a particular substance could be scratched only by another higher up. The softest material, talc, was considered as having a hardness of 1·0, while that of diamond was taken as 10, the intermediate minerals in order of increasing hardness being gypsum, calcite, fluorite, apatite, orthoclase, quartz, topaz, and corundum. This test, although over a century old, is still used in conjunction with other physical characteristics in the preliminary identification of minerals. A more recent test is the Bierbaum microcharacter test in which the specimen is moved under a diamond point loaded up to 3 grammes to produce a groove in it: the hardness number is then taken to be 10,000 divided by the square of the width of the groove in microns.

Other widely used tests are the Brinell tests which originated in 1900, or the Diamond pyramid test which was developed in 1922. In the standard Brinell a hardened steel ball of 1 cm. diameter is forced into the surface of the specimen under a load of 3,000 kg.; this load is removed after 30 seconds and the diameter of the permanent impression is measured. The Brinell hardness number (H_B) is calculated as load in kg./area of indentation in sq. mm. There are certain difficulties with this test; the harder the specimen, the greater is the danger of deforming the steel ball during indentation, which means of course that the hardness values obtained will be lower than they should be. This tendency becomes quite marked for materials with a Brinell hardness index of over 500. The use of diamond instead of steel would of course obviate this problem in part, but diamond balls cannot be machined, and although spheres made from sapphire or tungsten carbide have been used for tests these are more brittle than steel and may shatter under load.

The diamond pyramid indenter has the advantage over a ball of giving geometrically similar impressions at all loads and an indenter with an angle of 136° between opposite faces was chosen by the originators of this test (R. Smith and G. Sandiland) because it corresponded to the tangential angle of the 'ideal' ball impression—considered to have a diameter equal to 0·375 times that of the ball. This test being used on the Vickers hardness machine gives rise to the Vickers hardness number, H_V, which is calculated in much the same manner as the Brinell number. When the Vickers and Brinell hardness scales are compared it is found that they are almost identical up to a Brinell hardness of about 500: above that value the Brinell values are lower because of the deformation of the ball.

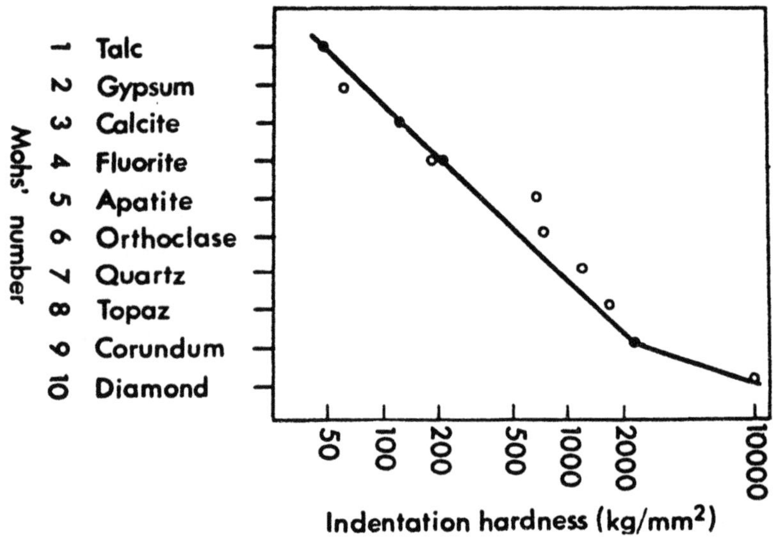

FIG. 10.1 Mohs' hardness number M plotted against indentation hardness. Each Mohs' interval corresponds to an increase in indentation hardness by a factor of about 1·6. (Taken with permission from B. W. Mott, 1964.)

The Vickers and Mohs hardness numbers can be compared and Tabor has shown by experiment that scratch hardness can be related remarkably closely to indentation hardness, as shown in Figure 10.1. This result confirms the great care with which Mohs chose his standard minerals and provides the basis for expressing the hardness of a mineral from the indentation hardness in terms of a fraction of the Mohs number.

Difficulties sometimes arise with small specimens of brittle materials, such as hard minerals or glass, which may shatter under high loads.

Under those conditions loads of a few grammes are often used and tests under these conditions are usually referred to as measures of 'micro-hardness'. H_V values obtained for a given homogeneous material measured with a load of a few grammes are often higher than those at a load of one kilogramme or more, and this has led to controversy as to whether the term 'micro-hardness' really has any definable physical meaning. In other words here as in psychology a change in the conditions of the measuring process may lead to considerable changes in the result and to discussion regarding the validity of the particular conditions of measurement used.

There are many other ways of determining hardness besides a static indentation one. These include (1) a ball, cone, or a number of small spheres may be dropped from a definite height on to a specimen and the hardness may be expressed in terms of the indentation size and energy of impact. (2) A diamond tipped weight may be dropped from a fixed height and the height of its rebound be measured. (3) A hard sphere attached to a pendulum may be made to strike against a test piece and the amplitude of the first swing or the time oscillation of a number of swings may be taken as a measure of hardness. (4) The specimen may be subjected to a sliding or rotary motion or to a particular type of cutting operation and the resistance to wear of the specimen may then be taken as a measure of its hardness.

Mott (1964) comments that 'these and indentation tests involve different combinations of physical properties so that although they may place various samples of a given class of material in roughly the same order of changing hardness the result will not necessarily allow proper comparisons between different types of material.'

Nowadays of course we understand relations between these various measures better because we have some fundamental understanding of the physical characteristics of the materials being tested, i.e. the basic configuration of atoms—known as the unit lattice cell—and deviations from this in practice. However, to go into these more fundamental and causal inventions would take us too far afield; after this brief excursion into some of the problems presented by the concept of 'validity' in physical science we must return to those facing the psychologist in dealing with tests of such multidimensional concepts as extraversion and neuroticism.

Fundamentally we may say that the problem of validity has two complementary aspects. In the first place we have the problem of *negative validity*, i.e. the presence in the measuring process of certain biases which would tend to invalidate the proper measurement of the quality in which we are interested. Typical of such biases for instance are response sets of various kinds which may range from the well-known acquiescence response set, or tendency to answer yes to all questions, to desirability response set, i.e. the tendency to answer all questions in a desirable direction. It is clear that if negative validity in a test is strong, i.e. if these response sets account for a good deal of the total variance of the test, then the test cannot be highly valid.

In the second place we have *positive validity*, i.e. some degree of measure of the success of the test in measuring that which it attempts to measure. As previously pointed out this cannot be easily determined by reference to one single perfect criterion as such a criterion is practically never available; consequently various indirect methods have to be used in order to demonstrate validity. None of these methods by itself can ever suffice to validate the test; the final conclusion regarding the value of the test must be drawn from a consideration of all the available evidence. In this chapter we will briefly consider first of all the negative validity of the M.P.I. and we will then carry on with a consideration of its positive validity.

In dealing with the question of negative validity we will make use of Martin's (1964) response style theory based on a factor analysis of a variety of measures of acquiescence and social desirability tests. He discovered three main factors and his general conclusion is summarized by him as follows. 'When a subject is confronted with a questionnaire item the formal content of the item may invoke a tendency to respond in terms of social desirability. In this case acquiescence (of any type) will be minimal and responses will tend to be consistent as between an item and its contradictory. If however such clear guidance is not available because the item is neutral for social desirability (and he may be idiosyncratic in finding it so) the subject may be guided in his reply by what he considers to be rational or authentic. Inevitably such a judgement would be based, like social desirability, on notions of consensus derived from social interaction or communication. . . . In a sense the subject is conforming to what is generally accepted as truth just as in social desirability he conforms to some generally acceptable standard of self-description. The conditions surrounding the emergence of Factor 1, acquiescence, make it highly probable that we are dealing with a "primitive belief" factor. . . . This factor properly measured would probably serve as an indicator of readiness to accept "common sense" truths. Finally if the subject finds little guidance in either SD or rational acquiescence he must fall back on his own tendency to acquiesce or dissent. This is the most ambiguous situation of the three.'

The theory makes no assertions about the relative power of these factors. Clearly some items and item clusters strongly invoke one tendency while being neutral for the others. There are individual differences however in the tendencies evoked by all three variables and since they do not correlate it is improbable that any great number of individuals is equally affected by two tendencies. The theory would predict that individuals give primacy to one tendency only and that this prime factor would be a major personality variable for the person concerned (especially in the areas of persuasability and conformity). It is our duty therefore to investigate the presence or absence of these three types of response style in experiments conducted with the M.P.I. or the E.P.I. and to assess the degree to which they contribute negative validity to the measurement of extraversion and neuroticism. (It is, of course, possible that response style may contribute positive instead of negative validity; this may be illustrated by a hypothetical example. In both the E.P.I. and the M.P.I. the neuroticism scale tends to be made up of questions the key answer for which is 'yes'. Let us suppose that the more emotional and neurotic a person is the more he is likely to demonstrate acquiescence. In this case then the more neurotic person would tend to endorse more neuroticism items not only because he is more neurotic but also because of his acquiescence response set. Thus response set would confer a certain amount of positive validity on the scale instead of subtracting from the total validity possessed by the scale. It has been argued in the literature that something of the kind has happened in relation to the authoritarianism scale, in the sense that most of the items are keyed in such a way that a 'yes' response gives a high score on authoritarianism. If now authoritarians also possess an acquiescence response set then it can be argued that the scale acquires additional validity through this association with acquiescence response set. There is no evidence that anything of the kind has taken place in relation to personality questionnaires and no claims for positive validity of response set will be entertained here. We will maintain rather that to the extent that responses are determined by response set to that degree is the scale itself invalidated.)

The first study carried out in this connection by Eysenck (1962) dealt with what Martin calls the 'primitive belief' factor of acquiescence, as well as with the response set of 'indecisiveness', i.e. the tendency of some subjects to give large numbers of '?' responses. The hypotheses investigated in this study were as follows: (1) Personality inventories such as the M.P.I. do not show evidence of 'acquiescence' response set. (2) Personality measures E and N do not show evidence of correlation with 'extreme' response set, or its inverse, 'indecisiveness'. (3) 'Indecisiveness', as measured by the number of '?' responses marked, has a high degree of consistency from test to test. (4) Content scores on authoritarianism scales are not independent of 'acquiescence' response set, but show a positive correlation. (5) Content scores on authoritarianism scales are not independent of 'indecisiveness' response set, but show a negative correlation.

Ten measures in all were used in this study. They are listed below, together with the numbers which will be used to refer to the various measures. (1) M.P.I. Extraversion scale. (2) M.P.I. Neuroticism scale. (3) Number of '?' answers in M.P.I. (4) Content score on the Jackson-Messick (1957) version of the F scale. (5) Acquiescence score on the

Jackson-Messick (1957) version of the F scale. (6) Number of '?' answers on the Jackson-Messick (1957) version of the F scale. (7) Hysteria scale of the MMPI. (8) Psychopathic deviate scale on the MMPI. (9) Psychasthenia scale of the MMPI. (10) Number of '?' answers on the Hy, Pd, and Pt scales.

These ten sets of scores were obtained from tests administered to 137 neurotic inpatients at Belmont and Netherne Hospitals. Psychiatric diagnoses were available for these subjects; the number of cases within each category is indicated by the number in parentheses: Psychopaths (10), Hysterics and Anxiety Hysterics (29), Personality Disorders (17), Anxiety States (20), Reactive Depressions (19), Obsessionals (5), and Others (37). Patients were both male and female (no sex differences were observed on any of the scales) and ranged in age from twenty-five to fifty (no age differences were observed).

The various psychiatric groups fell into the predicted order on the E scale; differences on the N scale were not statistically significant. The mean scores of the various groups were: Psychopaths = 31·5; Hysterics = 22·2; Depressives = 21·9; Others = 21·3; Personality Disorders = 19·7; Anxiety States = 19·0; Obsessionals = 17·4. While the hysteric group is the second most extraverted group, it is close to the dysthymic groups, and not significantly differentiated from them.

The ten sets of scores were intercorrelated, and a factor analysis carried out. Hotelling's principal components method was used, and rotation carried out according to Thurstone's principle of simple structure. Four factors emerged which would be identified with reasonable accuracy.

Factor I has high positive loadings on the N, Hy, Pd, and Pt scales, and a high negative loading on E; it is clearly the well-known questionnaire neuroticism factor. The presence of the E scale here is due to a fact several times before encountered. While the N and E scales are independent in normal samples, they correlate together to the extent of 0·4 or thereabouts in neurotic samples. In this particular group the correlation is actually even higher than usual ($r = -0{\cdot}58$), thus giving rise to the high factor loading of −0·73 for the E scale.

The second factor has high positive loadings on all three '?' counts and may thus be labelled a factor of *indecisiveness* or '?' response set, depending on whether we are willing to make the suggested psychological interpretation of the observed factor of more frequent choice of a non-committal answer. The actual correlations between the three quite independent '?' counts average above 0·6, a value which may be inserted in the Spearman-Brown prophecy formula to give a rough idea of the reliability of the total combined score. Even more interesting than this verification of our third hypothesis is the fact that the 'content' score of the F scale has a loading on this factor of −0·65. Hypothesis 5 thus finds empirical support, and we may conclude that persons who score high on the F scale, purified of its response set component, tend to have very definite opinions, and to shun 'wishy-washy' non-commital replies. The actual correlations of 'content' with the three '?' counts are: −0·17, −0·56, and −0·31.

Factors 3 and 4 are of relatively little interest, each containing only one high loading. Factor 3 may be identified as 'anti-fascist', the only high loading being a negative one for the content score of the F scale, and Factor 4 may be identified as one of acquiescence response set, this score having the only high loading on it. The actual correlation between content and set on the F scale is 0·21; this very slight positive correlation finds expression in the low positive loading of the content score on Factor 4 (0·30). Hypothesis 4 is thus also verified, although not at a very high level of certainty. (The observed correlation is just below the 0·01 level of *p*.) It is interesting that E has a negative loading on Factor 3; this agrees with the theory linking E and F (Eysenck, 1954).

The failure of the N scale to have a positive loading on Factor 4 supports hypothesis I, and indicates that the measurement of neuroticism is not complicated by the acquiescence response set. The failure of E and N to have loadings on Factor 2 supports hypothesis 2, and suggests that the measurement of extraversion and neuroticism is not complicated by 'indecisiveness' response set. It is concluded therefore that the results support all five hypotheses, at least as far as the particular sample tested is concerned.

It would probably not have been reasonable to expect the emergence of acquiescence responses based on readiness to accept 'common sense truth' in a questionnaire such as the M.P.I. and therefore the above findings are not unexpected.[1] We must now turn to an examination of a much more likely hypothesis that 'yea' and 'nay' saying tendencies, i.e. what Martin calls the subject's own tendency to acquiesce or dissent, account for a reasonable proportion of the variance of the M.P.I. score. The first study on this point was carried out by Eysenck and Eysenck (1963c).

Two scales were constructed for the measurement of neuroticism, each containing 24 items similar to those used in the M.P.I. but worded in a slightly simplified fashion so as to make them suitable for subjects with below average intelligence and education. These two scales, designated 'N_A' and 'N_B', are all scored in such a way that a 'Yes' answer is indicative of neuroticism, and a 'no' answer indicative of stability. In addition, four eight-item scales of extraversion were

[1] Relevant in this connection is a somewhat similar study by Soueif (1965), in which he administered 8 scales from the M.P.I. and Guilford's STDCR (in Arabic form) together with the PFCL (Personal Friend Check List—Soueif, 1958) to 215 Egyptian subjects. The PFCL was scored for 3 different response sets, and intercorrelations between the eleven scales factor analysed. The 3 main factors to emerge were N, E and 'extreme vs. moderation' response set.

constructed in a similar manner; these will be referred to as A, B, C and D. In scales A and C a 'Yes' answer was indicative of extraversion, while in scales B and D a 'No' answer was indicative of extraversion. The correctness of the system of scoring was checked by means of a factor analysis of all the items concerned in this study.

Two sets of predictions were made on the hypothesis that response set might play a part in answers to questions of this type. If there was indeed a tendency for people to answer 'Yes' regardless of the actual content of each question, then Extraversion scales A and C should correlate positively with N_A and N_B, as on all these scales the 'Yes' answer would be indicative of extraversion in the one case, neuroticism in the other, thus producing a positive correlation between extraversion and neuroticism. On the other hand Extraversion scales B and D should correlate negatively with N_A and N_B, because on these scales a 'No' answer measures extraversion while the 'Yes' answer measures neuroticism. The size of the differences found would then be an index of the extent of the influence exerted by response sets on these questionnaires.

The other hypothesis relates to the intercorrelations between the four sets of extraversion items. If response set plays a part in the answering of the questions then the correlations between congruent sets (AC and BD, i.e. sets where 'Yes' or 'No' answers respectively contribute towards a high score on extraversion), should be larger than the correlations between incongruent sets (AB, AD, BC, CD, i.e. sets where in the one case 'Yes', in the other case 'No', is the answer contributing to a high score on extraversion).

The questionnaire was applied to a sample of 500 subjects, roughly equally divided as to sex and containing a great variety of subjects from both working and middle class occupations. While the sample could on no account be considered representative, it would be much more similar to a proper representative sample than is usual in inquiries of this kind.

The results of the study as they relate to hypotheses 1 and 2 are given in Tables 10.1 and 10.2; it will be seen that they bear out the hypothesis of the existence of a small but definite response set in these data. Scales A and C correlate approximately $+0{\cdot}12$ with N_A and N_B while scales B and D correlate approximately $-0{\cdot}14$ with N_A and N_B. These results, when viewed against the fact that a correlation of 0·085 would be significant at the 5 per cent level and one of 0·115 at the 1 per cent level, significantly support the hypothesis. It will, of course, be noted that the results, although statistically significant, are so only because of the very large number of subjects involved; in absolute terms the correlations are, of course, very low and indicate that for most practical purposes response set can be disregarded in inquiries of this kind, and is of academic rather than practical interest. The figures from Table 10.2 suggest a similar conclusion; here also there is little doubt about the significance of the differences between the congruent and incongruent group correlations, but these differences are not large, and it will be seen that two of the four incongruent group correlations are actually larger than one of the two congruent group correlations.

TABLE 10.1

Correlations with two N scales with four E scales

	N_A	N_B
A	0·16	0·16
B	−0·13	−0·16
C	0·08	0·06
D	−0·15	−0·15

TABLE 10.2

Correlations between E scales congruent and incongruent for response

Congruent groups	Incongruent groups
AC = 0·60	AB = 0·48
BD = 0·45	AD = 0·35
	BC = 0·46
	CD = 0·34

The experiment was repeated by Eysenck and Eysenck (1964a) but on a much larger group of subjects. The same sets of items were used as before; the questions were printed in random order on a questionnaire together with 28 buffer items and were administered to 1,655 normal subjects of both sexes and 210 neurotics under treatment at various hospitals, also on both sexes. Both middle class and working class groups were equally represented, and although it could not be claimed that the sample was a truly random one, nevertheless it was probably not too unrepresentative of the British population. The results of the study are given in Table 10.3; product moment correlations have been averaged by the inverse hyperbolic tangent transformation. It will be seen that for both neurotics and normals congruent values (0·52 and 0·50) are larger than the incongruent ones (0·42 and 0·42). The results again suggest that acquiescence response set does indeed influence responses, although only to a mild degree, and that it does so for normals and neurotics alike.

TABLE 10.3

Correlations between E scales congruent and incongruent for response

	Congruent correlations			Incongruent correlations	
	Normals	Neurotics		Normals	Neurotics
A C	0·539	0·591	A B	0·499	0·511
B D	0·468	0·448	A D	0·345	0·217
			B C	0·481	0·596
			C D	0·352	0·318
Average	0·504	0·523		0·422	0·422

Correlations between the neuroticism questionnaires and the four extraversion scales would be expected to be higher for A and C than for B and D because of congruence and incongruence of 'yes' responses respectively; 'higher' in this connection means either 'greater in absolute amount if with positive sign', or 'less than absolute amount if with negative sign.' Correlations between N (N_A+N_B) and the four E scales are: 0·023, −0·097, −0·035 and −0·094 for normals, and 0·039, −0·109, −0·121 and −0·140 for the neurotics. Of the differences, only those involving E_A are statistically significant (at the 1 per cent level), and only for the very large normal group. There is slight support here for the postulation of a response set but the set is not very powerful.

A single experiment was carried out to investigate the problem of desirability response set by Eysenck and Eysenck (1963b). This study is concerned with the problem of 'desirability' in relation to the same two dimensions of personality. The questionnaire employed in this investigation contained 75 questions, to be answered by ringing either the 'Yes' or the 'No' answer; no '?' answers were permitted. Twelve questions were scored for the N variable, 54 questions for the E variable, and 9 questions formed a 'lie scale' (L). The N items were all taken from the M.P.I.; the E items were partly taken from the M.P.I. but other items were added from several studies carried out in an attempt to improve and extend the M.P.I. Each of the items used for the N and E scales had been shown to have high loadings on the appropriate factor in at least two, and sometimes as many as ten, independent factor analyses; not all of these analyses have been published.

The experiment consisted in having each questionnaire filled in twice, with an interval varying from one or two days to several weeks. On the first occasion, subjects were simply instructed to complete the inventory; on the second occasion, they were instructed to fill it in in such a way as to give the best possible impression of themselves, i.e. to put themselves in the best light. They did not know on the first occasion that they would be required to fill in the questionnaire again. In other words, on the second occasion they were asked to fake responses, and the main purpose of this study is to compare the 'truthful' responses and the 'fake good' responses. Our anticipation was that faking would shift the N scores towards a lower level, would leave the E scores relatively untouched, and would increase the level of 'lie' responses. It was also anticipated that while the mean E score would remain unchanged, there would be a tendency for both high and low E scores to shift responses towards a more average level, thus reducing the variance of E scores.

Ten groups of subjects were studied, giving a total of 873 Ss in all. The composition of these groups is shown in Table 10.4; it will be seen that the majority of Ss were University students (675, in all). All the Ss except for one group of U.S. students and a group of U.S. parents, teachers and housewives, were British; all the British Ss were English except for the Belfast group, who were of course Irish.

TABLE 10.4

	n
(1) Belfast students	163
(2) Non-student group (Housewives, evening classes, etc.)	85
(3) Working-class group	57
(4) Sheffield students	38
(5) Exeter students	89
(6) Non-student U.S. group (Housewives, parents, teachers, etc.)	57
(7) Belfast law students	66
(8) U.S. students	185
(9) Welsh students	32
(10) Manchester students	101
Total	873

Table 10.5 gives the means and the S.D.s, for E, N and L, of all the groups for both administrations of the questionnaire; these two administrations are referred to as A and B, respectively. Also given are the differences (A−B) between the two administrations. Analyses of variance were carried out to determine whether the differences between groups were significant; the results are indicated in Table 10.6. It is clear that the groups are differentiated with respect to E and N, but only slightly; with such small numbers the F values given suggest that differences may be safely disregarded. When we look at the B scores we find much higher F values for N and L, and a somewhat higher F value for E as well. The groups are obviously rather different in their 'faked' responses, particularly for N and L. For A−B, only L responses show a really high F value.

Inspection of the A scores reveals that the U.S.A. students are the most extraverted group; this might not come as a surprise. On the other hand, the U.S.A. non-student group (mostly Palo Alto housewives and other wage-earners) has the lowest E score; this might not have been anticipated. However, the F ratio is so low as to indicate that search for significance (in the psychological sense) would seem to be useless. The same is probably true of N, where the working class group has the highest score. This group also has the highest L score, which is unexpected; usually high L scores go with low N scores. This difference is startlingly large, and almost entirely responsible for the significance of the F ratio. No previous data on class comparisons are available for 'Lie' scale scores, so that we cannot tell whether this finding is unusual.

The working class group is again outstanding with respect to the B neuroticism scores, where they have far and away the highest scores, and also with respect to the Lie scores, where their score is now the lowest, by a long chalk. It would appear that this group is responsible for the

TABLE 10.5

	N	Age	Sex M	Sex F	A E	A N	A L	B E	B N	B L	A – B E	A – B N	A – B L
Means													
1.	163	18·822	70	93	28·748	6·736	1·601	30·454	1·632	7·325	– 1·706	5·104	– 5·724
2.	85	33·341	36	49	26·541	5·953	1·788	29·059	1·941	5·800	– 2·518	4·012	– 4·012
3.	57	41·491	50	7	28·772	7·035	2·807	31·018	4·632	4·860	– 2·246	2·403	– 2·053
4.	38	18·895	18	20	30·579	7·026	1·316	34·316	2·395	7·500	– 3·737	4·631	– 6·184
5.	89	19·820	33	56	28·112	6·213	1·416	29·966	1·944	5·449	– 1·854	4·269	– 4·033
6.	57	37·579	17	40	26·491	4·982	1·737	32·211	1·386	6·456	– 5·720	3·596	– 4·719
7.	66	20·727	48	18	29·288	6·773	1·515	32·652	2·318	6·697	– 3·364	4·455	– 5·182
8.	185	19·286	73	112	30·730	6·708	1·411	32·897	1·178	7·795	– 2·167	5·530	– 6·384
9.	32	23·875	15	17	27·719	5·031	1·281	30·969	0·875	5·969	– 3·250	4·156	– 4·688
10.	101	22·792	52	49	27·624	6·495	1·653	32·337	2·079	5·248	– 4·713	4·416	– 3·595
Standard deviations													
1.	163	2·261	70	93	8·220	3·226	1·451	5·891	1·641	1·993	10·455	3·237	2·340
2.	85	10·672	36	49	8·814	3·387	1·559	5·803	2·607	2·530	9·643	2·966	2·628
3.	57	13·791	50	7	8·604	2·988	1·931	7·749	3·074	2·532	11·189	4·697	3·476
4.	38	1·843	18	20	8·494	3·192	1·276	9·367	2·626	2·501	14·757	3·582	3·021
5.	89	2·443	33	56	9·449	3·379	1·629	7·541	2·465	2·884	11·253	3·704	2·909
6.	57	11·260	17	40	8·289	3·254	1·653	5·621	2·266	2·529	8·525	3·417	2·944
7.	66	5·058	48	18	8·372	3·042	1·756	6·607	2·513	2·219	10·687	2·962	2·833
8.	185	3·637	73	112	7·353	3·202	1·385	4·949	1·958	1·748	8·175	3·133	2·074
9.	32	3·087	15	17	7·722	2·706	1·276	4·617	1·100	2·559	9·281	2·919	2·507
10.	101	3·232	52	49	7·516	3·142	1·439	6·834	2·444	2·823	9·001	3·686	3·128

Means (top half) and S.D.s (bottom half) of E, N and L scores for 10 groups of Subjects under conditions A and B, and A – B.

main differences discovered between our ten groups, both for the A and the B administrations; a discussion of the possible reasons for this will be postponed until later.

TABLE 10.6

Analysis of variance

	(A)	(B)	(A − B)
E	2·944*	4·907**	1·433 NS
N	3·017*	13·312**	5·570**
L	4·931**	18·611**	21·003**

NS = Not significant * $P < 0·05$ ** $P < 0·01$

Difference scores (A − B) for E range between 1·706 and 5·720; in other words, there is a slight tendency for Ss to make themselves out as more extraverted when 'faking good'; the extent of this tendency is only about ⅓ S.D., which is almost negligible from the psychological point of view, although the unanimity of the shift (it is shown by all ten groups) leaves little doubt about its validity. For N the difference scores range from −2·403 to −5·530; all groups agree in faking a lowering of their neuroticism scores by over one S.D. This is a very large shift, although one might perhaps have expected an even larger one. On the L scores, too, there is a strong and unanimous shift towards greater lying, from between 2·053 to 6·384 points, corresponding to between 3 and 4 S.D.s; this is a large shift for all groups except the working class group. On the

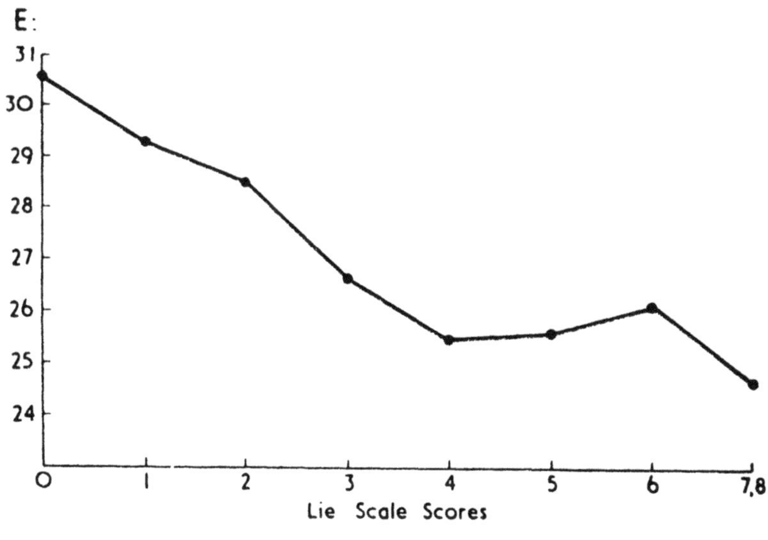

FIG. 10.2 Diagram showing relationship between score on the E scale as a function of different scores on the Lie scale. (From Eysenck and Eysenck, 1963b.)

whole, these figures bear out our expectation of a large shift for N and L, and a small or non-existent shift for E. It will also be noted that the predicted shrinkage of the variance for E scores from A to B does actually take place for all groups but one. Variances for N are lower, and for L higher, under condition B as compared with condition A, indicating a shift towards greater uniformity among Ss with respect to N, and towards greater heterogeneity with respect to L.

We may now turn to a consideration of the relationship between the Lie scale and the E and N scales. An increased tendency to lie (assuming that it is this which is measured by the L scale) is associated with introversion; L scorers of zero have high E scores (30·6) while Ss scoring 7 or above have E scores of 24·6. The regression does not depart significantly from linearity and is highly significant by analysis of variance. E scores under condition B show no significant relation to L, and it follows of course that change scores (A – B) show a tendency for liars to have negative change scores, i.e. to pretend to greater extraversion; this tendency is highly significant by analysis of variance.

Liars pretend to less neuroticism than do non-liars, as is shown in Figure 10.3. There is a drop from a score of 7·1 (L score zero) to a neuroticism score of 3·0 for Ss with lie scores of 7 or above; this regression is linear and highly significant by analysis of variance. There is a non-significant relation between N and L under condition B, and a highly significant linear one between L and change scores (liars change least). This last relation is demonstrated in Figure 10.4.

We must first of all deal with the odd behaviour of the working class group which, while on the whole showing the same tendencies as the other groups, changed much less than the others with respect to N and L. Our own interpretation would link this with Orne's (1962) concept of the 'demand characteristic' of the testing situation, which may be assumed to be rather different for working class subjects, unfamiliar with the very notion of an 'experiment', as compared with relatively sophisticated University students. Indeed, while the 'faking' instructions were accepted readily by all the other groups, the working class Ss showed clearly that they thought this to be a crazy idea. This curious behaviour should certainly be followed up, and the adequacy of this hypothesis be tested; our data do not enable us to judge its value.

As regards the main enquiry, we find that no hypothesis is tenable which would ascribe a large portion of the variance of the scores obtained under condition A to desirability response sets, i.e. a tendency for Ss to give answers which were socially accepted, and making Ss out to have desirable characteristics. If this were so, then little change should have taken place from condition A to condition B; yet this change was quite large, particularly on the L scale. With a possible 'desirability' score of 9 points, Ss only averaged a score of 1·5 under condition A; under instructions to 'fake good' they produced a change to almost 6·5 equal to between 3 and 4 S.D.s. Clearly desirability played relatively little part in their answers to the questions. Changes in N scores point in the same direction. These results are in good agreement with the independent evidence showing that E and N scales are valid when compared with external criteria (to be reviewed below); no such validity could be demonstrated if a large portion of the variance were due to desirability responses.

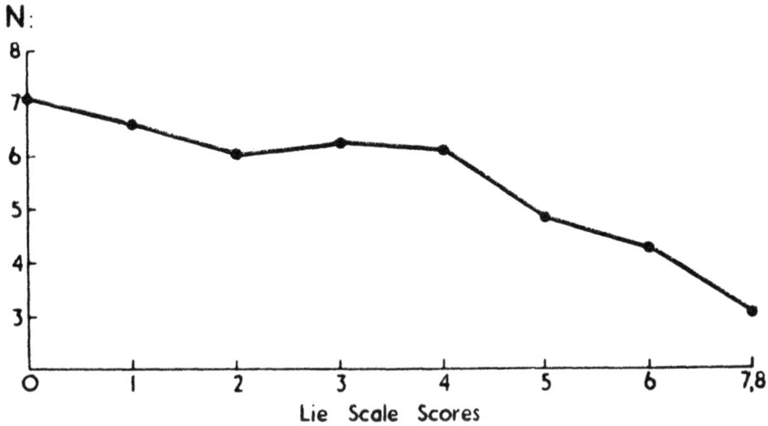

FIG. 10.3 Diagram showing relationship between score on the N scale as a function of different scores on the Lie scale. (From Eysenck and Eysenck, 1963b.)

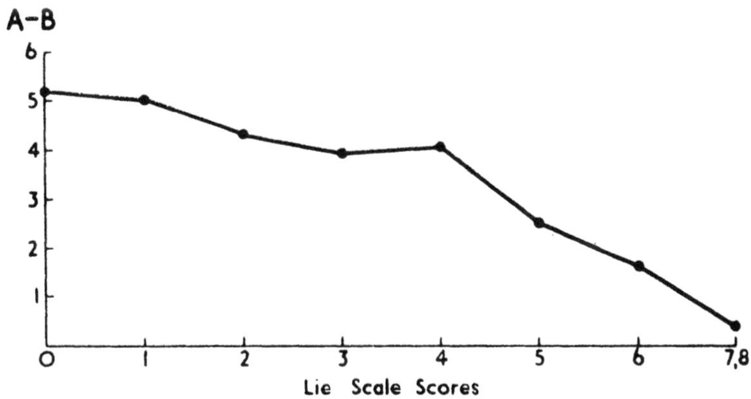

FIG. 10.4 Diagram showing change scores on the N scale as a function of different scores on the Lie scale. (From Eysenck and Eysenck, 1963b.)

This does not mean, of course, that desirability responses are completely absent in our questionnaire answers; such an hypothesis would be rendered untenable by the relations demonstrated between L scores and the E and N scales. It will be remembered that 'liars' pretend to less neuroticism than do non-liars; non-liars only catch up when *instructed* to 'fake good'. Extreme liars have already put themselves into the best possible light under condition A; they have no room left for 'faking good', and accordingly do not change under condition B. These results can be explained best if we assume that the L scale is a good measure of 'desirability' response set (faking good) on the part of Ss; only relatively few Ss engage in this practice to any significant extent, and these can be spotted by their high L scores. For the great majority, desirability response set may be disregarded. It is clear from Figure 10.3 that there is little change in N score while L scores are between 0 and 4; it is with scores of 5 and above that there appears to be a strong tendency to 'fake good'. (This agrees reasonably well with Gibson's figures (1962) who shows, with a scale twice as long, that a score of 10 is indicated as a cutting-off score; it also agrees with Eysenck's original suggestion (1953) to use 10 as the cut-off point with the 18-item scale.) Only 46 Ss have scores on the L scale of 5 or above, thus leaving 95 per cent of the sample as being relatively unaffected by desirability response set. (475 Ss, or well over half, have L scores of 0 or 1.)[1]

The relation between L and E is a little puzzling if we follow this line of thought. We have found that under 'faking good' conditions there is a slight trend towards extraversion, and one would have thought that liars would follow this trend and have higher E scores. The facts are actually opposite; liars have low E scores, and change correspondingly more towards extraversion under instruction to 'fake good'. We may here have a genuine relation between introversion and tendency to give desirable responses, which is only slightly attenuated by the somewhat greater desirability of extraverted responses. In other words, we would ascribe the relation between lying and low N scores to the effects of the former on the latter (liars fake good), and we would ascribe the relation between lying and low E scores to the effects of the latter on the former (introverts lie more). This hypothesis cannot be proved to be correct on the basis of our data; it would require an independent investigation, specially planned for the purpose, to make an evaluation possible. An alternative hypothesis might be framed in terms of the greater socialization postulated by Eysenck (1964b) as characteristic for introverts. The 'Lie' scale items all refer to *unusually* good behaviour patterns, such as never lying, cheating, losing one's temper, et cetera. It is possible that there may be genuine differences here between introverts and extraverts which might account for the observed relations between L and E. In

[1] Braun and Gomez (1966) have also studied the effects of faking instructions on the E.P.I. and come to similar conclusions. 'Although faking instructions can alter scores on the E.P.I., the Lie scale detects faking rather effectively. When Ss attempt to conceal their faking, a smaller percentage make Lie scores above the crucial point, but in the process they do not reduce their Neuroticism scores as markedly.'

support we might quote such investigations as those of Fine (1963) showing that extraverts are guilty of more traffic violations and accidents than introverts, and of S. B. G. Eysenck (1961) showing that unmarried mothers are more extraverted than married ones. The relationship between psychopathic behaviour and Extraversion has been confirmed quite frequently (Eysenck, 1964b), as has that between tender-mindedness and introversion (Eysenck, 1954). This alternative hypothesis might therefore repay investigation.

A study by Farley (1966) throws further light on this problem of social desirability and Lie Scale scores. He took as his point of departure the fact that Martin and Stanley (1963) had found a negative correlation of −0·61 with their own social desirability (SD) scale for N, but that the E scale did not correlate with SD; the L scale correlated 0·39 with SD. Farley used the E.P.I. and the more widely used Edwards scale (ESD) in a replication of this study; he also included the Crowne and Marlowe (1964) scale of SD. There is a marked difference between these two scales. The ESD is based on the notion that a socially desirable response is a True response to any item with a high social desirability scale value (as assigned by judges), and a False response to any item with a low social desirability scale value. The ESD has been constructed in terms of this definition of SD responding; it consists of 39 items drawn from the MMPI. Crowne and Marlowe have criticized the ESD as a measure of social desirability on the grounds that it is contaminated by psychological item content; it is not possible to sort out SD response bias from genuine endorsement of symptomatology. These authors (1960) have therefore developed an SD scale (MC-SD) which is supposedly free from pathological item content, and is based on a generalized motivational interpretation of SD responding. (See Heilbrunn, 1964, for a review of the whole issue of SD and psychopathology. Katkin's (1964) work suggests that the exclusion of pathology from the MC-SD scale is not complete.)

Using 100 subjects, Farley found that the ESD scale correlated with N (−0·60), but not with E or L. The MC-SD scale correlated most highly with L (0·55), and very little with N (−0·30) or E (−0·22). The marked reduction in correlation for N, and the marked increase in correlation for L, as we pass from the ESD scale to the MC-SD scale, both argue strongly for the two conclusions that (1) social desirability response set plays little part in N scores, and that (2) the L scale is a good measure of SD variance, unalloyed by pathological content, and may therefore be used as a suppressor variable. The slight remaining correlation between N and the MC-SD scale may find an explanation either in terms of Katkin's demonstration of pathological content in the MC-SD scale, or in terms of some genuine SD variance in the N scale, or most likely both.

It is along these lines that one should evaluate Blackburn's (1965) suggestion 'that the M.P.I. might be subject to response set of the denial-omission kind.' Using a repression-sensitization scale, he found a correlation between repression and N ($r = -0{\cdot}54$), and also between repression and E ($r = 0{\cdot}33$). He concluded that 'those who tend to deny or minimize deviant personality features score lower than those who admit or endorse unfavourable features.' He fails to discuss the likelihood that pathological content in the repression-sensitization scale may account for the correlation with N. The correlation with E is more interesting and may represent true 'repression' effect; there is independent evidence for such an hypothesis in the experimental work of Eriksen (1954).

As a summary of these various studies we may perhaps say that one form of response set plays no part in M.P.I. and E.P.I. scores. Two types of response set appear to play some part, but only a minor one, in the generation of M.P.I. and E.P.I. scores; namely the tendency to give 'yes' or 'no' answers regardless of content, and the tendency to put oneself into a desirable light. The latter tendency can be measured to some extent by having recourse to the Lie scale incorporated in the E.P.I. and in some forms of the M.P.I. Much further research will undoubtedly be necessary before we can be reasonably certain about the actual relationships between Lie scale, N scale and E scale, but the evidence suggests quite strongly that the Lie scale does measure to some extent at least desirability response set.

Control over acquiescence response set appears to be rather more difficult particularly as the neuroticism scales are made up of items which are keyed predominantly on the 'yes' items. A fairly obvious suggestion would be that of rewriting half the items in such a way that 'no' could be the keyed response, but such a suggestion is somewhat unrealistic. It has been our experience that most questions can be worded much more naturally in one direction than in the other, and in the case of neuroticism items, which consist essentially of a long list of symptoms, it is very much more natural to word them in such a way that the 'yes' response is related to the admission of that symptom. Take as an example an item such as 'Do you have frequent headaches?' It is of course possible to reword this in some such way as 'Do you have very few headaches?'; but in our experience this phrasing gives rise to certain difficulties. People having had no headaches at all during the last year or so are very doubtful about whether to answer yes or no; logically it might be argued whether the category 'very few' includes or excludes *no* headaches, but practically all subjects frequently raise questions about this type of wording. This might of course be overcome by phrasing the questions in this way. 'Do you never have any headaches?' This wording too, however, gives rise to difficulties because people who perhaps have one headache a year are again in doubt whether to say 'yes', which would be in line with the intention of the question, or 'no' which would be the literal truth. Semantic analysis and grammatical propriety suggest that even without the use of double negatives the questions of the neuroticism scale can be reworded so as to give a different keying, but actual experimentation (mostly not reported) suggests that such rewording gives rise to difficulties of understanding and response, which are at least as grave as those the rewording is intended to remedy. Other remedies such as forced choice responses have also been tried, but success has not been such as to suggest that these alternative methods would be any more valid than those actually used. For the time being at least, therefore, we must accept the limitations set on the validity of our scales by the presence of a certain limited amount of response set. (Our conclusions with respect to response set in the M.P.I. are very much in accord with Rorers (1965) general conclusions of the importance of these factors in relation to questionnaires as a whole; we have not attempted here to duplicate his excellent survey.)

11

THE VALIDITY OF THE M.P.I. POSITIVE VALIDITY

WE must now turn to a consideration of positive validity, i.e. evidence that questionnaire responses of subjects to the M.P.I. do in fact correlate with reasonable criteria of their outside behaviour. One very fundamental method that is obviously relevant in this context is the method of *nominated groups*, i.e. the investigation of agreement between questionnaire response and independent ratings by outside observers. The first study to be described here was carried out by S. B. G. Eysenck (1962).

Members of the Psychology Department in the Institute of Psychiatry were asked to nominate friends or acquaintances, known to them for some while, who seemed to them to be outstandingly extreme on either the *extraversion* or *neuroticism* dimension, or both. In other words, they were asked to pick people, on the basis of their *behaviour*, if this seemed to them to be extremely extraverted, extremely introverted, extremely stable, or extremely neurotic. Some judges chose candidates who seemed to them to be high on both dimensions. To guide the judges, the following definition of extreme extraversion and introversion was shown to them:

'The typical extravert is sociable, likes parties, has many friends, needs to have people to talk to, and does not like reading or studying by himself. He craves excitement, takes chances, often sticks his neck out, acts on the spur of the moment, and is generally an impulsive individual. He is fond of practical jokes, always has a ready answer, and generally likes change; he is carefree, easygoing, optimistic, and likes to "laugh and be merry". He prefers to keep moving and doing things, tends to be aggressive and lose his temper quickly; altogether his feelings are not kept under tight control, and he is not always a reliable person.'

'The typical introvert is a quiet, retiring sort of person, introspective, fond of books rather than people; he is reserved and distant except to intimate friends. He tends to plan ahead, "looks before he leaps", and distrusts the impulse of the moment. He does not like excitement, takes matters of everyday life with proper seriousness, and likes a well-ordered mode of life. He keeps his feelings under close control, seldom behaves in an aggressive manner, and does not lose his temper easily. He is reliable, somewhat pessimistic, and places great value on ethical standards.'

For neuroticism, it was suggested they nominate people who seemed to them to behave as if they had a large number of neurotic symptoms, and those whom they would expect to break down fairly easily given some degree of stress. On the other hand, the stable group required was to contain people who seemed so non-neurotic to the judge concerned that only the very greatest stress would produce neurotic symptoms and behaviour, or a tendency to break down.

The judges were asked to make sure that the subjects were neither psychologists, nor married to psychologists, and that their English was adequate to answer the many questions contained in the inventory. The subjects thus nominated were then asked, by the judges, to fill in a questionnaire of 140 items, as well as the Maudsley Personality Inventory. The questionnaire consisted of 18 lie items adapted from the M.P.I. Lie scale, as well as 122 items that seemed relevant to either extraversion or neuroticism. Only findings relating to the M.P.I. scales of extraversion and neuroticism, and the Lie scale, are discussed here. Completed questionnaires were sent directly to the author by the subjects, and were not seen by the judges; they were anonymous and identified by a code word.

In addition to age and sex 4 scores for each subject were obtained: (a) Extraversion (from the M.P.I.); (b) Neuroticism (from the M.P.I.); (c) Lie score; and (d) Number of Queries ('?' responses) given throughout the questionnaire. Altogether 22 people took part in the study as judges; there were 99 subjects in all, but it will be noted that the total of the number in the sub-groups exceeds this number because 21 subjects were nominated for two dimensions and therefore featured in two groups. The means and standard deviations of each group (those *named* as extraverts (E), introverts (I), stable (S) and neurotic (N) were computed for Extraversion, Neuroticism, Lie Scale and Number of Query scores, respectively, and are given in Table 11.1, together with the sex distribution of the sample. In addition, t tests were computed to test the significance of differences between the groups. These results are given in Table 11.2.

The results show at a very high level of significance that nominated extraverts and introverts differ significantly with respect to extraversion, the difference being one of 18 points. Extraverts are 10 points above the population mean, introverts 8 points below it. The two groups do not differ significantly on neuroticism. Nominated neurotics score higher on neuroticism than do nominated stable people, the difference being almost 15 points. The neurotics are 10 points above the population norms; the stables are 5 points below it. The two groups also differ with respect to extraversion, the difference being just over 8 points and fully significant statistically. The reasons for this have been discussed elsewhere in this book, and it has been shown that they can be derived from the general theory of personality on which the M.P.I. is based. The nominated groups do not differ significantly on the Lie scale, the number of queries, or in age.

TABLE 11.1

n	28 E	38 I	29 S	25 N	Pop. Means
E	35·357	16·921	29·207	20·720	24·91
N	19·893	22·658	15·034	29·680	19·89
L	7·964	9·368	7·103	8·560	
?	11·143	13·474	13·000	14·800	
Age	36·250	34·421	34·759	36·440	
σ^2E	64·164	87·696	88·599	96·293	94·28
σ^2N	108·470	162·447	105·677	131·477	121·44
σ^2L	24·036	35·320	24·667	41·090	
σ^2?	128·571	195·553	190·143	192·833	
σ^2age	103·750	97·602	82·547	92·840	
n(M	13	24	15	10	
F	15	14	14	15	

Means and variances of nominated groups

TABLE 11.2

		E	N	L	'?'	Age
n = 64	^{t}EI	8·395	0·940	1·025	0·724	0·735
n = 54	^{t}SN	3·239	4·950	0·940	0·477	0·659

Significance of observed differences by t test

It will be seen that the differentiation between introverts and extraverts by the judges was more successful than the discrimination between neurotics and normals. This was predicted on the assumption that extraverted behaviour is more easily observable by the outsider, whereas neuroticism is more characterized by subjective internal conditions, such as anxiety and other symptoms, which may not give rise to observable differences in behaviour.

Taking the population mean as cutting point there was a discordance between judges and questionnaire scores in 25 per cent of the cases nominated for stability-neuroticism, and in 21 per cent of the cases nominated for extraversion-introversion. These discrepancies could have arisen either because of errors by the judges, or faked responses by the subjects, or because of shifting criteria of what constitutes the population mean. The experiment was not designed to throw much light on this problem, although many incidental observations suggested certain hypotheses which will be investigated in future studies. It is of interest, though, to consider the relevance of the lie scale to this problem. It had been anticipated that subjects nominated as neurotics but having low neuroticism scores might have high lie scores, on the assumption that the judges were correct and that the subjects were faking their responses. This was not found to be so, the correlation between Lie scale and neuroticism being actually positive for this group (0·168). In contrast this correlation proved to be negative for the nominated stable group (−0·135). While both correlations are small and insignificant they nevertheless suggest that the hypothesis that low scoring neurotic subjects were faking their answers cannot be supported.

An attempt was made at a more detailed comparison by giving the same questionnaire that had been used in the above study to three hundred university and evening class students, 140 male, 160 female (Eysenck and Eysenck, 1963a). Factor analysis was undertaken of 124 items in the scale for this group of 300 subjects. The essential comparison of the study was of the factor loadings of any given item with the degree to which that item differentiated between the E and I or the S and N nominated groups. This differentiating property of the item will be designated the D (difference) score; it is calculated by subtracting the number of endorsements by nominated introverts from that given by nominated extraverts (D_E), and by subtracting the number of endorsements by nominated stable subjects from that given by nominated neurotic subjects (D_N). The main hypothesis under examination predicts that items with high D_E scores will also have high loadings on the E factor while items with D_N will have high loadings on the N factor (both loadings and D scores can be positive or negative, of course, and in the above sentence the word 'high' is understood as meaning 'high positive'; a high negative value would be called 'low'. This convention is followed throughout our description of this experiment).

The 124 items used in the analysis were selected from the total number in the questionnaire on *a priori* grounds. They were divided into two groups, as the electronic computer was unable to accept the total set. In addition to the 62 personality questions there was also included in each matrix of intercorrelations scores for age and sex, the number of '?' responses, and the 'Lie' scale score. Product moment correlations were run between the 68 variables in each case, and a principal components analysis performed; three factors were taken out in each of the two analyses. Rotation was undertaken in accordance with Thurstone's principle of simple structure, and the first two factors were clearly identified as neuroticism and extraversion. (Evidence for this identification will be given below.) The third factor had high and almost identical loadings in the two analyses for 'Age' (0·511 and 0·491) and for the 'Lie' scale score (0·430 and 0·441). The 'Lie' score also had negative loadings on Neuroticism (−0·226 and −0·217). The number of '?' responses had negative loadings on Extraversion (−0·135 and −0·186). Loadings on sex for E and N are quite low, being 0·182 and 0·162 in the first analysis, and −0·229 and 0·145 in the second (maleness being scored 1 point, femaleness 0 point). The third factor with its high loadings on age and lie scores is not of great psychological interest, and will not be discussed further.

Our identification of the E and N factors may be questioned. The first line of evidence, of course, lies in the similarity of the items defining each factor with the trait-names used in describing the types. More objective, perhaps, is the evidence presented in the next section, relating to the responses of the nominated groups. A third line of evidence relates to the similar pattern of factor loadings emerging from the present study as compared with the original factor analysis of the M.P.I. items (Eysenck, 1956). If we look at the N items in this original study, we find that none of them has loadings on the E factor in the present study of more than 0·25; all have loadings on the N factor of between 0·25 and 0·58, with the median in the 0·45–0·49 interval. Looking at the E items of the original study, we find that only 3 have N loadings in excess of 0·25 (none as high as 0·35). E loadings range from one exceptionally low one of 0·13 to 0·62, with the median in the 0·40–0·44 interval. No item is in the wrong quadrant. These results suggest substantial similarity between the two studies, although the samples of subjects were quite different, and although the matrix of items in which the M.P.I. items were embedded in the present study was not used at all in the original work. For the new items, i.e. those not contained in the original M.P.I., a prediction was made in each case as to the expected position of the item in the two-dimensional framework of the N and E factors, nearly all of these predictions were in fact borne out, although not always at acceptable levels of significance. Lengthy discussion of these predictions would not seem necessary as they are all rather obvious, and can mostly be deduced from the general theory of extraversion and neuroticism (Eysenck, 1957).

The results of the validation study are given in the original report which lists the items on which factor loadings were available, D_E and D_N scores, and E and N factor loadings. These detailed results, to which reference will be made in the discussion, can be summarized conveniently in the form of four correlations. D_E correlates 0·883 with the E loadings, and −0·270 with the N loadings; D_N correlates 0·676 with the N loading, and −0·525 with the E loading. (Correlations of 0·17 and 0·23 are significant at the 5 and 1 per cent levels respectively for $N = 124$.) We thus find that in both cases the predicted positive relation between D_E and E loading, and D_N and N loading, is indeed observed, assuming a very high value in the former case. In addition, however, there is also a less welcome correlation of considerable magnitude between D_N and the E loading (and to a much lesser extent between D_E and the N loading). These require some detailed discussion.

It is possible to formulate an hypothesis to account for the apparent tendency for judges to choose their N and S groups in such a way that these two groups are also differentiated in terms of introverted and extraverted questionnaire answers. This hypothesis relates to our demonstration (Eysenck, 1956b), already discussed in some detail, that there are two forms of social shyness, one introverted and the other neurotic. This hypothesis, it will be remembered, suggests that 'the introvert does not *care* to be with other people; the neurotic is *afraid* of being with other people.'

These two types of social shyness are of course easily differentiated by introspection, and consequently accessible to questionnaire probing, but they are confounded when we apply a simple behavioural criterion, as both lead to non-social behaviour, however different the underlying motivation. Thus to the observer social shyness will often appear to be associated with neuroticism, as well as with introversion, and he will be unable in most cases to distinguish 'introverted shyness' from 'neurotic shyness'. Thus our judges, in choosing the N and S groups, might have been expected to have based their choice partly on overt lack of sociability in the candidates they selected as members of the N group. It is likely that in doing this they selected erroneously a number of unsociable introverts. For these individuals the D_N scores should be high on 'introverted social shyness' items; at the same time these items would have high negative loadings on extraversion.

Let us now look at the items in the questionnaire having loadings of −0·35 or more on extraversion, and D_N scores of 10 or higher. There are 8 such items: they deal with keeping in the background on social occasions, being quiet in a social group, being shy with persons of the opposite sex, limiting one's acquaintances to a select few, having difficulties in 'losing oneself' at a lively party, being remote and distant except with intimate friends, being naturally reserved, and tending towards pessimism. With the exception of the last item (which only just qualified for inclusion in this group) all are indeed, as expected 'social shyness' items of the introverted kind, with uniformly low neuroticism loadings (all are below 0·27) and uniformly high D_E scores (ranging from 17 to 28). In the opposite quadrant (high E loading, low D_N scores) there are only 4 items if we use the same criterion as before, to which may perhaps be added another 4 which are only slightly outside the area specified. These 8 items deal with preferring rapid action, being (and being regarded as) lively, being able to have a good time at a party, liking to mix with people socially, being happy-go-lucky, being talkative, and keeping in close touch with things around one. These items are rather more mixed, only 3 obviously belonging to the 'sociable extraversion' kind. On the whole, however, the data seem to bear out the hypothesis quite well.

If this conclusion is acceptable, it follows that the discrepancies between ratings and self-ratings are in effect more likely to argue against the acceptance of the ratings, as these confound two possible causal determinants of observed 'sociable' and 'unsociable' behaviour. Thus the results of this experiment suggest unambiguously that as far as *extraversion* is concerned, self-ratings and behaviour as rated by others agree well; as far as neuroticism is concerned, the picture is rather less clear, but if our argument be accepted, then we may regard the self-ratings as valid, and the ratings as rather less so. This conclusion is in good agreement with the theory put forward by S. B. G. Eysenck (1962) that 'extraverted behaviour is more easily observable by the outsider, whereas neuroticism is more characterized by subjective internal conditions, such as anxiety and other conditions, which may not give rise to observable differences in behaviour'. It may finally be suggested that the method of nominated groups may be of considerable use in analysing problems of validity in this field.

The method of nominated groups was again employed in a rather larger study by Eysenck and Eysenck (1964b) in which the authors raised the question of the intelligence of judges as a possible determiner of the accuracy of their judgements. The test of personality used was the E.P.I. The measure of intelligence used was a well-standardized British test; this was administered in person to candidates who applied to become members of an organization (Mensa) which made the possession of a high I.Q. the prime requisite of membership. Candidates were first required to complete Form A of the test under unsupervised conditions; only those who succeeded were then admitted to the supervised test (Form B). Testing was carried out by the organization, not by the present writer, but appears to have been done conscientiously and well. From the results, two groups were formed which differed in intelligence, as defined by the test chosen. The intelligent group, with I.Q.s above 148 on this test, will be denoted M in this study, and was made up of individuals who passed the test; the less intelligent group, with I.Q.s below 148 on this test, will be denoted P in this study, and was made up of individuals who failed the test. (The S.D. of this test being unusually high, the tested I.Q. of 148 corresponds roughly to one of 130 on the Binet or the Wechsler scale.) Names of members of both groups were kindly furnished us by the secretary of 'Mensa'. These two groups constitute the judges; they were circulated with the E.P.I. and invited to take part in the general scheme of research (which was not at this stage specified). Out of about 1500 M-group members, 751 filled in the original questionnaire; out of 317 P-group members, 229 did. Details regarding the E and N scores of these subjects are given in Table 11.3, together with the scores for the E.P.I. standardization group of 1931 (which, of course, did not contain either M or P members).

TABLE 11.3

	E		N		
	M	σ	M	σ	n
M	20·213	7·541	17·177	8·985	751
P	22·699	7·709	18·432	8·840	229
Control Group	26·264	7·742	19·557	9·038	1931

It will be seen that apart from being more intelligent than the general population, the M group, and to a lesser extent the P group, is slightly less neurotic and much less extraverted. The former may be a reflection of the preponderance of middle-class members in both M and P; the latter is possibly a function of the rather cognitively-oriented type of society to which subjects belonged, or aspired to belong. 92 M and 27 P members were retested about one year later in person when they came to the Institute of Psychiatry in order to carry out some personality tests; the retest reliability for E and N was found to be 0·88 and 0·84 for M members, and 0·94 and 0·92 for P members. The correlation between E and N for the standardization group was —0·04; for the M and P groups it was —0·24 and —0·15.

M and P members were asked to act as 'judges' or selectors, and to choose one extreme extravert and one extreme introvert each from among their acquaintances. They were furnished with descriptions of 'typical' extraverts and introverts, as already presented above.

From nominations made by M and P members, 302 and 92 replies respectively were received from nominated extraverts, and 335 and 88 replies respectively from nominated introverts. The mean E and N scores of these groups are shown in Table 11.4. It will be seen that the nominated extraverts have E scores of 31, while the nominated introverts have E scores of 16, i.e. almost exactly one-half as large. Both differ significantly from the population mean of 26, the introverts more so than the extraverts. On N the nominated extraverts have lower scores than the nominated introverts, but the difference is slight (18 as against 20). This may be compared with the population mean of 20. It is apparent that, as in the previous studies, judges have no difficulty in identifying individuals who are extreme in extraversion or introversion, and it is also apparent that in doing so they do not fall into the error of confounding introversion and neuroticism to any considerable degree. The more intelligent M-group members do not judge extraversion better than the less intelligent P-group members. This argues against I.Q. as an important element in judging personality, although at lower levels it may of course exert a stronger influence.

TABLE 11.4

	E		N			
	M	σ	M	σ		n
M	31·106	6·702	17·215	9·129	Extraverts	302
P	31·773	6·758	18.761	9·054		92
M	16·030	6·968	19·812	9·333	Introverts	335
P	15·924	6·064	19·739	10·284		88

Among the nominees discussed above, many had no partners; i.e. some judges nominated an extravert who forwarded his questionnaire to us, but either failed to nominate an introvert, or nominated one who failed to forward his questionnaire. Similarly, some introverts had no matching extraverts. In all, there were 225 matched pairs nominated by M members, and 75 matched pairs nominated by P members. Table 11.5 gives the correlations between the E and N scores of judges, and the E and N scores of nominees, separated into extraverted and introverted nominees. The argument underlying this calculation was as follows. In the group of extraverted nominees, a high E score constitutes a 'good' choice, while in the group of introverted nominees, a high E score constitutes a 'poor' choice. If extraverted judges are better (or worse) than introverted judges in making good choices, then their E scores should correlate positively (or negatively) with the E scores of their choices. A similar argument applies to the N scores of the nominees, although there of course both a positive or a negative correlation would indicate the judges of the particular type of personality being correlated with N were erroneously choosing too many (or too few) extraverts or introverts because in their minds this dimension was adulterated with N. The figures in Table 11.5 do not suggest any relationship between judges' personality and accuracy of judgement, being uniformly low. (Levels of significance required for the 5 per cent and 1 per cent level of significance for the M and P groups respectively are 0·13 and 0·18 for M, and 0·22 and 0·29 for P.)

TABLE 11.5

	$E_{nom} E_x$	$E_{nom} N_x$	$N_{nom} E_x$	$N_{nom} N_x$		n
E group	0·104	−0·069	0·028	−0·023	Mensa	225
	−0·039	−0·128	−0·048	−0·006	P	75
I group	0·139	0·056	−0·094	0·044	Mensa	225
	0·105	0·090	−0·146	0·221	P	75

It will have been noticed that in the M and P groups, both of which were more introverted than the standardization group, N and E correlated negatively, while in the standardization group the correlation was quite negligible. These figures suggest the possibility that introverted groups in general may be characterized by a negative relationship between E and N, while the opposite may be true of extraverted groups. This hypothesis can, of course, be tested on our nominated E and I groups. The actual correlations for M-nominated introverts and P-nominated introverts were −0·19 and −0·10; those for the nominated extravert groups were −0·06 and +0·01. The evidence is slight but significantly in favour of the existence of a negative relationship between E and N among introverts; this is in good agreement with the finding of a curvilinear regression line reported in connection with the M.P.I. (Eysenck, 1959a).

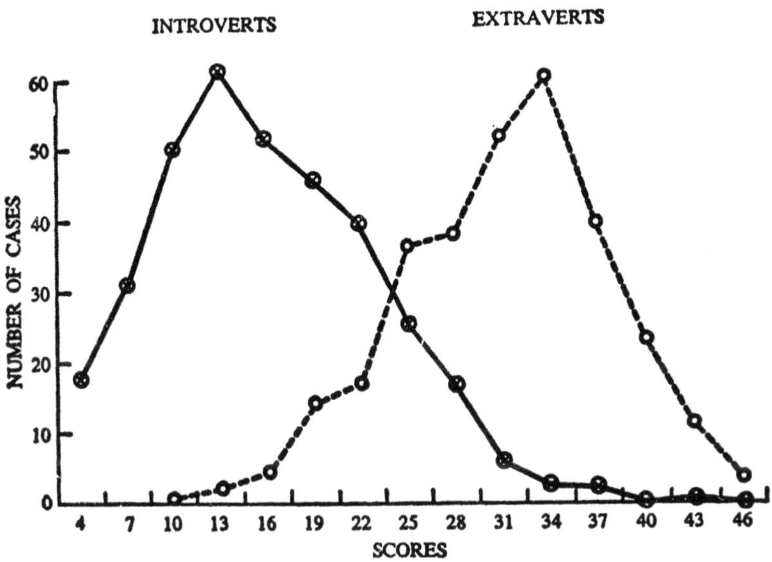

FIG. 11.1 E scores on 225 nominated introverts and 225 nominated extraverts. (From Eysenck and Eysenck, 1964b.)

A diagrammatic representation of the E and N scores of 225 nominated introverts and 225 nominated extraverts may make the comparative study of overlap between them easier. This is shown in Figure 11.1 where the ordinate shows the number of cases and the abscissa the actual E scores achieved by members of these two groups. The lines will be seen to cross at a score of just below 25 which is of course the mean of the whole population. A great majority of nominated extraverts have scores higher than that, a great majority of nominated introverts have scores lower than this. How can we account for the overlap existing between these two groups? There are three possibilities. The first is that judges are less than perfect in nominating extraverts and introverts, and that sometimes they are mistaken. The second possibility is that scores on the questionnaire are less than perfectly valid, and that sometimes genuine introverts obtain extraverted scores and vice versa. There is little doubt that both these sources of errors are in fact active and have contributed to the amount of overlap observed. There is however a third possibility which may be put in this way. Each judge is supposed to nominate two persons one of whom is to be more extraverted than the other, while the other is to be more introverted than the first. Let us suppose that judge 1 chooses the most extraverted and the most introverted of his circle of acquaintances, the average E score of whom is 36. As it happens the most extraverted person of his acquaintance has a score of 46, the most introverted one of 26. Judge 2 also makes a choice in his circle of acquaintances the mean E value of whom is 14. As it happens the most extraverted of his acquaintances has an E value of 24, the most introverted one of 4. In both cases the judge is perfectly correct in ranking the two members concerned, there being a difference of 20 points in the right direction between the extraverted nominee and the introverted nominee. If however we take the four chosen subjects together we find that there is considerable overlap in the distribution, the introverted subject of judge 1 being more extraverted than the extraverted subject of judge 2. Thus we may obtain overlap in spite of perfect validity of judgement and perfect validity of questionnaires simply because the mean E value of the acquaintances of a given person may be quite different to the E value of the acquaintances of another person. No independent study has been made of this possibility but examples not essentially dissimilar to the imaginary one given above have been observed and suggest that not all the overlap is due to errors either in ratings or self ratings.[1]

To these studies of nominated groups we may with advantage add such experiments as have been done by comparing the N scores of nominated neurotics and normals, i.e. comparisons between clinical groups and subjects not under psychiatric treatment. There would be little point in giving an extensive resumé of work done along these lines; we may refer the reader to Figure 7.3 given above and also to the extended discussion in Eysenck (1953). Taking all this work together we arrive at the conclusion that there is considerable evidence of the validity of the E and N scales when our criterion is that of rated everyday behaviour. Admittedly these ratings themselves are undoubtedly far from perfectly valid and must be considered only one criterion of validity among many others, but the considerable degree of congruence between ratings and self ratings seems to eliminate the possibility that either of these two methods of assessment depends entirely on error variance. Our reasoning here is based on the fact that the hypothetical sources of error to which these two methods are subject are quite distinct and do not overlap. The questionnaire relies essentially in its appraisal

[1] Vingoe (1966) has recently replicated some of this work on nominated groups with American subjects; the results agree well with those reported above.

of extraversion, say, on statements by the subject of his liking for parties, his impulsiveness, his desire for action, his carefree mood, etc. Ratings on the other hand rely on observed behaviour, i.e. on whether or not the subject does frequently go to parties, whether he is or is not impulsive in his everyday life, whether he tends to indulge in action rather than in thought, and so forth. It is certainly true that observation may be biased and inaccurate, and that self report may be subject to response set and other sources of error; the fact that both sources of information agree substantially suggests that there is some validity attaching to both.

Our next source of evidence will be dealt with rather more summarily. Here we are relying essentially on a method of validation which may be defined as follows. Extraversion-introversion and neuroticism are two dimensions of personality which are considered to be produced by certain physiological, biochemical and neurological pecularities of the organism. We have already indicated that a chain of arguments and deductions may be constructed by means of which predictions can be made from these hypothetical causes to experimental and everyday behaviour of the individual. Our next source of validation therefore consists essentially of reports of the testing of certain predictions made from these general theories. We have already noted, for instance, that dysthymics tend to be introverted, psychopaths and criminals extraverted. In so far as these behaviour patterns are predicted from our general theory their verification may be used as verification of the measuring instrument, i.e. the M.P.I. or the E.P.I. Similarly it has been predicted that unmarried mothers would be more extraverted than married mothers or unmarried women and S. B. G. Eysenck (1961) has shown that this is indeed so. Again Eysenck (1965c) has argued that there should be a relationship between cigarette smoking and extraversion and the results have certainly borne out the existence of such a relationship.

Many other predictions could of course be made along similar lines and can be tested empirically. Thus we would expect extraverted people to be more changeable, to have an employment history showing a large number of jobs held usually for relatively short periods; we would expect them to move about more, giving up their houses or flats frequently and exchanging them for others. We would expect extraverts to be more inconstant in their personal relationships, having for instance a greater number of divorces than introverts. We would expect introverts to show more 'brand' loyalty, i.e. to change less frequently the type of toothpaste, petrol, cigarette or motor car used by them. There is at least anecdotal evidence for most of these deductions and one properly designed but unpublished study demonstrating that in fact introverts show greater brand loyalty than extraverts. We also expect sexual perversions to be more frequently practised by extraverts, and the fact that clinically sexual perversions seem to be tied in with psychopathy suggests that this prediction too would probably be verified if a proper study were undertaken to test it. Our theory thus provides a large nomological network which makes possible the verification or falsification of the theory, and no doubt in the next few years many more studies will be carried out in this field. At the moment all that can be said is that in so far as predictions have in fact been made and studied the outcome has been a positive one.

A recent unpublished study by P. J. Taylor is of some interest in this connection. Using 149 men who had had at least 5 years of continuous service with a petrol refining company, he calculated for each person (a) total number of sickness absences, (b) total number of reported occupational injuries, (c) total number of treatment room attendances, and for a three year period only (d) total number of latenesses and (e) total number of absences other than sickness, holiday, education and union meeting. E, N and L scores on the M.P.I. were obtained, and the following correlations calculated:

TABLE 11.6

	a	b	c	d	e
E	0·22	0·23	0·26	0·15	0·23
N	0·17	−0·06	0·11	0·17	0·07
L	−0·15	−0·14	−0·16	−0·19	0·00

Single underlinings indicate significance at the 5 per cent level, double underlinings significance at the 1 per cent level. It will be seen that E plays a prominent part in these various activities, very much as predicted, with a general tendency for N to come into the picture at a rather less conclusive level.

Similar results were obtained by Dr. R. Cooper, from the University of Liverpool, who studied 55 female operators in the tobacco industry, engaged in extremely simple and routine tasks. Using the E.P.I. he found the following correlations:

TABLE 11.7

	E	N
Total days sick	0·39	0·08
Frequency of lateness	0·41	−0·11
Job adjustment	−0·35	−0·19
Permitted absence frequency	0·36	0·16

Both studies agree on the importance of E in determining undesirable behaviour in industrial situations, such as lateness, absences, frequency of sickness, poor job adjustment, and so forth. N clearly plays a much less important role.

More important from the scientific point of view, and also the most convincing proof, however, is the series of studies carried out to test experimental laboratory predictions made from the general theory of extraversion/introversion and neuroticism. We have already mentioned some of these studies such as, for instance, the predicted relationship between conditioning and introversion (Eysenck, 1965b). It would be impractical to discuss a great variety of studies carried out in this connection and we have instead listed some thirty or so with references in Table 11.8 below which will give the reader an idea of the variegated nature of the deductions which have been made and will lead him into this particular section of the literature. (The table is modified from one given by Eysenck and Rachman, 1965.)

TABLE 11.8

Experimental studies of introversion-extraversion

	Variables	Introversion	Extraversion	Reference
(1)	Intellectual function	Low I.Q.—vocabulary ratio	High I.Q.—vocabulary ratio	Himmelweit (1945) Foulds (1956)
(2)	Perceptual rigidity	High	Low	Canestrari (1957)
(3)	Speed-accuracy ratio	Low	High	Himmelweit (1946)
(4)	Level of aspiration	High	Low	Himmelweit (1947) Miller (1951)
(5)	Intra-personal variability	Low	High	Eysenck (1947)
(6)	Sociability	Low	High	Eysenck (1957)
(7)	Repression	Weak	Strong	Eriksen (1954)
(8)	Social attitudes	Tender-minded	Tough-minded	Eysenck (1954)
(9)	Rorschach test	High M	High D	Eysenck (1956a)
(10)	Conditioning	Strong	Weak	Eysenck (1965b)
(11)	Reminiscence	Low	High	Eysenck (1962b)
(12)	Figural after-effects	Small	Large	Eysenck (1955)
(13)	Stress reactions	Overactive	Inert	Davis (1948) Venables (1955)
(14)	Sedation threshold	High	Low	Shagass (1957)
(15)	Perceptual constancy	Low	High	Ardis and Fraser (1957)
(16)	Time judgement	Longer	Shorter	Claridge (1960) Eysenck (1959b)

TABLE 11.8 (*contd.*)

	Variables	Introversion	Extraversion	Reference
(17)	Verbal conditioning	Good	Poor	Eysenck (1959c)
(18)	Visual imagery	Vivid	Weak	Costello (1957)
(19)	Perception of vertical	Accurate	Inaccurate	Taft and Coventry (1958)
(20)	Spiral after-effect	Long	Short	Claridge (1960)
(21)	Time error	Small	Great	Claridge (1960)
(22)	Vigilance	High	Low	Claridge (1960) Bakan (1960)
(23)	Problem solving performance decrement	Little	Much	Eysenck (1959d)
(24)	Sensory thresholds	Low	High	Eysenck (1967)
(25)	Pain tolerance	Low	High	Eysenck (1967)
(26)	Sensory deprivation tolerance	High	Low	Eysenck (1967)
(27)	Alternation behaviour	Little	Much	Eysenck (1967)
(28)	Glandular reactivity	High	Low	Eysenck (1967)
(29)	E.E.G. arousal	High	Low	Eysenck (1967)
(30)	Adaptation	Slow	Quick	Eysenck (1967)

A perusal of the experiments listed in this Table as well as the many others which could have been listed, in addition to the physiological studies of Savage on EEG, Shagass on sedation threshold, and others quoted in a preceding section suggest that along many of these lines of research verification of the predictions made on the basis of our theory has not been entirely lacking, and in so far as positive results have been achieved we may regard this as validating the M.P.I. and the E.P.I.

In our discussion of validity we have not dealt with factorial validity or concurrent validity. Our reason for omitting factorial validity is simply that the whole of this book is essentially devoted to an examination of this concept, and that therefore a discussion of it here would be out of place. Concurrent validity would imply that our scales would correlate with other scales constructed to measure extraversion/introversion and neuroticism/stability. Except incidentally we have not paid much attention to this problem, partly because it has been dealt with already in the American manual of the M.P.I. with positive results, and partly because Part II of this book is devoted to an examination in very great detail of the concurrent validity of the Eysenck, Cattell and

Guilford Personality Questionnaires.[1] While on the whole concurrent validity of the M.P.I. is quite satisfactory, it should be noted that this particular method of demonstrating validity is of very uncertain value. Suppose that all the other measures of validity we have adduced were positive, but that concurrent validity were lacking; what would our conclusion be? Surely it would be that the M.P.I. and the E.P.I. are in fact adequate measures of the concept of extraversion and neuroticism as here defined, and that the other measures which did not correlate with these questionnaires were in fact poor measures. The fact that correlations are on the whole quite substantial suggests merely that all these different devices tend to measure much the same extraversion and much the same neuroticism; this agreement is a measure of reliability rather than of validity and adds very little to what we have found out already.

Consider just one example of research on concurrent validity. Knapp (1965) has published a comparison of E.P.I. scores and scores on the Personal Orientation Inventory (Shostrom, 1963, 1964), a measure which attempts to quantify Maslow's concept of self-actualization (1954). It consists of 150 paired-opposite statements of values and yields measures for 14 scales representing value areas which are held to be of major significance in the development toward self-actualization. Basing himself on the theoretical statements of the authors of these two questionnaires, Knapp argued that 'it would be expected that mean scores on the measure of self-actualization should be lower for a highly neurotic group than for a group comparatively low on neuroticism.' Subjects were 136 university students. Ninety-four of these received both forms of the E.P.I., the remainder only form A. Correlations of the P.O.I. scales with the N and E scales of the E.P.I. are shown in Table 11.9. Also shown are the results of another analysis, in which a sample of 'high' neurotic and a sample of 'low' neurotic subjects were chosen on the basis of their scores on the N dimension of the E.P.I. Mean scores on the P.O.I. for these two groups are presented in the Table, as well as results of statistical tests of significance; it will be seen that on every scale of the P.O.I. the high N group is significantly lower than the low N group, thus supporting the hypothesis. 'Self-actualization is seen to be positively and significantly related to the lack of neurotic symptoms and tendencies.'

This study is of interest in several ways. It serves to bring together two notions semantically and conceptually quite different, i.e. neuroticism and failure of self-actualization. It shows that response set cannot have had much influence on the results of the E.P.I., as the two inventories make use of quite different methods of scoring. Several other interesting

[1] A large number of concurrent validity studies have been carried out by Bendig (1957, 1959, 1960, 1963; Bendig and Hoffman, 1957); others will be found in Eysenck (1960c).

TABLE 11.9

Correlations between the Personal Orientation Inventory (POI) and the E.P.I. Tests of significance are given for differences between a 'high' neurotic group and a 'low' neurotic group on POI scales. Taken with permission from Knapp (1965)

POI	Correlations with EPI N = 94		Total group (N = 136)		High N group (N = 38)		Low N group (N = 35)		
scale and symbol	Neuroticism	Extraversion	M	SD	M	SD	M	SD	CR
Time competence (Tc)	−0·57**	0·11	16·30	2·80	14·45	2·81	18·20	2·24	6·33**
Inn directed (I)	−0·35**	0·33**	79·20	9·67	74·00	9·33	84·14	8·29	4·07**
Self-actualizing value (SAV)	−0·27**	0·18	18·25	2·75	17·08	2·64	19·03	2·77	3·07**
Existentiality (Ex)	−0·11	0·30**	19·48	3·67	18·97	3·66	21·06	3·08	2·66**
Feeling reactivity (Fr)	−0·08	0·30**	14·74	2·81	14·16	2·90	15·34	2·71	1·81*
Spontaneity (S)	−0·34**	0·39**	10·35	2·61	9·24	2·25	11·69	2·30	4·59**
Self-regard (Sr)	−0·52**	0·36**	10·98	2·64	9·32	2·34	12·83	1·61	7·51**
Self-acceptance (Sa)	−0·17	0·10	15·50	3·18	14·66	3·84	16·54	2·91	7·49**
Nature of man (Nc)	−0·21*	−0·05	11·56	1·99	10·95	1·91	12·46	1·65	3·62**
Synergy (Sy)	−0·25*	0·06	6·44	1·37	6·11	1·29	6·77	1·07	2·38**
Acceptance of aggression (A)	−0·09	0·37**	15·65	3·21	14·89	3·11	16·17	3·32	1·69*
Capacity for intimate contact (C)	−0·24*	0·26**	16·61	3·38	15·92	3·53	17·97	3·23	2·59**

* $p < 0.05$ ** $p < 0.01$

findings are discussed in the original paper, and it would take us too far to take these up in detail. But withal the writer would feel that what has been demonstrated has been the *reliability* of inventory measurement of emotionality, rather than the *validity* of either instrument. This may be a purely semantic question, but let us assume that the correlations had been zero throughout: would this have disproved the validity of either instrument? It would have shown Knapp's hypothesis to be wrong, and it would have demonstrated the existence of two orthogonal traits, neuroticism and self-actualization, but it would have left intact the possibility that each inventory measured what it was supposed to measure.

It might be objected that this is not a proper example of concurrent validity as the two measures are not measuring identical traits. This, however, is merely a question of semantics; the naming of concepts and factors is of course quite arbitrary. Consider another example. Cattell has published a Neuroticism Scale Questionnaire (NSQ), which consists of forty items arranged on four scales (I, tenderminded-toughminded; F, depression-cheerfulness, E, submissiveness-dominance, and a unipolar measure of anxiety). Kear-Colwell (1965) has provided us with correlations of these measures and the E and N scales of the M.P.I. on 106 cases. The NSQ correlated 0·60 with N and −0·50 with E; thus one measure of neuroticism (NSQ) correlated almost as highly with a measure of extraversion as with another measure of neuroticism! This would suggest a failure of concurrent validity. In reality all that is demonstrated is the well-known fact that what Eysenck calls neuroticism, Cattell calls anxiety, and what Cattell calls neuroticism is a mixture of Eysenck's N and introversion (Adcock, 1965). This is well illustrated when we consider the individual correlations of the four scales, particularly F and anxiety. The former correlates 0·24 with N, but −0·54 with E; it is therefore a fairly pure measure of the latter trait. Anxiety correlates 0·74 with N (a value almost identical with that reported in another similar study by Robinson *et al.*, 1965), but only −0·44 with E. (The sample consisted mainly of neurotic patients, and thus a sizeable negative correlation between N and E is expected, as pointed out previously.) The relationships observed make perfectly good sense, and do not in any sense suggest absence of concurrent validity; they merely highlight the semantic vagaries of writers of inventories!

The unsatisfactory nature of Cattell's system of nomenclature becomes apparent when we include the Taylor MAS in our consideration. Anxiety as defined by this scale is a mixture of N and introversion, i.e. it corresponds to Cattell's neuroticism. Thus Anxiety is not a unifactorial concept, as is made clear by Fenz and Epstein's analysis of the MAS (1965). The matter is discussed in some detail in Eysenck (1960f).

This concludes the first part of this book. It will be seen that we are still left with a number of problems which are important and which require a solution. We have three main sets of data, i.e. those produced by Guilford, by Cattell and by Eysenck; each of these workers has largely carried out his research in isolation from the others and there is no direct comparison available between their different factors. The question thus arises for instance why the primary factors, i.e. the traits, which emerge from the work of these three writers, are not more alike than in fact they are. The reader who will compare these sets of 15 or so main traits isolated by Guilford, Eysenck and Cattell will certainly find some similarities but these are far less marked than the differences. This is curious as all workers started off with very similar sets of items and it clearly becomes an interesting and important problem to see to what extent similarities are in fact noticeable across these three sets of inventories.

Another problem which arises is that of the relationship between the higher order or type factors which may emerge from the intercorrelations between the traits emerging from studies of the three authors noted. There is evidence that in each case we obtain a neuroticism and an extraversion factor, and there is some evidence in the literature to suggest that these correlate reasonably highly together. However, there is no study comparing all three systems in one single comparison and equally there is no one study which carries its analysis through from the original items, i.e. which relies from the beginning on correlations between single items rather than groups of items.

The third problem that arises is related to sex. Most factorial studies in the literature have not taken seriously the possibility that intercorrelations between items may be quite different for male and female samples and that different factors may result from such analyses. What is usually done is to carry out analyses on either male, female or mixed samples indiscriminantly and to carry out comparisons between the two sexes, if at all, then only by comparing their scores on the final questionnaires, factors, etc. This is clearly inadmissible and evidence is required to show whether in fact men and women show the same structure of personality or whether they do not.

Another important question relates to the presence and growth of the factors of extraversion and neuroticism in children. At what stage can personality questionnaires be meaningfully given to children? At what stage will we find the emergence of a factor of neuroticism or one of extraversion? Are these two factors independent in children as they are in adults or does the degree of correlation vary with age? Are there any differences between the sexes with respect to factor structure and are they differentiated with respect to scores on extraversion or neuroticism? Do these scores in turn change with age? There has been very little work reported in the literature on these questions apart from some studies carried out by Cattell, and it will hardly be denied that they raise important problems both from the theoretical and the practical points of view.

Another problem similar to the one presented by children is that presented by patients subnormal in intellect. Are they capable of answering questionnaires properly and will they show similar type factors as do normal people? Are their responses sufficiently reliable to make testing worthwhile? Here again is a whole area of research which has been comparatively neglected hitherto. These and other theoretical and practical questions will form the subject matter of the rest of this book which is concerned almost entirely with the report of empirical investigations carried out during the last few years.

PART TWO
Trait and Type Factors

12

THE DUAL NATURE OF EXTRAVERSION

S. B. G. Eysenck and H. J. Eysenck[1]

THE publication of the M.P.I. and various factorial studies connected with it aroused a certain amount of interest, and a number of critical discussions appeared, which raised fundamental problems obviously requiring an answer. Two of the main problems to appear were raised expressly by Carrigan (1960) in her excellent review of 'Extraversion/Introversion as a Dimension of Personality'. The first problem to be raised by Carrigan was the relation between extraversion and adjustment; her final comment was that 'A clear-cut answer cannot be given' (p. 351). It will be remembered that studies with the M.P.I. have usually shown a correlation of between 0·15 and 0·20 between neuroticism and introversion, with rather higher values for maladjusted samples; this might be interpreted as showing a lack of orthogonality between the two factors. An alternative explanation of course would be that this correlation is an artefact produced by a faulty selection of items. It is clearly impossible to find items having loadings only on one or the other of the two type factors with which we are concerned; in the ordinary way each item will have at least some slight loading on the factor which it is not supposed to be measuring. If now in the selection of items there is a lack of balance in the positive and negative loadings on the factor which is not supposed to be measured by a given item, then an artificial positive or negative correlation between extraversion and neuroticism can easily appear. The possibility exists that in the M.P.I. there are too many items from the dysthymic quadrant, i.e. having

[1] The results reported in this chapter, and their discussion, are reproduced, with permission, from Eysenck and Eysenck, 1963.

loadings both on neuroticism and introversion, and that it is due to the presence of these items that the two factors appear as correlated. This possibility, and the questions raised by the existence of the positive correlation between introversion and neuroticism in the M.P.I., were one of the reasons for carrying out the research underlying the production of the Eysenck Personality Inventory (E.P.I.) which is essentially an improved version of the M.P.I. (Eysenck and Eysenck, 1964).

Another problem raised by Carrigan relates to the *unidimensionality* of extraversion. Her conclusion here is that: 'The unidimensionality of extraversion/introversion has not been conclusively demonstrated' (p. 355); she further points out that several joint analyses of the Guilford and Cattell questionnaires show 'that at least *two* independent factors are required to account for the intercorrelations between the E-I variables'. The nature of these two factors is suggested by a quotation from Mann (1958), where in his discussion of his own results he suggests the possibility that 'Factor 3 corresponds to the American conception of extraversion with its emphasis on sociability and ease in interpersonal relations, while Factor 4 corresponds to the European conception of extraversion with its emphasis on impulsiveness and weak superego controls' (p. 108). This distinction already appeared in the Guilfords' (1934) paper on 'Factors in a typical test of Introversion/Extraversion', where they tried to account for the failure of American researchers to validate McDougall's predictions by arguing that while American workers have been largely concerned with the 'social factor' which appears in their analysis as Factor *a*, McDougall has been largely concerned with 'impulsiveness', or Factor *c* in their analysis. Carrigan concludes that 'a good case can be made for identifying Social Extraversion as a factor of "well adjusted" extraversion'. Lack of self control on the other hand may reflect 'maladjusted extraversion'. While this possibility exists of course it must remain somewhat doubtful whether sociability and impulsiveness would really turn out to be quite unrelated; in Eysenck's theoretical scheme sociability and impulsiveness would be two of the many traits which through their correlation define the factor of extraversion. It is clearly a purely empirical problem whether in fact sociability and impulsiveness items are or are not correlated and a special experiment was carried out to throw light on this problem (Eysenck and Eysenck, 1963d). (A replication of this study has been reported by Sparrow and Ross, 1964.) A special questionnaire was constructed containing 66 extraversion/introversion and neuroticism items; the items used are given in Table 12.1. Also included was a score from a Lie scale containing 18 items; sex, age (dichotomized), and the number of '?' responses. All seventy items were intercorrelated by means of product moment correlations, and four factors extracted using the method of principal components. These were then rotated (retaining orthogonality) into a close approximation to Thurstone's simple structure solution, graphical methods being used. Three hundred subjects in all were used of whom 133 were male and 167 female; the mean age of the sample was 27·73.

TABLE 12.1

	E	N	S v. Imp	IV
1. Do you sometimes say the first thing that comes into your head?	0·211	0·279	0·173	−0·233
2. Can you usually solve a problem better by studying it alone than by discussing it with others?	−0·153	−0·050	−0·011	−0·079
3. In a group, do you hate having to introduce people to each other?	−0·288	−0·113	−0·300	0·101
4. Do you very much enjoy good food?	0·207	−0·048	−0·095	−0·008
5. Are you a person who is not much given to cracking jokes and telling funny stories to your friends?	−0·356	−0·016	−0·328	−0·112
6. Do you often crave excitement?	0·369	0·323	−0·103	0·342
7. Do you drink alcohol only in moderation usually?	0·018	−0·253	−0·068	−0·097
8. Do you enjoy practical jokes?	0·349	−0·069	0·035	0·617
9. Would you rate yourself as an impulsive individual?	0·406	0·422	−0·200	−0·305
10. When you are drawn into a quarrel do you prefer to 'have it out' to being silent hoping things will blow over?	0·196	−0·016	0·124	0·011
11. Do you mind selling things, or soliciting funds for a cause in which you are interested?	−0·233	0·057	−0·228	−0·047
12. Do you like to be in a situation with plenty of excitement and bustle?	0·516	0·070	0·085	0·145
13. If you want to learn about something would you rather do it by reading a book on the subject than by discussion?	−0·304	0·022	−0·210	−0·228
14. Do you often act on the spur of the moment without stopping to think?	0·400	0·372	−0·349	−0·232
15. Are you reserved and distant except to intimate friends?	−0·477	−0·117	−0·379	0·211

TABLE 12.1 (*contd.*)

	E	N	S v. Imp	IV
16. When the odds are against your succeeding in some enterprise, do you think it worth while to take a chance?	0·230	−0·006	−0·156	0·111
17. Can you readily get some life into a rather dull party?	0·591	0·113	0·184	−0·079
18. Are you ordinarily a carefree individual?	0·603	−0·218	−0·194	0·156
19. Do you enjoy working alone?	−0·295	−0·014	0·014	−0·259
20. Do you enjoy opportunities for conversation so that you rarely miss a chance of talking to a stranger?	0·403	0·138	0·196	−0·070
21. Do you have difficulty in falling asleep easily at bedtime?	−0·159	0·380	0·081	0·054
22. Are you inclined to stop and think things over before acting?	−0·372	−0·311	0·396	0·221
23. Lie scale.	0·177	0·277	−0·102	−0·029
24. ? responses on questionnaire.	0·085	−0·031	−0·160	0·130
25. Age.	0·069	0·222	0·092	0·347
26. Sex.	−0·007	−0·163	−0·001	0·303
27. Do you tend to be slow and deliberate in your movements?	−0·400	0·051	0·112	0·359
28. Do you often need cheerful, sympathetic company to 'cheer you up'?	−0·057	0·644	0·042	0·115
29. Do you feel it essential to plan ahead carefully before beginning any undertaking?	−0·276	−0·132	0·258	−0·072
30. On the whole, do you prefer the company of books to people?	−0·420	0·030	−0·153	−0·186
31. If you are annoyed by something, do you find it absolutely necessary to 'let off steam'?	0·201	0·290	0·027	−0·181
32. Is your motto to take matters of everyday life with proper seriousness rather than to 'laugh and be merry'?	−0·475	0·068	0·274	−0·162
33. Do you tend towards an over-cautious pessimism?	−0·454	0·281	0·227	−0·162
34. Do you often have a restless feeling that you want something but do not know what?	0·100	0·537	−0·066	0·111
35. Would you describe yourself as an easy-going person not concerned to be precise?	0·373	0·005	−0·335	0·042

	E	N	S v. Imp	IV
36. Do you tend towards a rather reckless optimism?	0·468	0·115	−0·313	0·088
37. Would you do almost anything for a dare?	0·313	−0·138	−0·236	0·234
38. When people shout at you, do you shout back?	0·254	0·189	−0·239	0·065
39. Other things being equal, would you prefer the job of a farmer to that of a life insurance salesman?	−0·200	−0·027	−0·022	0·045
40. Are you given to acting on impulses of the moment which later land you in difficulties?	0·392	0·419	−0·372	−0·102
41. Would you rather spend an evening by yourself than go to a dull party?	−0·368	−0·122	−0·130	−0·261
42. Does your natural reserve generally stand in your way when you want to start a conversation with an attractive stranger of the opposite sex?	−0·450	−0·008	−0·235	0·196
43. Are you happiest, when you get involved in some project that calls for rapid action?	0·500	−0·102	−0·181	−0·049
44. Do you sometimes feel happy, sometimes depressed, without any apparent reason?	0·075	0·541	−0·139	−0·029
45. Do you usually take the initiative in making new friends?	0·531	0·049	0·320	−0·048
46. Would you rate yourself as a lively individual?	0·627	−0·062	0·129	−0·088
47. Would you be very unhappy if you were prevented from making numerous social contacts?	0·490	0·180	0·223	0·053
48. Are you inclined to be moody?	−0·197	0·668	0·022	0·149
49. Do you have frequent ups and downs in moods, either with or without apparent cause?	−0·055	0·717	0·086	0·048
50. Do you prefer action to planning for action?	0·393	−0·060	−0·327	0·036
51. Are you inclined to keep in the background on social occasions?	−0·653	0·000	−0·382	0·167
52. Is it difficult to 'lose yourself' even at a lively party?	−0·548	0·045	−0·124	0·114
53. Do you ever feel 'just miserable' for no good reason at all?	−0·087	0·653	−0·045	−0·187

TABLE 12.1 (*contd.*)

	E	N	S v. Imp	IV
54. Do you often find that you have made up your mind too late?	−0·048	0·326	−0·081	0·267
55. Do you like to mix socially with people?	0·557	−0·080	0·298	−0·014
56. Have you often lost sleep over your worries?	−0·210	0·482	0·029	−0·010
57. Are you inclined to limit your acquaintances to a select few?	−0·442	0·022	−0·353	−0·029
58. Are you often troubled about feelings of guilt?	−0·161	0·452	−0·032	0·060
59. Are your feelings rather easily hurt?	−0·106	0·378	−0·109	−0·176
60. Do you like to have many social engagements?	0·623	0·116	0·210	0·021
61. Are you inclined to be shy in the presence of the opposite sex?	−0·499	−0·023	−0·249	0·259
62. Do you nearly always have a 'ready answer' for remarks directed at you?	0·448	−0·070	0·074	−0·175
63. Would you rate yourself as a happy-go-lucky individual?	0·638	−0·066	−0·292	0·158
64. Have you often felt listless and tired for no good reason?	−0·087	0·532	−0·136	0·036
65. Are you inclined to keep quiet when out in a social group?	−0·609	−0·014	−0·380	0·129
66. Can you usually let yourself go and have a hilariously good time at a gay party?	0·633	0·029	0·200	0·016
67. Do you like work that requires considerable attention?	−0·128	−0·173	0·058	−0·051
68. Do other people regard you as a lively individual?	0·634	−0·042	0·141	−0·161
69. Do you often feel disgruntled?	−0·093	0·632	0·042	0·177
70. Do you like to play pranks upon others?	0·359	−0·023	−0·044	0·618

Factor loadings on the first 4 factors are given in Table 12.1; the fourth factor has high loadings on only two items and is clearly a doublet as both of these are concerned with playing practical jokes on other people. Factor 1 is an E factor, Factor 2 an N factor; identification in terms of item content is clear and in line with previous analyses and identifications. It is the third factor on which interest hinges, and for the purpose of discussion this factor has been plotted against Factor 1 in Figure 12.1. For the sake of clarity items scored in the introverted direction have been reversed; these items have an R after their number. Paying attention only to items having saturations of 0·25 or more on E we can see that these split up very evenly into two groups which have been indicated in the diagram by enclosed lines. One group contains exclusively items having reference to sociability (S), the other a little less

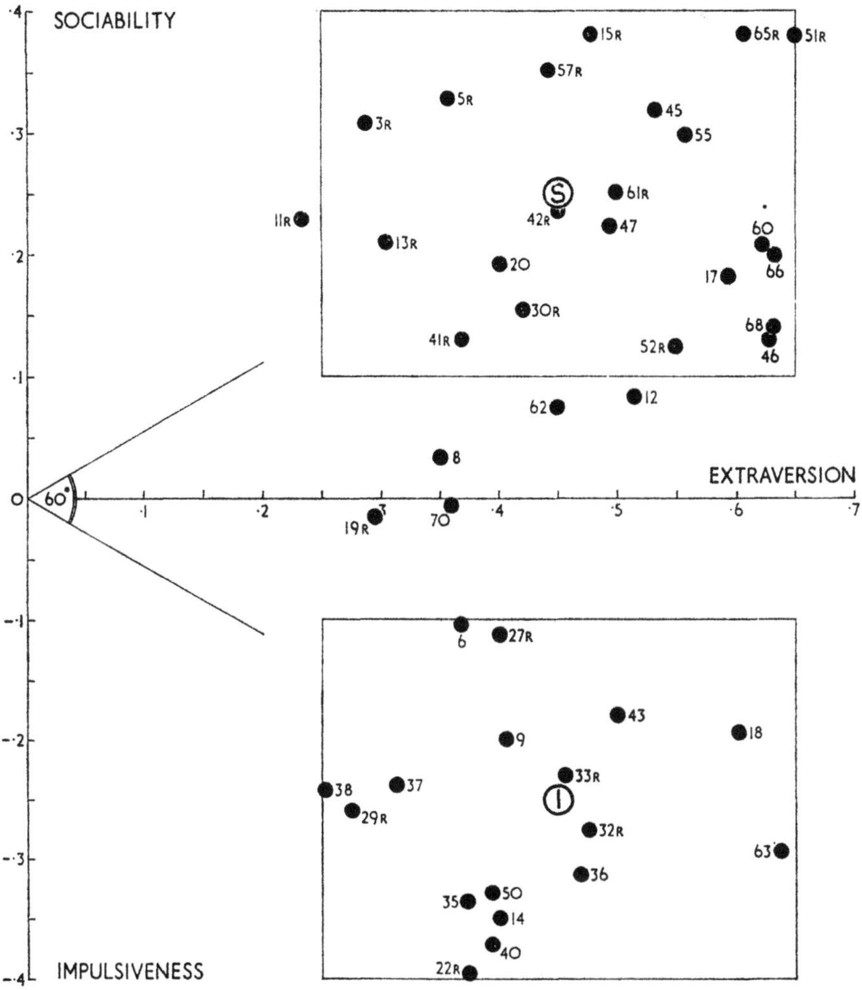

FIG. 12.1 Items defining Sociability and Impulsiveness components of Extraversion.

exclusively, items having reference to impulsiveness (Imp.). Items typically defining the former are; keeps in background on social occasions (R), quiet in social group (R), reserved and distant (R), limits acquaintances to a select few (R), likes to mix socially with people, etc. Typical items defining the latter factor are: thinks things over before acting (R), acts on impulse, acts on spur of moment, easygoing person, prefers action to planning for action, tends towards reckless optimism, would do almost anything for a dare, happy-go-lucky, plans ahead (R), etc. The S group is perhaps more homogeneous than the Imp. group of items and it is possible that a more appropriate name for the latter group might be found; for the purpose of this book the term 'impulsiveness' will be used without prejudice to alternative interpretations. The two aspects of this bipolar factor are seen to correspond well to the two types of extraversion postulated by the Guilfords (1934) and Mann (1958).

As an independent check on two of the points raised the questionnaire was administered to another similar sample of 300 subjects and scores obtained for neuroticism, using the standard procedure of the M.P.I. for this purpose. (All the M.P.I. questions have been included in the present questionnaire.) Also scored were sociability and impulsiveness, using in each case the most highly loaded 14 questions on that factor (i.e. those with the highest positive and negative loadings; these two groups are by accident well matched for saturation on the E factor). The correlation between S and Imp. was 0·468 ($P<0{\cdot}01$); N correlated $-0{\cdot}133$ with S and 0·166 with Imp. (both significant at the 0·05 level), suggesting that these factors too were reasonably but not quite independent of abnormality, as indeed has been suggested by their loadings on N in the original factor analysis. N and E (i.e. S+Imp.) correlated $-0{\cdot}011$; in other words, the two factor scores are quite independent. We thus find that S correlates negatively with abnormality and Imp. positively, thus leaving a zero correlation between N and E, where $E = S+Imp.$ In geometric terms, imagine N to protrude from the plane of the paper in Figure 12.1 at right angles; the plane of the paper could be tilted so as to raise Imp. and lower S in the third dimension without affecting the orthogonality between N and E.

This study suggests that there is some truth in the suggestion that *sociability* is an aspect of extraversion which shows some correlation with good adjustment, whereas *impulsiveness* is an aspect of extraversion which shows some correlation with poor adjustment; it is also clear however that these two aspects of extraversion are by no means independent but show a reasonably close relationship as indicated by the correlation between S and Imp. of approximately 0·5. It also appears from this study that neuroticism and extraversion are independent. The data may be useful in exemplifying our discussion of the possible artefacts which may arise in relating extraversion and neuroticism. Suppose that a questionnaire is constructed of extraversion which contains more sociability than impulsiveness questions; such a questionnaire would produce a *negative* correlation between extraversion and neuroticism. If a different questionnaire were constructed in which the number of impulsiveness items exceeded the number of sociability items a *positive* correlation would be expected between extraversion and neuroticism. Clearly there is something extremely arbitrary about the use of a correlation between completed questionnaire scales as an arbiter of the independence or otherwise of these personality variables, and within limits it is clearly possible to produce almost any desired result by suitable selection of items. A different procedure is needed and accordingly other experiments were undertaken which are recorded in the next sections.

Before doing so, however, we must note the apparently inconsistent findings reported by Barratt (1965), who claims that 'the Barratt Impulsiveness Scale (BIS) has never significantly correlated . . . with any anxiety or emotional stability scale. Also, in five separate factor analyses using different Ss the relative relationship of the impulsiveness and anxiety measures has been orthogonal and invariant even though different marker variables were used in the different factor analyses'. Thus, where we find some evidence for impulsiveness to be slightly positively correlated with neuroticism, Barratt claims complete independence. A look at his factor analytic results, however, does not support his claims. In the first place, his BIS is not a univariate measure of impulsiveness, but is made up of five factors, which he designates as lack of persistence, social optimism, lack of motor inhibition, aggression-autonomy, and action oriented; clearly the naming of the scale is inappropriate, and the questions contained in it appear to measure a variety of extraverted traits of which impulsiveness is only one. It is interesting to note that these five traits all load on a general factor of extraversion in his analysis, a factor on which the highest loading is carried by Guilford's R scale, i.e. the very scale which formed the starting point for the development of the M.P.I. extraversion scale. The loading of R on this factor is 0·86, while the five Barratt scales have loadings ranging from 0·34 to 0·74. The appropriate Cattell and Thurstone scales also have appropriate loadings on this factor. The BIS, it may be concluded, is not a true measure of impulsiveness, but rather a general E scale misnamed; it may, however, be admitted that the scale is deficient in sociability items, so that some degree of correlation with N might be expected.

Contrary to Barratt's claim, such a relationship is in fact found in his own data. His second factor, which may be identified as N (or anxiety, as he prefers to call it), has high loadings on the appropriate Cattell, Thurstone, Guilford and Taylor scales; it also is found, however, to load several of the Barratt scales, notably lack of motor inhibition (0·51) and aggressiveness-autonomy (0·32). Lack of persistence also has a small loading (0·22). Barratt's results, therefore, fit in perfectly with our own, provided we are willing to regard his BIS as a measure of the E factor with sociability items removed. As such, his studies give valuable support to our own experiments.

13

THE UNITARY NATURE OF EXTRAVERSION

H. J. Eysenck and S. B. G. Eysenck[1]

WE have seen in the preceding section that impulsiveness and sociability are correlated, and that the notion of a second-order factor of extraversion is in fact built upon correlations of first-order factors of this kind. However, it is often suggested that higher-order factors are little better than statistical artefacts, and that more 'reality' (whatever that may mean) adheres to first-order factors. We shall take up this argument again later on; here we shall merely report an experiment to illustrate our view that such an opinion is exactly the opposite of the truth.

Consider the conception of a factor as in some sense an underlying cause of the observed correlations (Eysenck, 1953). The correlation of any given test with that factor would then be an index of the degree to which that test measured that factor, i.e. its validity. If a criterion test could be found which correlated sufficiently highly with a given factor, i.e. which had sufficiently high validity as a measure of that factor, then it would be possible to use this test in a search for an answer to the problem posed above. If the factor was unitary in nature, then the tests (or test items) constituting it should have correlations with the criterion which were *proportional* to their factor loadings, and if the factor was independent of another factor, then the criterion should not correlate significantly with any test (item) constituting this other factor.

The choice of the criterion test would of course be crucial in this argument. In the first place, the criterion should be chosen from a domain different to that from which the tests making up the factor were

[1] The results reported in this chapter, and their discussion, are reproduced, with permission, from Eysenck and Eysenck, 1967.

chosen. If the factor were determined by the inter-correlations between inventory items, then the criterion should not be an inventory item or a compound of inventory items. It could be a psychiatric diagnosis, as for instance in the studies using criterion analysis (Eysenck, 1950, 1952), or it could be some objective behavioural test, or even some physiological reaction measure. Even more important is a second desideratum. The criterion should be chosen in such a way that it embodied a theory which predicted that it would be a good measure of one factor, but not of the other. Only by relating the criterion in some such way to explicit psychological (or physiological) theories about the nature of the factor in question can we hope to escape from the tautological arguments implicit in factor analysis.

The theory here chosen asserts that introversion is a product of cortical arousal, mediated by the reticular formation; introverts are habitually in a state of greater arousal than extraverts, and consequently they show lower sensory thresholds, and greater reactions to sensory stimulation. The theory in question has been discussed in great detail elsewhere (Eysenck, 1967), as has the evidence regarding these and other deductions from it; on the whole the evidence, both physiological and psychological, appears to be in line with predictions made from the theory. The test used in the present investigation is the lemon test, so called because it measures the salivary reaction of subjects to the stimulus of having four drops of lemon juice placed upon the tongue for twenty seconds. The test was originally suggested by Corcoran (1964), who has furnished data regarding its reliability and validity as a measure of extraversion. The score on the test is the amount of salivation produced under lemon juice stimulating conditions, as compared with the amount of salivation produced under neutral conditions, i.e. when no lemon juice is present. Extreme extraverts show little or no increment in salivation, while extreme introverts show an increment of almost 1 gram; intermediate groups show intermediate amounts of increment. Eysenck and Eysenck (1967) have found a correlation of 0·71 on 50 male and 50 female Ss between increment scores and introversion, as measured by the E.P.I.; the correlation with N was effectively zero. No sex differences were observed.

The present analysis is concerned with results on the lemon test obtained from 45 men and 48 women, i.e. a total sample of 93 Ss; all these subjects formed part of the population of the above-mentioned study; 7 subjects were dropped because of failure to complete the questions in the inventory. This inventory (the E.P.I. Form A) contains 57 questions, of which 24 measure E, 24 measure N and the remainder constitute a Lie scale. (The actual items are reproduced on a later page.) The scores of the 93 Ss on the Lemon Test and the 57 questions of the E.P.I. were intercorrelated, and the resulting 58×58 matrix of product-moment correlations factor-analysed by means of the principal components method, and rotated by means of the Promax Programme (Hendrickson and White, 1964). The first factor to emerge was clearly identified as extraversion, the second as neuroticism. Item 58 is the increment score on the lemon test; the lemon test score has a loading of −0·74 on extraversion, and a completely insignificant one of 0·02 on neuroticism. The analysis was repeated for men and women separately; the factor loadings were −0·70 and −0·60 respectively on the E factor, and 0·02 and −0·06 on the N factor. Factor-analytically, then, the lemon test seems to be a pure (univocal) measure of introversion.

If, as pointed out above, the lemon test may be regarded as a relatively pure criterion test of E, then (1) its correlations with the individual items of the E scale should be proportional to the factor loadings of that scale, and (2) its correlations with the individual items of the N scale

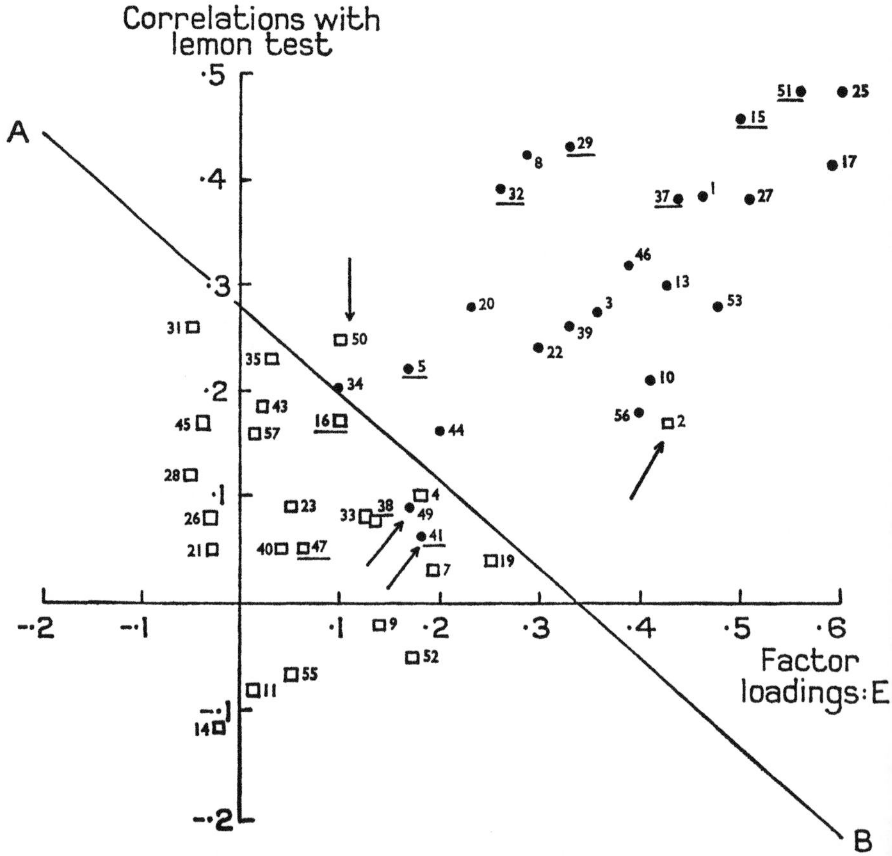

FIG. 13.1 Factor loadings on extraversion (abscissa) and correlations with lemon test (ordinate) of neuroticism items (squares) and extraversion items (circles).

should be effectively zero. Such a test might have been carried out on the factor loadings obtained in this study; however, it might have been objected that such a comparison capitalizes on whatever non-relevant factors were present on the occasion of this experiment and might have influenced both the E.P.I. responses of the Ss and their lemon test scores. Consequently we have chosen to use factor loadings obtained in a different and much larger study, using 500 Ss, half men, half women, who had been given the same items, together with another 50 items. This whole matrix of 107 × 107 items had been factor analyzed in the same manner as the matrix discussed above, i.e. by means of the principal components method, followed by Promax rotation. In this manner the scales are weighted against our hypothesis; not only are the factor loadings derived from a different population to that from which the item correlations with the lemon test are obtained, but in addition the factor analysis was carried out on a sample of items different from, and larger than, that used in our present experiment and factor analysis.

Results are shown in Figure 13.1, where factor loadings have been plotted along the abscissa, the item correlations with the lemon test along the ordinate. Items constituting the E scale have been printed as dots, items constituting the N scale, as squares. L scale items, being irrelevant to this comparison, have been omitted in order not to confuse the picture. Items with negative loadings larger than 0·10 have been reversed in sign (multiplied by −1); these items have been indicated in the Figure by underlining. It will be seen that practically all the E items have both high factor loadings on the extraversion factor and reasonable correlations with the lemon test, whereas N items have low loadings and low correlations. The line A–B has been drawn at the (arbitrary) level approximating a correlation value of 0·3, to divide the diagram into two parts; to the right (i.e. in quadrant I) are the high loading—high correlation values; to the left are the low loading—low correlation values[1]). The former should be E items, the latter N items; it will be clear that in fact this is so. There are only two N items to the right of the line, and two E items to the left; arrows have been inserted to point to these four values. It will be seen that for all items (both E and N) having loadings of 0·20 or above, correlations with the lemon test are 0·15 or higher; at loadings below 0·15, only three are above 0·20. There is thus a remarkable correspondence between the two sets of values.

It is obvious to the eye that the correlation values are roughly proportional to the factor loadings for the E items; a correlation was made both with and without regard for signs. Both correlations are positive, with the former of course much larger; the actual values are 0·97 and

[1] The line is actually slanted towards the right because the average size of the factor loadings is greater than the average size of the correlations in the ratio of 6/5; in order to compensate for this, the intercepts of the line on abscissa and ordinate have been changed from 0·3 to be in roughly the same proportion.

0·71. Both are sufficiently large to allow us to say that the predicted proportionality is in actual fact found, thus supporting the view that the items of the E.P.I. extraversion scale measure a factor which is, as far as this experiment is concerned, unitary. This outcome is particularly reassuring in view of the fact that the criterion test used was chosen on the basis of quite specific theories regarding the psychological and physiological nature of extraversion and introversion; only by thus extending the circular arguments of factor analysis and linking them with psychological theories of broader coverage can we bring together the psychometric and experimental approaches.

14

THE ORTHOGONALITY OF PERSONALITY STRUCTURE

H. J. Eysenck, A. Hendrickson and S. B. G. Eysenck

WE have dealt in Chapters 12 and 13 with the first point raised by Carrigan (1960), i.e. that of the *unidimensionality* of extraversion; we now propose to investigate her other point, i.e. the *independence* of E and N. Any attempted solution clearly raises methodological problems of great complexity, and it is for this reason that several alternative methods of rotation have been used in this study; only in this way can we be sure that our answer is not implicit in the particular method of analysis chosen. (See also Farley, 1967.)

Use was made of the newly constructed Eysenck Personality Inventory (Eysenck and Eysenck, 1964), which is an improved version of the Maudsley Personality Inventory. This consists of 108 questions concerning the E and N aspects of personality; it also contains a separate Lie scale, but no use was made of this in the present investigation. The choice of questions was based on previous experiments with the M.P.I., numerous factor analytic studies carried out at the Institute in the past, mostly unpublished, and a thorough review of the factor analytic literature (Eysenck, 1960e).

The E.P.I. was administered to 500 Ss, half males and half females; these differed widely in age, education and social class, although the better educated and the middle classes were over-represented to an extent which would make it impossible to consider this a random sample of the population. Comparison of means and standard deviations obtained on this sample with those contained in the manual of the

E.P.I. for diverse groups makes us believe that departure from randomness cannot have been very serious. Administration was anonymous, to encourage frank answers, and was carried out in group form. Standard instructions were used. To make discussion of the results meaningful adapted versions of the 108 questions are presented below. Age and sex were always entered on the forms, and constituted two additional variables for analysis.

TABLE 14.1

1. Like plenty of excitement and bustle around you
2. Often need understanding friends to cheer you up
3. Like working alone
4. Often got a restless feeling that you want something but do not know what
5. Often long for excitement
6. Sometimes feel happy, sometimes, sad, without any real reason
7. Hate having to introduce people to each other
8. Put your thoughts into words quickly
9. Usually carefree
10. Sometimes sulk
11. Stop and think things over before doing anything
12. Find it very hard to take no for an answer
13. Generally feel that things will sort themselves out and come right in the end somehow
14. Moody
15. Generally do and say things quickly without stopping to think
16. Mood often go up and down
17. Rather lively
18. Ever feel 'just miserable' for no good reason
19. Suddenly feel shy when you want to talk to an attractive stranger
20. Often lost sleep over your worries
21. Do almost anything for a dare
22. Often make up your mind too late
23. Like planning things carefully, well ahead of time
24. Often worry about things you should not have done or said
25. Often do things on the spur of the moment
26. Feelings rather easily hurt
27. Generally feel that things are bound to work out badly for you
28. Often felt listless and tired for no good reason
29. Like mixing with people
30. Often feel 'fed up'
31. Call yourself happy-go-lucky
32. Mind often wander when you are trying to attend closely to something
33. Prefer reading to meeting people
34. Often 'lost in thought'
35. Nearly always have a 'ready answer' when people talk to you
36. Sometimes bubbling over with energy and sometimes very sluggish
37. Usually stay in the background at parties and 'get togethers'
38. Daydream a lot
39. When you get annoyed you need someone friendly to talk to about it

40. Often think of your past
41. Like going out a lot
42. Often troubled about feelings of guilt
43. Prefer to have few but special friends
44. Call yourself tense or 'highly-strung'
45. When people shout at you, you shout back
46. Often feel lonely
47. Usually shy with the opposite sex
48. After you have done something important, you often come away feeling you could have done better
49. Usually let yourself go and enjoy yourself a lot at a gay party
50. Ideas run through your head so that you cannot sleep
51. Mind selling things or asking people for money for some good cause
52. Touchy about some things
53. Like practical jokes
54. Sometimes get so restless that you cannot sit long in a chair
55. Usually do things better by figuring them out alone than by talking to others about it
56. Have 'dizzy turns'
57. Often get into a jam because you do things without thinking
58. Get palpitations or thumping in your heart
59. Other people think of you as being very lively
60. Get attacks of shaking or trembling
61. Rather be at home on your own than go to a boring party
62. An irritable person
63. When you are drawn into a quarrel, you prefer to 'have it out' to being silent hoping things will blow over
64. Worry about awful things that might happen
65. Mostly quiet when you are with other people
66. Have many nightmares
67. Very much like good food
68. Ever get short of breath without having done heavy work
69. Rather plan things than do things
70. Suffer from 'nerves'
71. If there is something you want to know about, you rather look it up in a book than talk to someone about it
72. Troubled by aches and pains
73. Like the kind of work that you need to pay close attention to
74. Get nervous in places like lifts, trains or tunnels
75. An easy-going person, not generally bothered about having everything 'just so'
76. Sweat a lot without exercise
77. Hate being with a crowd who play jokes on one another
78. Get very bad headaches
79. Like doing things in which you have to act quickly
80. Call yourself a nervous person
81. When you make new friends, it is usually you who makes the first moves, or does the inviting
82. Bother you to have people watch you work

TABLE 14.1 (*contd.*)

83. Slow and unhurried in the way you move
84. Give up easily when things go wrong
85. Like talking to people so much that you would never miss a chance of talking to a stranger
86. Worry too long after an embarrassing experience
87. Find it hard to fall asleep at bedtime
88. Sometimes feel life is just not worth living
89. Be very unhappy if you could not see lots of people most of the time
90. Easily hurt when people find fault with your work
91. Sometimes say the first thing that comes into your head
92. Say you were fairly self-confident
93. Find it hard to really enjoy yourself at a lively party
94. Often feel self-conscious when you are with superiors
95. Usually keep 'yourself to yourself' except with very close friends
96. Troubled with feelings of inferiority
97. Easily get some life into a rather dull party
98. Worry about your health
99. Take everyday things very seriously rather than laughing them off
100. Often get 'butterflies in your tummy' before an important occasion
101. Like playing pranks on others
102. Hate to do more than one thing at a time
103. If the pay and hours were the same, you would rather be a farmer than insurance salesman
104. Prefer romantic stories to adventure stories
105. Like cracking jokes and telling funny stories to your friends
106. Feel uncomfortable in anything but everyday clothes
107. When the odds are against you, you still usually think it worth taking a chance
108. Suffer from sleeplessness

A matrix of product-moment correlation coefficients was computed and factored by the principal components method, unities being inserted in the principal diagonal of the matrix. All latent roots of the matrix were calculated. The number of factors was made equal to the number of latent roots greater than 1·00, following a suggestion by Guttman (1954). Thirty-three latent vectors were accordingly computed; these unrotated factors constitute the first solution we will have to consider (Solution One). The unrotated factors were then rotated to orthogonal simple structure according to the varimax method of Kaiser (1958). This constitutes our second solution (Solution Two). A further transformation to oblique simple structure was carried out by using the Promax method of Hendrickson and White (1964), with k = 4 for all columns. Three higher order analyses based on the intercorrelations between the oblique primary factors were computed using a procedure suggested by Hendrickson and White (1964).[1] Nine second order, four

[1] The procedure is to compute an orthogonal matrix, $H_{12} = A_1F_2$, where A_1 is the matrix of oblique factor loadings at the primary level and F_2 is the matrix of

third order, and two fourth order factors were computed. This constitutes Solution Three.

For reasons which will become clear later on, another varimax solution was attempted by going back to the unrotated factors, and rotating the first two by themselves to the varimax criterion. It was not deemed necessary to use a Promax rotation because the simple structure seemed to be quite adequate with the orthogonal solution. This will be named Solution Four.

The relative sizes of the factor contributions as produced by Solutions One and Two were plotted, and it was found that the main effect of the varimax rotation was, as expected, to distribute the variance much more evenly among the factors. (In the principal components analysis the first two factors were 2 and 3 times as large as any other.) Table 14.2 sets out the loadings of the first six factors in Solution One, as well as the total communalities. Close inspection of factors 1 and 2 discloses that they are very similar to the classical N and E factors as these have emerged from many previous analyses, N being characterized by mood swings, lack of concentration, worries, psychosomatic symptoms, nervousness, sensitivity, and inferiority feelings, and E by sociability, liveliness, impulsiveness, a happy-go-lucky disposition, and jocularity. Fig. 14.1 shows a plot of all items having loadings of 0·40 or above on one of the two factors; there are no items having such loadings on more than one factor, a fact which suggests that our choice of items to measure E and N has been reasonably successful. Simple structure is quite well marked, in spite of the fact that these are *unrotated* factors. (When a varimax rotation was attempted (Solution Four) to produce simple structure the resulting changes were minimal; the two factors produced by this solution are given in Table 14.2 for the sake of comparison, labelled J_1 and J_2).

TABLE 14.2

	F_1	F_2	F_3	F_4	F_5	F_6	h^2	J_1	J_2	K_1	K_2
Sex	0·23	−0·01	−0·24	0·46	−0·28	0·15	0·67	0·23	−0·04	0·14	−0·05
Age	0·27	0·43	0·29	−0·07	0·06	0·03	0·68	0·33	0·38	0·26	0·47
1	0·04	0·53	0·09	0·03	−0·03	0·06	0·62	0·12	0·52	0·13	0·61
2	0·54	0·21	0·04	0·23	−0·04	0·05	0·60	0·57	0·13	0·46	0·07
3	0·03	−0·33	−0·06	0·06	0·08	−0·10	0·59	−0·02	−0·33	−0·03	−0·21

unrotated factor loadings at the second order. F_2 is found by factoring ϕ_1, the matrix of intercorrelations between the oblique first order factors. The H_{12} matrix, which has as many rows (variables) as the first order solution by only as many columns (factors) as the second order solution, is then rotated to simple structure by varimax and Promax. The ϕ_2 produced as a result of this rotation is then factored to produce F_3, etc. The procedure is carried out until the F_n matrix has only a single factor or $\phi_n = I$. The advantage of this procedure rather than the more traditional method of higher order analysis is that it avoids the inaccuracies of analytic rotation with few variables in the matrix. For instance, if F_2 were rotated instead of H_{12}, we would have as many variables as there were factors in the first order solution; in this case, 33 instead of 110.

	F_1	F_2	F_3	F_4	F_5	F_6	h^2	J_1	J_2	K_1	K_2
4	0·43	0·31	0·23	0·06	0·03	0·03	0·57	0·47	0·24	0·35	0·33
5	0·24	0·46	0·16	0·08	−0·02	0·00	0 64	0·31	0·42	0·31	0·58
6	0·40	0·25	0·22	0·19	−0·03	−0·11	0·65	0·43	0·19	0·29	0·15
7	0·33	−0·06	0·34	−0·31	−0·01	−0·14	0·81	0·32	−0·11	0·38	−0·10
8	−0·38	0·07	−0·33	0·04	0·23	−0·19	0·66	−0·37	0·13	−0·38	0·09
9	−0·21	0·36	0·07	−0·01	−0·11	−0·08	0·52	−0·15	0·39	−0·09	0·30
10	0·39	0·13	0·15	−0·15	−0·03	−0·28	0·65	0·41	0·07	0·37	0·01
11	−0·29	−0·17	0·21	0·05	0·44	0·17	0·63	−0·31	−0·12	−0·26	−0·02
12	0·21	0·18	−0·08	0·08	−0·00	−0·15	0·66	0·23	0·15	0·17	0·07
13	−0·08	0·22	0·17	0·19	0·07	−0·06	0·59	−0·05	0·23	−0·08	0·18
14	0·45	0·10	0·13	−0·10	−0·06	−0·37	0·72	0·46	0·03	0·42	0·08
15	0·31	0·29	−0·09	0·02	−0·32	−0·25	0·63	0·35	0·24	0·28	0·18
16	0·46	0·19	0·13	0·11	−0·01	−0·36	0·60	0·48	0·12	0·40	0·15
17	−0·15	0·58	−0·11	0·03	0·17	−0·03	0·68	−0·06	0·60	−0·12	0·42
18	0·46	0·13	0·17	0·15	−0·12	−0·20	0·62	0·47	0·06	0·38	−0·01
19	0·43	0·01	0·43	0·03	0·11	0·23	0·63	0·43	−0·05	0·44	0·01
20	0·37	0·00	−0·36	0·11	0·17	−0·02	0·66	0·37	−0·06	0·27	−0·11
21	0·18	0·41	−0·11	−0·27	−0·05	−0·17	0·52	0·24	0·38	0·27	0·40
22	0·50	0·07	0·09	0·07	−0·05	−0·03	0·56	0·50	−0·01	0·46	−0·01
23	−0·04	−0·06	0·00	−0·08	0·49	0·04	0·66	−0·05	−0·05	0·01	−0·09
24	0·50	−0·01	0·07	0·29	0·04	0·08	0·55	0·49	−0·08	0·40	−0·11
25	0·19	0·43	0·03	0·07	−0·11	−0.09	0·60	0·25	0·40	0·19	0·39
26	0·48	−0·10	0·05	0·34	0·13	0.03	0·62	0·46	−0·17	0·37	−0·21
27	0·45	0·04	−0·16	−0·32	−0·13	0·05	0·60	0·45	−0·03	0·50	−0·04
28	0·50	0·13	0·08	0·02	−0·02	−0·19	0·61	0·51	0·05	0·46	−0·03
29	−0·27	0·50	−0·12	0·28	0·14	0·12	0·64	−0·19	0·53	−0·30	0·45
30	0·59	0·05	0·12	−0·04	−0·01	−0·20	0·61	0·59	−0·04	0·54	0·04
31	−0·10	0·56	−0·01	−0·20	−0·07	−0·07	−0·61	−0·02	0·57	0·00	0·39
32	0·45	0·19	0·18	0·05	−0·13	−0·03	0·61	0·47	0·12	0·44	0·13
33	0·26	−0·50	−0·03	−0·22	−0·09	−0·28	0·65	0·18	−0·53	0·28	−0·45
34	0·45	0·07	0·03	0·08	0·12	−0·10	0·62	0·46	0·00	0·00	0·04
35	−0·30	0·13	−0·28	0·09	0·15	−0·26	−0·70	−0·28	0·17	−0·31	0·18
36	0·36	0·25	0·12	0·18	0·05	−0·25	0·55	0·39	0·19	0·36	0·17
37	0·29	−0·50	0·29	−0·04	0·10	−0·04	0·66	0·21	−0·54	0·28	−0·30
38	0·37	−0·03	0·03	0·19	−0·09	−0·01	0·68	0·36	−0·08	0·28	−0·10
39	0·28	0·15	−0·00	0·28	0·15	0·11	0·59	0·30	0·11	0·25	0·04
40	0·36	0·19	0·06	0·02	0·22	0·02	0·56	0·38	0·13	0·35	0·03
41	0·02	0·59	0·08	0·09	−0·05	0·27	0·61	0·11	0·58	0·04	0·55
42	0·50	0·05	−0·03	0·10	0·10	0·18	0·58	0·50	−0·03	0·36	−0·15
43	0·17	−0·24	0·03	0·22	0·14	−0·13	0·61	0·13	−0·26	0·16	−0·20
44	0·38	−0·03	−0·35	0·05	0·13	−0·11	0·64	0·37	−0·09	0·30	−0·06
45	0·14	0·30	0·04	−0·07	0·09	−0·29	0·63	0·18	0·28	0·22	0·21
46	0·63	−0·06	−0·03	−0·02	−0·05	0·07	0·58	0·61	−0·15	0·57	−0·13
47	0·39	−0·18	0·34	−0·15	0·05	0·22	0·63	0·36	−0·24	0·43	−0·11
48	0·22	0·05	0·04	0·14	0·16	−0·02	0·60	0·22	0·02	0·22	0·01
49	−0·23	0·60	−0·12	0·16	0·01	0·07	0·74	−0·14	0·63	−0·20	0·43
50	0·38	−0·05	−0·27	0·07	0·26	0·02	0·62	0·37	−0·11	0·24	−0·07
51	0·08	−0·22	0·10	−0·01	−0·15	−0·12	0·74	0·05	−0·23	0·09	−0·19
52	0·28	0·08	0·12	0·13	0·23	−0·22	0·61	0·29	0·04	0·21	−0·03
53	0·10	0·44	0·23	−0·49	0·17	−0·10	0·71	0·16	0·42	0·18	0·37
54	0·34	0·32	0·06	0·08	0·02	−0·14	0·59	0·38	0·27	0·30	0·34
55	−0·07	−0·09	0·02	−0·13	0·19	−0·13	0·61	−0·08	−0·08	−0·01	−0·04
56	0·42	0·05	−0·26	−0·22	0·01	0·03	0·63	0·42	−0·01	0·42	0·03

	F_1	F_2	F_3	F_4	F_5	F_6	h^2	J_1	J_2	K_1	K_2
57	0·51	0·31	−0·12	−0·10	−0·10	−0·17	0·58	0·55	0·23	0·50	0·22
58	0·32	0·12	−0·11	−0·16	0·14	0·17	0·62	0·33	0·07	0·26	0·06
59	−0·10	0·51	−0·15	0·07	0·06	−0·16	0·70	−0·02	0·52	−0·08	0·29
60	0·53	0·03	−0·20	−0·16	−0·02	0·15	0·59	0·53	−0·05	0·48	−0·06
61	−0·04	−0·22	0·05	0·34	0·06	−0·24	0·61	−0·07	−0·21	−0·08	−0·21
62	0·33	−0·13	−0·13	−0·08	−0·05	−0·33	0·56	0·31	−0·18	0·32	−0·09
63	−0·13	0·30	0·05	0·15	0·17	−0·07	0·70	−0·08	0·32	−0·14	0·26
64	0·55	0·04	−0·12	0·08	−0·01	0·10	0·55	0·55	−0·04	0·47	−0·06
65	0·30	−0·33	0·28	−0·14	0·09	0·06	0·57	0·25	−0·37	0·33	−0·25
66	0·31	0·02	−0·35	−0·18	−0·08	0·11	0·54	0·31	−0·03	0·26	−0·10
67	−0·05	0·17	0·14	0·11	0·28	−0·14	0·54	−0·02	0·18	−0·04	0·19
68	0·32	−0·05	−0·17	−0·25	−0·02	0·01	0·55	0·31	−0·10	0·35	−0·09
69	0·17	−0·19	−0·04	−0·29	0·28	−0·09	0·54	0·14	−0·21	0·25	−0·17
70	0·48	−0·01	−0·29	0·07	0·11	0·15	0·68	0·47	−0·08	0·40	−0·04
71	0·10	−0·26	0·05	−0·08	0·18	−0·13	0·70	0·60	−0·27	0·16	−0·20
72	0·31	−0·04	−0·34	−0·06	0·23	−0·04	0·64	0·30	−0·09	0·27	−0·18
73	−0·19	−0·10	−0·07	−0·03	0·35	0·02	0·62	−0·20	−0·07	−0·19	−0·03
74	0·38	−0·05	−0·32	−0·09	−0·05	0·13	0·72	−0·37	−0·11	0·40	−0·14
75	−0·04	0·24	0·21	0·03	−0·31	0·16	0·64	−0·00	0·24	−0·02	0·05
76	0·16	−0·01	0·03	−0·21	0·15	0·05	0·62	0·16	−0·03	0·21	0·03
77	−0·06	−0·04	−0·20	0·39	−0·08	−0·16	0·72	−0.13	−0·43	−0·10	−0·34
78	0·35	0·02	−0·34	−0·09	0·12	−0·08	0·61	0.35	−0·03	0·32	0·01
79	−0·18	0·33	−0·10	−0·01	0·15	−0·14	0·55	−0·13	0·35	−0·20	0·43
80	0·52	−0·06	−0·32	−0·03	0·03	0·19	0·71	0·51	−0·14	0·45	−0·15
81	−0·13	0·31	−0·19	0·07	0·04	−0·01	0·71	−0·08	0·33	−0·16	0·28
82	0·47	−0·08	0·24	0·05	−0·10	0·03	0·55	0·45	−0·15	0·45	−0·06
83	0·11	−0·18	0·16	−0·19	−0·04	0·14	0·67	0·08	−0·19	0·18	−0·25
84	0·36	−0·02	−0·03	−0·07	−0·20	0·08	0·68	0·35	−0·07	0·46	−0·09
85	0·09	0·20	−0·26	−0·18	−0·02	0·03	0·59	0·12	0·18	0·14	0·07
86	0·50	−0·18	−0·10	0·14	0·12	0·20	0·56	0·47	−0·25	0·40	−0·31
87	0·33	0·05	−0·46	−0·12	0·04	0·12	0·74	0·33	0·00	0·28	−0·05
88	0·56	−0·05	−0·09	−0·04	−0·14	0·01	0·62	0·55	−0·13	0·55	−0·07
89	0·10	0·39	0·00	0·08	0·04	0·18	0·61	0·16	0·37	0·24	0·23
90	0·44	−0·10	0·05	0·33	0·15	−0·02	0·64	0·42	−0·16	0·36	−0·14
91	0·21	0·12	0·05	0·12	−0·28	−0·11	0·74	0·23	0·09	0·16	0·02
92	−0·45	0·17	−0·03	0·06	0·25	−0·25	0·82	−0·42	0·24	−0·46	0·17
93	0·27	−0·56	0·02	−0·16	−0·08	−0·15	0·69	0·18	−0·59	0·23	−0·41
94	0·49	0·02	0·17	0·06	0·13	0·13	0·56	0·49	−0·05	0·46	−0·09
95	0·23	−0·43	0·13	−0·01	0·19	−0·14	0·61	0·16	−0·46	0·28	−0·38
96	0·49	−0·17	0·04	0·07	−0·04	0·16	0·67	0·46	−0·24	0·43	−0·25
97	−0·12	0·48	−0·30	−0·14	−0·00	−0·11	0·62	−0·05	0·49	−0·07	0·25
98	0·26	0·05	−0·16	−0·02	0·17	0·06	0·70	0·26	0·01	0·19	−0·03
99	0·22	−0·26	−0·15	−0·00	0·34	−0·03	0·64	0·18	−0·29	0·18	−0·23
100	0·26	0·14	0·27	0·27	0·33	0·16	0·64	0·28	0·10	0·18	0·13
101	0·06	0·40	0·25	−0·48	0·10	0·09	0·69	0·12	0·39	0·15	0·36
102	0·26	0·02	0·19	−0·12	0·13	0·01	0·64	0·26	−0·02	0·37	0·02
103	−0·04	−0·21	0·06	0·13	−0·03	−0·03	0·66	−0·07	−0·20	−0·09	0·13
104	0·14	0·07	−0·16	0·30	−0·09	0·23	0·64	0·15	0·05	0·15	0·02
105	−0·03	0·45	0·10	−0·29	0·25	−0·03	0·62	0·04	0·45	0·05	0·36
106	0·30	−0·09	0·06	−0·33	0·03	−0·14	0·58	0·28	−0·13	0·41	−0·19
107	−0·07	0·26	0·07	0·12	0·13	−0·13	0·62	−0·03	0·27	−0·12	0·22
108	0·40	0·01	−0·47	−0·11	−0·02	0·08	0·75	0·40	−0·05	0·32	−0·07
	11·94	7·54	3·83	3·34	2·66	2·45	—	11·84	7·64	10·43	5·63

There are several interesting points in Fig. 14.1. (1) The striated area is free of items, suggesting an approach to simple structure. But this is possibly due, not to any inherent tendency towards simple structure in nature, but to the selection of items, based on theory and previous experience. There might be little difficulty in finding items to fit into this space if this were thought desirable. Equally, simple structure could of course be made more obvious if some items were left out, such as those numbered 5, 25, 21, 4, 6 and 57. The width of the sheaf of arrows delineating N or E is an *arbitrary function of the subjective decisions made before the commencement of the experiment*, in so far as these relate to the choice of items. (2) It follows from our particular choice of having a rather broad sheaf that some E items will have loadings on N which are not negligible, and equally, some N items will have loadings on E. Thus, sociability items measure E, but have negative correlations with N, while impulsiveness items also measure E, but correlate positively with N; this is very much in line with our earlier work (see Chapter 12). Inferiority feelings and sensitivity measure N, but have an introverted component, while mood-swings and lack of concentration measure N, but have an extraverted component. (3) It will be seen that the arrows (clusters of items) marked 'sociability' and 'shyness' are almost at right angles, and hence uncorrelated. This may seem strange at first, as one might have expected them to be negatively correlated. However, as we

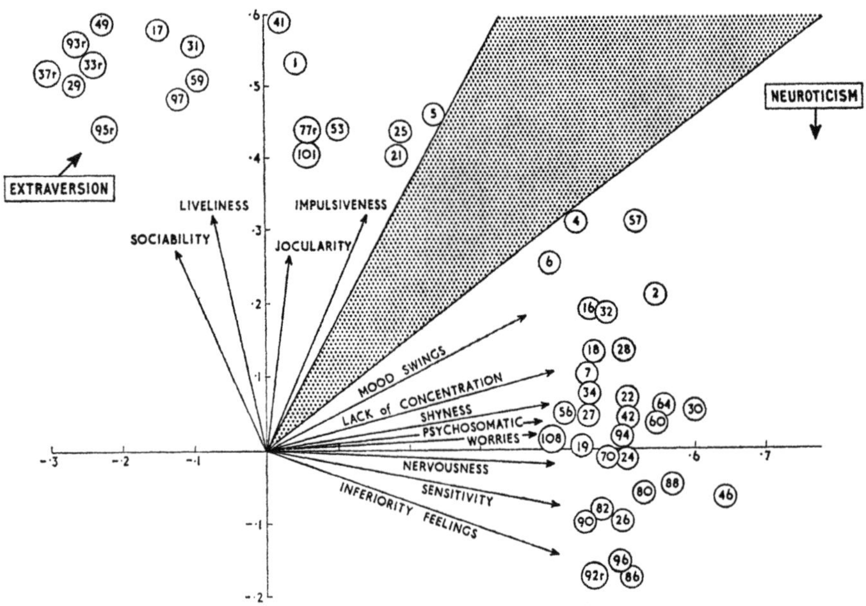

FIG. 14.1 Diagram showing position of all items having loadings of 0·4 or above on either of the first two factors. (Principal components solution.)

have shown in Part One, Guilford's S factor (social shyness) does not constitute a unitary factor, but is in fact made up of two groups of almost completely unrelated items identifiable as *neurotic shyness* and *introverted lack of sociability*. It would be a mistake to subsume these two independent factors under one label, as is unfortunately customary.

How about the next few unrotated factors with at least moderate factor contributions? F_3 has its highest loadings on items suggesting Nervousness and Sleeplessness; F_4 on Jocularity items; F_5 on Impulsiveness items; F_6 on Moodiness items. F_7 and F_8 (not given in Table 14.2) suggest factors of Pessimism and of Sociability.[1] None of these factors is quite unambiguous, and readers will be able to check our interpretations by reference to the loadings as given in Table 14.2. In any case it is only the first two factors which make any sizeable contribution to the variance, and which enable unambiguous interpretations to be made.

We now turn to a consideration of Solution Two (Table 14.3). Only factors with factor contributions of 2·00 and over will be considered, as the others tend to have only one or two high loadings. In order to characterize each factor, loadings of 0·4 and above will be relied on exclusively; we believe that low loadings are liable to obscure the picture rather than clarify it. (Very occasionally, items with loadings just short of 0·4 are given to clarify the nature of a factor; such items are placed in brackets.) There are fourteen factors; the sizes of the factor contributions are given in brackets in each case. Varimax factors will be designated by V, followed by their number. (Signs of loadings are not specified; they are always in line with common-sense interpretation.)

TABLE 14.3

V_1 (4·56):	*Mood-swing*	Characterized, in order of loading, by items 6, 18, 28, 4, 16, 36, 30
V^2 (4·44):	*Sociability*	Characterized, in order of loading, by items 49, 93, 37, 33, 41, 65
V_3 (3·18):	*Jocularity*	Characterized, in order of loading, by items 53, 101, 77, 105
V_4 (3·11):	*Impulsiveness*	Characterized, in order of loading, by items 15, 11, 25, 57, 91, 23
V_5 (2·99):	*Sleeplessness*	Characterized, in order of loading, by items 108, 50, 20
V_6 (2·80):	*Inferiority*	Characterized, in order of loading, by items 96, 94, 86
V_7 (2·61):	*Quick-wittedness*	Characterized, in order of loading, by items 35, 8, 47, 19
V_8 (2·57):	*Liveliness*	Characterized, in order of loading, by items 59, 17, 31, 97

[1] Nearly all these factors can be traced in the factor analytic literature (cf. Eysenck, 1960, for summary).

TABLE 14.3 (*contd.*)

V_9 (2·46):	*Nervousness*	Characterized, in order of loading, by items 80, 70, 44
V_{10} (2·42):	*Irritability*	Characterized, in order of loading, by items 14, 10, 62, 16
V_{11} (2·28):	*Psychosomatic*	Characterized, in order of loading, by items 68, 78, 56, 48
V_{12} (2·17):	*Masculinity*	Characterized, in order of loading, by items 'sex', 34
V_{13} (2·07):	*Uninterpreted*	Characterized by item 34
V_{14} (2·05):	*Sensitivity*	Characterized, in order of loading, by items 52, 100, 102, 90

Fourteen Varimax factors with latent roots above 2·00

There are obvious similarities between some of these factors and some from the unrotated solution; F_3 of Solution One is similar to V_5 of Solution Two; F_4 resembles V_3; F_5 resembles V_4, F_6 resembles V_2; F_8 resembles V_2. There is no match in Solution Two for F_7, which in any case was very ill-defined. The main difference between the two solutions lies of course in the complete disappearance of E and N, or rather their fragmentation into 'independent' factors. Thus our original E is now distributed among factors 2, 3, 4, 7; the original N is now distributed among factors 1, 5, 6, 8, 9, 10 and 13. Humpty-Dumpty has had his fall;

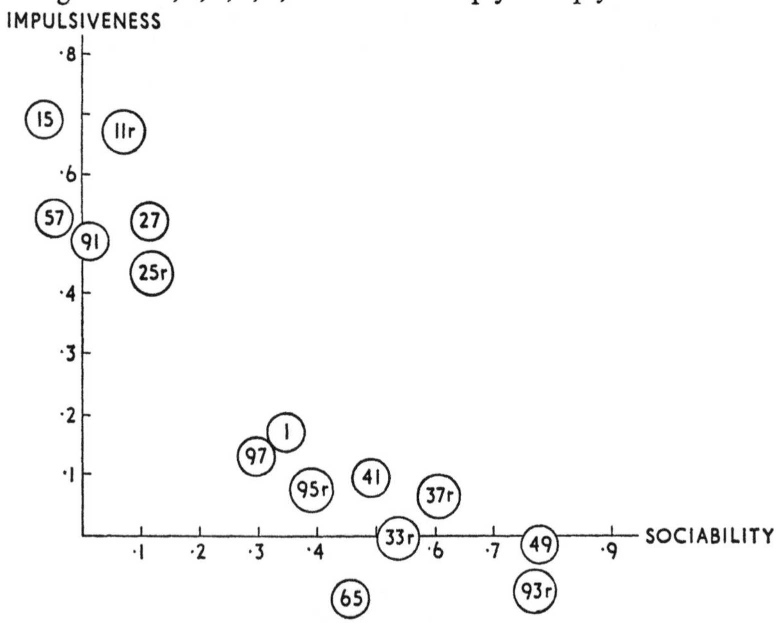

FIG. 14.2 Diagram indicating positions of items having loadings of 0·3 or above on Varimax factors 'impulsiveness' and 'sociability'.

can Solution Three put him together again? To answer this question, let us first of all consider in some detail just what varimax has done, and how it has done it.

Consider Fig. 14.2 where we have plotted varimax factors 2 (Sociability) against 7 (Impulsiveness); items measuring in the opposite direction have had their loadings multiplied by −1, and are marked 'r' (for 'reversed') in the figure. It will be seen that varimax has done an excellent job of finding an adequate simple structure despite the restriction to orthogonality. For the sake of interest, we have marked the average position of the Sociability and Impulsiveness items in Fig. 14.1 with arrows; the angle between them is 50°, giving a correlation between the two clusters of 0·64. Transformed into a scalar product this becomes approximately 0·20, which is close to the average intercorrelation of the two groups of items.[1] The two clusters are clearly not orthogonal or independent, and varimax has resulted in a solution which suggests a statistical artefact.

Varimax rotation adopts two conventions; one is simple structure, defined in terms of the 4th powers of loadings, the other is orthogonality between factors. In case of conflict between these two conventions, orthogonality is retained; thus in the case of the relation between sociability and impulsiveness orthogonality is not empirically discovered, but imposed by fiat. The existence of all-embracing factors such as E and N is rendered impossible by the same token; their failure to emerge is implicit in the conventions adopted *a priori*. However, we may continue our analysis by going on to Solution Three; the Promax method of rotation, while still maximizing simple structure imposes no *a priori* conception upon the angles between factors and allows them to become oblique (Hendrickson and White, 1964). This freedom implies the obligation to carry the analysis farther into the correlations between factors, thus giving rise to higher-order factors.

Below are given the main Promax factors, labelled F_1 through F_{22}; as before we have given in each case the defining variables with loadings above 0·40 (see Table 14·4). It will be clear that in so far as matching factors are available from the varimax solution, there is considerable similarity; Promax appears to be superior, however, in providing many more interpretable factors, and in making the Interpretation of factors existing in both solutions easier. (Full tables of factor loadings on all factors are available for inspection at the Institute of Psychiatry.) These effects of removing the constraint of orthogonality are of course not unexpected, but it is noteworthy that the clarification of factors, particularly the smaller and weaker ones, was quite considerable. Neverthe-

[1] It is interesting to note that Sheldon's two Extraversion factors (Viscerotonia and Somatotonia) emphasize this same dichotomy; Viscerotonia emphasizes sociability (sociophilia), Somatotonia emphasizes impulsiveness, activity and restlessness (Eysenck, 1960).

less, Cattell (1965) seems to overstate the case when he says, in comparing his 16 P.F. factors and those of the Guilford-Zimmerman scales, that these 'can never be aligned, for one has arrived at orthogonal and the other at oblique factors'. Comparisons of our V and F factors indicates considerable similarity; characterization is nearly always in terms of the same items in both cases. There is no difficulty here in aligning these orthogonal factors with the corresponding oblique ones.

Tables 14.5 and 14.6 give details of the second and third order factors, and show the gradual secretion of items to the major factors of neuroticism and extraversion, which emerge quite clearly at the fourth order level. The naming of the intermediate factors is somewhat arbitrary, and should not be taken too seriously; several of them are almost impossible to identify, such as P_8^2 and P_9^2. However, it is with the highest order factors that our main interest lies, and the loadings of these two factors, designated K_1 and K_2, are given in Table 14.2, for comparison with F_1, F_2, and J_1, J_2. The conclusion that we are again dealing with N and E is strengthened by computing the Wrigley-Neuhaus (1955) coefficient of factor similarity between the two E and the two N factors (J_1 vs. K_1, and J_2 vs. K_2). For N the coefficient was 0·9823, and for E it was 0·9511;

TABLE 14.4

Factor		Items in order of loading
P_1	*Mood-swings*	6, 18, 4, 30, 28, 16, 2, 36, 5, 46, Age, 22, 32, 24, 54, 88
P_2	*Sociability*	49, 93, 29, 37, 33, 65, 1, 41, 92, 46, 17
P_3	*Jocularity*	53, 77, 101, 105
P_4	*Impulsiveness*	15, 57, 11, 25, 91, 5, 21
P_5	*Sleeplessness*	108, 87, 50, 20
P_6	*Inferiority feelings*	96, 86, 94, 24
P_7	*Quick-wittedness*	8, 35, 7, 47, 19, 65, 94
P_8	*Liveliness*	59, 97, 17, 31
P_9	*Nervousness*	80, 70, 44, 92
P_{10}	*Irritability*	14, 10, 62, 45, 16
P_{11}	*Psychosomatic*	78, 68, 56
P_{12}	*Masculinity*	2, 104, 46, Sex, 39, 88, 26, 90
P_{13}	*Day-dreams*	38, 34, 46, 30, 42, 82
P_{14}	*Sensitivity*	52, 100, 90, 26, 102, 82
P_{15}	*Age*	Age, 61, 5, 41
P_{16}	*Personal tempo*	83, 79
P_{17}	*Optimism*	13, 92, 46
P_{18}	*Serious-mindedness*	99, 92, Age
P_{19}	*Excitability*	76, 7, 1, 5, 54, 102
P_{20}	*Self-confidence*	92, 107, 88
P_{21}	*Out-goingness*	81, 19
P_{22}	*Hypochondriasis*	98 (64, 72, 42, 56)

Twenty-two Promax first-order factors

TABLE 14.5

Factor		Items in order of loading
P_1^2	*Nervousness*	56, 74, 46, 27, 30, 57, 108, 78, 80, 87, 66
P_2^2	*Irritability*	62, 45, 44
P_3^2	*Self-confidence*	7, 92
P_4^2	*Shyness*	19, 100, 47, 90, 94, 4, 26, 24
P_5^2	*Rhathymia*	31, 41, 97, 17, 21, 1, 37, 53, 59, 105, 75, 89, 93, 101, 85
P_6^2	*Worry*	42, 20, 50, (24)
P_7^2	*Unconcern*	75, 83, 84
P_8^2	*Impulsiveness*	23, 69, 105, 51
P_9^2	*Impulsiveness*	91, (5)

Nine second-order Promax factors

TABLE 14.6

Factor		Items in order of loading
P_1^3	*Neuroticism*	88, 92, 46, 90, 64, 24, 42, 44, 26, 2, 86, 96, 108
P_2^3	*Sociability*	7, 29, 33, 95, 41, 65
P_3^3	*Excitement*	5, 1, 32, 54, 36
P_4^3	*Jocularity*	105, 53, 77, 101

Four third-order Promax factors

both values are high enough to show the essential identity of the factors in question, and thus the essential identity of the statistical solutions.

Our results enable us to give an answer to the two questions raised by Carrigan (1960). There are not *two* types of extraversion—sociability and impulsiveness—but merely one, made up of both sociability and impulsiveness, as well as jocularity, liveliness, quick-wittedness, optimism, easy-going, etc. In this, our present study agrees well with a previous one (Eysenck and Eysenck, 1963d). As regards the relation between extraversion and adjustment we find complete independence. This is shown both by the unrotated principal components solution and by the Promax analytically-rotated oblique solution; the correlation between N and E in the latter, although statistically free to assume any value at all, turned out to be $-0{\cdot}05$. On both these points, therefore, the results bear out Eysenck's (1947) original contentions.

At the same time, the results go some way to answer certain criticisms made by Cattell (1965) of Eysenck's general approach. Cattell makes the following points. (1) 'Simple structure is inherent in natural data.' (2) 'A factor is given the property of being something more than a classificatory principle . . . it is given the status of an *influence or cause.*' (Cattell's italics.) (3) Eysenck and others 'assert that a very "broad" primary factor is the same thing as a second order factor'; this 'confusion' he believes to be associated with a failure to recognize that second order factors are causally related to primary factors. Cattell goes in some detail into this third point. 'It is in fact true that there is a general resemblance of the first and second ... primaries, when rotated in inadequate space, to the second orders pattern'; says Cattell, but 'the imitation of the true second orders by these pseudo-second orders is poor'. And he calls attention 'to the misleading inferences and constructions in personality theory deriving from the use of what have been called pseudo-second order factors'.

Our own position with respect to these three points is clear. (1) The proposition that 'simple structure is inherent in natural data' seems to us not so much wrong as meaningless; it is certainly not a verifiable scientific statement. If accepted at all, it must be accepted on faith; we do not share this faith. We believe that while simple structure may often be useful in facilitating analysis, its applicability to the psychological analysis of any particular set of data has to be demonstrated independently. (2) A factor as such cannot be 'given the status of a cause' on the basis of any statistical manipulation. Its extraction from a matrix may *suggest* to us causal relations which can then be experimentally verified or disproved, but by itself factor analysis is merely a classificatory device.

These two points are questions of logic and argument; the third point is subject to empirical study. Do our data bear out Cattell's contention that 'the imitation of the true second orders by these pseudo-second orders is poor'? K_1 and K_2 fulfil all the requirements for 'true' higher order factors; J_1 and J_2 are clearly 'pseudo-second orders'. We have already reported that the Wrigley-Neuhaus coefficient of factor similarity give values of 0·98 for N and of 0·95 for E. Both coefficients indicate identity rather than poor resemblance.

Peterson (1960), himself a co-worker of Cattell's, has carried out an interesting comparison of the generality of primary factors as compared with 'pseudo-second order factors', over four populations of different ages, using Cattell's variables and data. He concluded that 'the degree of resemblance between child and adult factor patterns was generally unimpressive'. The 'mean loading correlation for all factor pairs for which identity is claimed ... is 0·42; ... the mean correlation for all other (non-matching) factor pairs is 0·17'. Peterson then proceeded to an alternative solution, rather along the lines of our two-factor varimax procedure; two factors were found at each age level which were identified with general neuroticism and introversion-extraversion. 'The degree of resemblance between representations of these factors at the various age levels was then assessed, and correlations between loadings on common marker variables were found to be in the neighbourhood of 0·80.' Even in Cattell's own work, therefore, 'pseudo-second order factors' are very much superior to simple structure factors as far as reproducibility is concerned.

Which of our solutions, then, is the correct one? We would suggest that this is a meaningless question; factor analysis is a tool designed to help in our quest for knowledge, but it cannot by itself disclose either the 'true' structure or the 'true' causal relationships involved in a particular domain. Unless the truth is known to us already, so that factorial solutions can be assessed by comparison with the 'true' solution, we can only use the information furnished by factor analysis as hypotheses, leading to further experimental study. We would postulate E and N as causal influences in behaviour, not because they emerge so repeatedly and strongly from factorial studies (Eysenck, 1960e), but because of psychological theories and arguments related to findings in learning theory, genetics, physiology, biochemistry, perception, anatomy, psychopharmacology and many other disciplines (Eysenck, 1957; 1967). It is because we can deduce the existence of E and N, and their relationship, from these more fundamental and general theories that we lay stress on the factorial findings supporting our general position, not vice versa; factorial analysis must ultimately play its part as a component of the hypothetico-deductive approach which characterizes science generally (Eysenck, 1950), rather than play a lone, esoteric game with mathematical symbols.

It is for the same reason that we would prefer the hierarchical model of personality structure originally suggested by Eysenck (1947) to the 'reticular' one suggested by Cattell (1965). Cattell argues against the heirarchical conception on statistical grounds, but the main arguments in favour of this model derive from experimental findings and theoretical considerations of a non-statistical kind. Causal hypotheses of factors as inherited autonomic lability underlying neuroticism, or inherited over-responsiveness of the activating or synchronizing parts of the ascending reticular formation underlying extraversion and introversion (Eysenck, 1963b), lead us inevitably to a psychological theory of hierarchical components of behaviour, structured along lines of greater generality at the top, and greater specificity at the bottom. Statistical analysis supports this view, but cannot by itself prove it. Neither, however, can the statistical data quoted by Cattell disprove the hierarchical hypothesis; as always in purely statistical arguments, there is a fatal degree of subjectivity attaching to the argument which makes decisions arbitrary rather than compelling.

In spite of this belief that factorial solution can never be objective and compelling, but must be subjective and permissive, it is possible to designate certain solutions as better or worse in terms of various psychological criteria. Thus the primary factors in the Promax solutions were more clearly marked and more readily interpreted than were the varimax factors; this finding lends some modest support to Cattell's preference for oblique factors, as against Guilford's insistence on orthogonal ones. The question of the superiority of the fourth order E and N factors over the varimax two-factor solution (or indeed over the Hotelling Principal Components solution) is not one which we believe to be answerable at the moment; fortunately the similarities are so marked as to make a choice unnecessary. From the point of view of questionnaire construction (the whole analysis was done with the express purpose of developing the E.P.I. as an improved version of the M.P.I.) E and N scales scored according to either solution would be expected to correlate very highly together.

We may conclude that our results support a view of personality which stresses the importance of two main factors, neuroticism and extraversion-introversion; which asserts the independence of the two factors from each other; and which postulates that each of these factors can be analysed into component 'sub-factors' which in certain types of rotational analysis appear as 'primary factors'. If interest is centred mainly on the two central factors, N and E, then a principal components solution gives a perfectly adequate approximation; a varimax rotation of the first two factors to be extracted may or may not improve this approximation. Primary factors can also be extracted from such a solution, but they are not as clearly marked and identified as might be wished.

If interest is centred mainly on a greater number of primary factors, then varimax or Promax rotation is indicated, with the latter clearly superior as far as interpretability of the resulting factors is concerned. In addition, Promax allows us to extract E and N as higher order factors closely similar to those given by the original principal components solution. While it would clearly not be permissible to generalize our conclusions beyond the particular experiment here reported, we would say that the results suggest that Promax combines the best features of all the other methods, giving adequate estimates of both the primary and the higher order factors. Whether it would do so in connection with other groups of subjects, other collections of items, and other types of psychological problems cannot be decided on *a priori* grounds, but must await the outcome of further applications of the method.

15

A JOINT FACTORIAL STUDY OF THE GUILFORD, CATTELL AND EYSENCK SCALES

M. I. Soueif, H. J. Eysenck and P. O. White

IT is interesting that throughout the last dozen or so years the Guilford, Cattell and Eysenck questionnaires have run their separate way without any investigation being devoted to a comparative study of their similarities and differences. In view of the fact that it now seems established that all three sets of questionnaires give rise to higher-order extraversion and neuroticism factors, it seemed desirable to carry out a fairly comprehensive study to analyse the precise relationships between the three sets of questionnaires. Such an analysis of course can be done at two levels. In the first place it is possible to group the questions within each questionnaire into sets according to the primary factors postulated by each of three authors on the basis of their own factorial analyses. These scales can then be inter-correlated and factorial analyses carried out on the scales. This roughly is what has been done in this section. In the second place it is possible to intercorrelate the actual items in the three sets of questionnaires, to factor analyse these and to see to what extent the factors which emerge are in fact similar to or identical with those postulated by the authors concerned. This is essentially what has been done in the subsequent sections of this part.

Three questionnaires were used. The first is the Eysenck Personality Inventory, which consists of 48 items measuring neuroticism, 48 items measuring extraversion and a lie scale consisting of 18 items. The following 114 items have been adapted with permission from the Eysenck Personality Inventory, copyright 1963 by Educational and

Industrial Testing Service, San Diego. Apart from the addition of the lie scale items the list differs from that given in the last section by omitting some items which were not found to have high loadings on extraversion and neuroticism, and in order to avoid complications arising from re-numbering items we have thought it best to present the adapted items again. The items were grouped into 10 subscales on the basis of the analyses reported in the previous section; also, there are two lie scales, Forms A and B, made up by an arbitrary subdivision of the 18 items into two sets of 9. In addition an acquiescence scale was constructed, the purpose and nature of which will be explained presently.

TABLE 15.1

A

1. Often long for excitement
2. Often need understanding friends to cheer you up
3. Usually carefree
4. Find it very hard to take no for an answer
5. Stop and think things over before doing anything
6. If you say you will do something you always keep your promise no matter how inconvenient it might be to do so
7. Your mood often goes up and down
8. Generally do and say things quickly without stopping to think
9. Ever feel 'just miserable' for no good reason
10. Do almost anything for a dare
11. Suddenly feel shy when you want to talk to an attractive stranger
12. Once in a while you lose your temper and get angry
13. Often do things on the spur of the moment
14. Often worry about things you should not have done or said
15. Prefer reading to meeting people
16. Feelings rather easily hurt
17. Like going out a lot
18. Occasionally have thoughts and ideas that you would not like other people to know about
19. Sometimes bubbling over with energy and sometimes very sluggish
20. Prefer to have few but special friends
21. Daydream a lot
22. When people shout at you, you shout back
23. Often troubled about feelings of guilt
24. *All* your habits good and desirable ones
25. Usually let yourself go and enjoy yourself a lot at a gay party
26. You call yourself tense or 'highly-strung'
27. Other people think of you as being very lively
28. After you have done something important, you often come away feeling you could have done better
29. Mostly quiet when you are with other people
30. Sometimes gossip

31. Ideas run through your head so that you cannot sleep
32. If there is something you want to know about, you would rather look it up in a book than talk to someone about it
33. Get palpitations or thumping in your heart
34. Like the kind of work that you need to pay close attention to
35. Get attacks of shaking or trembling
36. You always declare everything at the customs, even if you knew that you could never be found out
37. Hate being with a crowd who play jokes on one another
38. An irritable person
39. Like doing things in which you have to act quickly
40. Worry about awful things that might happen
41. Slow and unhurried in the way you move
42. Ever been late for an appointment or work
43. Have nightmares
44. Like talking to people so much that you never miss a chance of talking to a stranger
45. Be very unhappy if you could not see lots of people most of the time
46. Call yourself a nervous person
47. Troubled by aches and pains
48. Of all the people you know there are some whom you definitely do not like
49. Fairly self-confident
50. Easily hurt when people find fault with you or your work
51. Find it hard to really enjoy yourself at a lively party
52. Troubled with feelings of inferiority
53. Easily get some life into a rather dull party
54. Sometimes talk about things you know nothing about
55. Worry about your health
56. Like playing pranks on others
57. Suffer from sleeplessness
58. Like plenty of excitement and bustle around you
59. Often have a restless feeling that you want something but do not know what
60. Nearly always have a 'ready answer' when people talk to you
61. You sometimes feel happy, sometimes sad, without any real reason
62. You usually stay in the background at parties and 'get-togethers'
63. As a child you always did as you were told immediately and without grumbling
64. You sometimes sulk
65. When you are drawn into a quarrel, you prefer to 'have it out' to being silent hoping things will blow over
66. Moody
67. Like mixing with people
68. Often lost sleep over your worries
69. Sometimes get cross
70. Call yourself happy-go-lucky
71. Often make up your mind too late
72. Like working alone

TABLE 15.1 (*contd.*)

73. Often felt listless and tired for no good reason
74. Rather lively
75. Sometimes laugh at a dirty joke
76. Often feel 'fed-up'
77. Feel uncomfortable in anything but everyday clothes
78. Your mind often wanders when you are trying to attend closely to something
79. Put your thoughts into words quickly
80. Often 'lost in thought'
81. Completely free from prejudices of any kind
82. Like practical jokes
83. Often think of your past
84. Very much like good food
85. When you get annoyed you need someone friendly to talk about it to
86. Mind selling things or asking people for money for some good cause
87. Sometimes boast a little
88. Touchy about some things
89. Rather be at home on your own than go to a boring party
90. Sometimes get so restless that you cannot sit long in a chair
91. Like planning things carefully, well ahead of time
92. Have 'dizzy turns'
93. *Always* answer a personal letter as soon as you can after you have read it
94. Usually do things better by figuring them out alone than by talking to others about it
95. Ever get short of breath without having done heavy work
96. An easy-going person, not generally bothered about having everything 'just-so'
97. Suffer from 'nerves'
98. Rather plan things than do things
99. Sometimes put off until tomorrow what you ought to do today
100. Get nervous in places like lifts, trains or tunnels
101. When you make new friends, it is usually *you* who makes the first move, or does the inviting
102. Get very bad headaches
103. Generally feel that things will sort themselves out and come right in the end somehow
104. Find it hard to fall asleep at bed-time
105. Sometimes told lies in your life
106. Sometimes say the first thing that comes into your head
107. Worry too long after an embarrassing experience
108. Usually keep 'yourself to yourself' except with very close friends
109. Often get into a jam, because you do things without thinking
110. Like cracking jokes and telling funny stories to your friends
111. Rather win than lose a game
112. Often feel self-conscious when you are with superiors
113. When the odds are against you, you still usually think it worth taking a chance
114. Often get 'butterflies in your tummy' before an important occasion

To obtain scales representing the most up to date thinking of Cattell and Guilford it would have been possible to collect items from reports appearing in the literature. However, this would have the disadvantage of (a) being restricted to analyses that had already appeared in the literature and being unable to make use of unpublished material, and (b) it would involve a certain amount of subjective decision on the part of the writers in interpreting the relative merits of different items. Accordingly we preferred to have Guilford and Cattell, respectively, make the choice of items themselves and consequently wrote to both authors soliciting their co-operation in this study and asking them to select (a) those primary personality factors which they considered from their own work to be the most firmly established, and (b) to select items to measure each of these factors which, again from their own work, they considered to have the highest loadings for these factors.

Cattell's work is represented by 15 scales comprising 99 items; it was considered best to leave out his scale dealing with intelligence, as this would not be expected to give any great discrimination among the subjects of this study. Guilford's work is represented by 13 scales containing 109 items. These two scales are reprinted below and we finally give another list showing the numbers of items included in each of the subscales for the Cattell and Guilford scales. The items constituting each inventory were reproduced in booklet form for administration. Each inventory had its own instructions printed at the top of the front page; these instructions are reproduced together with the inventories below.

TABLE 15.2

The following items have been paraphrased by permission of R. B. Cattell and I.P.A.T. To enable the reader to trace the actual items used the number and form of each item in the Cattell 16 PF scales are given in connection with each item. Starred items come from the 1962 edition, the others from the 1966 edition.

CATTELL INVENTORY

The following items deal with:

94B. 1. Guilt feelings
120B. 2. Attitudes to work methods
176B. 3. Occupational preferences
*141B. 4. Kinds of stories preferred as a child
114A. 5. Chance remarks made for effect
142B. 6. Extent of personal involvement in discussion on world affairs, etc.
34B. 7. Attitudes to how leisure time is best spent
116A. 8. Nervous habits
148A. 9. Attitude to authority
8B. 10. Dislike of jocularity
56A. 11. Wariness of possible dangers in unfamiliar surroundings

TABLE 15.2 (*contd.*)

119B.	12.	Moodiness
167B.	13.	Ways of dealing with difficult people
158A.	14.	Choice of recreation
21B.	15.	Preference for active games
*31A.	16.	Inability to brazen out a lie
163A.	17.	Subject preferences at school
*23A.	18.	Obsessional behaviour
139B.	19.	Optimism
86B.	20.	Ease of expression
*19B.	21.	Frustration tolerance
16A.	22.	Choice of employment
50B.	23.	Tiredness on waking
107B.	24.	Inhibitions in talking about sex
115A.	25.	Occupational preference
181B.	26.	Loudness of voice
9B.	27.	Attitudes to energies spent on social work
162A.	28.	Active versus passive ways of getting things done
74B.	29.	Ideas coming into one's mind
25B.	30.	Restlessness
46B.	31.	Preference for magazine articles of different kinds
109A.	32.	'Crossing bridges when one meets them' approach to work
62A.	33.	Topographical ability
*113B.	34.	Doubts about truthfulness in others
171A.	35.	Preference of learning methods
27B.	36.	Preference of reading matter
9A.	37.	Whether to interfere in quarrels
*28C.	38.	Attributes in choice of friends
61A.	39.	Difficulties in lecturing
142A.	40.	Types of holidays preferred
149B.	41.	Degree of emotional arousal evoked by occurrences
135A.	42.	Self rating on sociability
51A.	43.	Occupational preference
141A.	44.	Fear of catching diseases
32B.	45.	Fear of being tempted to use weapons
4A.	46.	Ability to deal with problems
26B.	47.	Occupational preference
145B.	48.	Social attitudes
136A.	49.	Showing one's feelings easily
113A.	50.	Need to expose an unfair person
183B.	51.	Carefreeness (self rating)
93A.	52.	Reaction to being slighted
*184B.	53.	Admitting regard for clever crooks
66B.	54.	Need for fresh air
45A.	55.	Social attitudes
38B.	56.	Mistrusting people
10A.	57.	Sociability
81B.	58.	Feeling uncomfortable with domestic employees
92A.	59.	Making one's point, at all costs

155B. 60. Attitudes to the motivation of lawyers
5B. 61. Undue worries intruding on thoughts
129B. 62. Frustration tolerance
80A. 63. Feeling unappreciated
172A. 64. Independence
99B. 65. Lack of concentration
88A. 66. Negativism towards forceful people
112A. 67. Occupational preference
97A. 68. Enjoying organizing things
27A. 69. Taking an active part in social affairs
92B. 70. Regarding a ruthless person with tolerance
29B. 71. Number of past regrets
*21A. 72. Changeable tastes and habits
26A. 73. Occupational preference
20B. 74. Verbalizing criticisms at restaurants
68B. 75. Mood resilience
72A. 76. Need for appreciation
126A. 77. Occupational preference
87A. 78. Reading matter preference
83B. 79. Need for a lot of social stimulation
56A. 80. Feelings of superiority
161A. 81. Self consciousness
123A. 82. Moods of feeling sorry for oneself
*66A. 83. Being thought soft-hearted
*38A. 84. Considering others odd
124B. 85. Psychosomatic symptoms under stress
51B. 86. Occupational preference
*66D. 87. Choice of recreations
41A. 88. Urges for physical work-out
33A. 89. Being considered eloquent
116B. 90. Being considered unworldly
*76D. 91. Optimism
*17B. 92. Needing frequent breaks for work efficiency
112B. 93. Occupational preference
84A. 94. Being considered happy-go-lucky
58A. 95. Frequency of social outings
151A. 96. Occupational preference
12B. 97. Reading matter preference
79A. 98. Feeling unwanted by others
47A. 99. Childhood activities

TABLE 15.2a

A	3, 36, 43, 47, 73, 77, 86, 96
C	33, 46, 61, 62, 63, 71, 98
E	11, 16, 26, 45, 60, 80
F	10, 14, 24, 51, 79, 89, 95
G	7, 27, 32, 37, 35, 94
H	20, 39, 42, 49, 57, 81

TABLE 15.2a (*cont.*)

I	17, 67, 74, 78, 87, 93, 97
L	34, 50, 56, 66, 84, 91
M	4, 6, 13, 25, 38, 55, 90
N	54, 58, 59, 83, 88, 92
O	1, 12, 19, 21, 52, 75
Q	2, 5, 15, 28, 31, 48, 72
Q_2	35, 68, 69, 70, 76, 85, 99
Q_3	9, 18, 22, 40, 44, 64, 82
Q_4	8, 23, 29, 30, 41, 65
A_e	5, 8, 13, 16, 18, 19, 24, 27, 28, 30, 36, 37, 39, 45, 61, 64, 68, 70, 72, 73, 74, 78, 81, 88, 91

TABLE 15.3

The following items have been paraphrased by permission of J. P. Guilford and the Sheridan Supply Company. To enable the reader to trace the actual items used the number and trait letters of the Guilford STDCR, GAMIN and OAgCo scales have been given in connection with each item. Starred items from the GAMIN inventory come from the complete edition of that inventory; non-starred items from the abbreviated edition.

Guilford Inventory

The following items deal with:

OAgCo 125.	1.	Honesty being a matter of fear of consequences
STDCR 137.	2.	Resentfulness when thwarted
OAgCo 83.	3.	Extreme dislike of a person or people
GAMIN 29.	4.	Self confidence
STDCR 77.	5.	Playing jokes or tricks on others
OAgCo 55.	6.	Touchiness
OAgCo 93.	7.	Trusting others
STDCR 143.	8.	Worry about losing in sports
OAgCo 59.	9.	Sympathizing with others
GAMIN 91.	10.	Arguing at meetings
*GAMIN.	11.	Sweating when roused emotionally
STDCR 2.	12.	Limiting circle of friends
STDCR 162.	13.	Easily aroused anger
OAgCo 50.	14.	Purported belligerence of others
STDCR 65.	15.	Mood changes
GAMIN 90.	16.	Feeling that one's merits are unrecognized by others
*GAMIN	17.	Restlessness when involved in inactive work
OAgCo 65.	18.	Belief that others mostly avoid duties if they can
STDCR 14.	19.	Worries over awful things that might occur
OAgCo 25.	20.	Belief that forgiving people deserve to be tricked
GAMIN 84.	21.	Ability to relax
STDCR 130.	22.	Concern if deprived of many friends and acquaintances
GAMIN 74.	23.	Ease of startle response
OAgCo 47.	24.	Tendency to be easily offended
OAgCo 41.	25.	Judging others as foolish

GAMIN 121. 26. Undue sensitivity to scraping sounds
OAgCo 81. 27. Ability to take it calmly when found fault with
OAgCo. 132. 28. Wanting to snub people who interfere with one's affairs
GAMIN 172. 29. Distractibility when working
STDCR 46. 30. Over carefulness
OAgCo 44. 31. Aggression when provoked
GAMIN 64. 32. Occupational preference (One masculine, one feminine)
GAMIN 83. 33. Feeling that one is not as good or capable as others
GAMIN 143. 34. Apprehensiveness at not being popular
GAMIN 99. 35. Working quickly but productively
GAMIN 171. 36. Frequent bouts of energy
STDCR 139. 37. Preference for leisure activities with or without friends
STDCR 13. 38. A carefree attitude to life
GAMIN 34. 39. Ability to get out of scrapes
STDCR 159. 40. Undue tiredness
GAMIN 52. 41. Feeling that one is not getting on as well as others
OAgCo 87. 42. Strong objections to being dictated to by next of kin and acquaintances
GAMIN 21. 43. Personal tempo of work and play
GAMIN 118. 44. Expressing beliefs at meetings when opposed to speaker
STDCR 170. 45. Feeling that things are never all that bad
OAgCo 112. 46. Resentment at being dictated to
OAgCo 140. 47. General compassion for nations
STDCR 105. 48. Periods of doing nothing but thinking or ruminating
GAMIN 112. 49. Attitudes to lack of personal hygiene in others
OAgCo 75. 50. Success achieved by constant vigilance
*GAMIN 51. Physical prowess and stamina
STDCR 41. 52. Occurrence of feeling fed-up
GAMIN 95. 53. Occupational preference (one masculine, one feminine)
GAMIN 122. 54. Ability to think of a 'ready defence' when necessary
STDCR 113. 55. Seriousness in attitude to work
STDCR 4. 56. Judgement of self as happy-go-lucky
OAgCo 53. 57. Belief that rich people get a fairer legal hearing
GAMIN 92. 58. Sleeplessness
GAMIN 135. 59. Wanting to do shooting sports
GAMIN 151. 60. Habit of hurrying from one task to another
GAMIN 30. 61. Enjoying activities requiring fast action
GAMIN 109. 62. Restlessness
STDCR 64. 63. Thoughts wandering
STDCR 110. 64. Liking funny rather than straight films
GAMIN 180. 65. Preference for social evening rather than boxing match
STDCR 85. 66. Need for privacy to meditate
STDCR 22. 67. Mood swings
*GAMIN 68. Frequent yearning for extra money
STDCR 156. 69. Wondering about motivation of other people's actions
STDCR 150. 70. Number of social outings
GAMIN 102. 71. Attitude to smell of sweat in others
GAMIN 120. 72. Compassion for injured animals
STDCR 99. 73. Enjoying talking of philosophical matters with others

TABLE 15.3 (*contd.*)

OAgCo 144.	74.	Belief that the majority need a person to guide or instruct them
GAMIN 104.	75.	Habits such as doodling or tapping
STDCR 161.	76.	Frequent discussions of the meaning of life
STDCR 166.	77.	Sociability
STDCR 171.	78.	Feeling uncomfortable in the presence of others
STDCR 122.	79.	Wanting to see as few people as possible
STDCR 165.	80.	General good health
STDCR 47.	81.	Need for constant stimulation and bustle
GAMIN 162.	82.	Wanting to be more robust
OAgCo 74.	83.	Feeling that matters are more satisfactory if attended to personally
STDCR 140.	84.	Generally feeling well and happy
STDCR 126.	85.	Believing one's future to be bright
STDCR 68.	86.	Frequently wondering why people do the things they do
GAMIN 16.	87.	Embarrassment at sitting in front row at meetings
OAgCo 77.	88.	Belief that possibilities to do well are as good now as 50 years ago
STDCR 173.	89.	Unhappy about introspecting
STDCR 76.	90.	Ability to stay happy even though one has problems
GAMIN 185.	91.	Willingness to challenge someone who cheats
STDCR 117.	92.	Sleeplessness over troubles
OAgCo 82.	93.	Finding out limitations of an expert
GAMIN 10.	94.	Inability to turn away unwanted Salesmen
GAMIN 72.	95.	Compassion for animals
GAMIN 152.	96.	Holding one's own when one's rights are threatened
STDCR 9.	97.	Improving work when told one has done well
OAgCo 43.	98.	Belief that others try not to associate with one
GAMIN 127.	99.	Nervous habits
GAMIN 58.	100.	Fear of dark
STDCR 138.	101.	Fluctuation of mood
GAMIN 160.	102.	Undue dislike of persistent sounds
GAMIN 139.	103.	Wish to alter one's looks
GAMIN 69.	104.	Fear of certain animals
GAMIN 105.	105.	Rushing to get somewhere although not pressed
GAMIN 111.	106.	Belief that often others dislike one
OAgCo 32.	107.	Belief that there is a great need for reform in traffic rules
STDCR 118.	108.	Liking to get together with others
OAgCo 21.	109.	Fears that someone may 'tune in' to one by telepathy

TABLE 15.3a

A	10, 39, 44, 54, 87, 91, 94, 96
A_g	3, 20, 25, 28, 31, 42, 46, 74
C	2, 8, 13, 15, 45, 63, 67, 97, 101
C_o	1, 7, 18, 50, 57, 83, 88, 93, 107
D	19, 40, 52, 80, 84, 85, 90, 92
G	17, 35, 36, 43, 51, 60, 61, 105
I	4, 16, 33, 34, 41, 68, 82, 103, 106

M	32, 49, 53, 59, 65, 71, 72, 95, 100, 104
N	11, 21, 23, 26, 29, 58, 62, 75, 99, 102
O	6, 9, 14, 24, 27, 47, 98, 109
R	5, 30, 38, 55, 56, 64, 81
S	12, 22, 37, 70, 77, 78, 79, 108
T	48, 66, 69, 73, 76, 86, 89
A_c	1, 11, 16, 18, 22, 30, 47, 49, 55, 58, 65, 77, 83, 89, 90, 94, 95, 101, 108

It seemed desirable to have some measure of acquiescence response set included in the inventories, and accordingly three separate acquiescence response set scales were constructed for the three questionnaires. We proceeded as follows. Any item which was supposed to be responded to by 'no' in order to count for one of the personality dimensions and was following another item required to be answered 'yes' was considered an element in the acquiescence scale. The subject was given a score of 1 if this item elicited a 'yes' response. Thus the Eysenck Inventory was scored for acquiescence on a scale comprising 7 items, the Cattell Inventory on a scale comprising 25 items and the Guilford Inventory on a scale comprising 19 items. The numbers of the actual items used in each case are indicated in the key numbers, names and abbreviations of the 43 scales comprised below.

TABLE 15.4

Factor numbers and names, as well as abbreviations, for Eysenck, Cattell and Guilford factors

Eysenck Personality Inventory		
1	Mood swings	M
2	Sociability	Soc
3	Jocularity	J
4	Impulsiveness	Imp
5	Sleeplessness	Sl
6	Inferiority feelings	Inf
7	Liveliness	L
8	Nervousness	N
9	Irritability	Irr
10	Sensitivity	Sens
11	Lie Scale A	Lie A
12	Lie Scale B	Lie B
13	Acquiescence	Ac 1
Cattell Personality Inventory		
14	Cyclothymic	A
15	Ego-strength	C
16	Dominance	E
17	Surgency	F
81	Superego-strength	G

TABLE 15.4 (*contd.*)

19	Parmia	H
20	Premsia	I
21	Protension	L
22	Autia	M
23	Sophistication	N
24	Guilt proneness	O
25	Liberalism	Q 1
26	Self-sufficiency	Q 2
27	Self-sentiment control	Q 3
28	Ergic Tension	Q 4
29	Acquiescence	Ac 2
Guilford Personality Inventory		
30	Ascendency	A
31	Agreeableness	Ag
32	Cycloid	C
33	Co-operativeness	Co
34	Depression	D
35	Activity	G
36	Lack of inferiority	I
37	Masculinity	M
38	Lack of nervousness	N
39	Objectivity	O
40	Rhathymia	R
41	Social shyness	S
42	Introspectiveness	T
43	Acquiescence	Ac 3

These scales were administered to volunteer subjects, nearly all of them English, and ranging in age from 18 to 40 years; the majority were below 30. Six hundred of the subjects were males, 600 were females. All females and most of the males were students in Training Colleges. However, a sizeable proportion of the male sample were either students in technical colleges or worked as technicians in the British Aircraft Corporation. Administration was anonymous and carried out in group form. One and the same tester (M. I. Soueif) carried out all the testing. Co-operation was excellent and from the very many requests which were received for scores on the personality questionnaires by the subjects it would seem that motivation to answer truthfully must have been reasonably high. It could not of course be claimed that this population was in any sense representative of the total population of Great Britain; those who took part in this experiment were younger, more intelligent and of a better social class than would be compatible with random sampling. Apart from the difficulty of actually obtaining a random sample for the purpose of filling in such very lengthy questionnaires it should be noted that there are certain advantages to our choice. Experience has shown that older people tend to be more suspicious of 'new fangled ideas' such as having to answer questionnaires of this kind, and tend to refuse far more frequently. Dull, poorly educated and generally lower social groups have shown a tendency in our experience to find questionnaires such as the Guilford and Cattell rather difficult to answer, and they often misunderstand the purpose of the questions. This is partly due to the American phrasing adopted, the use of particular American terms and also to the fact that these questionnaires were constructed for student populations, and are rather difficult to understand for dull and poorly educated subjects. The same argument applied to the Maudsley Personality Inventory, and furnished one of the reasons for simplifying the wording, so that the E.P.I. is now much more readily intelligible to subjects of I.Q.'s down to 80, and with substantial educational deficits. It would have been impossible to administer the three sets of questionnaires to a random sample of the population and retain any hope that they could be understood and filled in properly. While we thus recognize the limits which are placed on any interpretation by this method of selection, we feel that under the circumstances no other choice could have been made.

The scales were intercorrelated and the intercorrelations factor analysed separately for the two sexes. All work was carried out on IBM 7090 computing machines and the steps used in this study were identical with those described in the previous section; it seems unnecessary therefore to give the details again. It will be more advantageous instead to go straight to the discussion of the results.

At the highest order factor level the male sample gives two factors the loadings of which are given in Table 15.5. Inspection of the Table reveals that the first factor is clearly one of extraversion, the second one of neuroticism. For the female sample there is a difference in that three factors emerge at this level (cf. Table 15.6). Two of these are again clearly identifiable as extraversion and neuroticism. The third factor is rather difficult to identify and may be little but an artefact. It has its highest loading on scale 43, i.e. the Guilford acquiescence score, which is of course not a personality scale at all. The Cattell acquiescence score also has a high loading so that the possibility must be contemplated that we are dealing here with a factor identifying acquiescence response set. Against this interpretation speaks the fact that the Eysenck acquiescence scale has no loading on this factor. Furthermore, several personality scales do load this factor in particular Guilford's activity scale, Eysenck's sleeplessness scale, Guilford's cooperativeness scale (negatively), Eysenck's inferiority feeling scale, and Cattell's sophistication scale (negatively). It is difficult to make any psychological sense out of this grouping of scales and the absence of such a factor for the male sample, coupled with the prominence of acquiescence scales in this sample, lead us to suggest tentatively that possibly the suggestion that we are dealing here with a factor revealing response set should not be dismissed out of hand.

When we turn to a comparison of the extraversion and neuroticism factors we find considerable agreement between the two samples. Going through the four quadrants in turn we note that the choleric quadrant is characterized in both cases by the following scales: rhathymia, impulsiveness, protension, dominance, surgency, jocularity, sociability and liveliness; permia and masculinity have similar loadings for extraversion but have a lower loading on neuroticism for the male sample which brings them down into the sanguine quadrant. This is perhaps not surprising; masculinity and parmia (venturesomeness) are considered masculine virtues but feminine vices and consequently may go with a certain degree of neuroticism in women. The same is probably true of ascendency which also has similar loadings on extraversion for the two sexes but has a positive loading on neuroticism for the women and a negative one for the men.

In the melancholic or dysthymic quadrant we also have a considerable amount of agreement. Items prominent here are guilt proneness, depression, ergic tension, mood swings, irritability, cycloid, sleeplessness, nervousness and sensitivity. Inferiority feelings have a loading on neuroticism only in males; perhaps feeling inferior is more natural for women! Autia (bohemianism) has a loading on neuroticism for the women but not for the men; again this sex difference is readily intelligible in our particular culture pattern.

There are relatively few scales in the phlegmatic quadrant; we may note that the two sexes have in common the cyclothymia scale, superego strength, and agreeableness; the two lie scales also seem to lie in this quadrant although with a very low introversion component. As regards the sanguine quadrant the two sexes have the following scales represented here: ego-strength, lack of inferiority, objectivity, lack of nervousness, and liberalism; activity has a loading on extraversion for both sexes but is positively loaded on neuroticism for the men, negatively for the women. It is difficult to see why this should be so; the difference is possibly not large enough to require an explanation until its existence has been demonstrated in connection with new samples of male and female subjects.

There are considerable differences with respect to the acquiescence scales between the sexes. For the men, the Guilford and Cattell acquiescence scales lie close together in the choleric quadrant with reasonably high loadings on neuroticism. The Eysenck scale on the other hand has a high loading on introversion but none on neuroticism. For the women the Cattell acquiescence scale also lies in the choleric quadrant but has loadings so low as to be practically located at the origin. The Guilford acquiescence scale has a moderate loading on neuroticism but it is negative instead of positive. Only the Eysenck acquiescence scale

TABLE 15.5

Primary factor loadings; Men

1	−0·25	0·39
2	+0·60	0·08
3	+0·54	0·27
4	+0·25	0·55
5	−0·27	0·19
6	−0·42	0·24
7	+0·70	0·26
8	−0·41	0·05
9	−0·32	0·39
10	−0·40	0·32
11	+0·03	−0·52
12	−0·04	−0·34
13	−0·60	0·10
14	−0·14	−0·14
15	+0·36	−0·44
16	+0·33	0·06
17	+0·65	0·31
18	−0·20	−0·49
19	+0·44	−0·14
20	−0·45	−0·16
21	+0·15	0·47
22	−0·29	−0·01
23	−0·19	0·01
24	−0·51	0·25
25	+0·00	−0·54
26	−0·43	0·09
27	+0·04	−0·23
28	−0·29	0·39
29	+0·20	0·39
30	+0·49	−0·05
31	−0·11	−0·61
32	−0·25	0·47
33	−0·08	−0·52
34	−0·47	0·25
35	+0·46	0·24
36	+0·28	−0·49
37	+0·35	−0·12
38	+0·24	−0·41
39	+0·26	−0·46
40	+0·65	0·45
41	−0·56	−0·09
42	−0·26	−0·01
43	+0·18	0·41

TABLE 15.6

Primary factor loadings; Women

1	−0·09	0·47	0·19
2	0·53	0·11	0·10
3	0·37	0·15	0.25
4	−0·25	0·50	0·21
5	0·09	0·05	0·49
6	−0·54	−0·11	0·42
7	0·57	0·10	0·28
8	−0·02	0·10	0·23
9	0·08	0·53	0·08
10	−0·36	0·06	0·24
11	−0·11	−0·64	0·15
12	−0·09	−0·41	0·11
13	−0·50	−0·03	−0·05
14	−0·06	−0·16	−0·11
15	0·34	0·37	−0·29
16	0·37	0·31	−0·05
17	0·60	0·32	0·13
18	−0·16	−0·66	0·18
19	0·59	0·10	−0·10
20	−0·44	0·25	−0·29
21	−0·11	0·26	0·33
22	−0·07	0·58	0·35
23	−0·09	0·07	0·04
24	−0·39	0·29	−0·16
25	0·07	0·48	0·08
26	−0·59	0·20	−0·32
27	−0·29	−0·55	0·06
28	−0·19	0·49	0·15
29	0·20	0·07	0·39
30	0·68	0·16	0·02
31	−0·07	−0·37	−0·22
32	−0·04	0·53	0·15
33	0·02	−0·02	−0·42
34	−0·38	0·32	0·18
35	0·58	−0·15	0·66
36	0·51	−0·16	−0·35
37	0·29	0·19	−0·24
38	0·28	−0·14	−0·46
39	0·43	−0·09	−0·26
40	0·47	0·47	0·05
41	−0·48	0·02	−0·13
42	0·07	−0·04	0·16
43	0·05	−0·30	0·71

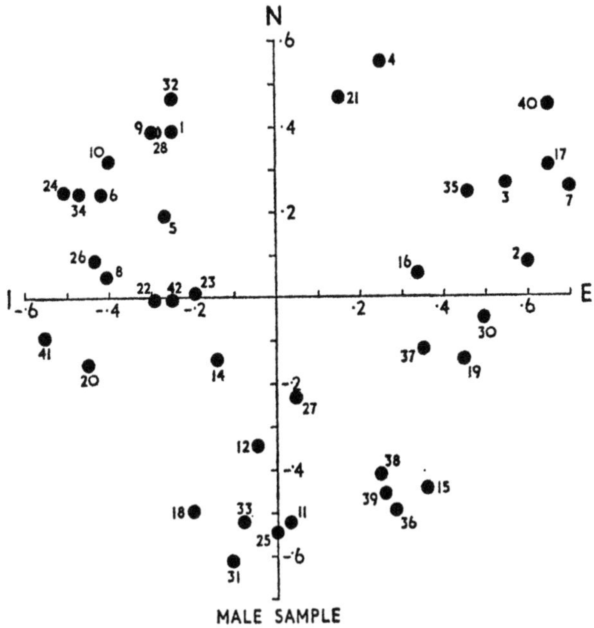

FIG. 15.1 Position of scales on two factor axes, for male subjects.

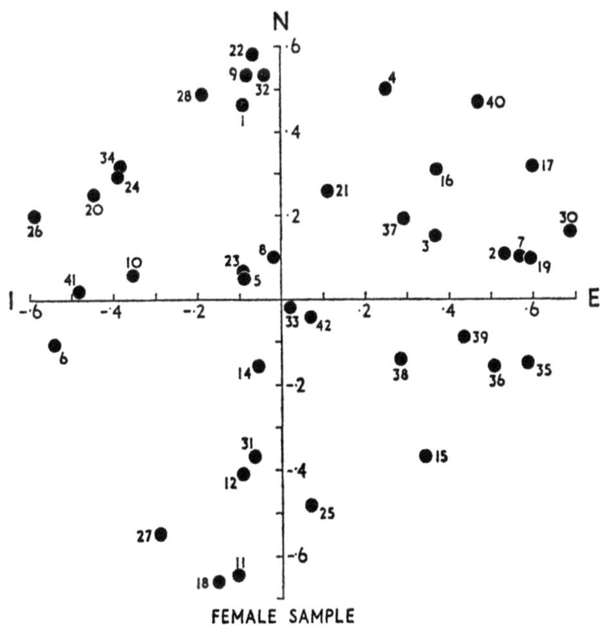

FIG. 15.2 Position of scales on two factor axes, for female subjects.

retains its position with a loading of −0·5 on the extraversion scale. These findings are perhaps in line with our suggestion that for the women the main part of the variance relating the Guilford and Cattell acquiescence scales has been taken over into a third factor. It is impossible from our results to verify this suggestion and it would require a separate experiment or perhaps a repetition of the present one to demonstrate to what extent our results are replicable. The items chosen for the acquiescence scale on the Eysenck questionnaire probably include too many extraversion-introversion questions to be considered free of content contamination; this may account for their having high loadings on this factor and giving results quite different from the Cattell and Guilford acquiescence scales. (The acquiescence scales have not been plotted in Figures 15.1 and 15.2, in order to keep the picture clearer as far as the proper personality scales are concerned.)

As far as the lie scales are concerned agreement between sexes is very high. Both scales have high negative loadings on neuroticism with the A scale in each case having higher loadings than the B scale; the slight loadings of both scales on the extraversion scale (negative) may be disregarded as being too small to be worthy of consideration. Can these loadings be interpreted as reflecting a desirability response set? We have already discussed experiments devoted to an investigation of this possibility and our conclusion then was that social desirability response set probably plays only a small part in the genesis of the neuroticism factor. No direct data are available to support this interpretation in connection with the present experiment but equally there is no good reason for assuming that different motivational factors were active in this experiment as compared with the previous one. The possibility arises that neurotic people as compared with unemotional stable people are in fact worse behaved in terms of the lie scale items, so that stable people are able to respond in the socially desirable sense more frequently than are neurotics, even though both groups are strictly telling the truth in each case. Possibly both social desirability and true behavioural differences may have played a part in producing the results we observe in these two factor analyses.

In interpreting the results of this study the reader should of course consult in each case the actual questions making up each of these questionnaires; simply to take the brief description of the scale afforded by its title as representing in fact the content of the scale may not be very reliable. To take but one example, it will be seen that in both the male and the female analysis Guilford's cycloid scale has a high positive loading on neuroticism whereas Cattell's cyclothymia scale has a low negative loading on this factor. This does not indicate an unreliability in the analysis but merely a different interpretation given to this very ill-defined term by these two writers. However, even interpreting the results of our two analyses simply in terms of the titles of the scales will show that on the whole our main contention is strikingly supported, namely that two independent factors resembling neuroticism and extraversion will emerge from our analysis of the intercorrelation of these three sets of scales. Our analysis enables us to calculate correlations between the final two factors; for the men this correlation is +0·16 for the women it is −0·10. These correlations are sufficiently near to zero as well as being in opposite directions to enable us to say that any departure from orthogonality for these two factors could only be very slight.

It may be interesting to retrace the growth of these uncorrelated super factors through the preliminary phases of correlated primary factors. Ten such factors were extracted for the men, and their loadings are given in Table 15.7. It will be seen that much the greatest portion of the variance is carried by the first two factors which are unambiguously identified as neuroticism and extraversion. The other factors are mainly doublets and perhaps of no great psychological interest. Factor 3 couples premsia and autia; Factor 4 opposes super-ego strength and rhathymia. Factor 5 opposes protension, i.e. paranoid suspiciousness, to agreeableness and co-operativeness, which is not perhaps unreasonable. Factor 6 couples the two lie scales for Forms A and B. Factor 7 has its main loading on the Cattell acquiescence scale. Factor 8 couples dominance, ascendency and masculinity. Factor 9 opposes sophistication to liberalism, as defined by the Cattell scales, and Factor 10 links sleeplessness and nervousness.

We may compare these results with those obtained from the females from whom also ten factors were extracted. These are given in Table 15.8. Here too the overwhelming weight of the variance is contributed by the first two factors identified respectively as neuroticism and extraversion. The third factor links the two lie scales of Forms A and B. The fourth opposes masculinity and dominance to cyclothymia. The fifth again opposes protension to agreeableness and co-operativeness. The sixth is largely made up of the acquiescence scale of Cattell. The seventh factor loads almost entirely on introspectiveness. The eighth is a doublet made up of premsia and autia. Factor 9 loads almost entirely on sophistication, and Factor 10 on sleeplessness as opposed to lack of nervousness. On the whole there is considerable similarity between the two solutions with only very occasional slight differences between them.

For the men, but not for the women, we next reach an intermediate stage, where four second order factors are extracted; there is nothing corresponding in the women's analysis who proceed straight from the ten first order factors to three second order factors or super factors. For the men we proceed from the original 10 first order factors to 4 second order factors and then to the two super factors we have already noted, which are therefore properly speaking third order factors. There is no obvious hypothesis as to these differences in number of levels. As

TABLE 15.7

1	−0·89	0·00	0·10	0·01	−0·02	−0·05	0·05	0·15	0·04	0·04
2	0·05	−0·84	0·07	0·07	−0·09	0·13	−0·12	−0·01	−0·04	−0·04
3	−0·07	−0·67	0·02	−0·38	−0·08	0·06	−0·05	−0·05	−0·02	0·06
4	−0·33	−0·42	−0·02	−0·37	0·07	−0·02	0·12	−0·03	0·12	−0·03
5	−0·16	−0·03	−0·01	−0·03	−0·11	−0·07	0·15	0·04	0·06	−0·71
6	−0·59	0·17	0·01	0·09	−0·02	−0·10	0·21	−0·24	−0·10	0·06
7	0·20	−0·71	−0·01	−0·07	0·11	−0·02	0·16	−0·00	0·06	−0·00
8	−0·17	0·02	−0·05	0·05	−0·12	−0·09	−0·10	0·01	0·07	−0·68
9	−0·82	−0·00	0·13	−0·06	0·03	0·10	−0·20	0·26	−0·00	−0·19
10	−0·58	0·01	0·05	0·22	−0·01	0·08	0·04	−0·18	0·03	−0·08
11	0·09	0·08	−0·04	0·13	0·06	−0·83	0·02	0·02	−0·13	−0·08
12	0·03	0·14	−0·08	0·17	0·07	−0·83	0·14	−0·00	0·15	−0·06
13	−0·01	0·78	0·03	0·21	0·05	0·41	0·19	−0·05	0·08	0·11
14	−0·18	−0·30	−0·42	0·46	−0·01	−0·10	−0·28	−0·08	0·08	0·16
15	0·45	−0·10	0·08	0·17	−0·18	0·07	−0·07	0·13	0·03	0·04
16	−0·05	−0·01	−0·08	−0·09	0·30	0·02	−0·10	0·76	−0·01	−0·00
17	0·04	−0·80	−0·02	−0·21	−0·01	0·15	0·01	0·05	−0·00	−0·04
18	0·01	0·10	0·11	0·69	−0·11	−0·12	−0·08	−0·08	−0·09	0·03
19	0·14	−0·53	−0·04	0·29	−0·08	0·13	−0·10	0·33	0·00	−0·15
20	−0·07	0·00	−0·78	0·22	−0·08	−0·10	−0·20	−0·13	0·05	0·08
21	−0·04	0·07	−0·01	−0·15	0·78	−0·02	−0·04	0·17	−0·17	0·10
22	0·15	0·02	−0·80	−0·21	−0·01	−0·04	−0·16	0·07	0·08	−0·15
23	0·03	0·17	0·09	0·14	0·15	−0·02	−0·50	0·07	0·52	0·05
24	−0·84	0·11	−0·02	0·12	−0·11	−0·02	−0·05	−0·06	0·01	0·06
25	0·04	0·07	0·13	0·22	0·13	0·02	−0·28	0·04	−0·82	0·12
26	0·28	0·38	0·01	−0·27	0·13	0·08	−0·21	−0·21	0·08	−0·41
27	0·08	−0·08	0·54	0·38	−0·03	−0·01	−0·23	−0·19	0·01	−0·09
28	−0·48	−0·02	−0·21	−0·19	−0·04	0·17	0·04	−0·10	−0·06	0·02
29	0·01	0·13	0·14	−0·33	−0·20	−0·07	0·89	−0·10	0·24	0·01
30	0·23	−0·15	−0·05	0·05	0·14	−0·02	0·18	0·58	0·03	−0·10
31	0·12	−0·05	−0·03	0·06	−0·21	−0·05	0·11	−0·23	−0·07	−0·07
32	−0·81	−0·00	−0·01	−0·01	0·02	0·04	0·08	0·23	0·10	−0·04
33	−0·01	−0·11	−0·02	0·10	−0·90	0·12	0·12	−0·09	0·01	−0·06
34	−0·66	0·14	0·02	0·01	−0·01	−0·11	−0·01	0·09	−0·04	−0·33
35	−0·14	−0·25	0·18	0·10	0·12	−0·09	0·49	0·26	−0·02	0·01
36	0·49	−0·02	−0·04	0·11	−0·20	0·02	−0·00	0·32	−0·03	−0·14
37	−0·06	0·07	0·14	−0·36	−0·10	−0·07	0·04	0·56	−0·03	0·09
38	0·35	0·17	0·06	0·09	−0·08	−0·07	−0·02	0·22	0·14	0·31
39	0·37	0·09	0·02	−0·15	−0·22	−0·08	−0·01	0·24	−0·05	0·09
40	0·08	−0·49	0·02	−0·54	0·17	0·02	0·11	0·06	0·09	0·16
41	−0·02	0·80	−0·04	−0·16	0·14	−0·07	−0·00	0·11	−0·06	−0·07
42	0·04	0·28	−0·45	0·21	0·05	0·10	0·28	0·22	−0·04	−0·08
43	0·08	−0·28	0·10	0·24	0·39	−0·07	0·32	−0·33	0·02	−0·11

TABLE 15.8

1	0·83	0·14	0·10	0·13	0·17	0·02	0·06	−0·10	0·03	0·09
2	0·06	0·91	0·04	−0·20	0·07	−0·11	0·05	0·02	0·07	−0·09
3	0·05	0·53	0·16	0·14	0·08	−0·02	0·23	−0·10	−0·14	0·18
4	0·34	0·55	−0·09	0·14	−0·02	0·21	0·15	0·11	−0·18	−0·07
5	0·05	−0·00	−0·02	0·10	0·02	−0·09	−0·12	0·16	−0·04	0·78
6	0·37	−0·14	−0·13	−0·05	0·08	−0·02	0·10	0·03	−0·44	0·07
7	−0·14	0·78	−0·09	0·02	−0·14	−0·02	−0·05	0·11	−0·17	0·07
8	0·35	−0·01	−0·22	−0·14	−0·04	0·07	−0·25	−0·06	0·44	0·38
9	0·84	0·09	0·17	0·04	−0·05	0·00	−0·04	−0·15	0·13	−0·12
10	0·50	−0·14	−0·00	−0·10	−0·06	−0·05	−0·27	0·04	−0·36	−0·19
11	−0·12	0·04	−0·74	0·00	0·19	−0·03	0·05	−0·09	0·08	0·04
12	−0·24	−0·07	−0·79	0·05	0·09	0·20	−0·08	0·13	−0·05	−0·01
13	−0·00	−0·88	0·25	−0·04	−0·20	0·03	−0·23	−0·03	−0·06	0·02
14	−0·08	0·40	0·22	−0·58	−0·01	−0·32	−0·15	0·19	0·08	−0·05
15	−0·35	0·07	0·08	−0·08	0·20	−0·01	−0·07	−0·20	0·10	−0·20
16	0·05	0·16	−0·13	0·63	−0·35	−0·30	−0·06	0·07	0·16	0·01
17	0·01	0·76	0·22	−0·05	−0·05	0·02	0·01	0·03	−0·01	0·08
18	0·14	−0·10	−0·16	−0·12	0·08	−0·40	−0·28	−0·28	−0·03	−0·02
19	−0·01	0·68	−0·10	0·06	0·05	−0·15	−0·28	0·16	0·06	−0·11
20	−0·18	−0·07	−0·12	−0·05	0·17	−0·08	−0·15	0·84	−0·22	0·13
21	−0·16	−0·13	0·15	0·01	−0·78	0·05	−0·12	−0·05	0·05	0·13
22	0·01	0·14	0·08	0·07	0·12	−0·07	−0·24	0·75	−0·02	0·12
23	0·06	−0·12	−0·01	−0·06	−0·12	−0·18	0·23	−0·13	0·73	−0·02
24	0·84	−0·09	0·07	−0·04	0·24	−0·02	−0·04	−0·05	−0·01	0·08
25	−0·20	−0·11	0·25	0·28	0·11	−0·56	−0·07	−0·19	−0·12	0·28
26	0·11	−0·50	−0·17	−0·04	−0·14	0·01	0·24	0·17	0·39	−0·06
27	−0·17	0·02	−0·11	−0·25	−0·04	−0·31	0·32	−0·25	0·10	−0·07
28	0·34	0·00	0·27	−0·15	−0·02	0·11	0·02	0·16	0·06	0·32
29	−0·01	−0·18	−0·10	−0·27	0·08	0·96	−0·16	−0·26	0·23	−0·02
30	0·09	0·35	−0·07	0·17	−0·13	0·06	−0·48	−0·07	0·06	−0·16
31	0·08	0·17	−0·27	0·09	0·81	−0·11	0·10	0·08	0·07	0·04
32	0·78	0·08	0·14	0·03	0·04	0·15	−0·11	−0·08	−0·01	−0·07
33	0·02	−0·01	0·06	0·00	0·78	0·16	−0·12	0·22	−0·10	−0·02
34	0·65	−0·18	−0·04	0·04	0·06	−0·04	−0·02	0·02	0·21	0·31
35	0·03	0·42	−0·13	0·17	−0·15	0·09	−0·28	−0·27	−0·32	0·19
36	−0·55	0·05	0·03	−0·03	0·12	0·13	−0·27	0·05	0·21	−0·02
37	0·01	−0·09	0·05	0·80	0·13	−0·22	0·03	0·01	−0·10	−0·04
38	−0·19	−0·03	−0·09	0·14	0·12	0·09	−0·04	−0·11	−0·03	−0·61
39	−0·32	0·03	−0·03	0·21	0·23	0·12	0·10	−0·15	0·34	0·13
40	0·03	0·41	0·25	0·10	−0·10	0·29	0·23	−0·10	−0·05	−0·09
41	−0·02	−0·87	−0·08	0·32	−0·15	0·04	−0·08	0·07	−0·07	−0·05
42	0·01	−0·17	−0·00	−0·07	−0·03	0·03	−0·80	0·25	−0·27	0·11
43	−0·16	0·35	−0·23	−0·39	−0·25	0·12	0·00	−0·10	−0·09	0·42

TABLE 15.9

Primary factor loadings

1	0·50	0·11	−0·10	−0·01
2	−0·11	−0·65	−0·03	−0·03
3	−0·01	−0·29	0·01	−0·40
4	0·39	−0·17	−0·10	−0·33
5	0·54	−0·01	0·12	0·17
6	0·61	0·26	0·14	0·04
7	0·04	−0·72	−0·03	−0·14
8	0·38	0·15	0·07	0·24
9	0·48	0·17	−0·14	0·02
10	0·56	0·10	−0·09	0·19
11	−0·24	0·17	0·51	−0·07
12	−0·18	0·14	0·26	0·00
13	0·21	0·33	−0·26	0·32
14	0·01	−0·03	−0·12	0·54
15	−0·58	−0·28	0·06	0·09
16	−0·12	−0·43	−0·15	0·09
17	0·07	−0·64	−0·05	−0·18
18	−0·23	−0·07	0·12	0·47
19	−0·22	−0·74	−0·08	0·35
20	0·22	−0·06	−0·02	0·60
21	0·44	−0·17	−0·06	−0·20
22	0·24	−0·05	−0·02	0·35
23	−0·53	0·30	−0·61	0·05
24	0·50	0·30	−0·06	0·14
25	−0·06	0·06	0·64	0·03
26	0·12	0·57	−0·06	−0·14
27	−0·39	0·13	−0·03	−0·05
28	0·59	0·11	−0·03	0·02
29	0·32	−0·09	0·03	−0·31
30	−0·15	−0·67	−0·04	0·18
31	−0·39	0·22	0·34	0·10
32	0·58	−0·02	−0·18	0·10
33	−0·38	0·07	0·18	0·22
34	0·61	0·25	0·07	0·11
35	0·24	−0·62	0·06	−0·00
36	−0·53	−0·30	0·09	0·21
37	−0·38	−0·00	0·05	−0·31
38	−0·74	−0·03	−0·12	−0·00
39	−0·62	0·04	0·14	−0·13
40	0·01	−0·32	−0·12	−0·55
41	0·11	0·65	0·07	−0·02
42	0·40	−0·32	0·03	0·58
43	0·53	−0·43	0·01	0·04

regards the nature of the four second order factors for the men these may be revealed by an inspection of the factor loadings which are given in Table 15.9. The first two factors are again neuroticism and extraversion. The third factor has its main loading on the lie scale with somewhat smaller negative loadings on sophistication and liberalism as defined by the Cattell scales. The fourth factor loads on cyclothymia, super-ego strength, premsia and lack of rhathymia. It is notable that most of these additional scales with the exception of the lie scale are from the Cattell questionnaire. It is interesting that the lie scales have very low loadings in this solution on Factors 1 and 2, i.e. there is here no evidence at all that they are connected with neuroticism or extraversion. It is possible from some points of view, particularly those of facilitating measurement, that this solution may be preferable to the higher order one we have discussed previously, where the lie scales figure quite prominently in the neuroticism factor loadings. We know of no criterion to decide between these possibilities.

All the interpretations given, and the whole discussion of results, hinges in large part on the replicability of the Eysenck, Guilford and Cattell factors which we have scored in order to obtain the various scales. If we may venture to look ahead at the results of analyses to be reported in later chapters, which investigate this very problem, we shall find that in actual fact the Eysenck factors are replicated reasonably well, the Guilford ones only very partially, and the Cattell ones hardly at all. This must mean, of course, that not too much attention should be paid to the outcome of the analyses reported in this section; particularly the position of the Cattell factors, in so far as they have not been replicated, cannot be regarded with much confidence as either supporting or invalidating the general theory with which we are here concerned. The reader will be in a better position to judge the results reported here after perusal of the results given in the next few sections.

16

FACTORS IN THE EYSENCK PERSONALITY INVENTORY

P. O. White, M. I. Soueif and H. J. Eysenck

WE have seen, in the previous section, how the questionnaires of Cattell, Eysenck and Guilford line up with respect to one another when each is scored in terms of a number of *a priori* scales, and the derived scales from the three questionnaires are factored in a single analysis. In this section we describe separate analyses for each of the questionnaires and, in a subsequent section, we will describe an analysis in which factors common to the three questionnaire batteries are determined. This two-stage process enables comparison to be made across questionnaires and requires neither that we factor all 322 questions within a single analysis, (this was not technically feasible at the time the analyses were carried out), or that we define our factors on an *a priori* basis as in the analysis described above.

The questionnaires, the samples, and the testing procedures have all been described in detail above. There were two groups of subjects (600 males and 600 females) and the Cattell (99 items), Eysenck (114 items) and Guilford (109 items) questionnaires were administered to all subjects. The responses to each questionnaire have been analysed separately within sexes making a total of 6 analyses.

Prior to discussing the substantive findings complete technical details of the analyses are now outlined. Since the same procedures were used for all six analyses they are described but once in general terms. To facilitate comparison with other descriptions, we will use the more general term 'variable' rather than item.

(1) Means, standard deviations and variances were computed for each variable.

(2) Product-moment correlations were computed between each pair of variables.

(3) A principal component model rather than an orthodox factor analysis model was utilized. That is to say, unities, rather than communality estimates were placed in the main diagonal. Thus instead of the mutually orthogonal unique factors implied by the latter procedure we imply, for each variable, a residual vector. The reasons for this choice are several. Firstly, the unities might well be considered as rough estimates to the unknown communalities in the factor model. Since it seems fairly generally to be acknowledged (see, for example, Harman, 1960, p. 88) that solutions are relatively insensitive to differences in communality estimates for very large matrices their use might seem justifiable on this basis alone. However, a very much more important reason for their choice is that, by placing unities in the diagonal and thus excluding 'unique' factors from the model, the resultant components, even after oblique rotation, lie within the test space. That is to say, the components are linear composites of the scores on the observed variables. Thus, for each individual a score may be 'computed' for each component and these scores may be correlated with measures outside the particular analysis. In the 'factor' model however, the factors do not lie in the test space. We may compute as their 'estimates' only projections of the factors on to the test space. The point of all this in the present context is that we subsequently make use of the computed component scores in relating the 'factors' (strictly speaking these are rotated principal components) among the three questionnaires. And, finally, our preferred method of communality estimation by refactoring was just not feasible in terms of the amount of computer time then available even if we had not had good reason to keep the factors in the test space.

(4) The number of 'factors' or components retained was dictated as well by several considerations. Firstly, each set of questions was designed, rather carefully, to span with from 6 to 10 marker variables per factor a rather well studied and clearly blocked out domain. The number of factors thus anticipated was at most 15 (for the Cattell questionnaire) for any one questionnaire. In this situation it might at first blush seem reasonable to fix the number of factors for each analysis at the number of factors for which there are markers. This however seems unwise since there is considerable support for the notion that 'under-factoring' may be catastrophic and that the problems due to 'over-factoring' though frequently very irritating may be coped with by thoughtful consideration. These points seem implicit in most of Cattell's writings on the number of factors problem (and have been stated explicitly by Kaiser (1964), for example). The well known 'roots greater

than one' criterion which is the number of latent roots greater than one in the correlation matrix with unit diagonals might be justified on several grounds. It is Guttman's (1954) well known *lower* bound for the number of factors. Further it corresponds identically both to Kaiser's (1962) *upper* bound as the number of factors with positive generalizability (see Cronbach *et al.*, 1963) and to Dickman's (1960) upper bound (on the common sense basis that it does not seem reasonable to accept factors which do not account for greater variance than do the original variables themselves). However, this criterion typically indicates as the number of factors between one-half to one-third the number of variables which, for the present analyses, is more than double the putative number for which the batteries were designed. Further, the computer time necessary for oblique rotation of such large numbers of factors was considered prohibitive. In consequence, the programme was set to retain the minimum of the number of roots greater than one and the number 20. In effect the number of factors was truncated to 20 for all of the first order solutions and the 'roots greater than one' criterion was effective for all higher order solutions. In view of the putative number of factors for the first order analyses this seems to be quite reasonable.

(5) A method suggested by Householder (see Wilkinson, 1960) was used to find an orthogonal similarity transformation to tridiagonalize the correlation matrix. Ortega's (1960) extension of the theory of Sturm sequences was applied to find the latent roots of the tridiagonal matrix, which are also those of the initial matrix. Wilkinson's (1958) method was utilized to compute the latent vectors of the tridiagonal matrix corresponding to roots greater than one and to transform these vectors to those of the original matrix. These latent vectors were then normalized such that, for each vector, the sum of squared elements was equal to the corresponding latent root. This is in accord with the standard metric convention that scores on all 'factors' or components have unit variance. Thus all unrotated solutions were in the standard 'principal axes' (Harman, 1960) form.

(6) Analytic rotation towards orthogonal simple structure was carried out by Kaiser's (1956, 1958) well-known *normalized varimax* procedure and the resultant solutions were transformed towards oblique simple structure using the *promax* procedure of Hendrickson and White (1964) which yields the primary factor pattern (matrix of factor loadings), the primary factor structure (matrix of correlations of variables with oblique factors), and the matrix of interfactor correlations which we shall refer to as the ϕ-matrix.

(7) The ϕ-matrix from the *promax* solution was itself factored using the methods of step 5 to yield a matrix relating the oblique promax factors to a set of orthogonal higher-order factors. This matrix was then pre-multiplied by the matrix of *promax* factor loadings derived

in step 6 to yield an orthogonal factor matrix relating the original variables to the orthogonal higher-order factors. In effect, the higher-order factors were projected onto the original variables.

(8) The matrix just described which relates the original variables to the orthogonal higher-order factors was then itself rotated via *varimax* and then *promax* toward oblique simple structure and yielded a primary factor pattern, a primary factor structure and a ϕ-matrix of intercorrelations among the oblique higher-order factors. This procedure of projecting the orthogonal higher-order factors onto the original varilables *before* rotation is due to Hendrickson and White (1966). It provides more vectors for the determination of the hyperplanes than does the Cattell-White (Cattell & White, 1962; Cattell, 1965) transformation which was formerly our preferred method for determining hierarchical factor solutions. The Cattell-White method rotates the matrix resulting from step 5 toward oblique simple structure and then projects the oblique higher-order factors onto the original variables. Consequently there are, at each rotational stage, markedly fewer vectors to determine the hyperplanes.

(9) Steps 7 and 8 were then repeated to yield solutions in terms of factors of successively higher order until a single higher-order factor was obtained. Thus, for example, in the analysis for the male subjects on the Cattell questionnaire we obtained 20 first-order factors, 7 second-order factors, 3 third-order factors and a single fourth-order factor.

The following set of formulae presents, for the more mathematical reader, the recurrence formulae relating the factors at level i to those at the previous level (i − 1). Equation (i) depicts the decomposition of ϕ_{i-1} into its latent roots and vectors. Equation (ii) indicates the rescaling of the latent vectors into the standard principal axes form. Equation (iii) projects the orthogonal level i factors onto the original variables. Equations (v)−(x) outline the steps in the *varimax*−*promax* transformations. The matrices $\triangle_i$ and D_i are diagonal matrices which rescale

Formulae for Factorization

(i) $\phi_{i-1} = L_i R_i L_i'$

(ii) $F_i = L_i R_i^{\frac{1}{2}}$

(iii) $H_i = A_{i-1} F_i$

(iv) $V_i = f_1(H_i)$

(v) $B_i = f_2(V_i)$

(vi) $\Omega_i = (V_i' V_i)^{-1} V_i' B_i \triangle_i$

(vii) $T_i = (\Omega'_i)^{-1} D_i$

(viii) $\phi_i = T_i' T_i$

(ix) $S_i = V_i T_i$

(x) $A_i = S_i \phi_i^{-1}$

columns so that Ω_i and T_i each are normalized with sums of squares equal to unity. We then increment i by 1 and repeat the cycle. For the first cycle, when $i = 1$, we set $A_0 = I$ (an identity matrix) and set ϕ_0 equal to the original correlation matrix.

It should be noted in passing that the *promax* formulation outlined in the table differs from that described in the Hendrickson-White (1964) paper and from that actually utilized in the programme used for the computations presented. This formulation, due to one of the present authors (P.O.W.), avoids explicit computation of the familiar reference vector structure and its consequent rescaling and thus contributes to a simpler statement of the key relationships involved in the hierarchical formulation. Use of a new *promax* programme (also due to P.O.W.) which implements the alternative formulation has verified that the reformulation is numerically (as well as theoretically) equivalent to the earlier formulation.

(10) Finally, component scores were computed for each individual on each factor or component at each level. The procedure used is now quite standard and is usually attributed to L. R. Tucker. It is outlined by Harman (1960) and will not be described further here.

At this point we consider the procedures which are used to relate the factors or components determined within each of the separate analyses to those determined within the other analyses. Two cases arise. Firstly, the sets of factors to be compared may be based on the same individuals. For example, for the male groups we have three sets of first-order factors determined, respectively, from the Cattell, the Eysenck and the Guilford questions. Since we have utilized the 'unities in the diagonal' model we are able to compute scores for each individual on each factor or component. Thus our task of relating the factors from the different questionnaires is quite straightforward; we have merely to compute directly the cross-correlations between the factor sets. This task will be undertaken in the next section.

The second case, however, is not so straightforward. Here the factors are not based upon the same individuals. For example, we have a set of first-order factors based on the Cattell questions for the male groups and a second set of first order factors, also based on the Cattell questions, but this time for the female groups. We cannot now compute a correlation directly as we did before since our factor scores are not based on the same individuals. Fortunately, H. F. Kaiser has provided what appears to be an adequate solution to the problem and White (1966) has provided a computer programme which implements the procedure. The Kaiser solution is given as the Appendix in this book. It is briefly described below.

The variable and factor vectors of one study are rotated rigidly to yield maximum congruence between the two sets of variable vectors and the cosines between the two sets of factor vectors are computed.

These cosines are interpreted 'as if' they are correlation coefficients and are used as coefficients of factor similarities.

Matrices of such interfactor coefficients are computed at each level on each questionnaire to assess the similarities and differences between the factors obtained for the male and female samples; these are discussed in this section.

In the following tables, factors for men and women are presented in conjunction, the pairing being in every case determined by the size of the factor comparison coefficient. Every factor in the male sample was compared with every factor in the female sample, and the highest congruence determined the pairing, thus eliminating subjective matching completely. Items are given in an abbreviated form, to save space, but the number of the item is always given so that the full form of the statement can be consulted in the appropriate questionnaire. Only items with loadings above 0·30 are given. The direction of each factor is determined by the accident of its extraction, so that as often as not the coefficient of factor comparison is negative; to make factors comparative one of them should then be multiplied by −1. This has not been done in the tables as it is a completely arbitrary step and can easily be done in the mind. The order of the factors and tables is also arbitrary; as far as possible we have chosen to discuss at the beginning the more obvious well-matched factors and leave the others to the end. The factor numbers for the male and female factors denoting the sequence of extraction are given in each Table to make later identification easier. All first-order factors are discussed before we go to on the second-order and higher-order factors.

Factor 1. *Sociability*. This factor is very clearly marked, and is virtually identical for both sexes, with a coefficient of factor similarity (to be abbreviated in future discussions to: C.F.S.) of 0·97.

TABLE 16.1

51	0·08	Do you find it hard to enjoy yourself at a lively party?
25	−0·83	Can you usually let yourself go and enjoy yourself a lot at a gay party?
62	0·78	Do you usually stay in the background at parties and get-togethers?
67	−0·71	Do you like mixing with people?
15	0·61	Generally do you prefer reading to meeting people?
17	−0·57	Do you like going out a lot?
108	0·56	Do you usually keep yourself to yourself except with very close friends?
74	−0·51	Are you rather lively?
27	−0·47	Do other people think of you as being very lively?
29	0·42	Are you mostly quiet when you are with other people?
58	−0·41	Do you like plenty of excitement and bustle around you?
20	0·39	Do you prefer to have few but special friends?

TABLE 16.1 (*contd.*)

53	−0·36	Can you easily get some life into a rather dull party?
101	−0·36	When you make new friends is it usually you who makes the first move or invites?

TABLE 16.2

62	0·87	Do you usually stay in the background at parties and get-togethers?
51	0·86	Do you find it hard to really enjoy yourself at a lively party?
25	−0·81	Can you usually let yourself go and enjoy yourself a lot at a gay party?
74	−0·71	Are you rather lively?
27	−0·66	Do other people think of you as being very lively?
29	0·57	Are you mostly quiet when you are with other people?
53	−0·55	Can you easily get some life into a rather dull party?
67	−0·44	Do you like mixing with people?
15	0·40	Generally do you prefer reading to meeting people?
11	0·34	Do you suddenly feel shy when you want to talk to an attractive stranger?
108	−0·34	Do you usually keep yourself to yourself except with very close friends?
17	−0·32	Do you like going out a lot?

Factor 2. *Impulsiveness.* This factor too is easily interpreted, having a C.F.S. of −0·93.

TABLE 16.3

8	0·78	Do you generally do and say things quickly without stopping to think?
109	0·66	Do you often get into a jam because you do things without thinking?
5	−0·63	Do you stop and think things over before doing anything?
13	0·60	Do you often do things on the spur of the moment?
106	0·53	Do you sometimes say the first thing that comes into your head?
22	0·37	When people shout at you do you shout back?

TABLE 16.4

8	−0·76	Do you generally do and say things quickly without stopping to think?
5	0·72	Do you stop and think things over before doing anything?
13	−0·71	Do you often do things on the spur of the moment?
109	−0·67	Do you often get into a jam because you do things without thinking?
91	0·56	Do you like planning things carefully well ahead of time?
105	−0·46	Do you sometimes say the first thing that comes into your head?
10	−0·41	Would you do almost anything for a dare?
70	−0·41	Would you call yourself happy-go-lucky?

Factor 3. *Mood Swings*. This factor has a C.F.S. of −0·95, indicating almost complete identity from male to female sample.

TABLE 16.5

61	0·94	Do you sometimes feel happy, sometimes sad, without any real reason?
9	0·89	Do you ever feel just miserable for no good reason?
73	0·72	Have you often felt listless and tired for no good reason?
19	0·66	Are you sometimes bubbling over with energy and sometimes very sluggish?
66	0·53	Are you moody?
59	0·42	Do you often have a restless feeling that you want something but do not know what?
76	0·43	Do you often feel fed-up?
7	0·39	Does your mood often go up and down?

TABLE 16.6

61	−0·94	Do you sometimes feel happy, sometimes sad, without any real reason?
9	−0·91	Do you ever feel just miserable for no good reason?
73	−0·72	Have you often felt listless and tired for no good reason?
7	−0·61	Does your mood often go up and down?
19	−0·55	Are you sometimes bubbling over with energy and sometimes very sluggish?
59	−0·51	Do you often have a restless feeling that you want something but do not know what?
76	−0·50	Do you often feel fed-up?
66	−0·45	Are you moody?
1	−0·33	Do you often long for excitement?

Factor 4. *Sleeplessness*. Another obvious but rather less important factor, with a C.F.S. of −0·91.

TABLE 16.7

57	−0·79	Do you suffer from sleeplessness?
104	−0·73	Do you find it hard to fall asleep at bed-time?
31	−0·65	Do ideas run through your head so that you cannot sleep?
68	−0·65	Have you often lost sleep over your worries?

TABLE 16.8

104	0·86	Do you find it hard to fall asleep at bed-time?
57	0·84	Do you suffer from sleeplessness?
31	0·69	Do ideas run through your head so that you cannot sleep?
68	0·66	Have you often lost sleep over your worries?
90	0·32	Do you sometimes get so restless that you cannot sit long in a chair?

Factor 5. *Jocularity*. This factor has a C.F.S. of −0·88, and is essentially restricted to three or four items.

TABLE 16.9

82	0·94	Do you like practical jokes?
56	0·91	Do you like playing pranks on others?
37	−0·78	Do you hate being with a crowd who play jokes on one another?

TABLE 16.10

82	−0·88	Do you like practical jokes?
56	−0·85	Do you like playing pranks on others?
37	0·71	Do you hate being with a crowd who play jokes on one another?
110	−0·36	Do you like cracking jokes and telling funny stories to your friends?

Factor 6. *Carefreeness*. Another rather small factor, with a C.F.S. of −0·80.

TABLE 16.11

70	−0·66	Would you call yourself happy-go-lucky?
3	−0·64	Are you usually carefree?
103	−0·59	Generally do you feel that things will sort themselves out and come right in the end?
96	−0·55	Are you an easy-going person, not generally bothered about having things just so?
99	−0·32	Do you sometimes put off until tomorrow what you ought to do today?

TABLE 16.12

103	0·64	Generally do you feel that things will sort themselves out and come right in the end?
3	0·54	Are you usually carefree?
70	0·32	Would you call yourself happy-go-lucky?

Factor 7. *Nervousness*. This is a rather more inclusive factor, with a C.F.S. of −0·82; this value suggests that in its manifestation there are possibly some interesting sex differences.

TABLE 16.13

47	0·78	Would you call yourself a nervous person?
97	0·75	Do you suffer from nerves?
26	0·63	Would you call yourself tense or highly-strung?
35	0·63	Do you get attacks of shaking or trembling?
92	0·51	Do you have dizzy turns?
45	0·42	Are you troubled by aches and pains?
55	0·40	Do you worry about your health?
100	0·35	Do you get nervous in places like lifts, trains or tunnels?

TABLE 16.14

47	−0·81	Would you call yourself a nervous person?
97	−0·79	Do you suffer from nerves?
26	−0·66	Would you call yourself tense or highly-strung?
35	−0·31	Do you get attacks of shaking or trembling?
98	−0·31	Would you rather plan things than do things?

Factor 8. *Sensitivity.* This factor has a C.F.S. of only −0·74; and this means inevitably that its naming is even more subjective than usual; again its expression in the two sexes is clearly not identical.

TABLE 16.15

14	−0·76	Do you often worry about things you should not have done or said?
50	−0·75	Are you easily hurt when people find fault with you or your work?
16	−0·69	Are your feelings rather easily hurt?
107	−0·66	Do you worry too long after an embarrassing experience?
23	−0·59	Are you often troubled about feelings of guilt?
40	−0·53	Do you worry about awful things that might happen?
52	−0·51	Are you troubled with feelings of inferiority?
83	−0·42	Do you often think of your past?
88	−0·40	Are you touchy about some things?
85	−0·38	When you get annoyed do you need someone friendly to talk to about it?
112	−0·38	Do you often feel self-conscious when you are with superiors?
11	−0·36	Do you suddenly feel shy when you want to talk to an attractive stranger?
49	0·36	Would you say you were fairly self-confident?
68	−0·32	Have you often lost sleep over your worries?

TABLE 16.16

14	0·78	Do you often worry about things you should not have done or said?
107	0·71	Do you worry too long after an embarrassing experience?
112	0·54	Do you often feel self-conscious when you are with superiors?
114	0·51	Do you often get 'butterflies in your tummy' before an important occasion?
23	0·49	Are you often troubled about feelings of guilt?
52	0·47	Are you troubled with feelings of inferiority?
11	0·39	Do you suddenly feel shy when you want to talk to an attractive stranger?
33	0·34	Do you get palpitations or thumping in your heart?

Factor 9. *Absent-mindedness.* This factor, with a C.F.S. of −0·58, is not very clearly defined, and is named only with great reluctance.

TABLE 16.17

80	−0·67	Are you often lost in thought?
21	−0·55	Do you daydream a lot?
78	−0·44	Does your mind wander when you are trying to attend closely to something?
4	0·32	Do you find it very hard to take no for an answer?

TABLE 16.18

34	−0·57	Do you like the kind of work that you need to pay close attention to?
41	0·52	Are you slow and unhurried in the way you move?
39	−0·43	Do you like doing things in which you have to act quickly?
78	0·43	Does your mind often wander when you are trying to attend closely to something?
28	−0·33	After having done something important do you feel you could have done better?

Factor 10. *Quick-wittedness.* This factor, with a C.F.S. of only 0·53, must be regarded with considerable doubt; quite possibly it is nothing but a statistical artefact.

TABLE 16.19

79	0·76	Can you put your thoughts into words quickly?
60	0·63	Do you nearly always have a ready answer when people talk to you?
44	0·59	Do you like talking to people so much that you never miss a chance of talking to a stranger?
10	0·38	Would you do almost anything for a dare?
63	0·36	As a child did you always do as you were told immediately and without grumbling?

TABLE 16.20

79	0·71	Can you put your thoughts into words quickly?
60	0·49	Do you nearly always have a ready answer when people talk to you?
112	−0·34	Do you often feel self-conscious when you are with superiors?
28	−0·33	After having done something important do you often feel you could have done better?

Factor 11. *Social shyness.* This factor has a C.F.S. of 0·60; it is not too clear how it differs from factor one, sociability. It seems that where factor 1 is more related to E, this factor may have an emotional-neurotic component. It, too, may be no more than a statistical artefact.

TABLE 16.21

72	−0·71	Do you like working alone?
89	−0·54	Would you rather be at home on your own than go to a boring party?
94	−0·46	Can you usually do things better figuring them out alone than by talking to others?
46	0·41	Would you be very unhappy if you could not see lots of people most of the time?
39	−0·35	Do you like doing things in which you have to act quickly?

TABLE 16.22

46	0·64	Would you be very unhappy if you could not see lots of people most of the time?
89	−0·52	Would you rather be at home on your own than go to a boring party ?
72	−0·46	Do you like working alone?
58	0·45	Do you like plenty of excitement and bustle around you?
20	−0·39	Do you prefer to have few but special friends?
108	−0·37	Do you usually keep yourself to yourself except with very close friends?
15	−0·33	Generally do you prefer reading to meeting people?

Factor 12. *Lie scales.* Items contained in the lie scales appear to give rise to one very clearly marked factor, with a C.F.S. of 0·92; this is shown below. There are, however, also no less than four other factors, with C.F.S. of 0·56, 0·58, 0·55, and 0·64, which contain a predominance of Lie items, mixed with various items from other scales. Little point would be served by printing all these tables, as no very clear picture emerges; it seems clear, however, that the Lie Scale is not as univocal as one might have desired.

TABLE 16.23

69	−0·84	Do you sometimes get cross?
12	−0·78	Once in a while do you lose your temper and get angry?
64	−0·34	Do you sometimes sulk?
88	−0·34	Are you touchy about some things?

TABLE 16.24

12	−0·80	Once in a while do you lose your temper and get angry?
69	−0·73	Do you sometimes get cross?
65	−0·39	When drawn into a quarrel do you prefer to have it out to being silent?
66	−0·35	Do you sometimes sulk?
88	−0·34	Are you touchy about some things?

The remaining factors do not match to any reasonable standard, nor are they easily interpreted; it seems best to regard them as statistical artefacts. One possible exception is a female factor identifiable as 'psychosomatic'; its highest match is male factor 'nervousness', which however has a higher C.F.S. with female nervousness. The second highest C.F.S. is shown below; the matching is clearly unsatisfactory, suggesting that possibly we are here dealing with a purely feminine factor.

TABLE 16.25

41	0·81	Are you slow and unhurried in the way you move?
42	0·39	Have you ever been late for an appointment or work?
105	−0·33	Have you sometimes told lies in your life?
71	0·32	Do you often make up your mind too late?
95	0·32	Do you ever get short of breath without having done heavy work?

TABLE 16·26

45	−0·83	Are you troubled by aches and pains?
92	−0·74	Do you have dizzy turns?
55	−0·69	Do you worry about your health?
95	−0·67	Do you ever get short of breath without have done heavy work?
102	−0·56	Do you get very bad headaches?
100	−0·45	Do you get nervous in places like lifts, trains or tunnels?
40	−0·34	Do you worry about awful things that might happen?
33	−0·31	Do you get palpitations or thumping in your heart?

At the second-order level of factor extraction, we find that both men and women have seven factors; of these only the first two or three, however, have more than a few items with loadings over 0·30. Factor 1 for the men is clearly a neuroticism factor which has taken into itself most of the primary factors related to this concept. For the women, the neuroticism factor is split in three, giving rise to factors 1, 3 and 8 as shown in the tables below. C.F.S.s show that male factor 1 is closely related to female factor 1 (−0·79) and female factors 3 (−0·64) and 7 (0·65). The separate meaning of the female factors is not immediately apparent, and any naming would be too subjective to be very valuable.

TABLE 16.27

66	−0·60	Are you moody?
26	−0·57	Would you call yourself tense or highly-strung?
68	−0·54	Have you often lost sleep over your worries?
97	−0·54	Do you suffer from nerves?
7	−0·53	Does your mood often go up and down?
50	−0·52	Are you easily hurt when people find fault with you or your work?

57	−0·52	Do you suffer from sleeplessness?
76	−0·52	Do you often feel fed-up?
55	−0·50	Do you worry about your health?
21	−0·49	Do you daydream a lot?
47	−0·49	Would you call yourself a nervous person?
73	−0·49	Have you often felt listless and tired for no good reason?
45	−0·48	Are you troubled by aches and pains?
107	−0·48	Do you worry too long after an embarrassing experience?
2	−0·47	Do you often need understanding friends to cheer you up?
16	−0·47	Are your feelings rather easily hurt?
104	−0·46	Do you find it hard to fall asleep at bed-time?
40	−0·45	Do you worry about awful things that might happen?
38	−0·42	Are you an irritable person?
102	−0·40	Do you get very bad headaches?
9	−0·39	Do you ever feel just miserable for no good reason?
23	−0·39	Are you often troubled about feelings of guilt?
61	−0·39	Do you sometimes feel happy, sometimes sad, without any real reason?
92	−0·38	Do you have dizzy turns?
31	−0·37	Do ideas run through your head so that you cannot sleep?
4	−0·36	Do you find it very hard to take no for an answer?
64	−0·35	Do you sometimes sulk?
1	−0·34	Do you often long for excitement?
14	−0·33	Do you often worry about things you should not have done or said?
33	−0·33	Do you get palpitations or thumping in your heart?
52	−0·33	Are you often troubled with feelings of inferiority?
59	−0·33	Do you often have a restless feeling that you want something but do not know what?
80	−0·32	Are you often lost in thought?
83	−0·32	Do you often think of your past?
109	−0·32	Do you often get into a jam because you do things without thinking?

TABLE 16.28

28	0·51	After having done something important do you often feel you could have done better?
41	−0·49	Are you slow and unhurried in the way you move?
112	0·49	Do you often feel self-conscious when you are with superiors?
47	0·43	Would you call yourself a nervous person?
52	0·41	Are you troubled with feelings of inferiority?
97	0·39	Do you suffer from nerves?
26	0·38	Would you call yourself tense or highly-strung?
49	−0·38	Would you say that you were fairly self-confident?
2	0·35	Do you often need understanding friends to cheer you up?

TABLE 16.29

35	0·47	Do you get attacks of shaking or trembling?
33	0·45	Do you get palpitations or thumping in your heart?
43	0·45	Do you have many nightmares?
104	0·38	Do you find it hard to fall asleep at bed-time?
67	−0·37	Do you like mixing with people?
68	0·36	Have you often lost sleep over your worries?
15	0·35	Generally do you prefer reading to meeting people?
57	0·33	Do you suffer from sleeplessness?
65	−0·33	When drawn into a quarrel do you prefer to have it out to being silent?
31	0·32	Do ideas run through your head so that you cannot sleep?
77	0·32	Do you feel uncomfortable in anything but everyday clothes?
110	0·32	Do you like cracking jokes and telling funny stories to your friends?
107	0·31	Do you worry too long after an embarrassing experience?

TABLE 16.30

80	−0·63	Are you often lost in thought?
21	−0·59	Do you daydream a lot?
83	−0·45	Do you often think of your past?
71	−0·43	Do you often make up your mind too late?
23	−0·39	Are you often troubled about feelings of guilt?
18	−0·35	Occasionally do you have thoughts and ideas you would not like other people to know about?
40	−0·34	Do you worry about awful things that might happen?
41	−0·33	Are you slow and unhurried in the way you move?
45	−0·33	Are you troubled by aches and pains?
55	−0·33	Do you worry about your health?
78	−0·33	Does your mind often wander when you are trying to attend closely to something?

Male and female factors 2 are extraversion factors; the C.F.S. is 0·93, indicating reasonable agreement.

TABLE 16.31

58	0·62	Do you like plenty of excitement and bustle around you?
70	0·60	Would you call yourself happy-go-lucky?
74	0·57	Are you rather lively?
27	0·54	Do other people think of you as being very lively?
82	0·53	Do you like practical jokes?
3	0·52	Are you usually carefree?
17	0·51	Do you like going out a lot?
56	0·51	Do you like playing pranks on others?
1	0·48	Do you often long for excitement?
10	0·46	Would you do almost anything for a dare?

37	−0·46	Do you hate being with a crowd who play jokes on one another?
39	0·45	Do you like doing things in which you have to act quickly?
67	0·43	Do you like mixing with people?
25	0·42	Can you usually let yourself go and enjoy yourself a lot at a gay party?
53	0·41	Can you easily get some life into a rather dull party?
13	0·40	Do you often do things on the spur of the moment?
51	−0·40	Do you find it hard to really enjoy yourself at a lively party?
62	−0·40	Do you usually stay in the background at parties and get-togethers?
110	0·39	Do you like cracking jokes and telling funny stories to your friends?
113	0·39	When the odds are against you do you still think it worth taking a chance?
46	0·34	Would you be very unhappy if you could not see lots of people most of the time?
89	−0·31	Would you rather be at home on your own than go to a boring party?

TABLE 16.32

74	0·63	Are you rather lively?
39	0·61	Do you like doing things in which you have to act quickly?
27	0·59	Do other people think of you as being very lively?
82	0·51	Do you like practical jokes?
53	0·50	Can you easily get some life into a rather dull party?
13	0·49	Do you often do things on the spur of the moment?
56	0·48	Do you like playing pranks on others?
58	0·48	Do you like plenty of excitement and bustle around you?
70	0·48	Would you call yourself happy-go-lucky?
3	0·46	Are you usually carefree?
37	−0·44	Do you hate being with a crowd who play jokes on one another?
110	0·43	Do you like cracking jokes and telling funny stories to your friends?
49	0·40	Would you say that you were fairly self-confident?
60	0·39	Do you nearly always have a ready answer when people talk to you?
25	0·38	Can you usually let yourself go and enjoy yourself a lot at a gay party?
62	0·38	Do you usually stay in the background at parties and get-togethers?
67	0·38	Do you like mixing with people?
46	0·37	Would you be very unhappy if you could not see lots of people most of the time?
15	−0·36	Generally do you prefer reading to meeting people?

TABLE 16.32 (*contd.*)

101	0·36	When you make new friends is it usually you who makes the first move or invites?
17	0·35	Do you like going out a lot ?
106	0·32	Do you sometimes say the first thing that comes into your head?
1	0·31	Do you often long for excitement?
51	−0·31	Do you find it hard to really enjoy yourself at a lively party?
109	0·31	Do you often get into a jam because you do things without thinking?

Male factor 3 has a C.F.S. with female factor 1 of −0·72; it suggests a physical or psychosomatic factor, but with only 3 loadings it would be unwise to insist on such an interpretation.

TABLE 16.33

102	0·57	Do you get very bad headaches?
95	0·44	Do you ever get short of breath without having done heavy work?
45	0·32	Are you troubled by aches and pains?

Male factor 4 has a C.F.S. with female factors 1 and 7 of 0·46 and −0·57; clearly this is another neuroticism factor, although it would not be possible to give it a distinctive name.

TABLE 16.34

11	0·52	Do you suddenly feel shy when you want to talk to an attractive stranger?
65	−0·46	When drawn into a quarrel do you prefer to have it out to being silent?
112	0·45	Do you often feel self-conscious when you are with superiors?
29	0·42	Are you mostly quiet when you are with other people?
60	−0·40	Do you nearly always have a ready answer when people talk to you?
79	−0·36	Can you put your thoughts into words quickly?
101	−0·36	When you make new friends is it usually you who makes the first move or invites?
49	−0·33	Would you say that you were fairly self-confident?
52	0·33	Are you troubled with feelings of inferiority?
53	−0·33	Can you easily get some life into a rather dull party?
71	0·32	Do you often make up your mind too late?

Factor 5 for both sexes is apparently a lie factor; C.F.S. is 0·76.

TABLE 16.35

69	−0·53	Do you sometimes get cross?
12	−0·50	Once in a while do you lose your temper and get angry?
81	0·45	Are you completely free from prejudices of any kind?
88	−0·41	Are you touchy about some things?
48	−0·39	Of all the people you know are there some whom you definitely do not like?
64	−0·37	Do you sometimes sulk?

TABLE 16.36

22	−0·56	When people shout at you do you shout back?
12	−0·52	Once in a while do you lose your temper and get angry?
38	−0·51	Are you an irritable person?
64	−0·49	Do you sometimes sulk?
65	−0·44	When drawn into a quarrel do you prefer to have it out to being silent?
63	0·32	As a child did you always do as you were told immediately and without grumbling?
66	−0·31	Are you moody?

Male factor 6 and female factor 4 (C.F.S. = 0·80) and M7 and F6 (C.F.S. = 0·48) appear to be lie factors, mixed up with other items; they defy proper interpretation, and are therefore not given here. Altogether one may say of the second-order factors, as was pointed out in an earlier section, that they represent a transition stage to the highest-order factors, and do not by and large give very meaningful results which lend themselves to interpretation. Some details have been given above so that the reader might see for himself the kind of configuration achieved; in future, unless these intermediary factors appear to make psychological sense, they will not be presented in detail so as to save space.

We must now turn to the main factors to emerge from our analysis, i.e. the third-order factors. Factor 1 in both male and female samples is clearly Neuroticism; the C.F.S. is 0·99954, suggesting almost complete identity for both sexes.

TABLE 16.37

2	0·57	Do you often need understanding friends to cheer you up?
112	0·54	Do you often feel self-conscious when you are with superiors?
7	0·50	Does your mood often go up and down?
66	0·49	Are you moody?
23	0·48	Are you often troubled about feelings of guilt?
52	0·46	Are you troubled with feelings of inferiority?

TABLE 16.37 (*contd.*)

64	0·46	Do you sometimes sulk?
78	0·46	Does your mind often wander when you are trying to attend closely to something?
9	0·45	Do you ever feel just miserable for no good reason?
11	0·45	Do you suddenly feel shy when you want to talk to an attractive stranger?
16	0·45	Are your feelings rather easily hurt?
50	0·44	Are you easily hurt when people find fault with you or your work?
61	0·44	Do you sometimes feel happy, sometimes sad, without any real reason?
76	0·44	Do you often feel fed-up?
14	0·43	Do you often worry about things you should not have done or said?
40	0·43	Do you worry about awful things that might happen?
19	0·42	Are you sometimes bubbling over with energy and sometimes very sluggish?
73	0·42	Have you often felt listless and tired for no good reason?
88	0·42	Are you touchy about some things?
107	0·42	Do you worry too long after an embarrassing experience?
71	0·41	Do you often make up your mind too late?
97	0·41	Do you suffer from nerves?
18	0·40	Occasionally do you have thoughts and ideas you would not like other people to know about?
47	0·40	Would you call yourself a nervous person?
85	0·39	When you get annoyed do you need someone friendly to talk to about it?
21	0·38	Do you daydream a lot?
49	−0·38	Would you say that you were fairly self-confident?
114	0·37	Do you often get butterflies in your tummy before an important occasion?
90	0·36	Do you sometimes get so restless that you cannot sit long in a chair?
1	0·34	Do you often long for excitement?
38	0·33	Are you an irritable person?
100	0·33	Do you get nervous in places like lifts, trains or tunnels?
109	0·33	Do you often get into a jam because you do things without thinking?

TABLE 16.38

66	0·56	Are you moody?
7	0·54	Does your mood often go up and down?
76	0·54	Do you often feel fed-up?
38	0·51	Are you an irritable person?
97	0·47	Do you suffer from nerves?
47	0·46	Would you call yourself a nervous person?
35	0·45	Do you get attacks of shaking or trembling?

68	0·45	Have you often lost sleep over your worries?
71	0·44	Do you often make up your mind too late?
40	0·43	Do you worry about awful things that might happen?
73	0·43	Have you often felt listless and tired for no good reason?
52	0·42	Are you troubled with feelings of inferiority?
64	0·42	Do you sometimes sulk?
2	0·41	Do you often need understanding friends to cheer you up?
19	0·41	Are you sometimes bubbling over with energy and sometimes very sluggish?
49	−0·41	Would you say that you were fairly self-confident?
57	0·41	Do you suffer from sleeplessness?
59	0·41	Do you often have a restless feeling that you want something but do not know what?
21	0·40	Do you daydream a lot?
23	0·40	Are you often troubled about feelings of guilt?
16	0·39	Are your feelings rather easily hurt?
50	0·39	Are you easily hurt when people find fault with you or your work?
112	0·39	Do you often feel self-conscious when you are with superiors?
9	0·38	Do you ever feel just miserable for no good reason?
26	0·38	Would you call yourself tense or highly-strung?
107	0·38	Do you worry too long after an embarrassing experience?
33	0·37	Do you get palpitations or thumping in your heart?
61	0·37	Do you sometimes feel happy, sometimes sad, without any real reason?
80	0·36	Are you often lost in thought?
92	0·35	Do you have dizzy turns?
104	0·35	Do you find it hard to fall asleep at bed-time?
1	0·34	Do you often long for excitement?
43	0·33	Do you have any nightmares?
95	0·33	Do you ever get short of breath without having done heavy work?
31	0·32	Do ideas run through your head so that you cannot sleep?
45	0·32	Are you troubled by aches and pains?
55	0·31	Do you worry about your health?

The second factor in each case is equally obviously Extraversion; the C.F.S. is 0·91758, which is smaller than in the case of of neuroticism, but still large enough to suggest substantial similarity.

TABLE 16.39

110	−0·51	Do you like cracking jokes and telling funny stories to your friends?
62	0·48	Do you usually stay in the background at parties and get-togethers?
15	0·46	Generally do you prefer reading to meeting people?

TABLE 16.39 (*contd.*)

74	−0·46	Are you rather lively?
29	0·43	Are you mostly quiet when you are with other people?
27	−0·41	Do other people think of you as being very lively?
30	−0·41	Do you sometimes gossip?
94	0·41	Can you usually do things better by figuring them out alone than by talking to others?
25	−0·40	Can you usually let yourself go and enjoy yourself a lot at a gay party?
87	−0·40	Do you sometimes boast a little?
108	0·40	Do you usually keep yourself to yourself except with very close friends?
67	−0·39	Do you like mixing with people?
51	0·37	Do you find it hard to really enjoy yourself at a lively party?
72	0·37	Do you like working alone?
49	−0·36	Would you say that you were fairly self-confident?
82	−0·36	Do you like practical jokes?
38	0·35	Do you like plenty of excitement and bustle around you.
70	−0·35	Would you call yourself happy-go-lucky?
101	−0·35	When you make new friends is it usually you who makes the first move or invites?
69	−0·34	Do you sometimes get cross?
56	−0·33	Do you like playing pranks on others?
46	−0·32	Would you be very unhappy if you could not see lots of people most of the time?
54	−0·32	Do you sometimes talk about things you know nothing about?
85	−0·32	When you get annoyed do you need someone friendly to talk to about it?
3	−0·31	Are you usually carefree?
53	−0·31	Can you easily get some life into a rather dull party?
86	0·31	Do you mind selling things or asking people for money for some good cause?

TABLE 16.40

17	−0·58	Do you like going out a lot?
25	−0·57	Can you usually let yourself go and enjoy yourself a lot at a gay party?
51	0·52	Do you find it hard to really enjoy yourself at a lively party?
58	−0·50	Do you like plenty of excitement and bustle around you?
62	0·49	Do you usually stay in the background at parties and get-togethers?
15	0·46	Generally do you prefer reading to meeting people?
29	0·46	Are you mostly quiet when you are with other people?
13	−0·45	Do you often do things on the spur of the moment?
22	−0·44	When people shout at you do you shout back?
74	−0·43	Are you rather lively?

27	−0·42	Do other people think of you as being very lively?
67	−0·42	Do you like mixing with people?
109	−0·42	Do you often get into a jam because you do things without thinking?
36	0·40	Would you always declare everything at the customs even if you knew you would never be caught?
110	−0·39	Do you like cracking jokes and telling funny stories to your friends?
8	−0·37	Do you generally do and say things quickly without stopping to think?
108	0·37	Do you usually keep yourself to yourself except with very close friends?
5	0·36	Do you stop and think things over before doing anything?
46	−0·36	Would you be very unhappy if you could not see lots of people most of the time?
70	−0·36	Would you call yourself happy-go-lucky?
37	0·35	Do you hate being with a crowd who play jokes on one another?
54	−0·35	Do you sometimes talk about things you know nothing about?
106	−0·35	Do you sometimes say the first thing that comes into your head?
113	−0·34	When the odds are against you do you still think it worth taking a chance?
1	−0·33	Do you often long for excitement?
32	0·33	Would you rather look something up in a book than talk to someone about it?
90	−0·33	Do you sometimes get so restless that you cannot sit long in a chair?
91	0·33	Do you like planning things carefully well ahead of time?
10	−0·32	Would you do almost anything for a dare?
19	−0·32	Are you sometimes bubbling over with energy and sometimes very sluggish?
65	−0·32	When drawn into a quarrel do you prefer to have it out to being silent?
75	−0·32	Do you sometimes laugh at a dirty joke?
98	0·32	Would you rather plan things than do things?
4	−0·31	Do you find it very hard to take no for an answer?
39	−0·31	Do you like doing things in which you have to act quickly?
86	0·31	Do you mind selling things or asking people for money for some good cause?

There is, in the male sample, a small additional factor which has a C.F.S. with F2 of 0·68344; it is made up of items usually associated with E, and it is not at all clear why it appears here split off from M2. In any case, the number of items concerned is very small, and no interpretation can be suggested.

TABLE 16.41

91	0·40	Do you like planning things carefully well ahead of time?
1	−0·38	Do you often long for excitement?
10	−0·37	Would you do almost anything for a dare?
102	0·33	Do you get very bad headaches?
77	−0·31	Do you feel uncomfortable in anything but everyday clothes?
89	0·31	Would you rather be at home on your own than go to a boring party?

Comments on the findings of this section will be kept brief, as obviously a more detailed discussion will be required when the results of the other two analyses have been given. However, one or two points appear worthy of comment. The first of these relates to the distribution of factors on a continuum from *tautological* factors (T-factors) at one end to *combinatorial* factors (C-factors) at the other. At the extreme, a T-factor would consist of several repetitions of the same question, and would then be seen for what it is—a simple reliability coefficient. While such extreme T-factors do not occur in the usual type of factor analysis, close approximations can be found. The factors of sleeplessness and jocularity, for instance, are very close to T-factors, in the sense that they are made up of very similar restatements of a particular question. Such factors are easy to identify and name, but they are of minimal psychological interest; they are likely to have high C.F.S.s almost by definition. C-factors are made up of dissimilar items, i.e. of items where the findings of a correlation does not involve a tautology; sensitivity and nervousness are examples of factors some way towards the C end of the continuum. Such factors are usually less easy to identify and name, and much subjectivity attaches to such efforts; in addition such factors tend to have lower C.F.S.s. This is true at the level of primary factors (first-order level); it would also seem to be true at the second-order level, and indeed at all intermediate levels up to the highest. When we reach the third-order factor level in the present investigation, however, we find factors (E and N) which are located towards the extreme C end of the continuum, which also have very high C.F.S.s, and which are easy to identify. We shall return to this discussion of T-factors and C-factors after a consideration of the Cattell and Guilford data.

How replicable are our factors, from one sex to the other, and from the study discussed in Section D to the present one? Similarity there certainly is, but little identity—except for the E and N. factors. It may be useful to give some more quantitative specification to these vague terms. Let us define 'identity' of factors in terms of C.F.S.s of above 0·90; close similarity in terms of C.F.S.s between 0·80 and 0·89; similarity in terms of C.F.S.s between 0·60 and 0·79. These limits are of course quite arbitrary, just as are significance levels, but they will serve up to a point in making our discussion less imprecise. We find that of the primary factors, identity is found in 4 personality factors and the Lie scale; close similarity in 3 personality factors; similarity in 2 personality factors and 1 Lie scale. Two personality factors and 3 Lie scales lie below the lower limit of this scale, implying only the most tenuous connection. Seven personality factors and 1 Lie scale are therefore fairly clearly identifiable across sexes, and (subjectively) across studies; yet in the main these factors are T-factors, and one would perhaps have been justified in showing some astonishment if these factors had failed to correspond in this fashion. The only psychologically interesting finding is the identity of the E and N factors; here we are clearly dealing with C-factors, and no *a priori* assumptions or tautological reasoning could have predicted the finding with confidence.

If we are right in asserting that high C.F.S.s (and in general replicability) of first-order factors is a function, in part, of the location of the factor towards the T-end of the continuum, then two consequences of some interest follow. In the first place, every statement or question can be made into a replicable factor by adding other statements or questions which paraphrase the original one. In the second place, factors which are characterized by high C.F.S.s replicability and easy interpretability are likely to be of little psychological interest, as being largely tautological. There would appear to be an infinity of such factors, and they are likely to vary in character with slight alternations in linguistic practice, precise wording of the questions, and other non-relevant changes. It would be idle to search in the universe of such factors for anything but reliability; these factors do not tell us much about human nature or human behaviour, but rather reassure us that questions are not answered at random. The moment that we leave the T-end and advance towards the C-end of the continuum, we find factors to be much less easy to interpret, C.F.S.s much lower, and psychological understanding much more difficult. This would suggest that higher order factors, such as E and N, which combine the virtues of combining divergent statements or questions with high C.F.S.s, are of much greater psychological interest and importance. We shall see in the next two sections whether this generalization is borne out by the data and analyses of Cattell's and Guilford's inventories.

17

FACTORS IN THE CATTELL PERSONALITY INVENTORY

H. J. Eysenck, P. O. White and M. I. Soueif

EVEN the most casual look at Cattell's factors will be sufficient to show that here we are dealing with factors located towards the C end of our C—T continuum; few if any of them are tautological. It would appear, therefore, that C.F.S.s would be likely to be appreciably lower than those observed in the E.P.I., and this deduction from the generalization made in the last section appears to be borne out in fact. Table 17.1 shows the number of primary factors in the Eysenck, Cattell and Guilford inventories which exceed 0·8, are below 0·6, or are intermediate; it will be seen that while 8 of Eysenck's factors have C.F.S.s in excess of 0·8, only one of Cattell's and 4 of Guilford's are in this category. When it is realized that 0·8 is a very lenient criterion indeed for factor comparison (we would prefer 0·9 as a minimum criterion for the assertion that two factors are identical), then it will be clear immediately that as far as Cattell's work is concerned there is very little evidence in our data to suggest that the factors which emerge have any marked degree of replicability. It might be objected that we are comparing male factors with female, and that possibly factors within one sex might be more reproducible than factors between sexes. This is of course possible, and we will soon turn to a comparison of our factors in both sexes with those suggested by Cattell on the basis of his own work; nevertheless it must be pointed out that neither Cattell nor Guilford in fact hold that men and women show different factor patterns. Both use the same items to measure their various primary factors in the two sexes, and although they mention occasional sex differences in scores on these questionnaires, there is no suggestion even of any differences in intercorrelation of items, or of factor patterns. As experimental disproof of the position advocated by Cattell and Guilford, therefore, our demonstration of low C.F.S.s between the sexes is perfectly acceptable; hardly any of the factors actually found in our analysis have sufficiently high C.F.S.s to enable one to say that a factor discovered on the male side has a unique and clear-cut, comparable factor on the female side. About 50 per cent of all factors have C.F.S.s which are below 0·6; none, in the case of Cattell, is above 0·9. This is a most disappointing finding when it is considered that both authors have spent thirty years or more in the production of their respective systems, and have carried out hundreds of factor analytic studies in the express hope of discovering invariant and replicable first-order factors.

TABLE 17.1

C.F.S.	Eysenck	Cattell	Guilford
0·80 and above	8	1	4
0·60—0·79	5	9	8
Below 0·60	7	10	8
Total	20	20	20

In considering these figures, it may be helpful to bear in mind the exact manner in which they were derived. First, a matrix was constructed of all the C.F.S.s of the 20 male factors with the 20 female factors, i.e. an asymmetrical 20 × 20 matrix. Next a search was made among the 20 C.F.S.s on the female side to find the one which gave the highest value for male factor 1. Next a similar search was made for factor 2, and so on. Too often for comfort several male factors had the same female factor as their highest C.F.S. choice; in that case the highest of these C.F.S.s determined which male factor this particular female factor would go with. In this way we are constantly maximizing the found C.F.S.s, a point which should lead to the discovery of a C.F.S. significant at the 0·05 level for each male/female comparison even if the C.F.S.s had been calculated on a purely chance basis. Unfortunately it is not possible to calculate p levels for C.F.S.s, but it is clear that the procedure used gives maximum chance to high C.F.S.s to emerge, and may load the dice too much in favour of high values; the failure of such values to emerge is therefore all the more surprising. (It will be clear that these considerations apply to a much lesser degree when second-order factors are involved, and not at all for third-order factors; with the latter, there are in fact no alternative choices, and hence no maximization). Table 17.2 below gives the C.F.S.s for all of the twenty factors extracted from Cattell's data; this table will be helpful on considering the actual factors in detail.

TABLE 17.2

Cattell C.F.S. Data

Male Factor	Female Factor	C.F.S.
1	2	0·77
2	15	−0·70
3	3	−0·66
4	5	−0·67
5	7	−0·84
6	17	−0·47
7	11	0·62
8	18	−0·28
9	16	0·63
10	8	0·37
11	12	0·54
12	10	0·38
13	1	0·65
14	14	−0·64
15	6	0·55
16	19	0·51
17	4	−0·52
18	13	0·51
19	9	−0·09
20	20	0·63

We must now turn to a consideration of the main Cattell factors, i.e. those having at least moderately high C.F.S.s.

Factor 1. *Physical activity*. This factor, having the highest C.F.S., is appropriately enough pretty much a T factor. It has no obvious match in Cattell's own system.

TABLE 17.3

15	0·78	Preference for active games
88	0·70	Urges for physical work-out
99	−0·70	Childhood activities
54	0·56	Need for fresh air
3	0·34	Occupational preferences

TABLE 17.4

88	−0·74	Urges for physical work-out
99	0·73	Childhood activities
15	−0·61	Preference for active games
54	−0·52	Need for fresh air

Factor 2. *Sensitivity*. This factor is not unlike one of the Eysenck ones; it finds no ready match in Cattell's system. To illustrate the difficulties in discovering whether such a match exists, and the subjectivity in

making a firm decision, consider the detailed facts. Five items from our factor 2 come from Cattell's factor 0 (1, 12, 19, 21, 75); of these one only occurs in our female sample. Two items come from Cattell's Q4 (30, 41), and three from C (46, 61, 63). One item each come from F (51) and from 0 (75); the former only appear in the female sample. Items 1, 30, 41, and 61 only appear in the male sample. (The word 'appear' means in this context, as explained before, 'has a loading of 0·3 or above.' This limitation may exclude items favourable to Cattell's hypotheses, but in actual fact serves more frequently to exclude chance intruders which would have hopelessly confused the picture. Clearly some objective criterion for inclusion must be adopted, as otherwise subjective and pseudo-psychological 'interpretation' could run riot.) The reader must decide whether he agrees that this picture of our factor 2 does not agree in any clear-cut way with Cattell's hypothesis of any of his factors; it is clearly a mixture of O, C and Q4, with several other factors of his thrown in as well. No such detailed comparisons will in future be made; the reader will be able to decide for himself by comparing the factors printed below with the key to Cattell's factors given on an earlier page.

TABLE 17.5

12	0·76	Moodiness
61	0·69	Undue worries intruding on thoughts
82	0·67	Moods of feeling sorry for oneself
1	0·60	Guilt feeling
30	−0·56	Restlessness
21	−0·47	Frustration tolerance
75	−0·47	Mood resilience
41	0·38	Degree of emotional arousal evoked by occurrences
63	0·35	Feeling unappreciated
46	−0·34	Ability to deal with problems

TABLE 17.6

46	0·64	Ability to deal with problems
75	0·59	Mood resilience
21	0·56	Frustration tolerance
19	0·53	Optimism
82	−0·52	Moods of feeling sorry for oneself
63	−0·42	Feeling unappreciated
12	−0·37	Moodiness
51	0·35	Carefreeness (Self rating)

Factor 3. *Jocularity.* This factor could also have been named carefreeness or sociability; items of all kinds are included, and no firm decision is possible. Of the Cattell factors, H and F are both heavily represented, with M. and Q1 also intruding.

TABLE 17.7

89	0·80	Being considered eloquent
49	0·71	Showing one's feelings easily
10	−0·68	Dislike of jocularity
42	0·59	Self rating on sociability
57	0·59	Sociability
51	0·48	Carefreeness (self rating)
20	−0·43	Ease of expression
39	−0·32	Difficulties in lecturing
5	0·31	Chance remarks made for effect

TABLE 17.8

10	0·65	Dislike of jocularity
89	−0·60	Being considered eloquent
6	0·45	Extent of personal involvement in discussion on world affairs etc.
5	−0·40	Chance remarks made for effect
51	−0·40	Carefreeness (self rating)

Factor 4. *Socially responsible.* This factor is difficult to name. In Cattell's system it is a mixture of Q2, A, G, C and H.

TABLE 17.9

68	0·79	Enjoying organizing things
96	0·71	Occupational preference
27	0·37	Attitudes to energies spent on social work
43	0·37	Occupational preference
36	0·31	Preference of reading matter

TABLE 17.10

69	−0·69	Taking an active part in social affairs
68	0·67	Enjoying organizing things
39	−0·51	Difficulties in lecturing
53	0·47	Admitting regard for clever crooks

Factor 5. *Sociability.* In view of the unusual way the questions are worded, this identification of factor 5 is made very hesitantly. The factor contains items from Cattell's factors A and I, predominantly, with M and Q1 also represented.

TABLE 17.11

47	0·83	Occupational preference
93	−0·73	Occupational preference
67	−0·62	Occupational preference
77	−0·54	Occupational preference
17	−0·49	Subject preferences at school
87	−0·47	Choice of recreations
25	−0·44	Occupational preference
3	0·43	Occupational preference
36	0·38	Preference of reading matter
86	0·35	Occupational preference
73	0·34	Occupational preference
43	0·33	Occupational preference
31	−0·31	Preference for magazine articles of different kinds

TABLE 17.12

25	0·71	Occupational preference
93	0·71	Occupational preference
17	0·69	Subject preferences at school
38	0·46	Attributes in choice of friends
96	0·42	Occupational preference
47	−0·38	Occupational preference
87	0·31	Choice of recreation

Factor 6. *Social shyness.* The same remarks apply here as in the case of factor 5. It is not easy to tell the two factors apart. Cattell's I and H are again involved, as are F, Q2 and Q3.

TABLE 17.13

86	−0·70	Occupational preference
73	−0·66	Occupational preference
79	0·39	Need for a lot of social stimulation
17	0·39	Subject preferences at school
95	0·37	Frequency of social outings

TABLE 17.14

95	0·81	Frequency of social outings
79	0·70	Need for a lot of social stimulation
14	−0·69	Choice of recreation
97	−0·39	Reading matter preference
76	−0·38	Need for appreciation
87	−0·36	Choice of recreations
42	0·32	Self rating on sociability
22	0·31	Choice of employment
57	0·31	Sociability

Factor 7. *Absentmindedness*. This factor is almost impossible to name, making very little psychological sense. It has several items in common with Cattell's Q4, with some admixture of Q3 and O.

TABLE 17.15

18	0·83	Obsessional behaviour
29	0·56	Ideas coming into one's mind
23	−0·32	Tiredness on waking

TABLE 17.16

29	−0·71	Ideas coming into one's mind
65	−0·60	Lack of concentration
18	−0·57	Obsessional behaviour
44	0·35	Fear of catching disease
1	−0·33	Guilt feelings
41	−0·33	Degree of emotional arousal evoked by occurrences
23	−0·32	Tiredness on waking

Factor 8. *Risk-taking*. Again little confidence is felt in the label. Cattell's factors A, C, E, G, M, Q2 and Q3 are all contained in it; no wonder perhaps that it is confused!

TABLE 17.17

40	0·73	Types of holidays preferred
11	0·63	Wariness of possible dangers in unfamiliar surroundings
64	0·52	Independence
85	−0·39	Psychosomatic symptoms under stress
62	0·34	Frustration tolerance
38	0·31	Attributes in choice of friends

TABLE 17.18

11	0·69	Wariness of possible dangers in unfamiliar surroundings
40	0·45	Types of holidays preferred
64	0·45	Independence
43	0·44	Occupational preference
32	−0·41	'Crossing bridges when one meets them' approach to work
77	−0·39	Occupational preference
96	0·33	Occupational preference

Factor 9. *Happy-go-lucky*. This factor is made up of items each of which comes from a different Cattell factor—F, G, L, N and Q1 are all represented.

TABLE 17.19

32	0·82	'Crossing bridges when one meets them' approach to work
83	−0·33	Being thought soft hearted
51	−0·32	Carefreeness (self rating)

TABLE 17.20

83	−0·75	Being thought soft hearted
56	0·43	Mistrusting people
72	−0·42	Changeable tastes and habits

Factor 10. *Ethico-religious.* This is the last of the factors having C.F.S.s exceeding the modest level of 0·6. It contains items from Cattell factors M, Q1, G, C, Q2 and I.

TABLE 17.21

53	0·67	Admitting regard for clever crooks
97	0·61	Reading matter preference
76	0·37	Need for appreciation
28	−0·36	Active versus passive ways of getting things done
71	−0·31	Number of past regrets

TABLE 17.22

78	−0·78	Reading matter preference
4	−0·66	Kinds of stories preferred as a child
13	0·34	Ways of dealing with difficult people
97	0·32	Reading matter preference

Little comment is required; the figures speak for themselves. There is very little support in these factors for the picture of personality structure which Cattell has presented at the first-order level of description; in every case two, three or more of Cattell's factors are mixed together to give rise to one of our factors. In no case is there a clear-cut agreement between the two sets of analyses; in every case is our factor a compound of items from various Cattell factors. Possible reasons for this state of affairs will be discussed later on; we must now turn to Cattell's higher-order factors.

The 8 male and 7 female second-order factors do not show any higher replicability than did the primary factors; there is one C.F.S. of 0·91 and one of 0·85, with all the others in the 70s and 60s, going as low as 0·35 in one case. The factors did not lend themselves to psychological interpretation, in spite of all efforts, and in order to save space we have not included them in our presentation. We will therefore go straight to the third-order factors, of which there are three for both the men and the women. The first of these is clearly neuroticism, with a C.F.S. of −0·98. The items are given below in Tables 17.23 and 17.24.

TABLE 17.23

65	0·54	Lack of concentration
82	0·53	Moods of feeling sorry for oneself
61	0·49	Undue worries intruding on thoughts
29	0·45	Ideas coming into one's mind
41	0·45	Degree of emotional arousal evoked by occurrences
72	0·44	Changeable tastes and habits
12	0·43	Moodiness
52	−0·43	Reaction to being slighted
30	−0·42	Restlessness
90	0·42	Being considered unworldly
98	0·42	Feeling unwanted by others
39	0·40	Difficulties in lecturing
23	0·39	Tiredness on waking
75	−0·39	Mood resilience
21	−0·38	Frustration tolerance
63	0·38	Feeling unappreciated
45	0·37	Fear of being tempted to use weapons
84	0·37	Considering others odd
1	0·34	Guilt feelings
58	0·33	Feeling uncomfortable with domestic employees
5	0·32	Chance remarks made for effect
64	0·32	Independence
69	0·32	Taking an active part in social affairs
57	−0·31	Sociability
83	0·31	Being thought soft hearted

TABLE 17.24

30	0·54	Restlessness
82	−0·52	Moods of feeling sorry for oneself
61	−0·50	Undue worries intruding on thoughts
12	−0·47	Moodiness
23	−0·42	Tiredness on waking
62	−0·42	Frustration tolerance
65	−0·42	Lack of concentration
63	−0·39	Feeling unappreciated
75	0·38	Mood resilience
21	0·37	Frustration tolerance
71	−0·37	Number of past regrets
90	−0·36	Being considered unworldly
46	0·35	Ability to deal with problems
72	−0·34	Changeable tastes and habits
83	−0·34	Being thought soft hearted
29	−0·32	Ideas coming into one's mind
98	−0·31	Feeling unwanted by others

Factor two equally clearly is Extraversion; it has a C.F.S. of 0·97. The items are given below in Tables 17.25 and 17.26.

TABLE 17.25

34	0·42	Doubts about truthfulness in others
17	−0·40	Subject preferences at school
38	−0·37	Attributes in choice of friends
15	0·36	Preference for active games
56	0·34	Mistrusting people
51	0·32	Carefreeness (self rating)
63	0·31	Feeling unappreciated

TABLE 17.26

57	0·59	Sociability
42	0·57	Self rating on sociability
22	0·53	Choice of employment
24	−0·51	Inhibitions in talking about sex
14	−0·49	Choice of recreation
51	0·45	Carefreeness (self rating)
89	0·41	Being considered eloquent
64	0·40	Independence
47	−0·36	Occupational preference
79	0·36	Need for a lot of social stimulation
97	−0·36	Reading matter preference
49	0·35	Showing one's feelings easily
10	−0·34	Dislike of jocularity
20	−0·34	Ease of expression
25	0·33	Occupational preference
95	0·33	Frequency of social outings
94	0·32	Being considered happy-go-lucky
52	0.31	Reaction to being slighted

Factor three presents something of a problem; it has a C.F.S. of −0·98, which suggests that it is not a statistical artefact. Judging by the items in it, we seem to be dealing with another kind of extraversion factor, perhaps more concerned with *socialization* than with *sociability*. We shall delay further discussion of this factor until we reach a later stage where the factors from one author are compared with those from both the others.

TABLE 17.27

42	0·57	Self rating on sociability
79	0·56	Need for a lot of social stimulation
14	−0·51	Choice of recreation
51	0·44	Carefreeness (self rating)
57	0·43	Sociability
59	0·41	Making one's point at all costs
50	0·40	Need to expose an unfair person
88	0·39	Urges for physical work-out
11	0·38	Wariness of possible dangers in unfamiliar surroundings
22	0·38	Choice of employment

TABLE 17.27 (*contd.*)

66	0·38	Negativism towards forceful people
89	0·37	Being considered eloquent
95	0·37	Frequency of social outings
28	0·34	Active versus passive ways of getting things done
24	−0·33	Inhibitions in talking about sex
64	0·32	Independence
54	0·31	Need for fresh air

TABLE 17.28

67	0·50	Occupational preference
47	−0·48	Occupational preference
93	0·48	Occupational preference
3	0·44	Occupational preference
7	−0·42	Attitudes to how leisure time is best spent
25	0·39	Occupational preference
39	−0·39	Difficulties in lecturing
20	−0·36	Ease of expression
38	0·36	Attributes in choice of friends
43	−0·33	Occupational preference
2	−0·31	Attitude to work methods
51	−0·31	Carefreeness (self rating)
68	0·31	Enjoying organizing things

This completes our examination of the factors extracted from Cattell's questionnaire. The main impression is that expectations raised by Cattell's writings are not fulfilled. His main factors are not replicable, either from our male to our female sample, nor from either of our samples to his own predicted grouping of items. Only at the third-order factor level do we encounter replicable factors, and these are not Cattell's factors, but N and E. In other words, Cattell's questionnaires may be used to measure these two type factors, and do so probably with the same degree of accuracy as do the Eysenck and Guilford questionnaires, but they should not be used to measure the Cattell primary factors, whose existence receives no support from this investigation.

18

FACTORS IN THE GUILFORD PERSONALITY INVENTORY

H. J. Eysenck, P. O. White and M. I. Soueif

WE have already commented on the fact that C.F.S.s for the Guilford questionnaire are intermediate between the Eysenck and the Cattell ones. Table 18.1 below shows the actual figures in some detail; optimum

TABLE 18.1

Guilford C.F.S. Data

Male Factor	Female Factor	C.F.S.
1	17	0·74
2	4	−0·94
3	3	0·63
4	19	0·51
5	9	−0·72
6	6	−0·61
7	10	−0·65
8	8	0·49
9	1	−0·90
10	13	0·84
11	12	0·42
12	5	0·85
13	11	0·75
14	18	0·54
15	15	0·51
16	7	0·76
17	14	0·31
18	17	−0·49
19	16	0·12
20	2	0·77

matching was attempted along the lines described in the preceding section. As before, we shall discuss all those pairs of factors whose C.F.S.s are above 0·60. Comparisons will also be made with the predicted factor patterns given by Guilford on the basis of previous work.

Factor 1. *Sociability*. This factor matches well across sexes, and it also matches well with Guilford's factor S (social shyness). There is little hesitation in naming this factor.

TABLE 18.2

108	−0·80	Liking to get together with others
70	−0·67	Number of social outings
22	−0·65	Concern if deprived of many friends and acquaintances
37	−0·61	Preference for leisure activities with or without friends
77	−0·60	Sociability
12	0·50	Limiting circle of friends
79	0·50	Wanting to see as few people as possible
65	−0·42	Preference for social evening rather than boxing match
5	−0·32	Playing jokes or tricks on others

TABLE 18.3

108	0·84	Liking to get together with others
79	−0·69	Wanting to see as few people as possible
70	0·66	Number of social outings
37	0·65	Preference for leisure activities with or without friends
22	0·52	Concern if deprived of many friends and acquaintances
77	0·44	Sociability
12	−0·40	Limiting circle of friends

Factor 2. *Moodiness*. This factor emerges as a mixture of Guilford's C and D factors (cycloid and depressed), with some intrusions from A and R.

TABLE 18.4

15	0·84	Mood changes
67	0·79	Mood swings
101	−0·78	Fluctuation of mood
40	0·68	Undue tiredness
52	0·47	Occurrence of feeling fed up
90	−0·47	Ability to stay happy even though one has problems
84	−0·42	Generally feeling well and happy
42	0·34	Strong objections to being dictated to by next of kin and acquaintances

TABLE 18.5

67	−0·87	Mood swings
15	−0·83	Mood changes
101	0·77	Fluctuation of mood
40	−0·70	Undue tiredness
52	−0·48	Occurrence of feeling fed up
90	0·45	Ability to stay happy even though one has problems
2	−0·40	Resentfulness when thwarted
81	−0·35	Need for constant stimulation and bustle
84	0·32	Generally feeling well and happy

Factor 3. *Carefreeness*. This matches to some extent with Guilford's Rhathymia, but with incursions from ascendancy and depression.

TABLE 18.6

30	−0·74	Overcarefulness
55	−0·66	Seriousness in attitude to work
56	0·43	Judgement of self as happy-go-lucky
39	0·42	Ability to get out of scrapes
54	0·42	Ability to think of a 'ready defence' when necessary
19	−0·40	Worries over awful things that might occur
38	0·38	A carefree attitude to life

TABLE 18.7

39	−0·82	Ability to get out of scrapes
54	−0·74	Ability to think of a 'ready defence' when necessary
30	0·58	Overcarefulness
55	0·52	Seriousness in attitude to work
56	−0·52	Judgement of self as happy-go-lucky
38	−0·32	A carefree attitude to life

Factor 4. *Sleeplessness*. This combines items from N (nervousness) and D (depression).

TABLE 18.8

58	0·83	Sleeplessness
92	0·72	Sleeplessness over troubles
21	−0·53	Ability to relax
80	−0·38	General good health

TABLE 18.9

58	0·78	Sleeplessness
92	0·74	Sleeplessness over troubles
21	−0·61	Ability to relax

Factor 5. *Dominance*. This is a mixture of Guilford's A, C, N and I factors, although the interpretation seems fairly clear and unobjectionable.

TABLE 18.10

46	0·74	Resentment at being dictated to
31	0·72	Aggression when provoked
28	0·69	Wanting to snub people who interfere with one's affairs
107	0·48	Belief that there is a great need for reform in traffic rules
26	0·34	Undue sensitivity to scraping sounds
93	0·31	Finding out limitations of an expert

TABLE 18.11

31	0·79	Aggression when provoked
46	0·61	Resentment at being dictated to
28	0·57	Wanting to snub people who interfere with one's affairs

Factor 6. *Optimism*. This is a mixture of Guilford's, D, C, R and Ag factors; the interpretation is not undertaken with any great faith.

TABLE 18.12

45	−0·69	Feeling that things are never all that bad
64	−0·59	Liking funny rather than straight films
85	−0·53	Believing one's future to be bright

TABLE 18·13

83	−0·69	Feeling that matters are more satisfactory if attended to personally
74	−0·56	Belief that the majority need a person to guide or instruct them
64	−0·50	Liking funny rather than straight films
19	−0·33	Worries over awful things that might occur
97	−0·32	Improving work when told one has done well

Factor 7. *Compassion*. This factor combines Guilford's M (masulinity) and Co (Co-operativeness) with O (Objectivity). There is also one item from the Ag scale.

TABLE 18.14

95	0·63	Compassion for animals
9	0·55	Sympathizing with others
72	0·51	Compassion for injured animals
1	−0·50	Honesty being a matter of fear of consequences
59	−0·45	Wanting to do shooting sports
74	−0·43	Belief that the majority need a person to guide or instruct them
18	−0·34	Belief that others mostly avoid duties if they can

TABLE 18.15

95	−0·78	Compassion for animals
72	−0·72	Compassion for injured animals
47	−0·44	General compassion for nations

Factor 8. *Inferiority*. This is almost entirely Guilford's factor I, with just a few intrusions.

TABLE 18.16

16	0·77	Feeling that one's merits are unrecognized by others
41	0·64	Feeling that one is not getting on as well as others
33	0·59	Feeling that one is not as good or capable as others
34	0·58	Apprehensiveness at not being popular
106	0·58	Belief that often others dislike one
98	0·50	Belief that others try not to associate with one
103	0·41	Wish to alter one's looks

TABLE 18.17

41	0·60	Feeling that one is not getting on as well as others
16	0·46	Feeling that one's merits are unrecognized by others
18	0·38	Belief that others mostly avoid duties if they can
89	0·38	Unhappy about introspecting
33	0·32	Feeling that one is not as good or capable as others
107	−0·31	Belief that there is a great need for reform in traffic rules

Factor 9. *Nervousness*. This is mainly Guilford's factor M, with several items from N thrown in, i.e. Lack of masculinity+nervousness.

TABLE 18.18

49	0·68	Attitudes to lack of personal hygiene in others
71	0·64	Attitudes to smell of sweat in others
99	−0·47	Nervous habits
72	0·39	Compassion for injured animals
95	0·32	Compassion for animals
102	0·32	Undue dislike of persistent sounds

TABLE 18.19

49	−0·67	Attitudes to lack of personal hygiene in others
71	−0·57	Attitudes to smell of sweat in others
102	−0·47	Undue dislike of persistent sounds
29	−0·46	Distractibility when working
26	−0·42	Undue sensitivity to scraping sounds
104	−0·34	Fear of certain animals

Factor 10. *Ascendancy.* This factor is almost entirely Guilford's Ascendancy and lack of Inferiority.

TABLE 18·20

10	−0·81	Arguing at meetings
44	−0·78	Expressing beliefs at meetings when opposed to speaker
87	0·59	Embarrassment at sitting in front row at meetings
96	−0·38	Holding one's own when one's rights are threatened
29	0·31	Distractibility when working

TABLE 18.21

4	0·58	Self confidence
24	−0·58	Tendency to be easily offended
94	−0·50	Inability to turn away unwanted salesmen
87	−0·49	Embarrassment at sitting in front row at meetings
91	−0·49	Willingness to challenge someone who cheats
96	0·44	Holding one's own when one's rights are threatened
34	−0·42	Apprehensiveness at not being popular
6	−0·37	Touchiness
33	−0·34	Feeling that one is not as good or capable as others

Factor 11. *Introspectiveness.* This factor contains all of Guilford's T-factor items, together with a few intrusions.

TABLE 18.22

86	0·75	Frequently wondering why people do the things they do
69	0·67	Wondering about motivation of other people's actions
76	0·66	Frequent discussions of the meaning of life
73	0·41	Enjoying talking of philosophical matters with others
66	0·40	Need for privacy to meditate
48	0·39	Periods of doing nothing but thinking or ruminating
64	−0·37	Liking funny rather than straight films

TABLE 18.23

86	0·78	Frequently wondering why people do the things they do
69	0·76	Wondering about motivation of other people's actions
76	0·66	Frequent discussions on the meaning of life
89	−0·39	Unhappy about introspecting
48	0·34	Periods of doing nothing but thinking and ruminating
53	−0·34	Occupational preference (one masculine, one feminine)
73	0·32	Enjoying talking of philosophical matters with others
109	0·31	Fears that someone may 'tune in' to one by telepathy

Factor 12. *Activity*. This factor corresponds well with Guilford's G (general pressure for overt activity).

TABLE 18.24

43	0·72	Personal tempo of work and play
51	0·64	Physical prowess and stamina
61	0·60	Enjoying activities requiring fast action
60	0·59	Habit of hurrying from one task to another
35	0·41	Working quickly but productively
36	0·39	Frequent bouts of energy
8	0·35	Worry about losing in sports
55	0·32	Seriousness in attitude to work

TABLE 18.25

60	−0·75	Habit of hurrying from one task to another
61	−0·71	Enjoying activities requiring fast action
51	−0·69	Physical prowess and stamina
36	−0·58	Frequent bouts of energy
43	−0·36	Personal tempo of work and play
12	0·32	Limiting circle of friends
37	0·31	Preference for leisure activities with or without friends

The results of this analysis differ from that carried out on Cattell's items in that the factors found coincide several times with those posited by Guilford to quite a remarkable extent. On other occasions it is found that two of Guilford's factors coalesce to give a perfectly interpretable single factor; Moodiness as a combination of cycloid and depressed, and Nervousness as a mixture of femininity and (Guilford's) nervousness are good examples. Even where several Guilford factors enter the picture, the factors involved are usually relatively easy to understand and interpret. We would conclude that the primary factors which emerge from the analysis of Guilford's items are psychologically superior to those which emerge from the analysis of Cattell's items.

The second-order factors will not be given here because although some of them can be interpreted with some confidence (Sociability is an outstanding example, with a C.F.S. of 0·92) the majority are rather mixed, and would not repay close scrutiny. We shall instead rather turn to the third-order factor level, where the men have two factors, the women three. The first factor is clearly neuroticism; it has a C.F.S. of 0·91.

TABLE 18.26

33	−0·58	Feeling that one is not as good or capable as others
34	−0·56	Apprehensiveness at not being popular
78	−0·55	Feeling uncomfortable in the presence of others
52	−0·54	Occurrence of feeling fed up
90	0·53	Ability to stay happy even though one has problems

TABLE 18.26 (*contd.*)

19	−0·52	Worries over awful things that might occur
56	0·52	Judgement of self as happy-go-lucky
2	−0·46	Resentfulness when thwarted
41	−0·46	Feeling that one is not getting on as well as others
67	−0·44	Mood swings
84	0·42	Generally feeling well and happy
27	0·41	Ability to take it calmly when found fault with
92	−0·40	Sleeplessness over troubles
16	−0·39	Feeling that one's merits are unrecognized by others
40	−0·39	Undue tiredness
103	−0·38	Wish to alter one's looks
80	0·35	General good health
6	−0·34	Touchiness
99	−0·34	Nervous habits
12	−0·33	Limiting circle of friends
15	−0·33	Mood changes
58	−0·33	Sleeplessness
21	0·32	Ability to relax
85	0·32	Believing one's future to be bright
109	−0·32	Fears that someone may 'tune in' to one by telepathy
10	0·31	Arguing at meetings
44	0·31	Expressing beliefs at meetings when opposed to speaker
101	0·31	Fluctuation of mood

TABLE 18.27

67	−0·56	Mood swings
34	−0·51	Apprehensiveness at not being popular
33	−0·50	Feeling that one is not as good or capable as others
92	−0·50	Sleeplessness over troubles
19	−0·49	Worries over awful things that might occur
40	−0·49	Undue tiredness
2	−0·47	Resentfulness when thwarted
52	−0·46	Occurrence of feeling fed up
15	−0·45	Mood changes
102	−0·44	Undue dislike of persistent sounds
6	−0·43	Touchiness
103	−0·43	Wish to alter one's looks
57	−0·42	Belief that rich people get a fairer legal hearing
109	−0·41	Fears that someone may 'tune in' to one by telepathy
14	−0·40	Purported belligerence of others
58	−0·40	Sleeplessness
78	−0·40	Feeling uncomfortable in the presence of others
82	−0·40	Wanting to be more robust
16	−0·38	Feeling that one's merits are unrecognized by others
75	−0·37	Habits such as doodling and tapping
41	−0·36	Feeling that one is not getting on as well as others

42	−0·36	Strong objections to being dictated to by next of kin and acquaintances
106	−0·36	Belief that often others dislike one
23	−0·35	Ease of startle response
24	−0·35	Tendency to be easily offended
25	−0·35	Judging others as foolish
18	−0·34	Belief that others mostly avoid duties if they can
29	−0·34	Distractibility when working
47	−0·34	General compassion for nations
48	−0·34	Periods of doing nothing but thinking or ruminating
87	−0·34	Embarrassment at sitting in front row at meetings
101	0·34	Fluctuation of mood
81	−0·33	Need for constant stimulation and bustle
90	0·33	Ability to stay happy even though one has problems
3	−0·32	Extreme dislike of a person or people
21	0·32	Ability to relax
63	−0·31	Thoughts wandering
69	−0·31	Wondering about motivation of other people's actions
84	0·31	Generally feeling well and happy

The second factor is equally clearly extraversion; it has a C.F.S. of −0·89, which is the lowest C.F.S. for a third-order factor we have so far encountered.

TABLE 18.28

56	−0·56	Judgement of self as happy-go-lucky
38	−0·53	A carefree attitude to life
61	−0·47	Enjoying activities requiring fast action
5	−0·46	Playing jokes or tricks on others
36	−0·46	Frequent bouts of energy
70	−0·46	Number of social outings
22	−0·42	Concern if deprived of many friends and acquaintances
54	−0·41	Ability to think of a 'ready defence' when necessary
59	−0·41	Wanting to do shooting sports
81	−0·40	Need for constant stimulation and bustle
60	−0·39	Habit of hurrying from one task to another
108	−0·39	Liking to get together with others
4	−0·36	Self confidence
17	−0·36	Restlessness when involved in active work
20	−0·35	Belief that forgiving people deserve to be tricked
77	−0·34	Sociability
18	−0·33	Belief that others mostly avoid duties if they can
39	−0·33	Ability to get out of scrapes
90	−0·33	Ability to stay happy even though one has problems
12	0·32	Limiting circle of friends
84	−0·32	Generally feeling well and happy
96	−0·31	Holding one's own when one's rights are threatened

TABLE 18.29

81	0·57	Need for constant stimulation and bustle
38	0·53	A carefree attitude to life
22	0·46	Concern if deprived of many friends and acquaintances
17	0·45	Restlessness when involved in inactive work
36	0·43	Frequent bouts of energy
68	0·42	Frequent yearning for extra money
70	0·42	Number of social outings
18	0·41	Belief that others mostly avoid duties if they can
39	0·38	Ability to get out of scrapes
20	0·37	Belief that forgiving people deserve to be tricked
54	0·37	Ability to think of a 'ready defence' when necessary
46	0·36	Resentment at being dictated to
28	0·34	Wanting to snub people who interfere with one's affairs
61	0·34	Enjoying activities requiring fast action
2	0·33	Resentfulness when thwarted
13	0·33	Easily aroused anger
5	0·32	Playing jokes or tricks on others
31	0·32	Aggression when provoked
59	0·32	Wanting to do shooting sports
56	0·31	Judgement of self as happy-go-lucky

The third factor is very small (3 items only) and has very low loadings; it will not here be interpreted.

TABLE 18.30

43	0·35	Personal tempo of work and play
44	0·35	Expressing beliefs at meetings when opposed to speaker
35	0·34	Working quickly but productively

Major comments and comparisons of the results in this section and those in other sections will be reserved until later. The main results of this analysis has been that again E and N emerge very clearly at the super-factor level, and give rise to acceptable C.F.S.s; first-order factors are more acceptable than those in the 1st section, and bear some resemblance to those postulated by Guilford, and also to those isolated in the analysis of the E.P.I.

19

COMBINED ANALYSIS OF CATTELL, EYSENCK AND GUILFORD FACTORS

P. O. White, H. J. Eysenck and M. I. Soueif

WE now describe the procedure utilized in combining the component scores from three separate questionnaires in a single analysis involving factors common to the three questionnaires at a given level in the factor hierarchy.

We construct a 3×3 supermatrix as follows: The diagonal submatrices (there is one corresponding to each of the three questionnaires) are the matrices of intercorrelations among the factors within questionnaires. These are the ϕ-matrices from the separate analyses. The off-diagonal submatrices are the cross-correlations between the corresponding sets of factors. They are computed directly from the component scores for individuals. The supermatrix may be schematized as follows:

$$\begin{matrix} R_{CC} & R_{CE} & R_{CG} \\ R_{EC} & R_{EE} & R_{EG} \\ R_{GC} & R_{GE} & R_{GG} \end{matrix}$$

Thus, R_{CC} contains the intercorrelations among the Cattell factors, R_{EE} contains the intercorrelations among the Eysenck factors and R_{GG} contains the intercorrelations among the Guilford factors. The off-diagonal submatrix R_{EC} contains the cross-correlations between the Eysenck factors and the Cattell factors. The other off-diagonal submatrices are similarly defined.

In illustration, let us consider the level 2 analysis for the male group. There are 7 second-order factors from the Cattell questionnaire, 7 second-order factors from the Eysenck questionnaire, and 7 second-order factors from the Guilford questionnaire. Thus, for this level 2 analysis the supermatrix is of the order 21×21 since there are 21 second-order factors in all. Rows 1—7 correspond to the Cattell second-order factors, rows 8—14 correspond to the Eysenck second-order factors and rows 15—21 correspond to the Guilford second-order factors.

The next step is to factor the supermatrix by the methods described earlier. That is to say we carry out a complete Hendrickson-White hierarchical analysis on this supermatrix. For convenience we refer to these factors among factors as superfactors to distinguish them from the ordinary higher-order factors within the separate analyses.

Since the variable vectors in these analyses are factors and since a number of the factors, particularly at the lower orders, are quite nebulous and do not themselves have particularly clear interpretations it is frequently extremely difficult to interpret the superfactors in terms of the loadings on these factors.

Consequently, it seemed desirable to compute the loadings on the superfactors of the original variables—in this case the questionnaire items themselves.

Let us come back to the level 2 analysis for illustration. We factor a 21×21 supermatrix of intercorrelations among the second order factors. Within this analysis we get 7 first-order factors, 3 second-order factors and a single third-order factor. Note that we use level to indicate the order of the factors from which the supermatrix is computed and order to indicate the order of the superfactors within this analysis. Thus there are 7 level 2 first-order factors and 3 level 2 second-order factors.

Let ${}_{C}A_{i}$, ${}_{E}A_{i}$, and ${}_{G}A_{i}$ refer to the i'th order factor loadings within the Cattell, Eysenck and Guilford batteries respectively and let ${}_{iC}A_{k}$, ${}_{iE}A_{k}$, and ${}_{iG}A_{k}$ refer to the submatrices of k'th order factor loadings in the level i supermatrix analysis. Thus, in the level 2 analysis the matrices ${}_{C}A_{2}$, ${}_{E}A_{2}$, and ${}_{G}A_{2}$ are the second-order factor matrices for the Cattell, Eysenck and Guilford analysis. The level 2 first-order factor matrix is of order 21×7. The matrices ${}_{2C}A_{1}$, ${}_{2E}A_{1}$, and ${}_{2G}A_{1}$ refer respectively to rows 1—7, rows 8—14 and rows 15—21 of this 21×7 matrix.

To project the level i-order k superfactors onto the original variables we compute the three submatrices ${}_{C}A_{i} \cdot {}_{iC}A_{k}$, ${}_{E}A_{i} \cdot {}_{iE}A_{k}$, and ${}_{G}A_{i} \cdot {}_{iG}A_{k}$. The first of these matrix products is the submatrix of loadings for the Cattell questions on the level i, k'th order factors. We return to our more specific example, for illustration. The submatrix of loadings for the Eysenck questions on the level 2 first-order factors is ${}_{E}A_{2} \cdot {}_{2E}A_{1}$. The first matrix in the product is of order 114×7, the second is of order 7×7 and, of course, the product is of order 114×7.

At this point we note that in the computations actually performed the entire supermatrix to be factored was computed by intercorrelating factor scores. Thus the diagonal submatrices are, because of minor rounding errors, not precisely equal to the corresponding ϕ-matrices.

This is offset by the guarantee that the supermatrices thus computed are Gramian and that all their latent roots are non-negative.

We now present a more general formulation. The subscripts i, j and k refer to levels, batteries and orders with j′ as an alternative subscript for batteries. The matrix ${}_iR_{jj'}$ is a submatric element of the level i supermatrix, ${}_iR$, which is factored to yield the level i factors of battery j and those of battery j′. The matrix ${}_iA_{jk}$ is the submatrix, for battery j, of loadings on the level i order k superfactors for the tests of battery j. It is computed as the product of two matrices. The prefactor, ${}_iA_{i}$, is the matrix of loadings on the order i factors of battery j for the tests of battery j. The postfactor, ${}_{ij}A_k$, is the matrix of loadings on the level i order k superfactors of the order i factors from battery j. The matrix ${}_i\phi_k$ is the matrix of intercorrelations among the level i order k superfactors and the matrix ϕ_{ji} is the matrix of intercorrelations among the order i factors from battery j. The structure matrix, ${}_iS_{jk}$ of intercorrelations between the tests of battery j and the level i order k superfactors, is computed as the product of the matrices ${}_iA_{jk}$ and ${}_i\phi_k$. Similarly, the structure matrix ${}_jS_i$, of intercorrelations between the tests of battery j and the order i factors of battery j, is computed as the product of the matrices ${}_iA_{jk}$ and ϕ_{ji}. Finally, the structure matrix ${}_{ij}S_k$ of intercorrelations between the order i factors from battery j and the level i order k superfactors, is computed as the product of the matrices ${}_{ij}A_k$ and ${}_i\phi_k$.

The reader may well be wondering at this point whether he can place much confidence in factors which are so far removed from the original observations. He might well note that the starting point for the analysis just described is a set of factors-among-factors and may suggest that perhaps we are just confounding error with more error. Such fears seem to be entirely unjustified. It will be seen, in the sections which follow, that it is precisely the higher order factors which appear in both sexes and appear in all three questionnaires.

At the third-order level, there were three factors for the men and four for the women; of these, however, only the first two in each case had a sufficient number of items with loadings above 0·3 to make interpretation possible. The first factor combines extraversion items from all three inventories, and is clearly identifiable as E; Table 19.1 shows the results for the men, and Table 19.2 the results for the women. For both sexes this is very much a C factor, not a T one; items deal with sociability (e.g. 42, 161, 171), liveliness (e.g. 126, 173), jocularity (e.g. 181, 209, 218), impulsiveness (e.g. 208, 112, 107), activity (e.g. 274, 88, 273), excitement (e.g. 79, 157, 294), carefreeness (e.g. 269, 51, 169) give clear evidence of the compound nature of this factor. The same items occur for both men and women, with very similar loadings; thus there is little reason to believe that E gives rise to different patterns of behaviour or self-description in the two sexes.

TABLE 19.1

C. 42	0·53	Self rating on sociability
C. 79	0·52	Need for a lot of social stimulation
E. 62	−0·51	Usually stay in the background at parties and get togethers
E. 25	0·49	Usually let yourself go and enjoy yourself a lot at a gay party
C. 14	−0·47	Choice of recreation
E. 53	0·47	Easily get some life into a rather dull party
E. 58	0·47	Like plenty of excitement and bustle around you
E. 82	0·47	Like practical jokes
E. 110	0·46	Like cracking jokes and telling funny stories to your friends
G. 38	0·46	A carefree attitude to life
G. 56	0·46	Judgement of self as happy-go-lucky
E. 56	0·44	Like playing pranks on others
E. 72	−0·44	Like working alone
E. 27	0·43	Other people think of you as being very lively
E. 108	−0·43	Usually keep 'yourself to yourself' except with very close friends
E. 29	−0·42	Mostly quiet when you are with other people
E. 51	−0·42	Find it hard to really enjoy yourself at a lively party
C. 51	0·41	Carefreeness (self rating)
E. 74	0·41	Rather lively
E. 109	0·41	Often get into a jam because you do things without thinking
C. 57	0·40	Sociability
E. 45	0·40	Be very unhappy if you could not see lots of people most of the time
G. 5	0·40	Playing jokes or tricks on others
G. 36	0·40	Frequent bouts of energy
G. 61	0·40	Enjoying activities requiring fast action
G. 70	0·40	Number of social outings
E. 37	−0·38	Hate being with a crowd who play jokes on one another
E. 70	0·38	Call yourself happy-go-lucky
E. 89	−0·38	Rather be at home on your own than go to a boring party
C. 59	0·37	Making one's point, at all costs
E. 17	0·37	Like going out a lot
G. 22	0·37	Concern if deprived of many friends and acquaintances
G. 81	0·37	Need for constant stimulation and bustle
C. 50	0·36	Need to expose an unfair person
C. 88	0·36	Urges for physical work-out
G. 54	0·36	Ability to think of a 'ready defence' when necessary
C. 11	0·35	Wariness of possible dangers in unfamiliar surroundings
C. 22	0·35	Choice of employment
E. 13	0·35	Often do things on the spur of the moment
E. 15	−0·35	Prefer reading to meeting people

G. 59	0·35	Wanting to do shooting sports
G. 60	0·35	Habit of hurrying from one task to another
C. 66	0·34	Negativism towards forceful people
C. 89	0·34	Being considered eloquent
C. 95	0·34	Frequency of social outings
E. 8	0·33	Generally do and say things quickly without stopping to think
E. 10	0·33	Do almost anything for a dare
E. 32	−0·33	If there is something you want to know about, you would rather look it up in a book than talk to someone about it
G. 17	0·33	Restlessness when involved in inactive work
E. 67	0·32	Like mixing with people
E. 94	−0·32	Usually do things better by figuring them out alone than by talking to others about it
G. 108	0·32	Liking to get together with others
C. 24	−0·31	Inhibitions in talking about sex
C. 28	0·31	Active versus passive ways of getting things done
E. 96	0·31	An easy going person, not generally bothered about having everything 'just so'
G. 18	0·31	Belief that others mostly avoid duties if they can
G. 20	0·31	Belief that forgiving people deserve to be tricked

TABLE 19.2

E. 17	−0·55	Like going out a lot
E. 25	−0·54	Usually let yourself go and enjoy yourself a lot at a gay party
C. 22	−0·53	Choice of employment
C. 57	−0·52	Sociability
E. 51	0·50	Find it hard to really enjoy yourself at a lively party
C. 42	−0·48	Self rating on sociability
E. 58	−0·47	Like plenty of excitement and bustle around you
E. 62	0·47	Usually stay in the background at parties and 'get togethers'
C. 24	0·45	Inhibitions in talking about sex
G. 38	−0·45	A carefree attitude to life
E. 15	0·44	Prefer reading to meeting people
E. 29	0·44	Usually quiet when you are with other people
C. 14	0·43	Choice of recreation
E. 13	−0·43	Often do things on the spur of the moment
G. 81	−0·43	Need for constant stimulation and bustle
C. 64	−0·42	Independence
E. 22	−0·42	When people shout at you, do you shout back
E. 74	−0·41	Rather lively
G. 22	−0·41	Concern if deprived of many friends and acquaintances
E. 27	−0·40	Other people think of you as being very lively
E. 67	−0·40	Like mixing with people
E. 109	−0·40	Often get into a jam, because you do things without thinking

TABLE 19.2 (*contd.*)

G. 56	−0·40	Judgement of self as happy-go-lucky
E. 36	0·38	Always declare everything at the customs, even if you knew that you could never be found out
G. 36	−0·38	Frequent bouts of energy
G. 70	−0·38	Number of social outings
C. 51	−0·37	Carefreeness (self rating)
E. 110	−0·37	Like cracking jokes and telling funny stories to your friends
C. 89	−0·36	Being considered eloquent
G. 17	−0·36	Restlessness when involved in inactive work
G. 39	−0·36	Ability to get out of scrapes
C. 25	−0·35	Occupational preference
C. 94	−0·35	Being considered happy-go-lucky
E. 8	−0·35	Generally do and say things quickly without stopping to think
E. 108	0·35	Usually keep 'yourself to yourself' except with very close friends
G. 54	−0·35	Ability to think of a 'ready defence' when necessary
C. 79	−0·34	Need for a lot of social stimulation
E. 5	0·34	Stop and think things over before doing anything
E. 45	−0·34	Be very unhappy if you could not see lots of people most of the time
E. 70	−0·34	Call yourself happy-go-lucky
C. 49	−0·33	Showing one's feelings easily
E. 37	0·33	Hate being with a crowd who play jokes on one another
E. 54	−0·33	Sometimes talk about things you know nothing about
E. 106	−0·33	Sometimes say the first thing that comes into your head
G. 61	−0·33	Enjoying activities requiring fast action
C. 10	0·32	Dislike of jocularity
C. 95	−0·32	Frequency of social outings
E. 113	−0·32	When the odds are against you, you still usually think it is worth taking a chance
E. 1	−0·31	Often long for excitement
E. 32	0·31	If there is something you want to know about, you would rather look it up in a book than talk to someone about it
E. 90	−0·31	Sometimes get so restless that you cannot sit long in a chair
E. 91	0·31	Like planning things carefully, well ahead of time
G. 68	−0·31	Frequent yearning for extra money

The second factor is identified equally clearly as neuroticism; all the items identified with this factor in the three separate analyses appear together in this one. Table 19.3 shows results for men, Table 19.4 for women; again the same items appear in both, with very similar loadings. Like E, N is clearly a C factor; all the different first-order factors noted in our previous discussions are represented.

TABLE 19.3

E. 2	−0·55	Often need understanding friends to cheer you up
E. 112	−0·53	Often feel self conscious when you are with superiors
G. 67	−0·53	Mood swings
C. 65	−0·49	Lack of concentration
E. 7	−0·49	Mood often goes up and down
G. 33	−0·49	Feeling that one is not as good or capable as others
C. 82	−0·48	Moods of feeling sorry for oneself
G. 19	−0·48	Worries over awful things that might occur
G. 34	−0·48	Apprehensiveness at not being popular
G. 92	−0·48	Sleeplessness over troubles
E. 66	−0·46	Moody
E. 78	−0·46	Your mind often wanders when you are trying to attend closely to something
G. 40	−0·46	Undue tiredness
G. 52	−0·46	Occurence of feeling fed up
E. 52	−0·45	Troubled with feelings of inferiority
C. 61	−0·44	Undue worries intruding on thoughts
G. 2	−0·44	Resentfulness when thwarted
E. 23	−0·43	Often troubled about feelings of guilt
E. 76	−0·43	Often feel 'fed up'
G. 15	−0·43	Mood changes
E. 11	−0·42	Suddenly feel shy when you want to talk to an attractive stranger
E. 16	−0·42	Feelings rather easily hurt
G. 102	−0·42	Undue dislike of persistent sounds
C. 29	−0·41	Ideas coming into one's mind
C. 41	−0·41	Degree of emotional arousal evoked by occurrences
E. 9	−0·41	Ever feel 'just miserable' for no good reason
E. 50	−0·41	Easily hurt when people find fault with you or your work
G. 6	−0·41	Touchiness
C. 72	−0·40	Changeable tastes and habits
E. 14	−0·40	Often worry about things you should not have done or said
E. 64	−0·40	Sometimes sulk
G. 78	−0·40	Feeling uncomfortable in the presence of others
C. 12	−0·39	Moodiness
C. 52	0·39	Reaction to being slighted
E. 21	−0·39	Daydream a lot
E. 40	−0·39	Worry about awful things that might happen
E. 49	0·39	Say that you were fairly self confident
E. 61	−0·39	Sometimes feel happy, sometimes sad, without any real reason
G. 103	−0·39	Wish to alter one's looks
G. 109	−0·39	Fears that someone may 'tune in' to one by telepathy
C. 30	0·38	Restlessness
C. 90	−0·38	Being considered unworldly
C. 98	−0·38	Feeling unwanted by others

TABLE 19.3 (*contd.*)

E. 46	−0·38	Call yourself a nervous person
E. 71	−0·38	Often felt listless and tired for no good reason
E. 97	−0·38	Suffer from 'nerves'
E. 107	−0·38	Worry too long after an embarrassing experience
G. 58	−0·38	Sleeplessness
E. 1	−0·37	Often long for excitement
E. 19	−0·37	Sometimes bubbling over with energy and sometimes very sluggish
E. 71	−0·37	Often make up your mind too late
G. 14	−0·37	Purported belligerence of others
G. 57	−0·37	Belief that rich people get a fairer legal hearing
G. 16	−0·36	Feeling that one's merits are unrecognized by others
G. 41	−0·36	Feeling that one is not getting on as well as others
G. 82	−0·36	Wanting to be more robust
C. 23	−0·35	Tiredness on waking
C. 39	−0·35	Difficulties in lecturing
C. 75	0·35	Mood resilience
E. 90	−0·35	Sometimes get so restless you cannot sit long in a chair
G. 90	0·35	Ability to stay happy even though one has problems
C. 21	0·34	Frustration tolerance
C. 63	−0·34	Feeling unappreciated
C. 84	−0·34	Considering others odd
E. 18	−0·34	Occasionally have thoughts and ideas that you would not like other people to know about
E. 85	−0·34	When you get annoyed you need someone friendly to talk to about it
E. 88	−0·34	Touchy about some things
G. 23	−0·34	Ease of startle response
G. 42	−0·34	Strong objections to being dictated to by next of kin and acquaintances
G. 101	0·34	Fluctuation of mood
G. 106	−0·34	Belief that often others dislike one
C. 45	−0·33	Fear of being tempted to use weapons
E. 109	−0·33	Often get into a jam because you do things without thinking
G. 75	−0·33	Habits such as doodling or tapping
G. 84	0·33	Generally feeling well and happy
E. 100	−0·32	Get nervous in places like lifts, trains or tunnels
E. 114	−0·32	Often get 'butterflies in your tummy' before an important occasion
G. 24	−0·32	Tendency to be easily offended
G. 25	−0·32	Judging others as foolish
G. 47	−0·32	General compassion for nations
G. 48	−0·32	Periods of doing nothing but thinking or ruminating
G. 87	−0·32	Embarrassment at sitting in front row at meetings
C. 1	−0·31	Guilt feelings
G. 21	0·31	Ability to relax
G. 29	−0·31	Distractibility when working

TABLE 19.4

E. 66	0·53	Moody
E. 7	0·51	Mood often goes up and down
E. 76	0·51	Often feel 'fed up'
G. 33	0·51	Feeling that one is not as good or capable as others
C. 82	0·50	Moods of feeling sorry for oneself
C. 61	0·49	Undue worries intruding on thoughts
G. 34	0·49	Apprehensiveness at not being popular
G. 52	0·49	Occurrence of feeling fed up
C. 30	−0·48	Restlessness
E. 38	0·48	An irritable person
G. 2	0·47	Resentfulness when thwarted
G. 78	0·46	Feeling uncomfortable in the presence of others
G. 90	−0·46	Ability to stay happy even though one has problems
G. 19	0·45	Worries over awful things that might occur
E. 97	0·44	Suffer from 'nerves'
C. 12	0·43	Moodiness
E. 46	0·46	Call yourself a nervous person
E. 35	0·42	Get attacks of shaking or trembling
E. 68	0·42	Often lost sleep over your worries
E. 71	0·42	Often make up your mind too late
G. 41	0·42	Feeling that one is not getting on as well as others
E. 73	0·41	Often felt listless and tired for no good reason
C. 75	−0·40	Mood resilience
E. 40	0·40	Worry about awful things that might happen
E. 64	0·40	Sometimes sulk
G. 56	−0·40	Judgement of self as happy-go-lucky
C. 65	0·39	Lack of concentration
E. 2	0·39	Often need understanding friends to cheer you up
E. 19	0·39	Sometimes bubbling over with energy and sometimes very sluggish
E. 52	0·39	Troubled with feelings of inferiority
E. 59	0·39	Often got a restless feeling that you want something but do not know what
G. 40	0·39	Undue tiredness
G. 92	0·39	Sleeplessness over troubles
E. 21	0·38	Daydream a lot
E. 23	0·38	Often troubled about feelings of guilt
E. 49	−0·38	Say you were fairly self confident
E. 57	0·38	Suffer from sleeplessness
C. 23	0·37	Tiredness on waking
E. 16	0·37	Feeling easily hurt
E. 50	0·37	Easily hurt when people find fault with you or your work
G. 103	0·37	Wish to alter one's looks
E. 9	0·36	Ever feel 'just miserable' for no good reason
E. 26	0·36	Call yourself tense or 'highly strung'
E. 112	0·36	Often feel self conscious when you are with superiors

TABLE 19.4 (*contd.*)

G. 84	−0·36	Generally feeling well and happy
C. 62	0·35	Frustration tolerance
E. 33	0·35	Get palpitations or thumping in your heart
E. 61	0·35	Sometimes feel happy, sometimes sad, without any real reason
E. 107	0·35	Worry too long after an embarrassing experience
C. 21	−0·34	Frustration tolerance
C. 46	−0·34	Ability to deal with problems
C. 63	0·34	Feeling unappreciated
E. 80	0·34	Often 'lost in thought'
G. 27	−0·34	Ability to take it calmly when found fault with
C. 71	0·33	Number of past regrets
E. 1	0·33	Often long for excitement
E. 92	0·33	Have 'dizzy turns'
E. 104	0·33	Find it hard to fall asleep at bedtime
G. 15	0·33	Mood changes
C. 29	0·32	Ideas coming into one's mind
G. 58	0·32	Sleeplessness
C. 83	0·31	Being thought soft hearted
C. 85	0·31	Psychosomatic symptoms under stress
E. 43	0·31	Have many nightmares
E. 95	0·31	Ever get short of breath without having done heavy work
G. 6	0·31	Touchiness
G. 80	−0·31	General good health

The third factor for the men is made up of Cattell items exclusively, and may thus be a statistical artefact, possibly due to the format of the questions; no psychological interpretation comes to mind. This factor is shown below in Table 19.5.

TABLE 19.5

C. 67	−0·50	Occupational preference
C. 47	0·49	Occupational preference
C. 93	−0·49	Occupational preference
C. 3	−0·46	Occupational preference
C. 39	0·40	Difficulties in lecturing
C. 7	0·39	Attitudes to how leisure time is best spent
C. 25	−0·39	Occupational preference
C. 20	0·37	Ease of expression
C. 38	−0·34	Attributes in choice of friends
C. 43	0·33	Occupational preference
C. 68	−0·33	Enjoying organizing things
C. 76	0·31	Need for appreciation

The third and fourth factors for the women are shown in Tables 19.6 and 19.7. The third factor is also made up exclusively of Cattell questions, and may also be just a statistical artefact due to questionnaire format. Factor four is made up exclusively of Guilford items; again some curious statistical artefact connected with questionnaire format is suggested, although it is not at all easy to pinpoint the precise feature responsible. In any case, these factors are very small, relatively unimportant, and difficult or impossible to interpret psychologically; it does not seem worth while to discuss them in any detail.

TABLE 19.6

C. 17	−0·45	Subject preferences at school
C. 38	−0·39	Attributes in choice of friends
C. 34	0·38	Doubts about truthfulness in others
C. 15	0·37	Preference for active games
C. 47	0·34	Occupational preference
C. 56	0·33	Mistrusting people
C. 93	−0·33	Occupational preference
C. 20	0·32	Ease of expression
C. 25	−0·32	Occupational preference
C. 2	0·31	Attitudes to work methods

TABLE 19.7

G. 44	0·38	Expressing beliefs at meetings when opposed to speaker
G. 35	0·37	Working quickly but productively
G. 43	0·37	Personal tempo of work and play
G. 10	0·31	Arguing at meetings
G. 93	0·31	Finding out limitations of an expert

Factors 1 and 2 are not entirely uncorrelated; for men and women respectively the correlations are −0·19 and −0·08. While negligibly small for all practical purposes these relations are probably genuine; both are in the same direction, and although no acceptable criterion of statistical significance is available, the large number of subjects used makes it possible that a very small but replicable correlation may obtain between neuroticism and introversion. On the other hand these data have gone through so many statistical procedures, each of necessity adding a certain amount of error, that we would not be justified in taking these correlations too seriously either. On a conservative estimate we might perhaps say that the data suggest that E and N overlap in their variances to the extent of 1 per cent; that is effectively to say that they are independent.

The items measuring the two dimensions are clearly separated. If we take a level of factor loadings of 0·4 as our minimum, we find that no E item has an N loading approaching this level, and of the N items none has an E loading approaching this level. This is an interesting empirical finding; theoretically there is no bar to items having loadings of 0·5 or even 0·7 on both factors simultaneously. Nor can this fact be explained in terms of item selection; the Eysenck Personality Inventory was admittedly constructed in such a way as to omit as far as possible items loading on both factors, but this is not true of the Cattell and Guilford items. These two authors explicitly tried to cover as much of personality as possible, and took considerable pains to choose items outside as well as inside the traditional E/N complex. Their failure to unearth items with high loadings on both scales is therefore likely to reflect a fact of nature; it also gives considerable support to the use of simple structure in deciding upon the position of factor axes in the personality field. The writer has always argued that simple structure and its applicability to a given field cannot be decided upon on the basis of *a priori* considerations, but has to be decided upon on a purely empirical basis; if items or tests can be found with equal ease inside the quadrants as on the axes, then clearly simple structure results in a purely superficial confirmation of factors effectively decided upon by item or test selection. This does not seem to be true in this case, and we may welcome this empirical validation of our choice of criterion for rotation.

We may conclude this part of the book by repeating our main finding, which is that primary factors are nonreplicable across sex for the most part, unless these factors are tautological, and that higher order or 'super-factors', i.e. E and N, are replicable across sex. Similarly, primary factors are not replicable from one investigator's set of questions to another's, while higher order or 'super-factors' are replicable. It would seem to follow that for experimental work and also for practical and applied work super-factors rather than primary factors are more likely to give useful and worth-while results; this conclusion will be discussed in some detail in the Epilogue.

PART THREE
Personality in Children

20

EXTRAVERSION AND NEUROTICISM IN CHILDHOOD

S. Rachman

THERE is growing agreement among child psychologists about the value of a bi-dimensional model of personality. Although the proposed models differ in details, it is possible to identify two dimensions which recur with extraordinary regularity. The dimension of extraversion closely resembles descriptions which have been variously called participation-withdrawal, sociable-isolated, approach-withdrawn, active-inactive. The second (Eysenckian) dimension, neuroticism, would seem to resemble the descriptions of ego-strength/ego-weakness, stable-unstable, emotionality and so forth. Bearing in mind the tremendous variations in sample selection, test construction and statistical treatment which are to be found in these studies, the consensus of opinion is quite remarkable. It would appear that the 'essence' of personality can survive practically any experimental vibrations. This trend is aptly described by Schaeffer's (1961) phrase—'converging conceptual models' for child behaviour. A similar development has also been noted in studies of adult personality. (Cf. Part I of this book.)

The crystallization of opinion among students of both adult and child personality is particularly interesting because, in both cases, the evidence is pointing towards the same two dimensions. This is encouraging and satisfying because it supports the idea of *continuity* in the growth of personality; it also raises the possibility of a unified theory of child and adult behaviour. The division of attention between child and adult psychology, although necessary, can lead one to regard children and adults as separate species. This convergence of models involving the same dimensions in both children and adults is therefore a reassuring event.

Furthermore, the emergence of similar dimensions in adult and child studies (usually independently conducted) strengthens the view that extraversion and neuroticism are viable and valuable concepts. The convergence of adult and child models of personality is also of psychobiological significance and accords very well with Eysenck's (1963) emphasis on the biological determinants of extraversion and neuroticism. *Extraversion and Neuroticism:* Cattell (1964) has expressed the view that 'every comprehensive personality theory may be said to contain at least implicit assumptions about the structure that personality assumes in the formative years .... research however has lagged far behind speculation.' It is to Cattell's credit that he is one of the few psychologists to have made a serious attempt at filling in the blank spaces. During the past decade he has examined personality at various ages ranging from early childhood through to adolescence and has sought to determine the feasibility of describing the personality of children and adults in the same terms. His results encourage the belief that this is possible and do indeed indicate some strong similarities between adult and child personality—even though they are assessed with different questionnaires, ratings and behavioural tests. In the investigations of four- and five-year-old subjects carried out with Peterson (Cattell and Peterson, 1959) for example, 81 *behavioural* response measures were used. The results are nevertheless comparable to those obtained from a *questionnaire* study of six- and seven-year-old children (Cattell & Coan, 1958), peer *ratings* among 10-14 year olds (Cattell & Gruen, 1954) and so forth.

The general nature and significance of Cattell's work is discussed elsewhere in this volume but it should be noted that his study of children has been criticized on methodological and rational grounds. Peterson (1961), for example, has argued that Cattell's results are more meaningful and reasonable if the multitude of factors are re-interpreted in terms of only the two largest factors, adjustment and introversion-extraversion. There is in fact a hint of this emphasis in Cattell's own work. Discussing the analysis of the behavioural tests given to the 4-5 year-old group, Cattell & Coan concluded that 'the factors checked here—but especially the general anxiety factor U.I. 24, the general neuroticism factor U.I. 23 and the extraversion-introversion factor U.I. 32—should provide a useful basis of determinate, uniquely-defined measures for those concerned with studies of personality development in childhood'. Re-considering Cattell's findings in terms of two-factor framework (adjustment and extraversion) Peterson found strong confirmation of their value across four different age-groups.

He re-analysed four of Cattell's studies by identifying the common elemental variables, tabulating the loadings on the common variables for all factors and then intercorrelating the loadings. All four studies involved rating procedures and the age-groups concerned were as follows: young students, 10-14 year-olds, 6-8 year-olds, 4 and 5 year-olds. The proportion of total variance accounted for by the first two factors was 46 per cent (31 per cent for factor 1). None of the remaining factors accounted for more than 6 per cent of the total variance. Arguing for efficiency in preference to sufficiency, Peterson suggests that the smaller factors, however real, are descriptively trivial. Accordingly he recommends that they be ignored in the interests of clarity, descriptive efficiency and scientific parsimony. His decision is amply justified by the demonstration that when the results of the four studies are compared in terms of the two dimensions only (i.e. adjustment and extraversion) a 'substantial resemblance' is revealed.

Factor 1 is 'primarily marked by obedience (in children), stability of interests and attitudes, responsibility, conscientiousness, good-natured, easy-going tendencies, patience, trust, good manners, freedom from jealousy, determination and perseverance, co-operativeness, modesty and emotional stability. Let us call it *General Adjustment*. Its resemblance to a reflection of the general neuroticism factor which Eysenck has so extensively discussed is rather striking.'

Peterson's second factor is 'principally marked by boldness, outgoing social tendencies, open expressiveness, gregariousness, energetic alertness, cheerfulness, attentiveness to others, and assertiveness. The resemblance to another factor emphasized by Eysenck, Introversion-Extraversion, is again fairly striking.'

The reliabilities of the two factors were found to be high and 'offer a reasonably solid basis for the development of more objective, economical measures of two evidently important personality traits.'

Peterson's re-analysis suggests the following propositions. Extraversion and neuroticism can be assessed reliably in children (even at the age of 4-5 years old). These dimensions are probably stable. They resemble the personality dimensions observed in adults.

Becker (1962) supports Peterson's view that a two-dimensional analysis of children's behaviour is demonstrable and useful. Parents and teachers were asked to rate the personality characteristics of a group of children. In the analysis, two major factors emerged; the first 'was empirically demonstrated to be equivalent to Peterson's introversion' and the second was described as 'the inverse of his adjustment factor.' Richards and Simons (1941) factor analysed the results obtained from ratings of nursery school children on the 30 Fels Child Behaviour Scales. Two clear factors emerged; one of them resembles Eysenck's neuroticism factor (or Schaeffer's love-hostility dimension; see below) and the other is suggestive of sociability (extraversion?). The third, doubtful, factor describes a mood component which the authors liken to introversion. Hewitt and Jenkins (1946) extracted information from 500 case-histories of problem children (mean ages 11-12) and ordered the data into 45 traits. They then carried out a modified form of cluster analysis which

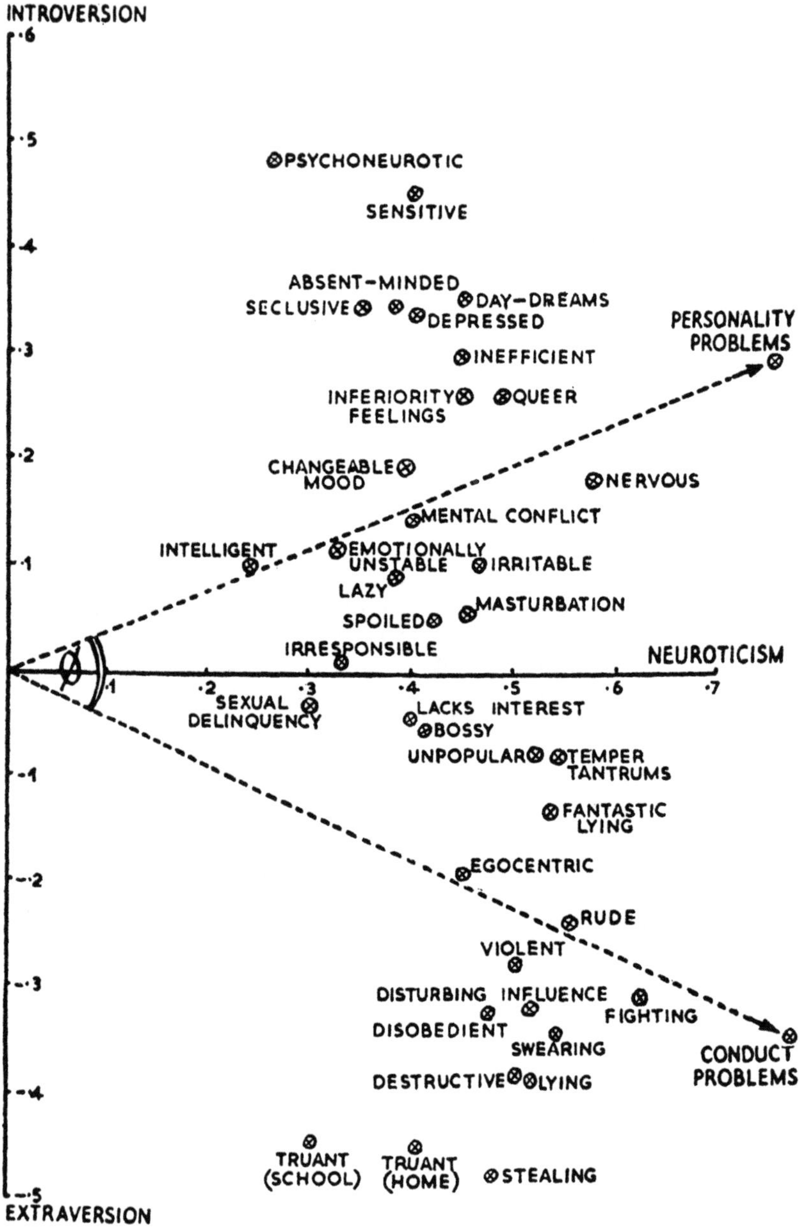

FIG. 20.1 Centroid analysis of behaviour problems in children. From Eysenck, 1960.

yielded 3 main clusters. The first one, 'unsocialized aggressive behaviour', included cruelty, malice, assaultive tendencies and fighting. The second cluster, 'socialized delinquency', included truancy, stealing, bad companions and gang activities. The third cluster, 'over-inhibited behaviour', included shyness, apathy, sensitiveness, submissiveness and seclusiveness. Similar findings emerge from Ackerson's (1942) study of behaviour problems in over 3000 children. He selected 162 traits and reported the inter-correlations between them. Himmelweit (1952) later carried out a centroid analysis on the data and obtained clear evidence of a general factor of neuroticism. Futhermore, a division between introverted and extraverted items also emerged (see Figure 20.1). In Himmelweit's analysis the two types of conduct disorder described by Hewitt and Jenkins (socialized and unsocialized) were not separated. The similarity of Himmelweit's results to those obtained from disturbed adults (Eysenck, 1957) is most marked. The children with 'personality problems' resemble the adult *dysthymic* groups described by Eysenck and the children with 'conduct problems' are similar to adult *hysterics*, psychopaths and criminals.

In discussing Cattell's work, it was pointed out that comparable results have been obtained from studies in which different assessment techniques were used. Three examples from independent investigations reinforce this view. The techniques used were ratings (Hallworth), questionnaires (Springob and Streuning) and behaviour tests (Koch).

Koch (1942) combined laboratory tests and time-sampling behaviour ratings in her study of pre-school children. Three main personality factors were obtained from the inter-correlations of the 38 variables involved. The first factor is suggestive of stability (as opposed to neuroticism). The second factor refers to social extraversion ('uninhibited and socially outgoing') and the third one is called 'lack of vigour'. In his recent study of 112 school children, Hallworth (1965) extracted 3 factors from teacher's ratings and self-report inventories. The two main factors were labelled 'extraversion' and 'emotional stability'. Springob and Streuning (1964) administered the California Personality Inventory (C.P.I.) to 226 boys and extracted five factors. There were two major factors; the first was self-acceptance and outgoingness (likened by the authors to extraversion) and the second, self-control which is compared to an adjustment factor. A similar result was reported by Mitchell and Pierce-Jones (1960) in their analysis of C.P.I. responses in adults.

Influenced no doubt by studies of the type mentioned here Slater, in 1962, proposed a two-dimensional model consisting of an introversion-extraversion scale and an ego-weak to ego-strong scale.

Similarly influenced by work of this nature (and more instances of theorizing and research could be quoted[1]) Schaefer (1961) attempted to

[1] See *The Structure of Human Personality* (H. J. Eysenck), Quay and Quay (1965).

structure these converging models into a circumplex scheme. 'There is,' he pointed out, 'substantial concurrence, both past and present, in two-dimensional conceptual models for social and emotional behaviour.' As can be seen in Figure 20.2, his scheme consists of an extraversion dimension and a love-hostility dimension. The latter description is preferred to 'neuroticism' because it 'emphasizes the quality of interpersonal relations of the dimension' and avoids its 'identification with psychoneurosis, to the exclusion of other patterns of maladjusted behaviour.' It is not clear what types of maladjusted behaviour Schaeffer

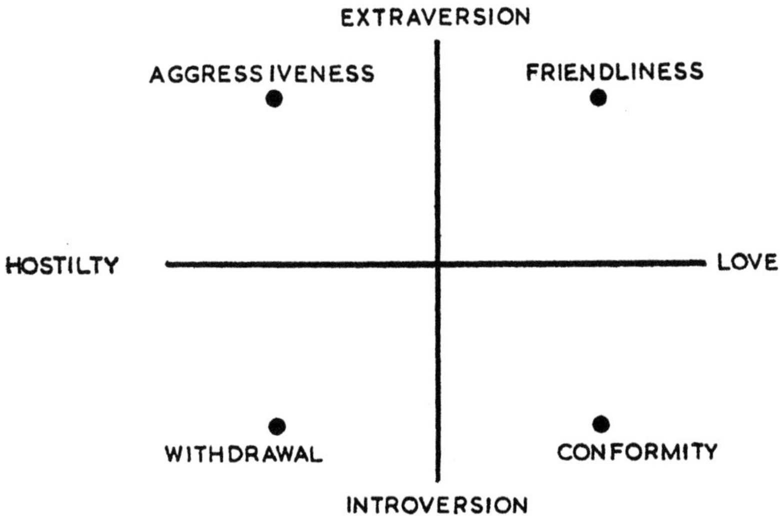

FIG. 20.2 Schaeffer's hypothetical model for social and emotional behaviour in children. Reprinted with permission from 'Parental Attitudes and Child Behaviour', edited by J. Glidewell. (C. Thomas, 1961.)

is referring to but it could as easily be argued that love-hostility is a misleading description. What, for example, is the relationship between love and conformity? While it would of course be desirable to agree on nomenclature, these differences are not of crucial significance. The similarity between these labels is emphasized by a recent study (Schaeffer *et al.*, 1966) in which the following result emerged. The first two factors 'clearly replicated this two dimensional structure with a clear factor of Extraversion-Introversion' and 'a general factor of Adjustment vs Maladjustment in the class room' (see Figure 20.3). In this same report, a slightly different procedure produced a love-hostility dimension instead; examination of the trait organization however makes it clear that the differences between the two dimensions are less than the names suggest.

More generally, Schaeffer's use of a circumplex model is a promising development which may yield an 'integrated view of a set of relationships'. It appears to be especially useful in attempting to bring parental and child behaviour into perspective. Another strength implicit in Schaeffer's approach is his use of the hierarchical approach to the organization of behaviour. In this approach, three levels of abstraction are involved; behaviour items, traits and factors (Eysenck, 1960).

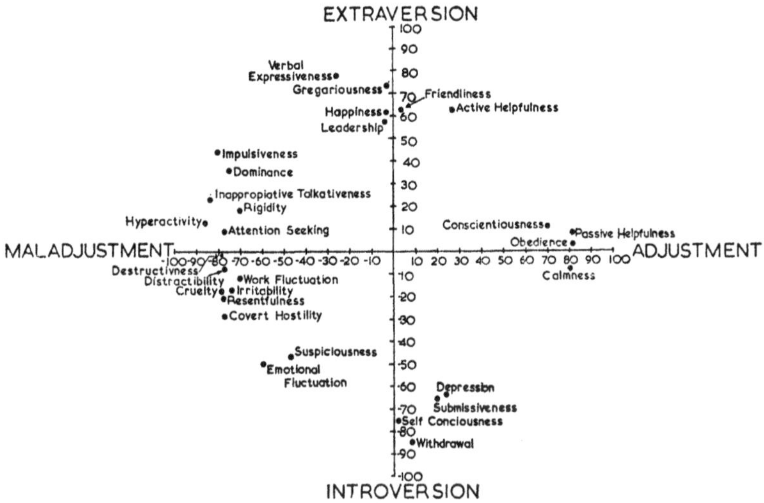

FIG. 20.3 Analysis of classroom behaviour ratings showing a Circumplex model in which two major dimensions emerge. Reprinted with permission from Schaefer, Droppleman and Kalverboer (1966).

It is not surprising that the experimental results and models discussed above differ in details. They were derived from widely differing samples, involved many techniques of assessment (mostly ratings, but also questionnaires and behaviour tests), and were computed and analysed in a variety of ways. The truly remarkable feature of this work is the extent of agreement which emerges. The dimensions of extraversion and neuroticism (or adjustment) appear to be viable and valuable concepts in child psychology.

It is also important to remember that when E and N are assessed directly (as in the case of the Junior Maudsley Personality Inventory—Furneaux & Gibson, 1961) the two dimensions are found to be independent. Callard and Goodfellow (1962) for example, obtained a correlation of −0·10 between E and N on this scale. This result was confirmed by Child (1964) who obtained a correlation of −0·07 between E and N, and by Crupley and D'Aoust (1965).

The Stability of Personality. One of the less obvious, but nevertheless significant, advantages of the dimensional analysis of personality was pointed by Emmerick (1964). He argues that the 'search for more encompassing dimensions offers an especially promising strategy for development analysis' on the ground that behavioural continuity may go undetected if small segments of behaviour are chosen for study. He quotes a convincing example from Kagan and Moss' (1962) longitudinal study in which it was found that apparently discontinuous segments of behaviour were later shown to be comparatively stable if they were subsumed under a single concept (e.g. masculinity).

There are clear indications from the Kagan and Moss and the MacFarlane *et al.* (1954) studies (among others) that certain types of behaviour do run a fluctuating course during childhood. Furthermore, the prediction of adult behaviour from childhood observations can be extremely difficult. It is also the case, however, that some degree of consistency and stability in children's behaviour *has* been convincingly demonstrated. In the presence of this apparently confusing evidence, Emmerick's suggestion has considerable appeal. It should follow of course that a major personality dimension, such as extraversion, would be a particularly appropriate yardstick for use in longitudinal research. In fact, the available evidence (although incomplete and sketchy) on the development of extraversion encourages the view that it is an enduring dimension and can be detected at a fairly early age. The neuroticism dimension does not seem, on present evidence, to be equally stable.

In their analysis of the ratings of children's behaviour from infancy through adolescence, Bayley and Schaefer (1963) found 'evidence for both consistency and change in overt behaviour,' (p. 94). Social and emotional behaviour appear to become more stable with age[1]—a trend which they liken to intellectual development. Their 'most striking finding' was the 'pervasive and relatively high correlations of early activity and rapidity with subsequent behaviour.' High motility in infancy may be a good predictor of later behaviour and would seem to be an innately determined attribute. The stability of motility measures during infancy has of course been reported in numerous studies (e.g. Fries & Woolf, 1954; Escalona & Heider, 1959; Thomas *et al.*, 1964).

The finding of greatest interest to the present discussion is that *early ratings of rapid, active behaviour are positively correlated with extraverted behaviour in the later years*. Further evidence, relating behaviour in early childhood to behaviour at 9 and 12 years of age, suggests that 'social extraversion may be relatively consistent from infancy to pre-adolescence.' The correlations with adolescent behaviour were 'not clear' and may be attributed to the inconsistencies which they observed to occur during the adolescent period.

Shyness and friendliness were reliably assessed at an early age and

[1] A common observation (see Kagan and Moss, MacFarlane *et al.*, for examples).

found to correlate rather well with behaviour in late childhood and adolescence. Early friendliness for example, showed positive correlations with the adolescent behavioural clusters of friendly, social and independent and negative correlations with timidity and reserve.

Early signs of emotional adjustment were found to be poor predictors of later behaviour. 'More enduring patterns of adjustment develop at later ages.' Sex differences in adjustment begin to emerge in late childhood with boys showing greater consistency. During adolescence however the boys' behaviour patterns tend to show greater fluctuations. Sex differences of this type were also noted by Kagan and Moss (among others). For example, they reported that aggression was found to be a more consistent trait in boys; dependency more consistent in girls. MacFarlane *et al.* (1954) obtained similar findings; boys are consistently more aggressive and from the age of 4½ onwards, girls are consistently more dependent.

The main findings of the Schaeffer and Bayley study can be summarized in this way. Ratings taken in early, middle and late childhood can be ordered within two-dimensional space; the introversion dimension is particularly consistent. The love-hostility dimension (Neuroticism?) is less consistent, with age and sex differences becoming marked in early adolescence.

In his short-term longitudinal study of 38 nursery-school children Emmerick (1964) obtained evidence of the stability of extraversion even in early childhood (3–4 years). He states that 'interpersonal-impersonal orientation was a highly stable and continuous organizer of personality variance throughout the four semesters, revealing the importance of this manifestation of extraversion-introversion in early social development'.

It is instructive to turn from this short-term study of young children to a longitudinal study bridging two decades. Tuddenham (1959) followed up 72 members of an adolescent growth study carried out in the late thirties. Of the 106 stability coefficients which he examined, 98 were found to be significant (but not spectacularly high). He extracted some clusters from the mass of correlational data and reported that the most stable of these included half the variables and clearly resembled extraversion-introversion. 'Among the stable variables for both sexes were several which connoted expressiveness and expansive spontaneity vs inhibition, and which may be closely related to an extraversion-introversion dimension' (p. 28). The most stable single variable for men was 'drive aggression'—a finding which concurs with that reported by Kagan and Moss. The most stable feminine variable was 'social prestige' which may or may not be related to Kagan and Moss's trait 'dependency.'

In similar vein, Bloom (1964) quotes the results of an unpublished longitudinal study by Tyler. Four hundred and two adolescent boys and 184 girls were given personality inventories to complete after a 4-year interval (17-21 years of age) and it was found that the re-test correlations for 'social introversion' and 'thinking introversion' were in the region of +0·60.

One of the most interesting studies in this connection is a follow-up reported by Burt (1965), the results of which fit in remarkably well with those of the Himmelweit (1952) analysis of Ackerman's data. Teachers' ratings were obtained on 763 children, of whom 15 per cent later became habitual offenders, while 18 per cent became neurotics. Assessments were obtained on the child's emotionality and his extraverted or introverted temperament; ratings of 'high-emotionality' were given to the highest 25 per cent in the group, and similarly 25 per cent were rated 'introverted' and 25 per cent 'extraverted.' Habitual offenders received ratings of 'high emotionality' in 63 per cent of all cases, neurotics in 59 per cent. Habitual offenders were rated 'extraverted' in 54 per cent of all cases, 'introverted' only in 3 per cent; neurotics were rated 'introverted' in 44 per cent of all cases, 'extraverted' only in 14 per cent. The results show reasonable predictive accuracy, and fit in well with theoretical expectation.

Sex Differences. Numerous attempts have been made to assess 'adjustment' in children; in recent years considerable effort has gone into the development and evaluation of anxiety scales. The most popular of these have been the CMAS (Children's Manifest Anxiety Scale) and the GASC (General Anxiety Scale for Children). Examples of neuroticism scales include the Junior Maudsley Personality Inventory and the Junior Eysenck Personality Inventory. Summing up the general findings from work in this field, Turland (1965) concluded that in practically all the studies reported, the girls had higher anxiety scores than the boys (see Castaneda *et al.* (1956); Costello & Brachman (1962); Rie (1963) for examples). This conclusion was also reached by Terman and Tyler (1954) in their detailed examination of the evidence from surveys and questionnaire studies. The emphasis in their assessment however, was on emotional stability rather than anxiety per se.

In general, the anxiety (or neuroticism) scores tend to show a slow decline with increasing age. The most frequent exceptions to this trend are found to occur in early adolescence. Sometimes, the increased scores are restricted to girls (Eysenck, S., 1965) but boys have occasionally shown similar changes (Rie, 1963). This upsurge of neuroticism during early adolescence has of course been independently noted in clinical investigations and surveys (Eysenck & Rachman, 1965).

Sex differences in extraversion have rarely been studied in children but Eysenck's (1965) results suggest a small, consistent trend towards higher E scores in boys. Gibson (1964) reported a similar (non-significant) trend on the Junior MPI, while Costello & Brachman (1962) found no sex differences with the same Test. The surrounding evidence is by no means clearcut; Terman & Tyler (1954) concluded that the evidence points to greater sociability in girls but that boys are more dominant and aggressive than girls at virtually all ages. The sexual differences in aggression have already been noted above. The MacFarlane study (1954) is concerned with behaviour *problems* and can add little to our knowledge of sex differences in extraversion. If anything however, it suggests that girls are more likely to develop dysthymic disorders than extraverted disturbances; boys are more prone to develop extravert disorders than introvert disorders.

Lie Scale. The incorporation of lie scales in questionnaires for children has produced some unexpected outcomes. The original purpose underlying the insertion of lie items was presumably to control for faking. Sarason *et al.* (1960) and Castaneda *et al.* (1956) among others, have reported non-significant relationships between L scores and anxiety (or neuroticism). On the other hand, Lunneborg (1964) and Lunneborg & Lunneborg (1964) obtained significant correlations between L scores and social desirability. In addition, Eysenck (1965) found that lie scores decline with age; a result which prompted her to regard (low) L as a measure of social maturity. Her view receives partial support from MacFarlane's (1954) longitudinal study in which it was reported that lying frequency declines with age. Moreover, social desirability scores also decline with age and (high) scores are correlated with lower intelligence (Crandall *et al.*, 1965).

The social significance of lie scores is an intriguing problem but from the practical point of view, these scores do not always seem to have a direct influence on adjustment scores obtained through questionnaires. However, Levitt (1957) obtained significant negative correlations between L scores and anxiety scores in a group of 322 Chicago children. The highest (negative) correlation was obtained from 4th-grade children and the overall correlation for the entire sample was $-0{\cdot}20$ ($p < 0{\cdot}001$). Similar relationships between N and lie scores were found by Gibson (1964) in a study involving the Junior MPI. Lie scores correlated with N Scores to the extent of $-0{\cdot}54$ in girls and $-0{\cdot}28$ in boys. Lie scores were not significantly correlated with E scores. The meaning of these findings is by no means clear; from a practical point of view, however, the simple equation of the N scores obtained by different subjects (without regard to their Lie scores) seems inadvisable at this stage.

An Overview. The utility of a bi-dimensional model in the description and analysis of childhood personality appears to be well established. There is indeed a striking 'convergence of conceptual models' which bear a strong resemblance to models of adult personality. It is suggested furthermore that the dimensions of extraversion and neuroticism could be utilised with great advantage in studies of personality in children. Developmental studies in particular would benefit from the application of these clear and stable dimensions.

Although the following propositions are presented partly as a succinct account of the available information, they are primarily intended as a guide for further explorations.

1. Extraversion and neuroticism can be assessed reliably in children (even at the age of 4-5 years ?).
2. These dimensions are stable.
3. They resemble the personality dimensions observed in adults.
4. Activity and rapidity in infancy are related to extraversion in childhood.
5. Boys are more stable (emotionally) than giıls (i.e. have lower N).
6. Boys are more aggressive (and possibly more extraverted) than girls.

21

PERSONALITY DIMENSIONS IN CHILDREN

S. B. G. Eysenck

IT is curious that children, as compared to adults, have attracted relatively little interest on the part of personality psychologists. Inventories and questionnaires are thick on the ground as far as adults (consenting or not) are concerned, but children are much less well catered for. Only two children's personality inventories are at all widely used in this country at the moment; one is the Cattell IPAT scale (Porter & Cattell, 1960), the other the Junior M.P.I. (Furneaux & Gibson, 1961). In both cases it should be noted that there have never been conducted proper item analyses and factor analyses for all the questions used, for all age groups, and for the two sexes separately; such detailed analyses are in our opinion necessary in order to take into account possible age and sex variations in factor structure, and in order to gain some more information on the organization of personality in children as they pass from one age to another. The present chapter reports in detail some of the work done in the construction of the Junior E.P.I. (S. B. G. Eysenck, 1965a; b); hardly any of this material has been made available hitherto in view of the severe space restrictions in the Manual which accompanies the inventory.

The scale was designed to measure the two major personality traits of neuroticism (stability/emotionality) and extraversion/introversion. (The inventory also contains a lie scale for the detection of faking.) The construction of an experimental set of 108 items was begun by carefully selecting, adapting and re-writing items contained in the adult version of the E.P.I., and adding further items. Items presented below (Table 21.1) are adapted with permission from the Junior Eysenck Personality

Inventory, copyright 1965 by Educational and Industrial Testing Service, San Diego. All references in this chapter will be to the items and numbers as given in this Table. (Occasionally reference to items in the course of the test will be in abbreviated form, or with the wording slightly changed so as to conform to the grammatical structure of the sentence.) From these items were finally chosen the 24 items which constitute the final E scale, and the 24 items which constitute the final N scale; the items in this Junior E.P.I. are also numbered, and these numbers are of course different to those in the Table below. Items adapted from the Junior E.P.I. are also printed in the text on a later page, and on that occasion the numbers of the items in Table 21.1 will also be given again for each item, to make comparisons easier.

TABLE 21.1

1. Like plenty of excitement going on around you
2. Often need kind friends to cheer you up
3. Like working alone best
4. Often get a feeling that you want something but you don't know what
5. Often long for exciting things to happen
6. Sometimes feel happy and at other times sad for no special reason
7. Shy of speaking first when you meet new people
8. Say things you are thinking quickly
9. Usually happy and cheerful
10. Sometimes go quiet when you are angry
11. Stop and think before doing things
12. Find it very hard to take no for an answer
13. Usually feel if things go badly that they will work out right in the end
14. Moody
15. Usually say things quickly without stopping to think
16. Sometimes feel specially cheerful and at other times sad without any good reason
17. Rather lively
18. Ever feel 'just miserable' for no good reason
19. Suddenly feel shy when you want to talk to someone you don't know
20. Find it hard to get to sleep at nights because you are worrying about things
21. Do almost anything if someone dared you to do it
22. Often make up your mind when it is too late
23. Like to plan things carefully before you do anything
24. Often worry about things you should not have done or said
25. Often make up your mind to do things suddenly
26. Feelings rather easily hurt
27. Usually feel that things are bound to work out badly for you
28. Often feel tired for no good reason
29. Like mixing with other children
30. Often feel fed up
31. Call yourself happy-go-lucky

32. Your mind often wanders off when you are doing a job
33. Rather be alone instead of meeting other children
34. Like to stick to one game for a long time
35. Nearly always have a quick answer when people talk to you
36. Sometimes bubble over with energy and sometimes do things seem an awful effort
37. Rather sit and watch than play at parties
38. Soon tire of your toys
39. When you get cross, it helps if you have somebody friendly to talk to
40. Often think of your past
41. Like going out a lot
42. Grown-ups think you are a naughty child
43. Like to have just a few really good friends you can trust
44. Often cry
45. When children shout at you, you shout back
46. Often feel lonely
47. (for boys) Usually shy when you meet girls
    (for girls) Usually shy when you meet boys
48. After you have done something important you afterwards feel you could have done better
49. Usually let yourself go and enjoy yourself at a gay party
50. Ideas run through your head so that you cannot sleep
51. Too shy to ask strangers to give you money for some good cause, like the Scouts
52. Touchy about some things
53. Like practical jokes
54. Sometimes get so restless that you cannot sit in a chair long
55. Usually do a job better by thinking it out alone than by asking others about it
56. Have 'dizzy turns'
57. Often get into trouble because you do things without thinking first
58. Get thumping in your heart
59. Other people think of you as being very lively
60. Get attacks of shaking or trembling
61. Rather be at home than at a dull party
62. Lots of things annoy you
63. When someone quarrels with you, you prefer to have it out rather than keep quiet hoping that things will blow over
64. Worry about awful things that might happen
65. Mostly quiet when you are with others
66. Have many frightening dreams
67. There are many foods you hate
68. Ever get short of breath without having done heavy work
69. Rather plan things than do things
70. Suffer from nerves
71. Often like a rough and tumble game
72. Troubled by lots of tummy aches
73. Like the kind of work that you have to keep thinking about and attending to

TABLE 21.1 (*contd.*)

74. Get frightened in places like lifts, trains or tunnels
75. An easy going person who does not worry about having things just so
76. Sweat a lot without having done much
77. Hate being with a crowd who play jokes on one another
78. Get very bad headaches
79. Like doing things where you have to act quickly
80. Call yourself a nervous person
81. When you make new friends you usually make the first move
82. Bother you if people watch you work at school
83. Slow and unhurried in the way you move
84. Give up easily when things go wrong
85. Like talking to people so much that you would talk to anybody you meet
86. Worry for a long while if you feel you have made a fool of yourself
87. Find it hard to go to sleep at bedtime
88. Sometimes feel life is just not worth living
89. Be very unhappy if you could not see lots of people most of the time
90. Easily hurt when people find fault with you or the work you do
91. Sometimes say the first things which come into your head
92. Usually feel fairly sure you can do the things you have to
93. Find it hard to really enjoy yourself at a lively party
94. Feel shy and awkward when you are with important people
95. Usually not say much except to your nearest friend
96. Feel you are no good and can't do anything right
97. Get a party going
98. Worry about getting ill
99. Take things very seriously rather than laughing them off
100. Often get 'butterflies in your tummy' before an important occasion
101. Like playing pranks on others
102. Hate to do more than one thing at a time
103. Very much afraid of the dark
104. On T.V. you like watching Cowboy films better than stories with animals in them
105. Like telling jokes or funny stories to your friends
106. Feel awkward when you are dressed up and in new clothes
107. Still think it is worth having a go at a game even if you are not sure you will win
108. Lie awake a lot during the night

The experimental form of the E.P.I. was administered to 6,760 school children between the ages of 7 and 16. Most of the children came from the Rotherham area, near Sheffield, but several London schools were also tested. It should be noted that the older children, i.e. those in the 15 and 16 year groups, are not as good a sample of the general population as are the younger children because some children in these age groups elect to leave school so that those who remain are self-selected to some degree. For this reason 16 year olds from youth clubs and some apprentices in industry who had left school were included in the oldest age group, but this device can hardly guarantee a proper sample. Since the 16 year old group is, by necessity, so heterogeneous it may be as well to interpret results for this age with some caution. Tests were administered in groups; for the younger ages, with some reading difficulties, the questions were read out as well by the tester. The children were not queried regarding their understanding of the questions it was thought that the results of the analysis of the data would be more revealing in this respect than the untutored introspections of young children.

The first analysis to be carried out involved intercorrelations of the 108 items for each age group separately, but with the sexes combined. There were thus 9 matrices of intercorrelations, the 16 year group being omitted because of the rather small number of cases, and because of its possible failure to be representative. Product-moment correlations were used throughout. Principal component factors were extracted, two for each matrix; our concern at this stage was entirely with the E and N factors, and we have shown in a previous chapter that the first two factors to emerge from a principal components analysis are very good approximations to the higher-order E and N factors which emerge from an oblique factor analysis. Such a more complex analysis, with emphasis on primary (first-order) factors will be presented subsequently. The emerging factors were rotated analytically according to the Promax programme, and the emerging factors interpreted as E and N. Table 21.2 shows the numbers of cases in each analysis, as well as the latent roots for the two factors. (The rotations involved were quite small; had they not been made at all the interpretation would have been equally clear.)

TABLE 21.2

Latent roots

n	Age	N	E	L
491	7	9·615	3·573	2·718
580	8	9·320	3·560	3·023
761	9	8·447	3·834	3·340
844	10	8·684	3·919	3·300
989	11	9·596	4·188	3·140
747	12	9·617	4·295	3·681
804	13	9·209	5·453	2·974
786	14	8·309	4·927	3·077
527	15	8·914	6·615	4·188

Also given in Table 21.2 are the results obtained from intercorrelating and factor analysing a lie scale of sixteen items 12 of which form part of the J.E.P.I. The scale was constructed by adapting and rewriting from the E.P.I. and adding others. The scale was given to a further set of school children not previously tested, amounting in all to 2,777. One factor only was extracted in each of the ten analyses carried out; this factor loaded on all the items and contributed latent roots as indicated in Table 21.2. Items and factor loadings are shown separately in Table 21.3.

24 N and 24 E items were selected from the 108 items in order to form the final Junior E.P.I. scale. The items were chosen on the basis of the following considerations: (1) High loadings on one factor. (2) Low loadings on the other factor. (3) Consistency of loadings over different age groups. Table 21.4 shows the factor loadings of all items, their original numbers on the 108 item list given in Table 21.1, and their loadings from E and N, the numbers of the items chosen for the J.E.P.I. have had an E or an N printed after them.

Inspection suggests reasonably close agreement, both for E and N, between loadings over age groups. However, a more exact method of comparison is required, and accordingly factor comparisons were carried out using the Kaiser (1960) method.[1]

The results of the factor comparisons are shown in Table 21.5; values concerning E are given above the leading diagonal, and values concerning N are given below the leading diagonal. It will be seen that all the values are reassuringly high, only falling below 0·9 on two occasions, and exceeding 0·98 most of the time. It is particularly interesting that there is no obvious decline in size of factor comparisons with age; the 7 year old children are not notably inferior to the 12 or 15 year olds in this respect. There is a tendency for the N factor to be more stable than the E factor, but the differences are not very large, and even for the E factor it cannot be said that factor comparisons suggest great variations in factor structure with increasing age. Our conclusion must be that: (1) neuroticism as a dimension of personality can be isolated as early as age 7 by means of questionnaires: (2) extraversion as a dimension of personality can be isolated as early as age 7 by means of questionnaires: and (3) both dimensions retain their identity from age 7 to age 15, and indeed to adulthood.

Additional questions inevitably arise, primarily related to the existence and nature of primary factors in these various groups, and also to the problem of sex differences in factor structure. We shall try to answer these two questions. In order to obtain data relating to the

[1] As explained before a preliminary orthogonal transformation to maximize the pairwise sum of inner products between variables vectors match variables as closely as possible in a common space, and the cosines of the angles between the two sets of factor vectors in this space are computed. Input to the programme is an orthogonal factor matrix for each study and the reference vector transformation matrix for each study. If the factor solution is orthogonal the corresponding transformation is an identity matrix.

and others whose experience with children suggested that there would be little if any understanding among 7 and 8 year olds of personality questions presented in this manner. Our own expectations were coloured by these forecasts, and we were agreeably surprised by the positive outcome of the analyses reported in these pages.

The primary factors discussed above are not of course orthogonal, and their intercorrelations give rise in turn to second-order factors; these are not reported here as they could not be interpreted. (It will be recalled that an identical phenomenon appeared in the case of the adult material discussed on a previous page.) When third-order factors were extracted, it was found (1) that 3 of these exceeded the minimum requirements, (2) that one of the three made relatively little contribution to the variance, and could not readily be interpreted, and (3) that 2 factors were readily identifiable as E and N respectively. It may be of some interest to compare these E and N factors with those given in Table 21.4. In order to save space, and make this comparison easier, we have given in Table 21.20 loadings only for the 48 items which make up the E and N scales of the Junior E.P.I. Table 21.20 also contains loadings for our small 16 year old sample, which consisted of 231 children only.

TABLE 21.19

Shyness — *Factor comparisons*

	7	8	9	10	11	12	13	14	15	16
7										
8	0·491									
9	0·703	0·787								
10	0·576	0·812	0·886							
11	0·514	0·785	0·816	0·886						
12	0·560	0·864	0·886	0·918	0·899					
13	0·612	0·864	0·873	0·951	0·686	0·873				
14	0·471	0·896	0·849	0·950	0·839	0·883	0·955			
15	0·419	0·824	0·774	0·862	0·794	0·829	0·945	0·899		
16	0·489	0·805	0·828	0·903	0·763	0·846	0·949	0·916	0·947	

Factor comparisons were again computed for E and N; the values were slightly lower than in the case of the principal components factors, but still in excess of 0·90 in the great majority of cases. Factor comparisons for E were again slightly lower. Greater stability would appear to attach to the principal components factors, as might have been expected in view of the extensive series of statistical manipulations which the Promax higher order factors have undergone; for this reason alone one might, in this situation, prefer the values given by the principal components analysis. However, no real choice is of course involved, in view of the fact that the final N and E items chosen from the whole list of 108 would probably have been much the same regardless of which of the two solutions had been preferred; the similarities are so great as to swamp the slight differences for all practical purposes.

We have already mentioned the third higher-order factor which appeared in our analyses, and dismissed it as uninterpretable. The possibility was considered that it might bear some similarity to the postulated factor of 'psychoticism' (Eysenck, 1960) which would be expected to emerge from a study such as this provided suitable questions were included. The following questions appeared more than once with loadings of 0·3 or above in the analysis; given in brackets after each number is the number of times the item did appear, and the key: 101 (5,Y); 42 (4,Y); 29 (3,N); 45 (3,Y); 71 (3,Y); 81 (3,N); 34 (2,Y); 54 (2,Y); 57 (2,Y); 67 (2,Y); 72 (2,Y); 100 (2,N); 106 (2,Y); 107 (2,N). The difficulty in deciding whether this factor can in any way be interpreted as 'psychoticism' lies obviously in the fact that very little is in fact known about the childhood behaviour of future psychotic patients. It is often suggested that such children are shy and withdrawn, but there is little evidence in favour of this notion, and much against it. Thus Robins (1966), in a large-scale follow-up study, found that 'the shy, withdrawn personality sometimes thought to be predictive of schizophrenia did not predict it in these children. None of the schizophrenics had been described as a shy or withdrawn child, and only one-sixth as avoiding others or seclusive. In more than half the pre-schizophrenics were noted incorrigibility, running away from home, theft, and poor school performance. Restlessness, irritability, and depression were all more common than was shyness. . . . The pre-schizophrenic who appears in child-guidance clinics seems most often to be a child with antisocial behaviour *accompanied* by severe non-antisocial symptoms.' Similar findings are reported from the Dallas Clinic (Michael *et al.*, 1957) and the Judge Baker Clinic (Nameche *et al.*, 1964). It must, of course, be added that with all these children there has been a (possibly severe) pre-selection in that only clinic children were followed up; the possibility remains that the majority of future psychotics are shy and withdrawn in childhood and do not come in contact with a child guidance clinic. In that case only the pre-morbid children who in addition to their psychotic disorder have other disorders which bring them in contact with the clinic would be spotted and followed up. In view of the absence of proper data on

TABLE 21.20

Third-order E and N factors

Item on final J.E.P.I.	Item on (108) form	N 7	E 7	N 8	E 8	N 9	E 9	N 10	E 10	N 11	E 11
1	1 E	−0·08	0·18	−0·01	0·04	0·01	0·22	−0·07	0·06	0·06	0·44
2	2 N	0·26	0·08	0·39	−0·03	0·27	−0·10	0·36	0·08	0·22	−0·29
3	35 E	−0·05	0·12	0·14	0·10	−0·03	0·31	−0·08	0·19	−0·15	−0·01
5	14 N	0·13	0·20	0·26	0·11	0·30	0·22	0·30	−0·05	0·21	−0·02
6	33 E	0·15	0·02	0·33	−0·12	0·07	−0·05	0·11	−0·13	0·04	−0·31
7	50 N	0·49	−0·08	0·24	0·04	0·47	0·04	0·33	−0·05	0·36	0·04
9	53 E	−0·03	0·14	0·09	0·17	0·10	0·19	0·07	0·25	−0·31	0·08
10	18 N	0·39	−0·08	0·50	0·05	0·48	0·05	0·37	−0·09	0·36	−0·00
11	17 E	0·05	0·27	−0·24	0·10	−0·07	0·25	−0·02	0·17	0·00	0·40
13	62 N	0·34	0·01	0·30	−0·05	0·47	−0·05	0·51	0·04	0·04	−0·22
14	79 E	−0·18	0·14	−0·03	0·29	−0·04	0·26	−0·08	0·20	−0·13	0·26
15	64 N	0·50	0·11	0·41	0·01	0·54	−0·02	0·45	−0·06	0·53	0·05
17	97 E	0·05	0·26	0·07	0·36	0·00	0·49	−0·11	0·19	−0·03	0·34
18	58 N	0·20	−0·08	0·48	0·19	0·29	0·19	0·15	−0·15	0·17	−0·04
19	81 E	−0·06	0·18	0·12	0·28	0·03	0·36	0·12	0·29	−0·17	0·15
21	90 N	0·41	0·05	0·28	−0·35	0·34	−0·10	0·31	−0·15	0·60	−0·07
22	105 E	0·02	0·16	0·07	0·30	0·16	0·16	0·02	0·21	0·02	0·28
23	28 N	0·16	0·04	0·42	0·11	0·36	0·09	0·46	−0·11	0·17	−0·20
25	9 E	−0·16	0·28	0·05	0·17	−0·14	−0·04	−0·03	0·03	−0·04	0·26
26	52 N	0·25	0·26	0·28	0·10	0·44	0·04	0·35	−0·22	0·36	0·13
27	29 E	−0·05	0·23	−0·32	−0·04	−0·01	0·22	−0·12	0·08	−0·05	0·31

TABLE 21.20 (*contd.*)

29	56 N	0·35	−0·02	0·24	0·06	0·24	−0·02	0·29	−0·06	0·14	−0·18
30	101 E	0·08	0·04	−0·08	0·35	0.09	0·37	0·20	0·34	−0·26	0·17
31	30 N	0·46	0·09	0·39	0·03	0·31	−0·04	0·40	−0·23	−0·03	−0·20
33	65 E	0·13	0·03	0·16	−0·24	0·01	−0·26	0·07	−0·41	−0·03	−0·38
34	54 N	0·28	−0·01	0·32	0·07	0·31	0·04	0·30	−0·05	0·09	0·10
35	25 E	0·19	0·26	0·27	0·09	0·09	0·31	0·24	0·15	−0·05	0·21
37	66 N	0·43	−0·01	0·38	0·12	0·38	0·00	0·34	−0·01	0·18	−0·09
38	49 E	−0·01	0·37	0·05	0·14	0·03	0·09	0·00	0·01	−0·05	0·37
39	26 N	0·17	−0·02	0·21	−0·16	0·36	0·01	0·22	−0·16	0·62	0·01
41	31 E	−0·14	0·33	0·14	0·16	−0·08	0·26	−0·06	0·24	0·06	0·14
42	86 N	0·51	0·00	0·28	−0·23	0·44	−0·04	0·37	−0·02	0·65	0·12
43	71 E	0·02	0·13	0·08	0·35	0·02	0·35	0·14	0·35	−0·13	0·38
45	12 N	0·26	0·14	0·16	−0·24	0·26	0·00	0·22	0·05	0·19	−0·01
46	41 E	0·00	0·38	0·21	0·20	−0·07	−0·02	0·01	0·15	0·02	0·30
47	88 N	0·31	−0·18	−0·06	−0·22	0·29	0·05	0·36	0·00	0·24	−0·05
49	59 E	−0·01	0·06	0·09	0·36	−0·00	0·10	−0·06	0·15	0·01	0·26
50	32 N	0·36	0·06	0·31	0·10	0·45	0·06	0·55	0·21	0·22	0·09
51	37 E	0·12	−0·07	0·14	−0·07	0·08	0·05	0·06	0·03	−0·06	−0·36
52	20 N	0·49	−0·10	0·24	−0·11	0·43	−0·01	0·27	−0·10	0·42	0·03
53	92 E	0·12	−0·12	0·03	0·27	0·00	0·38	−0·07	−0·06	−0·01	0·19
54	46 N	0·59	0·04	0·35	−0·09	0·52	−0·01	0·30	−0·33	0·24	−0·23
55	7 E	0·24	0·14	0·17	−0·14	0·23	−0·18	0·29	−0·18	0·42	−0·06
56	22 N	0·42	0·11	0·39	0·19	0·43	0·08	0·49	0·04	0·25	0·08
57	45 E	−0·13	0·42	0·18	0·36	−0·01	0·13	0·32	0·12	−0·11	0·02
58	16 N	0·17	−0·01	0·33	0·04	0·35	0·04	0·37	−0·02	0·35	0·00
59	93 E	0·11	−0·10	0·20	−0·03	0·20	−0·09	0·14	−0·08	0·05	−0·40
60	57 N	0·36	0·22	0·19	0·11	0·40	0·01	0·57	0·18	0·12	0·03

Third-order E and N factors

Item on final J.E.P.I.	Item on (108) form	12 N	12 E	13 N	13 E	14 N	14 E	15 N	15 E	16 N	16 E
1	1 E	0·11	0·27	0·17	0·30	0·13	0·26	0·11	0·37	0·19	0·46
2	2 N	0·29	−0·09	0·22	−0·12	0·11	−0·29	0·29	−0·09	0·37	0·09
3	35 E	−0·07	0·12	−0·01	0·20	0·00	0·29	−0·10	0·37	−0·21	0·30
5	14 N	0·26	0·04	0·34	0·05	0·18	−0·29	0·26	0·01	0·55	0·03
6	33 E	0·04	−0·36	0·05	−0·18	0·05	−0·21	0·09	−0·27	−0·24	−0·31
7	50 N	0·38	−0·04	0·51	−0·03	0·52	−0·01	0·38	−0·10	0·23	0·07
9	53 E	−0·02	0·29	0·17	0·27	0·18	0·38	−0·00	0·43	−0·25	0·42
10	18 N	0·40	0·03	0·30	−0·15	0·29	−0·21	0·40	0·09	0·49	−0·11
11	17 E	−0·04	0·37	0·11	0·40	0·12	0·36	−0·00	0·43	−0·12	0·48
13	62 N	0·55	−0·01	0·33	−0·26	0·33	−0·16	0·45	0·05	0·40	0·12
14	79 E	−0·01	0·26	0·07	0·35	−0·01	−0·32	−0·31	0·27	−0·40	0·37
15	64 N	0.53	−0·11	0·40	−0·14	0·30	−0·21	0·28	−0·08	0·37	−0·09
17	97 E	−0·02	0·36	0·06	0·48	0·11	0·42	−0·07	0·48	−0·27	0·50
18	58 N	0·36	0·04	0·43	0·11	0·28	−0·04	0·34	0·07	0·31	−0·04
19	81 E	−0·02	0·33	0·04	0·33	−0·10	0·19	−0·04	0·40	−0·07	0·24
21	90 N	0·38	−0·20	0·28	−0·25	0·26	−0·27	0·35	−0·18	0·42	0·01
22	105 E	0·09	0·35	0·20	0·41	0·20	0·28	−0·04	0·37	−0·02	0·50
23	28 N	0·47	−0·01	0·31	−0·22	0·33	−0·11	0·47	−0·00	0·27	−0·06
25	9 E	−0·06	0·14	−0·04	0·28	−0·07	0·22	−0·18	0·26	−0·38	0·15
26	52 N	0·34	−0·06	0·25	−0·00	0·29	−0·15	0·14	−0·00	0·23	−0·04
27	29 E	−0·05	0·23	−0·14	0·06	0·01	0·27	−0·13	0·21	0·16	0·23

TABLE 21·20 (*contd.*)

29	56 N	0·35	−0·03	0·40	0·04	0·26	−0·06	0·25	−0·06	0·20	−0·13
30	101 E	0·13	0·45	0·28	0·41	0·30	0·49	0·09	0·50	−0·09	0·43
31	30 N	0·47	−0·04	0·26	−0·23	0·26	−0·28	0·40	−0·05	0·47	0·11
33	65 E	0·09	−0·38	0·00	−0·34	−0·22	−0·51	0·03	−0·46	0·15	−0·44
34	54 N	0·44	0·12	0·44	0·19	0·33	0·04	0·20	0·14	0·03	0·42
35	25 E	0·18	0·25	0·34	0·21	0·26	0·32	0·09	0·24	0·09	0·27
37	66 N	0·48	−0·04	0·37	−0·07	0·37	−0·01	0·32	−0·06	0·06	−0·03
38	49 E	0·08	0·41	0·08	0·41	0·08	0·31	−0·03	0·53	0·01	0·45
39	26 N	0·33	−0·14	0·21	−0·21	0·14	−0·31	0·33	−0·20	0·44	−0·00
41	31 E	0·07	0·35	0·10	0·35	0·14	0·34	0·02	0·50	−0·17	0·46
42	86 N	0·42	−0·13	0·22	−0·34	0·27	−0·34	0·31	−0·25	0·42	−0·22
43	71 E	0·11	0·48	0·25	0·54	0·26	0·50	−0·06	0·50	−0·33	0·53
45	12 N	0·29	0·26	0·44	0·08	0·29	0·11	0·39	0·15	0·47	0·18
46	41 E	0·09	0·40	0·15	0·40	0·15	0·41	0·09	0·38	0·28	0·54
47	88 N	0·47	0·01	0·34	−0·07	0·32	−0·16	0·37	−0·04	0·49	−0·05
49	59 E	0·03	0·40	0·16	0·52	0·12	0·43	0·03	0·45	−0·11	0·51
50	32 N	0·33	0·04	0·46	0·00	0·40	−0·07	0·46	0·12	0·37	0·14
51	37 E	0·01	−0·28	−0·02	−0·29	0·01	−0·19	0·06	−0·38	−0·10	−0·54
52	20 N	0·30	−0·17	0·41	−0·09	0·44	−0·07	0·32	−0·16	0·35	0·05
53	92 E	0·01	0·32	−0·04	0·28	−0·12	0·20	−0·30	0·24	−0·48	0·05
54	46 N	0·34	−0·27	0·15	−0·33	0·12	−0·37	0·35	−0·18	0·25	−0·02
55	7 E	0·20	−0·23	0·06	−0·28	0·01	−0·37	0·03	−0·44	0·03	−0·37
56	22 N	0·43	0·11	0·37	−0·10	0·32	−0·11	0·33	0·08	0·52	0·20
57	45 E	0·24	0·36	0·26	0·23	0·37	0·26	0·16	0·38	0·30	0·23
58	16 N	0·41	0·02	0·32	−0·07	0·23	−0·23	0·34	0·04	0·38	0·07
59	93 E	0·17	−0·29	0·00	−0·36	0·00	−0·24	0·03	−0·45	−0·05	−0·49
60	57 N	0·48	0·24	0·47	0·01	0·51	0·18	0·52	0·30	0·42	0·29

this point interpretation of the third factor would seem pointless at this juncture.

We must now turn to the question of sex differences in factor structure. Separate analyses were made along the same lines as described above (Promax higher order analysis) of the boys and girls in the various age groups, and the results for the primary factors are given below in a series of tables. The psychosomatic factor is given in Table 21.21; the mood factor in Table 21.22; the sleeplessness factor in Table 21.23; the sociability factor in Table 21.24; the impulsiveness factor in Table 21.25; the jocularity factor in Table 21.26; and the social shyness factor in Table 21.27. For some sex-age combinations a given factor simply does not appear in the analysis, and the corresponding column has been left blank.

Second and third order factors were extracted, and again the latter clearly represent E and N. Factor comparisons were run for the seven primary factors as well as E and N, and the results are shown in Table 21.28. It will be seen that the results for E and N are reasonably satisfactory; there is no serious doubt that these two factors appear in very similar fashion among boys and girls. The position is quite different for the primary factors; factor comparisons are much lower throughout, and while a recognizable pattern does appear to emerge, yet clearly very much less confidence can be placed in the identity of these primary factors when comparing one sex with the other. Some of these differences may be due to features such as the advent of sexual maturity; note for instance the precipitate decline of the figures for the psychosomatic factor after the age of 12. We will take up this theme of sex differences again when we turn to sex-linked factor score changes over the years.

The relationship between E and N is of some interest; with adults the two factors are for all practical purposes orthogonal, but this may not be true with children. Table 21.29 shows the observed correlations between the two factors for both the principal components solution, rotated into oblique structure, and for the third order Promax factors. It will be seen that low negative correlations are the rule, averaging around the −0·20 to −0·25 mark. With the exception of the 7 year olds this pattern appears quite stable, although there are of course variations around this mean value and the children appear to differ in this respect from the adults. It will be noted that as age increases, i.e. among the 15 and 16 year olds, correlations are somewhat lower, and begin to approach the adult values; this may be a chance result, of course, but is possibly suggestive.

Data are also available for the correlations between scores on the Junior E.P.I. E and N scales. These need not of course be identical with, or even similar to, the correlations between the factors, and in view of the careful selection of the items one might expect the score correlations

TABLE 21.21

Psychomatic factor

No. on 108 item inventory	No. on J.E.P.I.	7 M	7 F	8 M	8 F	9 M	9 F	10 M	10 F	11 M	11 F	12 M	12 F	13 M	13 F	14 M	14 F	15 M	15 F	Adult M	Adult F
44	—	0·02	0·10	0·41	−0·07		0·08	0·18	0·39	0·24	0·32	0·24	0·16	0·25	0·09	0·33	0·31	0·81	0·06	—	—
56	29	0·40	0·49	0·36	0·58		0·51	0·00	0·59	0·42	0·55	0·57	0·38	0·48	0·19	0·08	0·40	−0·03	0·35	0·51	0·74
60		0·54	0·21	0·30	0·38		0·58	0·16	0·48	0·66	0·44	0·44	0·48	0·67	0·16	0·45	0·65	0·13	0·44	0·63	0·30
66	37	0·39	0·64	0·38	0·40		0·35	0·59	0·45	0·51	0·68	0·33	0·20	0·16	0·48	0·38	0·28	0·05	0·21	0·15	0·20
68		0·32	0·26	0·42	−0·01		0·24	0·03	0·15	0·29	0·60	0·25	0·14	0·30	0·20	0·21	0·22	0·25	0·07	0·27	0·67
70		0·44	0·18	0·55	0·31		0·44	0·01	0·32	0·67	0.37	0·01	0·76	0·86	0·07	0·19	0·52	0·16	0·83	0·75	0·08
72		0·67	0·19	0·48	0·63		0·70	0·65	0·45	0·51	0·60	0·03	0·18	0·49	0·66	−0·03	0·17	0·31	0·49	—	—
74		0·30	0·35	0·27	0·12		0·25	0·37	0·47	0·56	0·36	0·14	0·37	0·41	0·40	0·72	0·01	0·68	0·22	0·35	0·45
76		0·18	0·21	0·45	0·09		0·45	0·12	0·40	0·17	0·46	0·15	0·12	0·41	0·02	0·07	0·18	0·08	0·07	—	—
78		0·46	0·23	0·61	0·81		0·76	0·31	0·55	0·42	0·66	−0·04	0·20	0·21	0·17	0·07	0·60	0·15	0·44	0·18	0·56
80		0·44	0·65	0·61	0·34		0·44	0·05	0·27	0·78	0·39	−0·07	0·75	0·84	0·17	0·26	0·44	0·01	0·78	0·78	0·07
86		0·30	0·30	0·16	0·25		0·27	0·16	0·05	0·22	0·08	−0·04	−0·01	−0·10	0·34	0·12	−0·03	0·00	−0·01	−0·02	0·04
98		0·38	0·21	0·09	0·50		0·43	0·46	0·30	0·19	0·48	0·24	0·42	0·37	0·56	−0·03	0·15	0·10	0·13	0·40	0·69
103		−0·05	0·11	0·14	0·01		0·09	0·19	0·19	0·44	0·42	0·16	0·31	0·37	0·48	0·76	0·12	0·69	0·01	—	—

44	—	Often cry
56	29	Have 'dizzy turns'
60		Get attacks of shaking or trembling
66	37	Have many frightening dreams
68		Ever get short of breath without having done heavy work
70		Suffer from nerves
72		Troubled by lots of tummy-aches
74		Get frightened in places like lifts, trains and tunnels
76		Sweat a lot without having done much
78		Get very bad headaches
80		Call yourself a nervous person
86		Worry for a long while if you feel you have made a fool of yourself
98		Worry about getting ill
103		Very much afraid of the dark

TABLE 21.22

Moods factor

No. on 108 item inventory	No. on J.E.P.I.	7 M	7 F	8 M	8 F	9 M	9 F	10 M	10 F	11 M	11 F	12 M	12 F	13 M	13 F	14 M	14 F	15 M	15 F	Adult M	Adult F	No. on adult Qre.
2	2	0·73	0·35	0·05	0·01	−0·10	0·08	0·20	0·02	0·17	0·17	−0·02	0·25	0·10	0·03	0·10	0·28	0·07	0·04	0·19	0·25	2A
4		−0·02	0·47	0·15	−0·01	0·33	0·35	0·21	0·18	0·41	0·26	0·38	0·38	0·04	0·26	0·14	0·23	0·24	0·12	0·42	0·51	2B
6		0·66	0·53	0·56	0·62	0·75	0·67	0·68	0·78	0·76	0·74	0·75	0·83	0·75	0·81	0·87	0·84	0·84	0·88	0·94	0·94	4B
10		0·15	−0·08	0·03	−0·09	−0·04	0·12	0·34	0·39	0·18	0·23	0·26	0·12	−0·07	0·23	0·13	0·09	0·08	0·46	0·29	0·09	7B
14	5	0·08	0·24	−0·09	0·04	0·20	0·09	0·26	−0·02	0·15	−0·01	0·06	0·10	0·28	0·40	0·10	0·18	0·20	0·13	0·53	0·45	9B
16	58	0·37	0·62	0·31	0·34	0·59	0·67	0·79	0·63	0·73	0·68	0·71	0·84	0·79	0·84	0·88	0·89	0·94	0·89	0·69	0·61	7A
18	10	0·37	0·09	0·22	0·16	0·36	0·17	0·60	0·67	0·69	0·60	0·58	0·66	0·78	0·78	0·69	0·72	0·75	0·54	0·89	0·91	9A
27		0·28	0·03	0·55	0·10	0·04	0·06	0·15	0·18	0·26	0·06	0·14	0·12	0·15	−0·14	0·09	0·04	0·10	−0·01	—		—
28	23	0·28	0·16	0·00	0·34	0·12	0·09	0·33	0·21	0·12	0·44	0·42	0·36	0·25	0·45	0·18	0·25	0·13	0·15	0·72	0·72	16B
36		0·01	0·12	−0·01	0·15	0·18	0·00	0·15	0·19	0·21	0·15	0·56	0·23	0·09	0·35	0·01	0·31	0·46	0·19	0·66	0·55	19A

2	2	Often need kind friends to cheer you up
		Often need understanding friends to cheer you up
4		Often get a feeling that you want something but you don't know what
		Often get a restless feeling that you want something but do not know what
6		Sometimes feel happy and at other times sad for no special reason
		Sometimes feel happy sometimes sad without any real reason
10		Sometimes go quiet when you are angry
		Sometimes sulk
14	5	Moody
16	58	Sometimes feel specially cheerful and at other times sad without any good reason
		Mood often go up and down
18	10	Ever feel 'just miserable' for no good reason
27		Usually feel that things are bound to work out badly for you
28	23	Often feel tired for no good reason
		Often felt listless and tired for no good reason
36		Sometimes bubble over with energy and sometimes do things seem an awful effort

TABLE 21.23

Sleeplessness factor

No. on 108 item inventory	No. on J.E.P.I.	7 M	7 F	8 M	8 F	9 M	9 F	10 M	10 F	11 M	11 F	12 M	12 F	13 M	13 F	14 M	14 F	15 M	15 F	Adult M	Adult F	
20	52	0·30			0·51	0·68	0·68	0·71	0·52	0·64	0·39	0·67	0·70	0·77	0·78	0·75	0·80	0·74	0·70	0·65	0·66	Find it hard to get to sleep at night because you are worrying about things
50	7	0·14			0·63	0·57	0·70	0·69	0·61	0·70	0·32	0·68	0·83	0·77	0·62	0·71	0·83	0·71	0·77	0·65	0·69	Ideas run through your head so that you cannot sleep
66	37	0·17			0·33	0·26	0·52	0·09	0·14	0·27	0·01	0·28	0·04	0·17	0·22	0·26	0·20	−0·00	0·21	0·29	0·30	Have many frightening dreams
87		0·54			0·70	0·84	0·76	0·79	0·69	0·79	0·18	0·63	0·76	0·80	0·91	0·81	0·80	0·93	0.80	0·73	0·86	Find it hard to go to sleep at bedtime
108		0·74			0·55	0·85	0·71	0·77	0·67	0·75	0·25	0·48	0·66	0·84	0·82	0·77	0·77	0·89	0·74	0·79	0·84	Lie awake a lot during the night

TABLE 21.24

Sociability factor

No. on 108 item inventory	No. on J.E.P.I.	7 M	7 F	8 M	8 F	9 M	9 F	10 M	10 F	11 M	11 F	12 M	12 F	13 M	13 F	14 M	14 F
1	1	0·12				−0·07	0·06	0·03	0·32	0·21	0·14	0·04	0·16	0·05	0·55	0·30	0·45
29	27	0·41				0·29	0·47	0·70	0·78	0·22	0·61	0·15	0·03	0·22	0·60	0·57	0·78
33	6	−0·28				−0·67	−0·74	−0·72	−0·63	−0·28	−0·73	−0·12	−0·21	−0·24	−0·67	−0·50	−0·89
37	51	−0·02				−0·31	−0·46	−0·08	−0·17	−0·65	−0·08	−0·35	−0·25	−0·66	−0·65	−0·10	−0·08
41	46	0·05				−0·10	0·26	0·16	0·23	0·30	0·22	0·14	0·21	0·56	0·63	0·12	0·11
49	38	−0·10				0·10	0·36	0·13	0·13	0·71	0·29	0·43	0·61	0·71	0·73	−0·03	0·00
89		−0·04				0·07	0·05	0·20	−0·08	0·00	0·25	−0·14	0·02	0·10	0·19	0·29	0·48
93	59	−0·20				−0·17	−0·31	−0·12	−0·34	−0·31	−0·23	−0·59	−0·72	−0·57	−0·70	0·08	−0·07
105	22	−0·12				0·14	0·08	−0·06	0·00	0·07	0·23	0·02	0·22	0·18	0·40	0·16	0·13

No. on 108 item inventory	No. on J.E.P.I.	15 M	15 F	Adult M	Adult F	No. on adult Qre.	
1	1	0·53	0·49	0·41	0·06	1B	Like plenty of excitement going on around you
							Like plenty of excitement and bustle around you
29	27	0·63	0·76	0·71	0·44	10B	Like mixing with other children
							Like mixing with people
33	6	−0·65	−0·72	−0·61	−0·40	15A	Rather be alone instead of meeting other children
							Generally you prefer reading to meeting people
37	51	−0·59	−0·42	−0·78	−0·87	5B	Rather sit and watch than play at parties
							Usually stay in the background at parties and 'get-togethers'
							Like going out a lot
41	46	0·62	0·37	0·57	0·32	17A	Usually let yourself go and enjoy yourself at a gay party
49	38	0·68	0·50	0·83	0·81	25A	Usually let yourself go and enjoy yourself a lot at a gay party
							Be very unhappy if you could not see lots of people most of the time
							Find it hard to really enjoy yourself at a lively party
89		0·21	0·32	0·18	−0·04	46A	Like telling jokes, or funny stories to your friends
							Like cracking jokes and telling funny stories to your friends
93	59	−0·64	−0·59	−0·88	−0·86	51A	
105	22	0·15	0·29	0·19	0·22	53B	

TABLE 21.25

Impulsiveness factor

No. on 108 item inventory	No. on J.E.P.I.	7 M	7 F	8 M	8 F	9 M	9 F	10 M	10 F	11 M	11 F	12 M	12 F	13 M	13 F	14 M	14 F
11		−0·17		0·19	0·04		−0·70	−0·10	−0·14	−0·14	−0·70	−0·75	−0·54	−0·58	−0·33	−0·42	−0·48
15		0·15		−0·13	0·05		0·04	0·50	0·52	0·62	0·50	0·62	0·73	0·59	0·57	0·73	0·63
22	56	0·08		0·10	0·13		0·03	−0·00	0·47	0·25	0·11	0·27	0·44	0·31	0·38	0·28	0·18
23		−0·07		−0·03	−0·18		−0·67	−0·45	−0·10	−0·23	−0·18	−0·16	−0·20	−0·59	−0·11	−0·08	−0·20
25	35	0·19		0·37	−0·03		0·12	−0·22	0·69	0·40	0·16	0·22	0·15	0·30	0·50	0·35	0·27
38		−0·05		−0·01	0·20		0·09	0·23	0·05	0·08	0·00	0·11	0·25	0·08	−0·06	0·15	0·04
45	57	0·16		−0·04	0·13		0·06	0·13	−0·03	−0·07	−0·00	0·14	0·41	0·42	0·25	0·34	0·27
57	60	0·07		−0·13	0·58		0·01	0·08	0·15	0·24	0·25	0·40	0·44	0·55	0·67	0·59	0·57
91		0·61		0·06	0·45		−0·03	0·32	0·67	0·72	0·32	0·41	0·70	0·44	0·67	0·66	0·74

No. on 108 item inventory	No. on J.E.P.I.	15 M	15 F	Adults M	Adults F	
11		−0·70	−0·69	−0·63	−0·72	Stop and think before doing things
15		0·54	0·90	0·78	0·76	Usually say things quickly without stopping to think
22	56	0·22	0·22	0·15	0·24	Often make up your mind when it is too late
23		−0·36	−0·28	−0·27	−0·56	Like to plan things carefully before you do anything
25	35	0·46	0·50	0·60	0·71	Often make up your mind to do things suddenly
38		0·12	0·08	—	—	Soon tire of your toys
45	57	0·01	0·07	0·37	0·27	When children shout at you, you shout back
57	60	0·72	0·56	0·66	0·67	Often get into trouble because you do things without thinking first
91		0·66	0·82	0·53	0·46	Sometimes say the first things which come into your head

TABLE 21.26

Jokes factor

No. on 108 item inventory	No. on J.E.P.I.	7 M	7 F	8 M	8 F	9 M	9 F	10 M	10 F	11 M	11 F	12 M	12 F	13 M	13 F	14 M	14 F
21		0·03	0·18				0·09	0·30	−0·09	−0·02	0·16	−0·01	0·12	−0·03	0·11	0·23	0·50
53	9	0·08	−0·03				0·76	0·86	0·62	0·36	0·73	0·45	0·76	0·50	0·67	0·53	0·39
71	43	0·45	0·80				0·20	0·16	0·20	0·46	0·11	0·21	0·44	0·24	0·21	0·39	0·42
77		0·09	0·07				0·19	−0·13	−0·49	−0·08	−0·26	−0·55	−0·38	−0·73	−0·79	−0·72	−0·37
101	30	0·42	0·33				0·45	0·64	0·53	0·30	0·56	0·75	0·73	0·78	0·75	0·73	0·62
105	22	0·19	0·05				0·65	0·55	0·41	0·09	0·46	0·13	0·30	0·18	0·26	0·40	0·17

No. on 108 item inventory	No. on J.E.P.I.	15 M	15 F	Adults M	Adults F	
21		0·10	0·29	0·18	0·25	Do almost anything if someone dared you to do it
53	9	0·78	0·85	0·94	0·88	Like practical jokes
71	43	0·25	0·63	—	—	Often like a rough and tumble game
77		−0·67	−0·90	−0·78	−0·71	Hate being with a crowd who play jokes on one another
101	30	0·79	0·88	0·91	0·85	Like playing pranks on others
105	22	0·20	0·37	0·19	0·36	Like telling jokes and funny stories to your friends

TABLE 21.27

Shyness factor

No. on 108 item inventory	No. on J.E.P.I.	7 M	7 F	8 M	8 F	9 M	9 F	10 M	10 F	11 M	11 F	12 M	12 F	13 M	13 F	14 M	14 F
7	55	0·56	0·23	0·70	0·57	0·63	0·77	0·80	0·79	0·79	0·82	0·82	0·85	0·83	0·92	0·82	0·77
8		0·06	0·07	−0·16	−0·27	−0·20	−0·18	−0·51	−0·10	−0·15	−0·30	−0·30	−0·50	−0·09	−0·34	−0·37	−0·26
19		0·64	0·54	0·75	0·56	0·72	0·85	0·68	0·72	0·81	0·77	0·74	0·83	0·76	0·84	0·80	0·81
35	3	0·16	0·03	−0·03	−0·12	−0·10	−0·13	−0·33	−0·09	−0·04	−0·21	−0·26	−0·13	−0·05	−0·26	−0·53	−0·18
47		0·04	0·85	0·44	0·58	0·47	0·38	0·48	0·34	0·54	0·50	0·45	0·61	0·70	0·42	0·63	0·65
51		0·13	0·32	0·18	0·57	0·27	0·14	0·33	0·15	0·18	−0·07	0·43	0·13	0·21	0·24	0·24	0·28
65	33	0·01	0·05	−0·07	0·22	0·13	−0·01	0·07	0·34	0·18	0·29	−0·01	0·18	0·25	0·18	0·26	0·17
81	19	−0·08	0·12	−0·27	−0·19	−0·08	−0·07	−0·07	−0·27	−0·03	−0·37	−0·50	−0·48	−0·37	−0·59	−0·54	−0·57
85		−0·08	−0·10	0·03	−0·32	−0·02	−0·14	−0·29	−0·10	−0·08	−0·19	−0·21	−0·54	−0·31	−0·28	−0·12	−0·15
94		0·16	0·17	0·15	0·74	0·68	0·63	0·56	0·49	0·55	0·50	0·43	0·68	0·67	0·64	0·55	0·42
95		0·19	0·08	0·17	−0·06	0·04	0·01	0·33	0·16	0·18	0·26	0·15	0·20	0·32	0·39	0·38	0·26

TABLE 21.27 (*contd.*)

No. on 108 item inventory	No. on J.E.P.I.	15 M	15 F	Adult M	Adult F	No. on adult Qre.	
7	55	0·75	0·88	—	—	—	Are you shy of speaking first when you meet new people?
8		−0·29	−0·28	−0·76	−0·71	22B	Can you say the things you are thinking quickly? (Can you put your thoughts into words quickly?)
19		0·77	0·81	0·17	0·21	11A	Do you suddenly feel shy when you want to talk to someone you don't know? (Do you suddenly feel shy when you want to talk to an attractive stranger?)
35	3	−0·21	−0·17	−0·63	−0·49	3B	Do you nearly always have a quick answer when people talk to you? (Do you nearly always have a 'ready answer' when people talk to you?)
47		0·68	0·70	—	—	—	Are you usually shy when you meet girls? (for boys) Are you usually shy when you meet boys? (for girls)
51		0·15	0·29	−0·21	−0·01	29B	Would you be too shy to ask strangers to give you money for some good cause like the Scouts? (Do you mind selling things or asking people for money for some good cause?)
65	33	0·26	0·28	0·20	0·22	29A	Are you mostly quiet when you are with others? (Are you mostly quiet when you are with other people?)
81	19	−0·60	−0·53	−0·23	−0·13	44B	When you make new friends do you usually make the first move? (When you make new friends is it usually you who makes the first move, or does the inviting?)
85		−0·50	−0·31	−0·59	−0·19	44A	Do you like talking to people so much that you would talk to anybody you meet? (Do you like talking to people so much that you never miss a chance of talking to a stranger?)
94		0·57	0·62	0·22	0·34	55B	Do you feel shy and awkward when you are with important people? (Do you often feel self-conscious when you are with superiors?)
95		0·27	0·18	0·02	0·09	51B	Do you usually not say much except to your nearest friend? (Do you usually keep 'yourself to yourself' except with very close friends?)

TABLE 21.28

Factor comparisons; Boys versus Girls

		7	8	9	10	11	12	13	14	15
	E	0·991	0·718	0·635	0·968	0·972	0·933	0·986	0·847	0·958
	N	0·994	0·961	0·886	0·987	1·000	0·989	0·999	0·922	0·976
1st Order										
PSYCHOSOMATIC		0·797	0·746	—	0·711	0·805	0·517	0·484	0·322	0·118
MOODS		0·725	0·360	0·453	0·652	0·873	0·785	0·754	0·833	0·861
SLEEPLESSNESS		—	—	0·915	0·867	0·774	0·770	0·896	0·921	0·856
SOCIABILITY		—	—	0·637	0·736	0·539	0·430	0·735	0·576	0·743
IMPULSIVENESS		—	0·431	—	0·500	0·521	0·807	0·701	0·761	0·860
JOKES		0·501	—	—	0·781	0·256	0·483	0·824	0·739	0·841
SHYNESS		0·476	0·679	0·780	0·740	0·879	0·657	0·914	0·925	0·901

TABLE 21.29

Correlations between E and N

Age	Principal components	Promax
7	0·09	0·19
8	−0·10	−0·33
9	−0·27	−0·14
10	−0·20	−0·24
11	−0·30	−0·34
12	−0·27	−0·29
13	−0·25	−0·37
14	−0·21	−0·37
15	−0·15	−0·17
16	—	−0·13

TABLE 21.30

Relation between factors

E with N

	First sample				Second sample			
Ages	*n*	Girls	*n*	Boys	*n*	Girls	*n*	Boys
7	257	−0·017	234	−0·044	88	+0·037	108	−0·018
8	285	−0·088	295	−0·129	148	−0·006	138	−0·222
9	376	−0·117	385	−0·142	143	−0·210	135	−0·211
10	420	−0·163	424	−0·116	149	+0·047	141	−0·219
11	479	−0·133	510	−0·198	211	−0·089	178	−0·277
12	353	−0·161	394	−0·185	198	−0·310	163	−0·326
13	422	−0·046	382	−0·194	186	−0·061	175	−0·285
14	391	−0·127	395	−0·168	212	−0·039	155	−0·236
15	258	−0·173	269	−0·083	63	+0·030	50	−0·157
16	147	−0·156	84	−0·152	73	−0·052	63	−0·140

	E with L				N with L			
Ages	*n*	Girls	*n*	Boys	*n*	Girls	*n*	Boys
7	88	+0·157	108	+0·086	88	−0·392	108	−0·453
8	148	−0·124	138	−0·105	148	−0·438	138	−0·356
9	143	−0·020	135	+0·078	143	−0·401	135	−0·199
10	149	−0·036	141	+0·107	149	−0·314	141	−0·377
11	211	−0·067	178	−0·036	211	−0·259	178	−0·253
12	198	−0·015	163	−0·072	198	−0·219	163	−0·349
13	186	−0·241	175	−0·229	186	−0·325	175	−0·224
14	212	−0·144	155	−0·029	212	−0·335	155	−0·399
15	63	−0·367	50	−0·095	63	−0·368	50	−0·297
16	73	−0·338	63	−0·353	73	−0·196	63	−0·246

to approach somewhat more closely to zero. Table 21.30 gives the correlations of E with N, as well as those of E with L, and of N with L. For the E vs. N correlations we have two separate samples available; the first sample consists of the children on whom the factor analyses were carried out, the second sample consists of groups of London schoolchildren. It was thought wisest not to confine these calculations to the

TABLE 21.31

Extraversion norms

(a) Girls

	Final norms			First sample			Second sample		
Ages	*n*	*m*	S.D.	*n*	*m*	S.D.	*n*	*m*	S.D.
7	345	15·466	3·256	257	15·412	3·247	88	15·625	3·278
8	433	16·078	3·276	285	16·035	3·315	148	16·162	3·197
9	519	16·453	3·562	376	16·444	3·605	143	16·476	3·447
10	569	16·808	3·175	420	16·645	3·267	149	17·268	2·849
11	690	17·316	3·574	479	17·261	3·596	211	17·441	3·521
12	551	17·354	3·514	353	17·062	3·714	198	17·874	3·059
13	608	17·411	3·941	422	17·384	4·100	186	17·473	3·555
14	603	17·471	3·715	391	17·419	3·851	212	17·566	3·448
15	321	16·713	4·450	258	16·837	4·388	63	16·206	4·663
16	220	16·469	4·720	147	16·150	4·818	73	17·110	4·446

(b) Boys

Ages	*n*	*m*	S.D.	*n*	*m*	S.D.	*n*	*m*	S.D.
7	342	15·833	3·344	234	15·876	3·192	108	15·741	3·649
8	433	16·667	3·128	295	16·881	3·102	138	16·210	3·133
9	520	17·050	3·414	385	17·148	3·409	135	16·770	3·414
10	565	17·791	3·334	424	17·873	3·313	141	17·546	3·386
11	688	17·693	3·479	510	17·737	3·551	178	17·567	3·261
12	557	17·582	3·497	394	17·569	3·557	163	17·613	3·347
13	557	18·164	3·846	382	18·181	3·800	175	18·126	3·943
14	550	17·836	3·798	395	17·833	3·906	155	17·845	3·509
15	319	17·225	4·457	269	17·007	4·621	50	18·400	3·194
16	147	17·408	4·620	84	17·202	4·756	63	17·683	4·417

original sample only. The data show a much reduced negative correlation between E and N in both samples; for most age groups it might be said that the remaining correlation is almost entirely negligible, amounting to something slightly in excess of 0·15.

Correlations between N and L are rather large, averaging above −0·3 and in some cases exceeding −0·4. The size of the correlations appears to be largely independent of age and the data suggest that children with high lie scores will tend to have low neuroticism scores, possibly due to conscious attempts at faking. There is also a slight negative correlation for the older children between E and L, which is in good conformity with data found in adults. This may be interpreted as either showing a slight tendency for introverts to lie more, or else, and this may be the preferable interpretation, as an indication of a slight tendency for introverts actually to be better behaved (Eysenck, 1964). Scores on the J.E.P.I. show some interesting variation with age. Table 21.31 gives the figures for boys and girls separately, for E, and Table 21.32 does so for N. Lie scale norms are given in Table 21.33. Figure 21.1 shows the distribution of E scores with age in diagrammatic form; Figure 21.2 does the same for N. Figures 21.3a and 21.3b show the changing shapes of the score distributions for L as we go from the

TABLE 21·32

Neuroticism norms

(a) Girls

Ages	Final norms *n*	*m*	S.D.	First sample *n*	*m*	S.D.	Second sample *n*	*m*	S.D.
7	345	11·061	4·905	257	11·109	5·107	88	10·920	4·259
8	433	11·437	4·787	285	11·004	4·771	148	12·270	4·707
9	519	12·273	4·808	376	12·154	4·880	143	12·587	4·597
10	569	12·190	5·032	420	11·698	4·950	149	13·577	5·004
11	690	11·833	5·330	479	11·499	5·373	211	12·592	5·153
12	551	12·487	5·194	353	12·377	5·116	198	12·682	5·324
13	608	12·905	5·192	422	12·609	4·892	186	13·575	5·760
14	603	13·920	4·811	391	13·509	4·708	212	14·679	4·906
15	321	13·713	4·583	258	13·589	4·485	63	14·222	4·930
16	220	13·750	5·106	147	13·088	5·030	73	15·082	4·997

(b) Boys

Ages	*n*	*m*	S.D.	*n*	*m*	S.D.	*n*	*m*	S.D.
7	342	10·283	4·925	234	10·115	4·966	108	10·648	4·815
8	433	11·524	4·848	295	11·342	4·958	138	11·913	4·581
9	520	11·381	4·652	385	11·332	4·710	135	11·519	4·480
10	565	11·222	4·997	424	10·991	5·036	141	11·915	4·813
11	688	11·097	5·116	510	10·880	5·082	178	11·719	5·163
12	557	11·018	5·064	394	10·822	5·124	163	11·491	4·884
13	557	10·736	5·026	382	10·641	4·951	175	10·943	5·181
14	550	10·847	4·826	395	10·977	4·754	155	10·516	4·990
15	319	10·414	4·994	269	10·543	4·873	50	9·720	5·548
16	147	9·150	4·691	84	8·952	4·649	63	9·413	4·734

TABLE 21.33

Lie scale norms

Ages	Girls *n*	*m*	S.D.	Ages	Boys *n*	*m*	S.D.
7	88	9·080	1·931	7	108	8·083	2·392
8	148	7·757	2·332	8	138	6·667	2·662
9	143	7·308	2·595	9	135	5·785	2·669
10	149	5·624	2·722	10	141	4·851	2·667
11	211	5·493	2·645	11	178	4·792	2·618
12	198	4·444	2·856	12	163	4·141	2·755
13	186	3·489	2·450	13	175	3·057	2·181
14	212	3·108	2·267	14	155	3·032	2·337
15	63	2·778	2·498	15	50	2·160	2·510
16	73	2·123	1·958	16	63	2·571	2·198

young to the older age groups. Certain conclusions are apparent, even to visual inspection; these conclusions were verified by analysis of variance. E scores show boys more extraverted than girls; this finding recalls similar ones with adults. Extraversion increases with age, at least from 7 to 13; there is a slight decline after that age. Both sex and age contribute significant F values to the analysis of variance beyond the 0·001 level; no significance attaches to the interaction. As regards N,

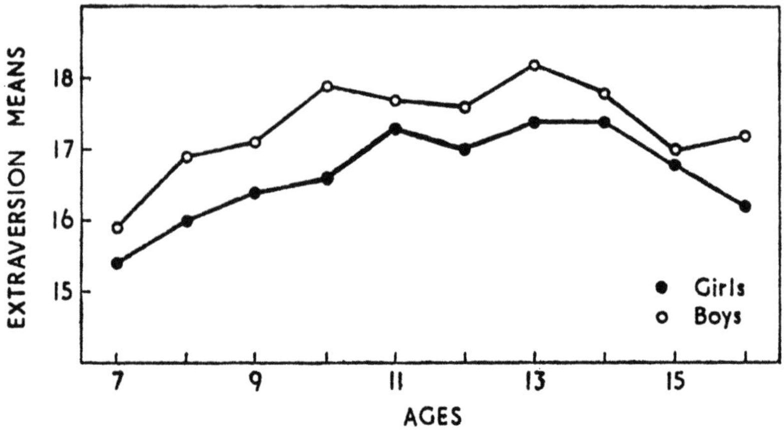

FIG. 21.1 Mean Extraversion scores plotted against age for the two sexes.

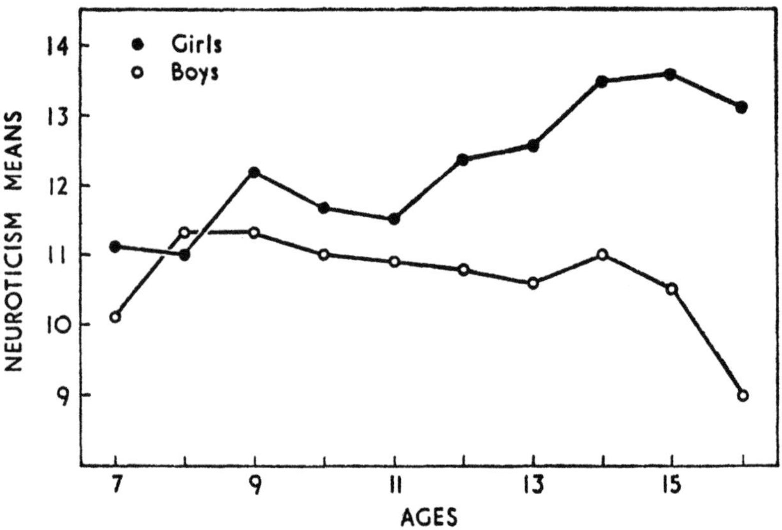

FIG. 21.2 Mean Neuroticism scores plotted against age for the two sexes.

analysis of variance showed that sex, age, and the sex by age interaction were all significant beyond the 0·001 level. It thus appears to be a fact that girls become more unstable with increasing age, whereas boys appear to remain at very much the same level. Here too results agree with adult findings, where women tend to have higher N scores than men.

The distribution of lie scale scores in percentages is given in Figure

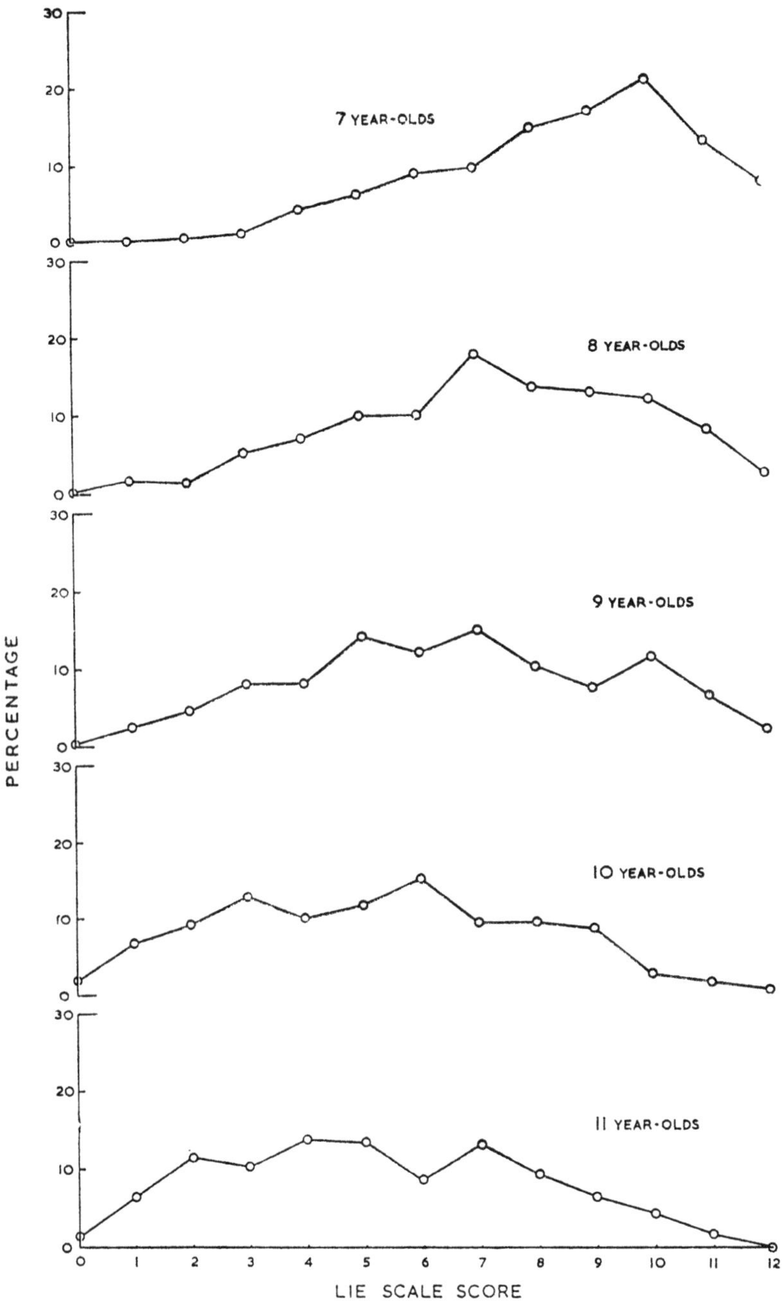

FIG. 21.3a The Distribution of Lie Scale scores, in percentages, for age groups seven to eleven years.

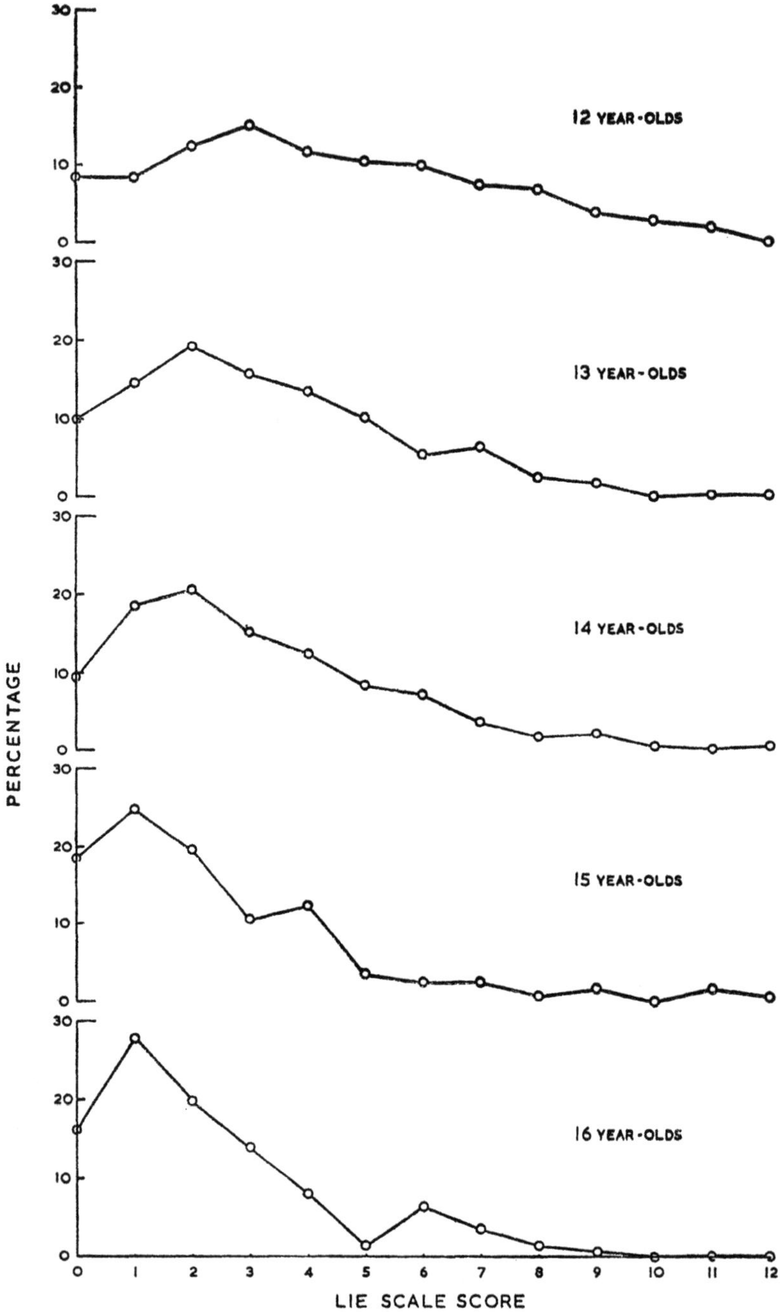

FIG. 21.3b The Distribution of Lie Scale scores, in percentages, for age groups twelve to sixteen years.

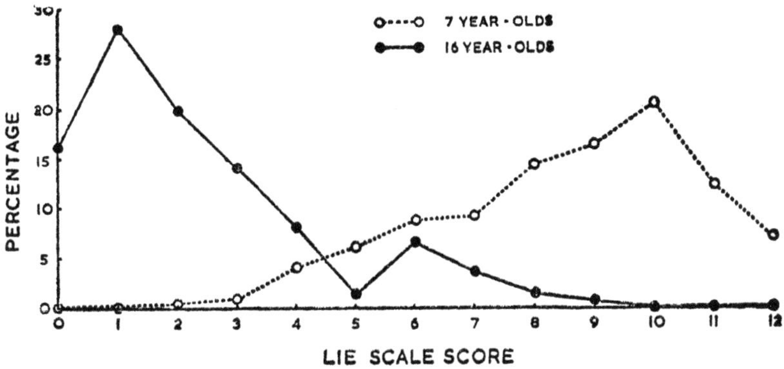

FIG. 21.4 The Distribution of Lie Scale scores, in percentages, for seven and sixteen year olds.

21.3 for the various age groups, and shows clearly the shift from high lying in the younger children to very low lying in the older boys and girls. This conclusion is particularly apparent in Figure 21.4 which gives the lie scores in percentages for the 7 and the 16 year olds. This is in good agreement with observational findings on the individual lying in children (McFarlane *et al.*, 1954).

Split half reliabilities for the scales, corrected for length by the Spearman Brown Prophecy Formula are given in Table 21.34. It will be seen that as expected there is no great change with age as far as the neuroticism scale is concerned but that there is a considerable increase in reliability with age as far as extraversion is concerned. For the lie scale, again as expected, there is a slight increase in reliability but this is of no practical significance.

More important perhaps than split half reliabilities are test retest reliabilities. These were obtained on 1,056 boys and 1,074 girls in all, the

TABLE 21.34

Split-Half Reliability

	E				N				L			
Ages	*n*	GIRLS	*n*	BOYS	*n*	GIRLS	*n*	BOYS	*n*	GIRLS	*n*	BOYS
7	257	0·651	234	0·602	257	0·819	234	0·815	88	0·409	108	0·607
8	285	0·633	295	0·581	285	0·802	295	0·785	148	0·665	138	0·636
9	376	0·694	385	0·676	376	0·804	385	0·804	143	0·716	135	0·728
10	420	0·655	424	0·670	420	0·803	424	0·839	149	0·751	141	0·725
11	479	0·721	510	0·718	479	0·841	510	0·836	211	0·718	178	0·669
12	353	0·748	394	0·705	353	0·850	394	0·841	198	0·767	163	0·733
13	422	0·798	382	0·778	422	0·836	382	0·834	186	0·719	175	0·712
14	391	0·756	395	0·810	391	0·821	395	0·828	212	0·635	155	0·684
15	258	0·862	269	0·864	258	0·823	269	0·847	63	0·765	50	0·779
16	147	0·868	84	0·862	147	0·890	84	0·812	73	0·667	63	0·737

time elapsing between test and retest being one month. The results are shown in Table 21.35. It will be seen that the reliabilities average between 0·7 and 0·8; they tend on the whole to increase with age for E, a little less so for N, while as far as L is concerned there is no obvious progression. All in all the test/retest reliabilities are a little lower than the split half reliabilities.

TABLE 21.35

Test-retest reliability

	Boys				Girls			
Ages	*n*	E	N	L	*n*	E	N	L
7	101	0·599	0·733	0·679	111	0·512	0·619	0·654
8	112	0·660	0·634	0·636	114	0·603	0·783	0·640
9	115	0·643	0·795	0·740	120	0·551	0·645	0·732
10	127	0·631	0·712	0·739	116	0·653	0·860	0·786
11	108	0·755	0·869	0·703	129	0·740	0·842	0·736
12	152	0·768	0·717	0·681	131	0·602	0·527	0·411
13	136	0·587	0·801	0·578	130	0·674	0·771	0·608
14	140	0·704	0·746	0·645	148	0·726	0·721	0·776
15	59	0·735	0·744	0·537	57	0·860	0·845	0·889
16	6	0·917	0·815	0·589	18	0·897	0·883	0·446
All	1056	0·691	0·751	0·776	1074	0·673	0·739	0·789

The general personality theory with which we are dealing regards E and N, as being uncorrelated with intelligence, and in adult samples this independence has usually been verified. It seemed desirable to duplicate this work with children, and all in all some 700 boys and girls have been tested on the Junior E.P.I. and their scores correlated with two intelligence tests. One of these (I.Q.$_1$) was a verbal test given in the school independently of the present investigation; the other test (I.Q.$_2$) was a practice test given prior to I.Q.$_1$ The correlations between the two tests for all the groups ran typically between 0·85 and 0·90. The results are given below in Table 21.36. It will be seen that as far as E is concerned there is no evidence of any correlation with I.Q.[1] As regards N there is a

[1] This statement is true strictly only of the overall correlations, including all ages. When we look at the finer grain of the tables, we can see a definite trend for positive correlations between E and IQ turning into negative ones as age increases. Thus at age 11 correlations are 0·22 for girls and 0·28 for boys: at 13 they are 0·09 and 0·00, and at 15 −0·16 and −0·13. These trends are significant statistically, and suggest that perhaps introverts are late developers. In a recent unpublished study D. Cookson and H. J. Eysenck found a marked positive relation between extraversion and both IQ and school achievement in a very large random sample of Staffordshire children, both boys and girls; thus the data given in Table 21.36 for that age are apparently replicable. Similarly, much research in the literature has shown the superiority of introverts at older ages and at University. Unfortunately no follow-up studies have been done with this hypothesis in mind; until this is done alternative theories to that of late developing of introverts cannot be ruled out.

slight trend towards negative correlations but this is too slight to be regarded as of any psychological significance. Children having high scores on the L scale show a significant tendency to be duller than average, a finding which agrees well with some unpublished data showing that adults of subnormal intelligence also tend to have very high lie scores. (It should be noted that the number of cases for the various groups given in Table 21.36 refers in each case to the correlations obtained with $I.Q._1$; when $I.Q._2$ was given a few of the children were absent, thus reducing total numbers by some 5 per cent at most.)

TABLE 21.36

Girls

		I.Q.1			I.Q.2		
Age	*n*	E	N	L	E	N	L
11	57	0·222	−0·076	−0·198	0·212	−0·115	−0·164
12	108	0·016	0·019	−0·214	0·074	0·020	−0·241
13	102	0·087	−0·051	−0·228	0·085	0·029	−0·334
14	64	−0·221	−0·399	−0·192	−0·295	−0·314	−0·204
15	33	−0·156	0·064	0·035	−0·105	0·253	0·082
16	9	−0·405	−0·351	−0·008	−0·115	−0·111	−0·000
All	373	0·004	−0·091	−0·195	0·022	−0·045	−0·242

Boys

		I.Q.1			I.Q.2		
Age	*n*	E	N	L	E	N	L
11	66	0·275	−0·240	−0·382	0·261	−0·256	−0·438
12	108	0·227	−0·179	−0·138	0·118	−0·100	−0·144
13	98	−0·000	−0·020	−0·173	−0·034	0·127	−0·283
14	30	0·283	−0·274	−0·410	0·234	−0·237	−0·423
15	24	−0·128	−0·109	−0·280	−0·078	−0·130	−0·033
16	8	0·037	0·489	−0·644	−0·062	0·521	−0·909
All	334	0·105	−0·155	−0·273	0·055	−0·070	−0·330

Too little is known about the validity of the Junior E.P.I. as yet to make any claims for its use, other than as an instrument for experimentation. Two hundred and twenty-nine child guidance clinic subjects have been tested and rated with respect to the extraverted or introverted nature of their symptoms, and it was found that the group as a whole was very significantly above the standardization group with respect to neuroticism, and that there was a very significant difference with respect to E between children showing extraverted symptoms and those showing introverted symptoms. It seems probable therefore that the scale may be valid in connection with clinical investigations.

Our belief in the likely validity of the scales in other connections must await confirmation from experimental studies of the kind which have demonstrated the validity of the M.P.I. and the E.P.I. (Eysenck, 1967);

however, it is noteworthy that there are many findings in relation to the adult scale which have been duplicated with the J.E.P.I. We have already mentioned the similarities in correlation patterns, the superior N scores of girls and women, and the superior E scores of boys and men. The age relation of lying demonstrated in our samples have also been discovered by other investigators along quite different lines. In this book we are concerned with the structure and measurement of personality, rather than with the validity of the inventories which are the outcome of our studies, hence the reader may pardon this very brief and perfunctory discussion of an issue which from many points of view might have been regarded as the most important of all.

It may be useful to give a brief summary of the major findings contained in this chapter. In the main, our results support the view that the general principles discovered in the analysis of the structure of adult personality recur in the analysis of the structure of personality of children. We find that among boys and girls extraversion and neuroticism are very clearly apparent, even at the youngest ages investigated; girls are somewhat more emotional, boys somewhat more extraverted. The primary factors into which E and N can be broken down are similar to those found among adults, and here too these primary factors are less consistent and less clear-cut than are the higher order factors of E and N. Scales of E and N have reasonable split-half and test-retest reliabilities, although for the youngest groups these leave something to be desired, particularly if measurement of individual cases, rather than group comparisons, are desired. Correlations with intelligence are small or non-existent. E and N are related (negatively) to a slight extent; the two factors have something like 5 per cent of the variance in common, the two scores something like 2 per cent, while among adults the factors appear quite orthogonal. This orthogonality is approached among the older groups of children. The relations between the L scale and the E and N scales are very much like those observed in our adult groups, L having a very small negative correlation with E and a larger negative one with N. On the whole, the extension of our general descriptive scheme of personality to children from 7 to 16 appears justified, and the possibility of measuring the major dimensions of personality in children, at least above the age of 8 or 9, appears clearly demonstrated.

22

PERSONALITY IN SUBNORMAL SUBJECTS

S. B. G. Eysenck

PERSONALITY differences are as pronounced among men and women in the subnormal IQ range as among normal or above-normal people, and these differences may play a decisive role in determining whether a given subnormal patient may have to spend his or her whole life in an institution, or will be able to leave and lead a more or less normal, self-supporting life. There is some evidence that the personality factors most relevant to adjustment of this kind are extraversion-introversion and neuroticism-stability (Eysenck, 1960e) and it seemed desirable to develop a measuring instrument for subnormals in order to make possible further research in this field. It is intended for subnormal subjects with IQ's between 50 and 80 who are hospitalized in institutions for the mentally subnormal; it is possible though perhaps unlikely that the norms collected from such patients may be applicable also to subnormals of similar IQ outside an institution, and without further research into this question use of the test should be restricted to hospitalized populations only.

In addition to the E and N scales, each of which consists of 20 items, there is also included a Lie scale (L), made up of 12 items; the purpose of this scale is to detect deliberate faking. The items of all three scales have been adapted from the E.P.I. and have undergone a process of successive refinement (S. B. G. Eysenck, 1966).

For the purpose of constructing the E.P.I. (W) for subnormal subjects, 124 questions, of which 18 were lie items, were administered to the standardization group. This consisted of 426 subjects (229 men, 197 women) with IQ's between 50 and 80, who were hospitalized in various institutions for the mentally subnormal. The items in the questionnaire were read individually to the subjects, and were marked in accordance with their answers by the examiner. A factor analysis (principal axes method) was carried out on the intercorrelations of the 106 personality items, and two factors extracted. A single factor was similarly extracted from the intercorrelations of the 18 lie items. The resulting factors were clearly identifiable as E, N and L. On the basis of this analysis, the 52 most suitable items were chosen for the final scale, i.e. 20 E, 20 N and 12 L items. Choice was determined by item loading on the relevant factor, and by lack of loading on irrelevant factors, as well as by a desire to have as little item content overlap as possible.

Some slight difficulties were experienced with the wording of a few of the items, and accordingly these items (10 in number) were reworded to make them easier of comprehension, but without changing in any way the sense of the item. This second version of the questionnaire was again factor analysed to make sure that the rewording had not changed the loading to any substantial extent. For this purpose 330 subjects who had taken part in the first test were retested with the revised inventory. It was found that differences in factor structure and loadings were minimal for the changed as well as for the unchanged items. The version here presented is of course the second, improved one.

The 52 items of the scale are given in Table 22.1 below; each item is preceded by an N, E or L to indicate the personality variable which is being measured.

TABLE 22.1

E1. Like plenty of excitement going on around you
N2. Worry about your health
E3. Nearly always have a quick answer when people talk to you
N4. Ideas run through your head so that you cannot sleep
L5. Sometimes get cross
E6. Like practical jokes
N7. Ever feel 'just miserable' for no good reason
E8. Rather lively
N9. Lots of things annoy you
L10. As a child you always did as you were told
E11. Like doing things where you have to act quickly
N12. Worry about awful things that might happen
E13. Get a party going
N14. Get thumping in your heart
L15. There are people you definitely do not like
E16. When you make new friends you usually make the first move
N17. Often felt tired for no good reason
E18. Like telling jokes or funny stories to your friends
N19. Touchy about some things

L20. Ever told a lie
E21. Usually happy and cheerful
N22. Suffer from nerves
L23. Sometimes put off until tomorrow what you ought to do to-day
E24. Like mixing with people
N25. Often feel fed-up
L26. Sometimes boast a little
E27. Like playing jokes on others
E28. Sometimes get so restless that you cannot sit in a chair long
E29. Usually let yourself go and enjoy yourself at a gay party
N30. Feelings rather easily hurt
L31. All your habits are good ones
E32. Like going out a lot
N33. Worry for a long while if you feel you have made a fool of yourself
E34. Other people think of you as being very lively
N35. Sometimes feel life if just not worth living
L36. Sometimes talk about things you know nothing about
E37. Usually feel fairly sure you can do the things you have to
N38. Often 'lost in thought'
E39. Say the things you are thinking quickly
N40. Find it hard to get to sleep at night because you are worrying about things
L41. Ever been late for an appointment or work
E42. Usually feel if things go badly they will work out right in the end
N43. Often feel lonely
E44. Slow and unhurried in the way you move
N45. Sometimes sulk
L46. If you say you will do something you always keep your promise
E47. Often long for exciting things to happen
N48. Often troubled with guilty feelings
L49. Now and then you lose your temper and get angry
E50. Very much enjoy talking to people
N51. Get attacks of shaking and trembling
L52. Sometimes have thoughts you would not like others to know about

The loadings of the 20 N and the 20 E items in this scale are given in Table 22.2 below; the L items were not included in the analysis, but analysed separately. These factors are the first two principal components, with latent roots of 5·954 and 3·420. Also given are the loadings of the same items when they were analysed as part of the 106 item inventories on a previous occasion.

It will be seen that the loadings are very similar, and that the factor pattern is reasonably replicable in a population of this kind. Furthermore, the loadings are very similar to those obtained with subjects of normal intelligence. It would seem, therefore, that our two main personality dimensions can be used for taxonomic purposes even in a population well below the average in intelligence.

TABLE 22.2

Item	N 1st analysis	N 2nd analysis	E 1st analysis	E 2nd analysis
1	0·09	0·03	0·42	0·34
2	0·45	0·46	−0·13	−0·15
3	−0·03	−0·04	0·40	0·37
4	0·52	0·54	0·05	0·04
6	0·04	0·03	0·42	0·43
7	0·53	0·56	−0·06	0·00
8	−0·17	−0·15	0·44	0·55
9	0·54	0·56	0·03	0·06
11	0·08	0·06	0·46	0·39
12	0·51	0·54	−0·03	0·02
13	0·06	0·05	0·49	0·46
14	0·46	0·45	0·08	0·03
16	0·07	0·05	0·40	0·32
17	0·49	0·53	−0·14	−0·04
18	0·06	−0·02	0·50	0·38
19	0·49	0·51	0·04	0·13
21	−0·11	−0·08	0·40	0·48
22	0·47	0·50	−0·06	−0·08
24	−0·05	−0·05	0·26	0·38
25	0·55	0·60	−0·04	0·09
27	0·17	0·05	0·34	0·12
28	0·55	0·50	0·12	0·03
29	−0·04	0·02	0·33	0·52
30	0·56	0·58	−0·07	0·01
32	−0·03	−0·01	0·31	0·40
33	0·46	0·50	−0·05	0·06
34	−0·06	−0·07	0·43	0·44
35	0·51	0·54	0·01	0·03
37	−0·08	0·00	0·19	0·32
38	0·56	0·52	0·01	−0·03
39	−0·06	−0·08	0·37	0·34
40	0·57	0·59	−0·10	−0·12
42	0·05	0·06	0·34	0·47
43	0·51	0·55	−0·11	−0·05
44	0·36	0·28	−0·04	−0·23
45	0·55	0·56	−0·06	0·03
47	0·29	0·30	0·36	0·48
48	0·52	0·52	−0·03	−0·03
50	−0·02	−0·01	0·48	0·52
51	0·53	0·53	0·04	−0·01

In view of the difficulties in reading and comprehension likely to be experienced by mental defectives, it is essential that subjects be tested individually. The examiner reads out each item to the subject, waits for a reply, and then marks the appropriate answer. Prior to the administration of the test the examiner reads out the instructions, and makes sure that they are understood. Questions regarding the instructions may be fully answered; questions regarding the individual items require a more carefully guarded reply. If possible, the examiner should simply re-read the item, perhaps slightly changing his tone or emphasis; if this does not produce comprehension, and if it is apparent that a particular word is not known to the subject, then and only then may the examiner re-phrase the wording by introducing a synonym, or by explaining the meaning of the question. Care should always be taken not to alter the meaning of the question, or to suggest a particular answer. If too many questions require an explanation, the value of the score becomes increasingly doubtful, and the examiner should make a note to this effect on the questionnaire.

Scoring of the completed form is accomplished by aligning the scoring key furnished with the form, and counting one point for each underlined answer uncovered by a hole in the appropriate key.

Reliability of the scales

Split-half reliability. Corrected by the Spearman-Brown formula, the reliability of the three scales was as follows: E = 0·70; N = 0·88; L = 0.70.

Test-retest reliability. The values to be quoted under this heading refer to the correlation between version 1 and version 2, and are therefore strictly speaking not test-retest correlations; however, as the changes were quite minimal we may perhaps accept these values as minimum estimates of the true values. On 78 subjects tested at Harperbury, the values were as follows: E = 0·71; N = 0·83; L = 0·92. Subjects tested at other institutions presented some difficulties in cross-identification, and have therefore been omitted.

The reliability of the scales is reasonable for the N variable, but rather low for E. This difference may be a reflection of the generally higher factor loadings of the N items as compared with the E items; only further experience with the scale will enable us to discover just why it is that N is more clearly marked in subnormals than E, a feature in which they resemble young children.

E and N are uncorrelated with each other, $r = -0{\cdot}073$, as are E and L, $r = -0{\cdot}028$. There is, however, a sizeable correlation between N and L, $r = -0{\cdot}595$. This is very much in line with the position in the field of normal adult and child personality measurement. Further research is required to indicate more clearly the causal implications of this relationship, and the optimal use of the L scale for correcting any intentional faking that may have taken place.

The mean age of the population was 35·633, with a S.D. of 14·925. None of the scales showed a meaningful correlation with age, the actual values being: E = −0·065; N = 0·010; L = 0·107.

TABLE 22.3

Means and standard deviations of the E, N and L scores for groups of different I.Q.

		E		N		L	
I.Q.	*n*	M	S.D.	M	S.D.	M	S.D.
Total	370	14·195	3·557	10·070	5·307	6·065	2·731
(50–59)	129	13·535	3·727	10·147	5·467	6·558	2·738
(60–69)	125	14·528	3·682	9·808	5·383	6·312	2·576
(70–80)	116	14·569	3·127	10·267	5·072	5·250	2·725

As regards sex, there were no differences with respect to E (M = 14·268±3·403; F = 14·110±3·736). Women, however, had much higher scores on N, as is indeed usually found with normal adults and children: M = 8·712±5·319; F = 11·634±4·857. On the L scale the males showed a slightly greater tendency to lie: M = 6·495±2·673; F = 5·570±2·721. Except for E, the sexes must clearly be kept apart in experimental and statistical analyses. It seemed desirable to investigate the possibility that scores on the three scales might be related to actual IQ level, and accordingly 370 patients on whom precise and comparable IQ measurements were available were subdivided into three groups on the basis of their intelligence test scores (cf. Table 22.3). It will be seen that differences on E and N are minimal; there is no reason to suspect that IQ is in any way related to a person's standing on these personality variables within the range sampled here. The data suggest, however, that a patient's tendency to lie increases as his IQ decreases, and this finding is well in line with the discovery that in children chronological age is negatively correlated with L scores: this means, of course, that mental age, and consequently IQ over the total range, is so correlated with L. Why this should be so, either in children or in subnormals, is a matter for conjecture.

EPILOGUE

Primary and higher-order factors

WE are now in a position to review the massive sets of data discussed in the preceding sections, and to draw some more general conclusions. Comments have already been made in connection with certain issues as they arose, but a more concentrated discussion has been postponed until all the data had been presented. This discussion can most profitably start with a consideration of a relatively old but still very live problem, viz. that of the primacy of first-order as opposed to higher-order factors. This problem is often linked with the names of the main protagonists of the two positions: Spearman, who advocated the primacy of higher-order factors (or 'g' factors, as they used to be called), and Thurstone, who advocated the primacy of first-order factors (or group factors, as they are called in England). It is often (erroneously) implied in text-books that the opposition is absolute, and can be decided on the basis of some crucial experiment; it is also often argued, or assumed, that such an experiment was in fact performed by Thurstone, and that the Spearman position was thereby made untenable. None of this is true.

Spearman (1927) maintained that intelligence tests selected so as not to show extraneous overlap in design or content would, when applied to an unselected population or random sample, give rise to intercorrelations which could be represented as a matrix of rank 1 (to use matrix algebra terms he himself did not in fact use). Thurstone (1938) showed that tests showing often quite extensive extraneous overlap in design or content failed, when applied to a very highly selected population of exceptionally intelligent university students, to give rise to correlations which could be represented as a matrix of rank 1. There was of course no real inconsistency between these results, and even with his highly selected university students Thurstone's data reveal the existence of a powerful general factor (Eysenck, 1939). Thurstone himself soon realized that it was in fact impossible to retain orthogonality of primary factors and simple structure, and made his choice in terms of the latter, with the explicit understanding that the correlations between factors in turn required resolution in terms of higher order factors; his later work provides ample evidence of a general factor of intelligence.

Nor did Spearman fail to discover group factors, such as verbal and numerical ability; indeed, it is difficult to see any justification for the legend that has grown up regarding his refusal to admit such factors. Even such very modern-sounding notions as 'divergent' tests and 'originality' or 'creativity' factors resulting therefrom were pioneered in his laboratory under the name of 'fluency' factors, and he even correctly anticipated the correlation between these factors and extraversion (Eysenck, 1967). We see therefore that the battle lines are wrongly drawn; both sides admit the existence of both kinds of factors—the most inclusive, general type of intelligence factor, as well as the most exclusive, limited group factor. The continuing argument between the English and the American schools is concerned, not with the admissibility of both kinds of factors, but rather with their usefulness. Americans believe that from the practical point of view a profile of many small factors is most likely to give accurate prediction; English psychologists believe that a few more inclusive factors have the advantage. As far as intelligence is concerned the evidence is certainly not compellingly in favour of the American point of view; indeed, such work as has been done tends to favour rather the English side (McNemar, 1964; Vernon, 1965). The writer has discussed the problems arising in the intelligence field (Eysenck, 1967); here we are more concerned with the similar problems which arise in the field of personality.

Theoretically, one would expect the American view to emerge victorious without any quibble. If we conceive of our superfactor(s) as made up of the correlations between many primary factors, then clearly we lose some variance in discarding that portion of the primary factor variance which is specific to each factor, and not part of the variance of the superfactor. This loss should show itself in the accuracy of prediction made possible by the different combinations of scores; unless the variance discarded has no correlation with the criterion, and cannot even be used as a suppressor variable, it must surely contribute to the overall prediction. This argument is so inviting that many applied psychologists have accepted it in the absence of any direct evidence; where such evidence has been presented it has often suffered from the usual error of capitalizing on chance deviations, a process which obviously favours that approach which produces the greater number of such deviations!

From the theoretical point of view this approach has obvious weaknesses which may be made more obvious by taking the argument a step further. If we lose variance by collapsing a number of factors into one, then obviously we also lose variance by collapsing a large number of tests into a smaller number of factors; why not use the variance contributed by the tests individually to predict the criterion? This direct approach via regression as an alternative to factor analysis is indeed preferred by many applied psychologists, and from the purely statistical point of view there is little that can be objected to it. We might even be prepared to go a little further and suggest that not tests but test items could be regarded as the atoms from which our prediction should be constituted; after all, the summing of individual items into a test score also loses variance which could be used for prediction! And now that computers are universally available, even the excuse that such large numbers of items impose an intolerable strain on the overworked statistician will not do any longer. Why then factor analysis at all?

The answer, usually, is taken to consist of the following considerations. The prediction criterion is constantly changing, as is the composition of the sample used, familiarity with the tests, the selection ratio, and many other parameters which crucially affect the exact prediction equation. Even where these factors do not change very much, we often wish to apply the knowledge gained in one situation to another, slightly different one; often we do not even know whether, and in what ways, the second situation differs from the first. Often we do not have the resources, or the time, to repeat the lengthy and expensive process which leads to the setting up of the proper regression equation on the basis of which we can make accurate predictions. Under such circumstances, a psychological understanding of the relation between criterion and test may help us in setting up a more satisfactory testing situation than would be possible by simply applying the old regression formula under changed circumstances. Indeed, without some psychological understanding of what we are doing we might not even be able to recognize that the circumstances had changed! And factors are believed to be purer in composition, and nearer to psychological concepts, than are tests which are compound mixtures difficult to 'read' without benefit of factorial dissection.

All this is true, but only if factors are invariant with respect to changes in sex, age, education, social class, or whatever variables may differentiate one group to whom the tests are to be applied from another. Thus factor invariance becomes the crucial issue in the debate between factor analysis and advocates of simple regression equation procedures. And it is curiously precisely in this respect that factor analysts have usually been uncommonly coy, refusing to carry out the necessary type of controlled investigation which alone can answer questions of this kind. We do, admittedly, have many investigations in which research workers look at patterns of loadings and identify these arbitrarily and subjectively as being, or resembling, a certain factor, but such alleged identifications often hide profound differences. When efforts are made to identify personality factors in samples of subjects differing in intelligence, or intelligence factors in samples of subjects differing in personality, then it is found that significant differences do in fact appear, not only in the nature of the factors, but in their very number (Eysenck and White, 1965). And we have seen in the studies reported in this volume that coefficients of factor similarity for most of the Cattell and Guilford factors are very low when male and female subjects are being compared. This issue is of course quite different from that of comparability of factor scores; two groups may differ greatly in factor scores, but have the same pattern of covariances, and consequently of factors, and conversely they may have identical factor scores, but quite different patterns of covariances, and consequently factors. The assumption of most factor analysts that factors extracted from one group will apply with equal force to other groups differing along various parameters from the original group is not one which can be accepted without definite proof in each particular case, and such evidence as exists suggests that for personality and intelligence test variables this assumption is not firmly grounded, and may be altogether fallacious. Our first conclusion, therefore, must be that factor invariance with change in sample along such parameters as sex, age, class and education must be rigorously demonstrated; it cannot be assumed without proof. No claims for the 'existence' of a factor can be entertained seriously until and unless such proof of invariance is given, or until the exact rules of change of factor composition with change of parameter are established.

Of all the factors examined, only E and N begin to approach such a status; they have been replicated with high accuracy in studies carried out on male and female subjects; they appear in different age groups, down to the age of 7; they are replicable in different European and non-European countries; they have appeared in groups of subjects differing widely in education and intelligence. They have been prominent in the psychological literature for some 2,000 years, and many workers, in many countries, using many different types of tests and measures, have unearthed evidence regarding their nature and existence (Eysenck, 1960e). None of this is true of the alleged Cattell and Guilford factors, whose existence is in fact not premised, in the form in which they are offered, on a single factor analytic study. Until much stronger evidence is offered, therefore, it is suggested that these factors be considered as suggestive, not as confirmed.

Our second point relates to the age-old practice of creating traits, types and factors by *fiat*, i.e. by simple introspective contemplation of reality as it presents itself to the author in question. It is this practice which is responsible for the low regard in which personality research is held by experimental psychologists; where there are hundreds of rival claimants in the field, all suggesting different solutions, the experimentalist may with reason be doubtful about the rigour with which these different results have been attained. The outstanding fact about such systems as those of Cattell and Guilford is not that they are objective, and based on correlation and factor analysis, but that they are subjective, and based on arbitrary and intuitive judgements. The building stones of a questionnaire are the items, and objectivity demands that factor analysis should begin at this level, i.e. with the intercorrelation and factor analysis of items. Yet this has in fact not been done; although

Guilford, for instance, began by establishing factors on the basis of small-scale factor analyses of some 20 or 30 items, he constructed his inventories on the basis of adding to these items others not selected on the basis of factor analysis, but by intuition and hypothesis. At no time did either he or Cattell intercorrelate all the items in his scales in one single analysis, to establish the fact that the postulated factors did in fact exist, and emerge with the correct items having high loadings on these and only these factors. As we have seen in the first part of this book (Part One), Guilford's factor S, assumed by him to be a unitary, univocal factor of social shyness, split into two quite uncorrelated parts when subjected to item analysis. And as shown in the second part of this book (Part Two), almost none of the factors discovered on the basis of intercorrelating items from Guilford's and Cattell's sets could be shown to be in fact made up from the items postulated to constitute this factor, and only those items.

Again, only E and N escape from this criticism. There are now many studies in the literature based on intercorrelations between items which yield these two factors, and it can be documented that identical items go to make up each factor on different occasions. It is difficult to over-emphasize the importance of this point. No rigorous analysis is possible when subjective estimates and judgements are allowed to come in through the back door, and no sophistication in factor analytic minutiae can make up for this vital error. Admittedly, the laboriousness of the procedure when many items are involved serves as an excuse for work done prior to the free availability of computers, but for work done since 1955 or thereabouts it must be said that failure to extend the process of factor analysis right down to the fundamental building stones of any inventory or questionnaire form a severe weakness which could easily have been overcome.

This leads us on to our third point. Subjective procedures often come into the analytic process itself, and we are firmly of the opinion that only analytic methods capable of being machine programmed are properly admissible for serious work in this field. The range of variation which is opened up by *coup d'oeil* procedures of rotation, particularly when there are many factors available for rotation, is too large to allow subjectivity subtly to push results towards preconceived ends; any subjective criteria for rotation must be spelled out exactly and precisely, and can be incorporated in analytic programmes, such as Promax. It should hardly need saying that such programmes should not impose restrictions upon the process of rotation which are not imposed by the intrinsic nature of the data; thus simple structure is admissible as a limitation, but orthogonality is not. Varimax is an excellent first step in rotation, but it must be used only as a first step to oblique factor solutions; if the analysis ends with Varimax, then we have not discovered orthogonality of factors, but imposed it, and our results may be, and usually are, not in accord with the facts. If factors are indeed orthogonal, then oblique rotation will reveal them to be so; if factors are oblique, orthogonal rotation will not reveal them to be so. No analysis imposing such restrictions on the data should be acceptable when more revealing types of analysis are available.

When such rules of objectivity are followed, what is the outcome? In the studies described in Parts Two and Three, we have seen that while primary factors emerge in considerable profusion, these seldom if ever agree precisely with those postulated by Cattell and Guilford, and on the average may be said to show marked disagreement on many vital points. Furthermore, while some factors show acceptable C.F.S.s from one sex to the other, the average level of comparability is not high enough to allow us to say that identical factors are obtained from males and females. Primary factors, with a number of exceptions, must be established separately for men and women, if they are to be used at all. It is possible (our results do not enable us to say) that the same is true for people with good and poor education, or for people above and below the age of 40, or for bright and dull subjects. The belief, sometimes echoed by text-book writers, that the main primary factors of personality description have been identified by Cattell or Guilford is clearly premature; this fact should have been obvious long ago, if only because of the lack of agreement between these two writers! Much long and arduous work still lies ahead before we can claim to know very much about the structure of personality at the primary level. At the highest level of generality, fortunately, the Eysenck, Cattell and Guilford systems show complete agreement, across sex, in the shape of the independent E and N factors postulated originally by Eysenck (1947).

What can we say about those primary factors which issue in acceptable C.F.S.s as compared with those which do not? We have already drawn attention to the continuum from T factors to C factors, and it will be remembered that C.F.S.s tended to be high for T factors, i.e. factors whose nature was tautological, and more similar to reliability coefficients, than for C factors, i.e. factors which combined divergent items with varying content. This conclusion may appear obvious, and hardly worth stating, but little has been found in the literature on this point, and it seemed worth while putting this hypothesis down in black and white as a basis for discussion. It would seem to follow from this argument, if the hypothesis be indeed accepted, that in our search for primary factors replicable across sex, age, social class, education and intelligence we should concentrate on T factors, and avoid C factors unless very strong evidence was available to suggest that such factors would be likely to be replicable. The fact that Cattell's factors were found to be particularly difficult to replicate emerges in part as a consequence of his preoccupation with C factors; Eysenck is more concerned with T factors, while Guilford is intermediate.

It might of course be argued that T factors are useless, just because they ask the same question with slight changes in emphasis. This is not true, for two reasons. In the first place, consider the Spearman-Brown prophecy formula, and the logic underlying it. If two sociability questions, asking the same question with only slight changes in wording, correlate 0·5 over a group of 1,000 subjects, then the score from the two questions combined is much more reliable than that from only one question. A scale of ten such questions would approach acceptable reliability, where one question by itself would fail to do so. Increase in reliability is not an unworthy goal, although it does not make much contribution to our psychological understanding of personality.

The second advantage of having a scale of ten or more questions, rather than one, lies in the very fact that we now have a scale. Individuals can be differentiated much more readily, and in greater detail, where the single question leaves us with only an either/or classification. Furthermore, the constituent questions of a scale can be chosen so as to call forth different proportions of agreements and disagreements. This feature, corresponding to the difficulty level of intelligence test items, has not been much emphasized in questionnaire construction, but it holds out much promise. A scale the top item of which is answered in the affirmative by all but the least sociable, while the bottom item is answered in the affirmative by none but the most sociable is an obvious improvement on a single item, even though again not much contribution may have been made to psychological insight. Our suggestion, in brief, is that primary factors are of use not so much in aiding our psychological understanding, but rather as aids in methodology, enabling us to construct psychometrically superior scales.

It may be objected that factor analysis is not the method of choice for this purpose, and that item analysis and other methods are superior, as well as less complex and time consuming. This is only partly true, and a single example will suffice to establish the need for factor analysis even at this stage. Consider Guilford's S factor. This consists of a number of questions ostensibly concerned with sociability, and assumed to measure one single factor. It is assumed by Guilford that this is a univariate factor, and one might think that here indeed we are dealing with a T factor of the purest water. Yet in fact we have shown that this factor breaks up into two quite unrelated ones; item analysis of the usual type would not have established this. Factor analysis (or some modification of factor analysis) was required to achieve this result, and it is suggested that every T factor must be shown to be univocal; it cannot be assumed to be so. Only when this demonstration has been successfully accomplished can we proceed to use the items involved to construct our scale according to the best precepts of psychometric practice.

It is our conviction that scales of sociability, impulsiveness, activity, carefreeness and so on, constructed along these lines, would be of considerable use to psychologists along both practical and experimental lines, even though they would add little directly to our psychological understanding. It is also our conviction that none of the existing scales, whether they have been constructed in part with the use of factor analysis, as in the case of Cattell and Guilford, or whether they have been constructed in studied disregard of factor analysis, as in the case of the Gough scales and the M.M.P.I., approach to this ideal sufficiently to accept them without many reservations. Here there would appear to be a job of considerable dimensions well worth the doing.

When we turn to the E and N scales, it is obvious that they approach the C end of the continuum; equally, it will be agreed that the proven existence of these two orthogonal factors does make an important contribution to our understanding of the psychology of personality. These relationships are not tautological; they could not have been predicted on a purely logical or *a priori* basis. The fact that they do exist, and are relatively invariant to changes in many parameters is an important psychological fact. Relatively accurate measurement of these two dimensions is possible, even with the crude instruments available to us at the present moment; no doubt these are susceptible to considerable improvement, but such improvement is unlikely to change in any major fashion the general picture outlined in this book.

We are now in a position to return to the question with which we started this chapter. What is the contribution that factor analysis can make to prediction, over and above that made by regression equation? The answer, essentially, is that in a completely stationary, unchanging situation, where identical predictions are made from identical samples, no improvement can be made by factor analytic treatment of data over regression equation treatment. But in the more frequently occurring real life situation, where constantly changing samples of applicants have to be tested to meet constantly changing criteria, and where the choice of tests is constantly being improved, factor analysis has many important advantages. T factors cut down the number of calculations to be done by grouping items in homogeneous tests; they also suggest psychological hypotheses regarding the importance of certain traits and abilities for the particular criterion chosen. C factors do the same job even more successfully because the grouping of items suggested by them is unexpected, and likely to lead to further research into the nature of the factors concerned; this research in turn is likely to throw added light on the reasons why these particular tests, rather than others, succeed in predicting the criterion. E tests predict success on occupations requiring high degrees of vigilance; psychological research into the reasons for this relationship has suggested likely hypotheses, and has elaborated new tests which may be even more successful at predicting occupational success in this line of work. The regression equation fails because it does nothing but a psychometric job of prediction; factor analysis adds psychological understanding and improvement of testing devices based on such understanding. Such understanding is essential when changes in sample or criterion, however subtle, throw out the finely calculated predictions of the regression formula.

We can now see what is possibly the main reason why the confident expectation that many primary factors would lead to better prediction than a few major ones has not been fulfilled. The primary factors which have been unearthed and used in personality research, such as the Cattell and the Guilford ones, fail because they are in fact not unitary, univocal combinations of items measuring the same fundamental trait, as is assumed by these authors; they are not invariant across such differences of sex, age, education or class as will inevitably arise in typical samples to whom the inventories are applied. Instead, they are half arbitrary, half accidental conglomerations of items sharing functional equivalence only to a limited degree, and thus quite unfitted to bear the burden imposed upon them by their originators. And what is true of these inventories is even more true, *a fortiori,* of such other inventories as have never been subjected even to the appearance of a factor analytic type of item selection. The task of primary factor extraction is not nearing completion, as some writers claim, it has hardly begun yet in any serious manner. By contrast, higher order factors emerge with credit from our studies; they are found to share functional equivalence to a substantial degree, and they do show invariance across many different parameters. Small wonder that from the point of view of meaningful prediction they are superior to primary factors lacking in these essential virtues.

Hitherto we have concentrated on practical application and prediction of diverse applied criteria. But more important, from the fundamental point of view, is the contribution which such factors may make to the furtherance of personality theory, and the understanding and explanation of human conduct. It is our contention that here too it is only the higher order factors which have been found to be capable of integration with our existing knowledge of psychological and physiological fact; both E and N can be understood in terms of such well-established concepts and structures as the limbic system, the visceral brain, and the ascending reticular formation (Eysenck, 1967). Primary factors, even should they escape the criticisms made of them above, would still be purely descriptive at the lowest level; causal theories regarding their mode of origin and working are still as far as ever from being linked with our knowledge of experimental and general psychology. There is admittedly still no agreement about the usefulness of, and need for, a psychological understanding of the nature of the tests and factors we use in our work, some psychometrists apparently thinking that statistical expertise in item manipulation can make up for lack of theoretical explanation, but to us it seems almost self-evident that without such theoretical explanation little improvement can be expected in the sad state of our present knowledge of personality. It is for this reason, more than any other, that we feel that the factors of extraversion and neuroticism hold far more promise than do the primary factors discussed in this book. Primary factors are either tautological or non-invariant; E and N are invariant and non-tautological. Furthermore, E and N find a ready explanation in theoretical psychology and experimental physiology; primary factors offer neither of these advantages. Unless a considerable change takes place in these well-established facts, it is difficult to avoid the conclusion that much work on personality in recent years has followed the wrong path.

APPENDIX

RELATING FACTORS BETWEEN STUDIES BASED UPON DIFFERENT INDIVIDUALS[1]

HENRY F. KAISER
University of Wisconsin, Madison
STEVE HUNKA
University of Alberta, Edmonton
JOHN BIANCHINI
Educational Testing Service, Berkeley

ABSTRACT

A METHOD for relating factors between studies based upon different individuals is developed. This approach yields a measure of relationship between all factors under consideration—a measure which may be interpreted as a correlation coefficient.

A problem of great interest in the application of factor analysis is to determine the relationship between factors of two different studies. Four cases may be distinguished, depending upon whether the same or different variables and upon whether the same or different individuals have been observed. For the two cases where the same individuals have participated in both studies, the correlation between factors (or their estimates) may be computed directly because of the common individuals. On the other hand, when the factors of two studies based upon different individuals are to be compared, no such obvious solution exists. Thus, how could it be possible to relate the factors of a study done in Alaska with the factors of another study done 47 years later in Alabama? For the case of 'different individuals, different variables', an objective solution is obviously impossible. However, if the same

[1] We are indebted to Professor Julius M. Sassenrath for suggesting this problem. Computations were done on the CDC 1604 of the University of Wisconsin Computing Centre under a grant from the University of Wisconsin Research Committee. Since this Centre is partially supported by the National Science Foundation and by the Wisconsin Alumni Research Foundation, these agencies are acknowledged. Mr. Edgar Arendt assisted in the computations.

variables were observed in Alaska and Alabama, a basis for comparison exists.

It is the purpose of this paper to propose a solution to the problem of relating factors between studies with different individuals, some of the same variables. The method presented below yields a measure of relationship between all factors of the two studies simultaneously—a measure which may be interpreted as a correlation coefficient.

The notion of 'relating' factors should be distinguished from the notion of 'matching' factors. For the problem of this paper—relating factors—we are interested only in assessing the degree of relationship between the factors for two completed studies taken as they stand, regardless of the strength of these relationships. On the other hand, when matching factors the problem is to rotate two sets of arbitrary reference factors, such as principal axes, to find two sets of factors which are as close together as possible, thus matching pairs of factors. Cattell (1944) and Tucker (1951) have attacked elegantly the problem of matching factors, but their methods seem to be irrelevant for the problem of relating factors.

The statement of the solution is first motivated in the following section by an appeal to geometric intuition. Next, the technical details of obtaining a numerical solution are outlined. As an example, the method is then applied to relating the factors between two anthropometric studies. Certain limitations of the procedure are discussed.

METHOD

For each of the two studies being compared, consider the geometric configuration of the test vectors and the factor vectors in the space where cosines of angles between vectors mean correlations, the space Holzinger and Harman (1941, Chapter 3) call the 'vector representation'. Thus for the first study with p_1 tests and q_1 factors, (p_1+q_1) vectors, all with a common origin, lie in a q_1-dimensional vector space, where the q_1 factor vectors are of unit length and the p_1 test vectors are of length equal to the square-root of their communalities. The cosine of the angle between any two vectors gives the correlation between the two variables represented. (Note that the test vectors do not represent the observed tests, but the common parts of the observed tests, i.e. the reflection of the original test vectors on to the common factor space.) For the second study, a similar configuration of (p_2+q_2) vectors lying in a q_2-dimensional vector space is easily visualized. For convenience designate the studies 'first' and 'second' so that $q_1 \geqq q_2$.

Now place both configurations of vectors in the same space with the same origin. Therefore, all $(p_1+q_1+p_2+q_2)$ test and factor vectors now lie in a q_1-dimensional vector space, a space in which the cosines of the angles between vectors within, but not between, studies represent observable correlations. A placement of this sort is not unique, for the correlations between the tests and factors of the first study with the tests and factors of the second study are not known. The problem is to find a unique, meaningful way of placing these two set of vectors. Consider the p, $p \leqq p_1$, $p \leqq p_2$, tests which are common to the two studies. The method of this paper is based upon the following principle: place the two sets of p vectors representing the p common tests pairwise as close together as possible, matching the common part of each test in the first study with its mate in the second. This may be quantified by requiring that the sum of the p inner products be maximized. It is made operational by rotating the complete set of vectors for the second study rigidly until the condition is met. After this rotation we measure the cosines of the angles between all pairs of the q_1+q_2 factor vectors. Within each of the two studies, these cosines of course give the actual correlations between the factors within the study. Between studies, however, these cosines are not correlations in the usual sense (because of there being no common individuals on which to base a correlation) but they may surely be taken as a measure of relationship between the factors represented, and a measure which certainly can be interpreted as a correlation coefficient.

The mathematics of the method will now be undertaken. First throw away the $(p_1-p)+(p_2-p)$ non-common test vectors, as they are of no concern. This leaves $2p+q_1+q_2$ vectors under consideration. Extend each of the $2p$ common test vectors to unit length, as the procedure will be applied with normalized test vectors: both in the senior author's alpha factor analysis (Kaiser and Caffrey, 1965) and his varimax rotational criterion (Kaiser, 1958), it has proved desirable to proceed with the common parts of tests normalized, and, to be consistent with these earlier procedures, test vectors will be normalized here.

Because of overwhelming advantages in simplicity, all vectors will be referred to an orthonormal basis, or co-ordinate system, with unit-length, mutually perpendicular axes. Four distinct situations arise in establishing the projections of the test and factor vectors on the axes of the orthonormal co-ordinate system. We review these four possibilities in some detail:

(a) *Uncorrelated (orthogonal) factors.* Simply take the final (probably rotated) factors as the co-ordinate axes. For a given study (the first, say), a matrix of order $(p+q_1)\times q_1$ may be written:

$$\begin{bmatrix} H_1^{-1}F_1 \\ \\ I \end{bmatrix} \qquad [1]$$

where F_1 is the $p\times q_1$ factor matrix for the p common tests and $H^2 = \text{diag}(F_1F_1')$, the diagonal matrix of reproduced communalities; thus

$H_1^{-1}F_1$ is simply the row normalized factor matrix. The $q_1 \times q_1$ identity matrix below $H_1^{-1}F_1$ in [1] is the loadings of the uncorrelated factors on themselves. Matrix [1] then gives the loadings of all common tests and factors on the (same) factors.

(b) *Correlated primary factors, transformed (rotated) from known uncorrelated factors by a known primary factor transformation* T_1. Take the known uncorrelated factors represented by F_1, e.g. principal axes, as the coordinate system. Then, for the first study, $H_1^{-1}F_1$ again gives the normalized loadings of the common tests on these factors; however, the loadings of the rotated primary factors on the unrotated factors is given by T_1', where T_1 is the transformation matrix which transforms F_1 into the oblique primary factors under consideration. Therefore, if in the first study, the loadings of all $p+r_1$ common tests and (rotated) oblique factors on the (unrotated) uncorrelated factors appear as the $(p+q_1) \times q_1$ matrix:

$$\begin{bmatrix} H_1^{-1}F_1 \\ \\ T_1' \end{bmatrix}, \qquad [2]$$

Typically this instance is rare, for the matrix T_1 is usually not known. (Operationally oblique rotation most often is carried out with respect to the computationally intermediate reference vectors.)

(c) *Correlated reference vectors, transformed (rotated) from known uncorrelated factors by a known reference vector transformation* Y_1. Since of course we want to relate primary factors, not reference vectors, we must obtain the loadings of the primary factors implied by the known reference vectors on the known uncorrelated factors, represented again by F_1. These loadings are again given by a T_1', where

$$T_1' = D_1 Y_1^{-1} = D_1(Y_1' Y_1)^{-1} Y_1'. \qquad [3]$$

Y_1 is the nonsymmetric reference vector transformation (often called 'lamba') and D_1 is the diagonal matrix which normalizes the rows of Y_1^{-1}. The complete matrix of projections of tests and factors are set out again as in [2], with T_1' calculated by [3].

(d) *Correlated primary factors, no known related uncorrelated factors.* Here an F_1 and a T_1 may be 'made up' by the multiple group method (Guttman, 1944). Let L_{11} be the known intercorrelation matrix of the primary factors (if L_{11} is not known, or cannot be determined from other matrices, insufficient information is available to proceed). Factor

L_{11} (most conveniently by the square root method) into a T_1 so that

$$L_{11} = T_1'T_1, \qquad [4]$$

and find the corresponding F_1 by

$$F_1 = B_1T_1^{-1} \qquad [5]$$

or

$$F_1 = A_1T_1' \qquad [6]$$

where B_1 is the (known) primary factor *structure* matrix, or A_1 is the (known) primary factor *pattern* matrix, for the common tests. Again, set out the projections of the common tests and factors, as in [2], using the T_1' from [4] and $H_1^{-1}F_1$, the row-normalized F_1, from [5] or [6].

Situations (a] and (c) above are conventional. Situation (b) will arise only in the rare instance of direct rotation, bypassing the reference vectors, and (d) occurs when direct solution for correlated factors are made, e.g. in direct cluster analysis. In the taxonomy above note that our T_1 is Thurstone's (1947) T', but Harman's (1960) T; our L_{11} is Thurstone's R_{pq} and Harman's Φ. Finally, for more detail regarding the matrix gymnastics of the interrelationships of primary factors and reference vectors, etc., see Harman (1960, Chapter 13).

We can now present algebraically an arbitrary placement of the $2p+q_1+q_2$ vectors of interest as the $(2p+q_1+q_2)\times q_1$ matrix:

$$\begin{bmatrix} H_1^{-1}F_1 & \\ T_1' & \\ H_2^{-1}F_2 & 0 \\ T_2' & 0 \end{bmatrix}, \qquad [7]$$

where the subscripts 1 and 2 refer to matrices for the first and second studies, and the zero matrices, for $q_1 > q_2$, indicate (q_1-q_2) columns of zeros; remember also that T_1 and/or T_2 are identity matrices when F_1 and/or F_2 represent the (uncorrelated) factors being related.

To find the necessary and sufficient conditions for rotating the test vectors of the second study as close as possible to the test vectors of the first study consider any two columns in the supermatrix [7]. Designate the two $p\times 1$ vectors of tests' loadings for the first study by u and v and the two $p\times 1$ vectors of tests' loadings of the second study by x and y. An orthogonal rotation—orthogonal to keep our orthonormal basis—of these two columns of the second study may be made, yielding new loadings X and Y, given by the standard formulas

$$X = x\cos\phi + y\sin\phi, \qquad [8]$$

$$Y = -x\sin\phi + y\cos\phi, \qquad [9]$$

where ϕ is the angle of rotation.

The criterion function for rotation—maximizing the pairwise sum of inner products between the two studies—is then

$$u'X+v'Y. \tag{10}$$

Upon differentiating [10] with respect to ϕ, using [8] and [9], and setting the derivative equal to zero, after a good deal of algebra, it is seen that the desired angle of rotation is given by

$$\phi = \tan^{-1}\left(\frac{u'y+v'x}{u'x-v'y}\right). \tag{11}$$

Thus, ϕ will be zero only if $u'y+v'x$, the numerator of the fraction in [11], is zero. By inspecting the second derivative of [10] it may be shown that when also $u'x-v'y$, the denominator of the fraction in [11], is positive, a maximum for the criterion function for the plane under consideration has been attained.

The above conditions are for any pair of columns in [7]; we now express these results for the matrix as a whole. Let K' be a $q_2 \times q_1$ transformation matrix,[1] with K orthonormal by columns—$K'K = I$—with which to postmultiply the $p \times q_2$ matrix $H_2^{-1}F_2$. This $p \times q_1$ product, $H_2^{-1}F_2K'$, is to have rows which 'match up' as well as possible with the rows of $H_1^{-1}F_1$ according to the conditions of the preceding paragraph, which, for the entire matrix, are that

$$(H_1^{-1}F_1)'(H_2^{-1}F_2K') \tag{12}$$

is symmetric, with positive diagonals.

To accomplish this let

$$C = (H_1^{-1}F_1)'(H_2^{-1}F_2) \tag{13}$$

a matrix of order $q_1 \times q_2$. According to [12], CK' is to be symmetric. Consider

$$G = CC', \tag{14}$$

a square symmetric matrix of order q_1 but rank only q_2 (assuming $q_2 \leqq p$). Now write G as

$$G = WM^2W' \tag{15}$$

where W is the $q_1 \times q_2$ matrix of unit-length column eigenvectors of G, and M^2 is the $q_2 \times q_2$ diagonal matrix of positive eigenvalues of G. Since $W'W = I$, G may be written further as

$$G = (WMW')(WMW')' = (WMW')(WMW') \tag{16}$$

where M is the diagonal matrix of positive square roots of M^2. This factoring WMW' of G obviously is symmetric. Since $K'K = I$, we may write

$$(CK')(CK')' = CC' = G = (WMW')(WMW'), \tag{17}$$

[1] In a preliminary dittoed draft of this paper, which had wide circulation, we defined this matrix as K rather than K'. Consistent with the convention of having the untransposed version of matrices 'tall', we have changed the former K to K'.

and consequently, we want to transform C with a K' so that it equals the symmetric matrix WMW':

$$CK' = WMW'. \qquad [18]$$

This K', then, is the desired transformation for rotating the common test vectors of the second study as close as possible to the corresponding common test vectors of the first study. Solving [18] for K' explicitly

$$K' = (C'C)^{-1}C'WMW'. \qquad [19]$$

This solution may be simplified[1] by rewriting [19]:

$$K' = [(C'C)^{-1}C'] [WM^2W'] [WM^{-1}W'] \qquad [20]$$

since $W'W = L$. Upon noting from [14] and [15] that $WM^2W' = CC'$, K' becomes:

$$K' = [(C'C)^{-1}C'] [CC'] [WM^{-1}W'],$$

$$K' = C'WM^{-1}W'. \qquad [21]$$

We have shown that the unit-length row vectors $H_2^{-1}F_2K'$ are as close as possible to their mates in $H_1^{-1}F_1$. However, finding $H_2^{-1}F_2K'$ is not of primary concern. Rather, in performing the rigid rotation of all $p+q_2$ row vectors of

$$\begin{bmatrix} H_2^{-1}F_2 \\ \\ T_2' \end{bmatrix} \qquad [22]$$

with K', the most basic interest is in the resulting factor vectors, the rows of $T_2'K'$—and their relationships to the factor vectors of the first study, the rows of T_1'. To measure the cosines of the angles between these two sets of factor vectors in this space where cosines mean correlations, inner products are taken. Designating the matrix of these inner products between studies by L_{12},

$$L_{12} = T_1'(T_2'K')'$$

$$L_{12} = T_1'KT_2 \qquad [23]$$

the rows of L_{12} represent the factors of the first study and the columns of L_{12} the factors of the second study. Remember again that T_1 and/or T_2, as in [7], will be identity matrices when the factors being related are represented directly by F_1 and/or F_2, rather than rotations of F_1, and/or F_2.

The cosines between all (q_1+q_2) factor vectors may be exhibited as

$$\begin{bmatrix} L_{11} & L_{12} \\ L_{21} & L_{22} \end{bmatrix} = \begin{bmatrix} T_1' \\ T_2'K' \end{bmatrix} \begin{bmatrix} T_1' \\ T_2'K' \end{bmatrix}'$$

$$\begin{bmatrix} L_{11} & L_{12} \\ L_{21} & L_{22} \end{bmatrix} \quad \begin{bmatrix} T_1'T_1 & T_1'KT_2 \\ T_2'K'T_1 & T_2'T_2 \end{bmatrix}. \qquad [24]$$

[1] We are indebted to Professor Ledyard R. Tucker for providing this simplification.

$L_{11} = T_1'T_1$ and $L_{22} = T_2'T_2$, of course, are actual intercorrelations within the two studies while L_{12} and its transpose L_{21} contain the proposed measure of relationship between factors between studies.[1]

EXAMPLE

For illustrative purposes, a small problem (but complicated because $q_1 > q_2$ and one set of factors is correlated and the other uncorrelated) will now be solved. In Table A1 is given the complete analysis reported by Thurstone (1946) of 12 anthropometric measurements on 100 adult North Ireland males. (The correlation matrix first appeared in a paper by Hammond (1942).) In Table A2 is given the orthogonally rotated varimax factors of the first two centroids of a correlation matrix of 14 anthropometric measurements on 50 London University male students. (These centroids were calculated by Cohen (1939–41).) The four Thurstone-Hammond rotated primary factors will now be related to the two orthogonal varimax factors by the method of this paper.

TABLE A1

Thurstone's Factor Analysis of 12 Anthropometric Measurements on 100 North Ireland Males

	Centroid F				Reference Vector Simple Structure V @ FY			
Stature*	72	−55	−15	−11	−04	76	−08	45
Sitting height	60	−34	−25	−48	−03	80	00	01
Shoulder breadth*	51	17	22	−06	05	03	49	19
Hip breadth	59	21	36	−11	−02	01	64	22
Span	79	−35	02	03	02	52	15	55
Chest breadth*	60	32	24	−16	10	01	65	10
Chest depth*	34	34	29	−26	−03	−07	59	−09
Head length*	45	31	−30	04	51	09	23	00
Head breadth*	28	29	−36	32	61	−08	05	11
Head height	23	16	−49	19	57	10	−11	01
Hand length	78	−41	01	23	07	46	07	71
Hand breadth	58	−15	38	31	−07	01	34	67

Reference Vector Transformation Y				Primary Factor Transformation T @ (Y′)⁻¹D				Primary Factor Intercorrelations L @ T′T			
27	40	47	46	40	69	70	50	100	16	06	07
54	−64	64	−45	45	−36	45	−42	16	100	38	03
−70	−42	58	32	−72	−32	42	27	06	38	100	02
39	−50	−17	70	35	−54	−36	71	07	03	02	100

*Variables marked with an asterisk are common to the two studies being related.

[1] P. O. White has noted the formal equivalence of this problem to the well-known 'orthogonal procrustes' problem. (Schönemann, P. H. *Psychometrika*, 1966, **31.**) He points out an even simpler form for K than that given in equation [21].

Let $C'C = UM^2U'$, $U'U = I$ denote the eigenvalue–eigenvector representation of $C'C$ analogous to that of CC' given in equations [14] and [15]. It follows that $C = WMU'$ and that $(C'C)^{-1} = UM^{-2}U'$. Substituting for C and $(C'C)^{-1}$ in equation [19] and noting that $W'W = U'U = I$ it is readily verified that $K = WU'$.

TABLE A2

Varimax factors from Cohen's centroids for 14 anthropometric measurements on 50 London University male students

Waist circumference	94	02
Pelvic circumference	91	07
Pelvic breadth	78	20
Head diagonal	70	27
Chest circumference	84	07
Chest depth*	71	18
Shoulder breadth*	52	44
Chest breadth*	70	15
Head length*	58	29
Stature*	15	93
Leg length	16	89
Arm length	11	85
Head breadth*	64	04
Trunk length	10	73

* Variables marked with an asterisk are common to the two studies being related. In Table A3, these variables from this study are reordered to be properly paired with their mates from Thurstone's study.

There are $p = 6$ variables in common to the two studies: stature, shoulder breadth, chest breadth, chest depth, head length, and head breadth. In Table A3 is outlined in detail the computations for obtaining the transformation K' and the final matrix L_{12} (or L_{21}) of our measure of relationship between the factors between the two studies.

At this point, it may be of interest to ascertain the quality of the fit of the two sets of test vectors after rotation with K'. A seemingly reasonable index, varying between zero and one for all problems, would be the mean cosine between the p pairs, given by

$$\frac{1}{p}\ \text{trace}\ [H_1^{-1}F_1KF_2'H_2^{-1}]. \tag{25}$$

For the present example, this index is 0·85, suggesting that the pairing of the six variables was reasonable. It may be wise also to look at the individual diagonals of $H_1^{-1}F_1KF_2'H_2^{-1}$ to see if any particular pair of purported common tests is badly matched—casting doubt on the validity of the assumption of the two tests being the same.

CAUTIONS

It is easy to fall in the trap of calling two variables from different studies the same merely because they have the same name. Even in the relatively clearcut universe of anthropometric measurements, the fallacy of calling the variable *height* (for adult men) the same variable as *height* (for teen-age girls)—simply because they are both designated 'height'—

TABLE A3*

Outline of computations for relating rotated primary factors of Tables 1 and 2

$$\begin{bmatrix} H_1^{-1}F_1 \\ T'_1 \\ H_2^{-1}F_2\,0 \\ T'_2\,0 \end{bmatrix} = \begin{bmatrix} 78 & -59 & -16 & -12 \\ 87 & 29 & 38 & -10 \\ 81 & 43 & 32 & -22 \\ 55 & 55 & 47 & -42 \\ 72 & 50 & -48 & 06 \\ 45 & 46 & -57 & 51 \\ 40 & 45 & -72 & 35 \\ 69 & -36 & -32 & -54 \\ 70 & 45 & 42 & -36 \\ 50 & -42 & 27 & 71 \\ 16 & 99 & 00 & 00 \\ 76 & 65 & 00 & 00 \\ 98 & 21 & 00 & 00 \\ 97 & 25 & 00 & 00 \\ 89 & 45 & 00 & 00 \\ 100 & 06 & 00 & 00 \\ 100 & 00 & 00 & 00 \\ 00 & 100 & 00 & 00 \end{bmatrix}$$

$$C = (H_1^{-1}F_1)'(H_2^{-1}F_2) = \begin{bmatrix} 321 & 199 \\ 199 & 08 \\ 03 & 02 \\ -15 & -27 \end{bmatrix} \qquad G = CC' = \begin{bmatrix} 1424 & 653 & 13 & -102 \\ 653 & 396 & 07 & -32 \\ 13 & 07 & 00 & -01 \\ -102 & -32 & -01 & 10 \end{bmatrix}$$

$$W = \begin{bmatrix} 90 & 42 \\ 44 & -89 \\ 01 & 00 \\ -06 & -20 \end{bmatrix} \qquad M^2 = \begin{bmatrix} 1747 & 00 \\ 00 & 82 \end{bmatrix}$$

$$K' = C'WM^{-1}W' = \begin{bmatrix} 62 & 78 & 01 & 03 \\ 77 & -61 & 00 & -20 \end{bmatrix}$$

$$L_{12} = T'_1KT_2 = \begin{bmatrix} 61 & -04 \\ 13 & 86 \\ 78 & 34 \\ 01 & 49 \end{bmatrix} \qquad \begin{bmatrix} L_{11} & L_{12} \\ L_{21} & L_{22} \end{bmatrix} = \begin{bmatrix} 100 & 16 & 06 & 07 & 61 & -04 \\ 16 & 100 & 38 & 03 & 13 & 86 \\ 06 & 38 & 100 & 02 & 78 & 34 \\ 07 & 03 & 02 & 100 & 01 & 49 \\ 61 & 13 & 78 & 01 & 100 & 00 \\ -04 & 86 & 34 & 49 & 00 & 100 \end{bmatrix}$$

* Decimal points omitted. To conserve space the entire table has been rounded to two places.

is possibly easily fallen into. In psychological testing this pitfall is undoubtedly worse because of the additional difficulty of having physically different tests[1] purporting to measure the same thing: who is to say that one psychologist's test of *ego-strength* is another's—or perhaps yet another's test of *emotional stability*? Because of this consideration, pairing two variables from different studies may be somewhat dubious unless the two sets of observations are samples from the same population and, if psychological tests, the observations are on exactly the same test. It is suggested that, except for a highly restricted and thus perhaps sterile class of problems for which the pairing of common tests is absolutely indisputable, there is an element of judgment in the application of the method developed in this paper.

More technical, but closely related, is the consideration that pairing two observed variables may be inappropriate because we are not matching the original variables, but rather their common parts (projections onto the common factor space). This difficulty will arise particularly when one study is based upon more variables than the other, allowing the first to have more factors. The common part of a variable from the first study could then be substantially different from its mate in the second study because of the opportunity of its converting specificity to commonness. Some serious effort indicates that a completely satisfactory resolution of this difficulty is not easy. While it is not suggested that one be so compulsively careful as to require only the same variables in the two studies being related (so that $p = p_1 = p_2$), gross differences in p_1 and p_2 and particularly in q_1 and q_2 are to be viewed carefully to check the appropriateness of pairing the common parts of two variables. In the above example where $q_1 = 4$ and $q_2 = 2$, it is comforting to note that the two sets of communalities are approximately equal.

The above limitations regarding the present technique have been pursued at some length because it would appear that the present method is particularly susceptible to being applied indiscriminantly to yield a substantial amount of nonsense by thoughtless investigators. However, this criticism seems inevitably to apply to any proposed solution to the problem of relating factors between studies based upon different individuals.

[1] E.g., different items, or different time limits, or different scoring procedures, etc.

BIBLIOGRAPHY AND AUTHOR INDEX

Numbers in italic type at the end of each entry refer to the page on which the reference is quoted.

ACKERSON, L. *Children's Behavior Problems*. Chicago Univ. Press, Chicago. 1942. *257*

ADAMSON, M. *Familles des plantes*. Vincent, Paris. 1763. *8*

ADCOCK, C. J. A comparison of the concepts of Cattell and Eysenck. *Brit. J. educ. Psychol.*, 1965, **35**, 90–7. *135*

ALLPORT, G. *Personality*. Constable, London, 1937. *29*

ARDIS, J. A. and FRASER, B. Personality and perception: the constancy effect and introversion. *Brit. J. Psychol.*, 1957, **48**, 48–54. *131*

ÅSTRÖM, J. and OLANDER, F. MPI kliniskt bruk. *Nordisk Psykiatrisk Tidsskrift*, 1960, **14**, 300–11. *93*

BAKAN, P. Extraversion-introversion and improvement in an auditory vigilance task. *Brit. J. Psychol.*, 1960, **50**, 325–32. *132*

BARRATT, E. S. Factor analysis of some psychometric measures of impulsiveness and anxiety. *Psychol. Rep.*, 1965, **16**, 547–54. *149*

BARTHOLOMEW, A. A. and MARLEY, E. The temporal reliability of the Maudsley Personality Inventory. *J. ment. Sci.*, 1959, **105**, 238–40. *59*

BAYLEY, N. and SCHAEFER, E. *Maternal Behaviour and Personality Development. Proc. Res. Council on Child Develop. & Psychiatry*, Iowa. 1960. *260*

BECKER, W. C. The matching of behavior ratings and questionnaire personality factors. *Psychol. Bull.*, 1960, **57**, 201–12. *42*

BECKER, W. C. Developmental psychology. In *Ann. Rev. Psychol.* (Ed. P. Farnsworth). 1962. *255*

BENDIG, A. W. Extraversion, neuroticism and manifest anxiety. *J. consult. Psychol.*, 1957, **21**, 398. *133*

BENDIG, A. W. College norms for and concurrent validity of the Pittsburgh revision of the MPI *J. psychol. Stud.*, 1959, **11**, 12–17. *133*

BENDIG, A. W. Extraversion, neuroticism and student achievement in introductory psychology. *J. educ. Res.*, 1960, **53**, 263–7. *90, 133*

BENDIG, A. W. Three factor analyses of the scales of the Maudsley Personality Inventory. *J. psychol. Stud.*, 1960, 11, 104–7. *133*

BENDIG, A. W. Factor analyses of the Guilford Zimmerman Temperament Survey and the Maudsley Personality Inventory. *J. gen. Psychol.*, 1962, **67**, 21–6. *42*

BENDIG, A. W. The relation of temperament traits of social extraversion and emotionality to vocational interests. *J. gen. Psychol.*, 1963, **69**, 311–18. *133*

BENDIG, A. W. and HOFFMAN, J. L. Bills' index of adjustment and the MPI *Psychol. Rep.*, 1957, **3**, 507. *133*

BERNAL, J. D. Science in history. Watts, London: 1957. *3*

BLACKBURN, R. Denial-admission tendencies and the Maudsley Personality Inventory. *Brit. J. clin. Psychol.*, 1965, **4**, 241–3. *115*

BLOOM, B. *Stability and change in human characteristics.* Wiley, New York. 1964. *261*

BOLARDOS, A. C. Validation of the Maudsley Personality Inventory in Chile. *Brit. J. soc. clin. Psychol.*, 1964, **3**, 148. *94*

BRAUN, J. R. and GOMEZ, B. J. Effects of faking instructions in the Eysenck Personality Inventory. *Psychol. Rep.* 1966, **19**, 388–90. *114*

BRENGELMANN, J. C., and BRENGELMANN, L. Deutsche Validierung von Fragebogen. *Z. exp. angew. Psychol.*, 1960, **7**, 291–331. *95*

BURT, C. The general and specific factors underlying the primary emotions. *Brit. Ass. Ann. Rep.*, 1915, **84**, 694–6. *28*

BURT, C. The analysis of temperament. *Brit. J. med. Psychol.*, 1937, **17**, 158–88. *28*

BURT, C. The factorial analysis of emotional traits. *Character & Person.*, 1939, **7**, 238–54, 285–99. *28*

BURT, C. *The Factors of the Mind.* Univ. of London Press, London. 1940. *28, 37*

BURT, C. The factorial study of temperamental traits. *Brit. J. Psychol.*, Stat. Sect., 1948, **1**, 178–203. *28*

BURT, C. Factorial studies of personality and their bearing on the work of the teacher. *Brit. J. educ. Psychol.*, 1965, **35**, 368–78. *60, 262*

CAINE, T. M. and HOPE, K. Validation of the Maudsley Personality Inventory E Scale. *Brit. J. Psychol.*, 1964, **55**, 447–52. *85*

CALLARD, M., and GOODFELLOW, C. Neuroticism and extraversion in schoolboys as measured by the JMPI. *Brit. J. educ. Psychol.*, **32**, 241–50. *259*

CANESTRARI, R. Sindromi psichiatriche e rigidita percettiva. *Riv. exp. di Freniatria.*, 1957, **81**, 1–10. *131*

CARRIGAN, P. M. Extraversion-introversion as a dimension of personality: a reappraisal. *Psychol. Bull.*, 1960, **57**, 329–60. *141, 155*

CASTANEDA, A., MCCANDLESS, B. and PALERMO, D. The Children's Form of the MAS. *Child Develpm.*, 1956, 316–26. *264, 263*

CATTELL, R. B. Parallel proportional profiles and other principles for determining the choice of factors by rotation. *Psychometrika*, 1944, 9, 267–83. *334*

CATTELL, R. B. Personality and motivation structure and measurement. Harrap, London. 1957. *36*

CATTELL, R. B. Personality and Social Psychology. R. Knapp, San Diego, 1964. *254*

CATTELL, R. B. Higher-order factor structures: reticular vs hierarchical formulae for their interpretation. In C. Banks and P. Broadhurst (Eds.) *Essays in Honour of Sir Cyril Burt.* University of London Press, London, 1965. *168, 170, 199*

CATTELL, R. B., BLEWETT, D. B. and BELOFF, J. R. The inheritance of personality. *Amer. J. Human Genetics*, 1955, **7**, 122–4. *49*

CATTELL, R. B. and COAN, R. W. Personality dimensions in the questionnaire responses of six and seven-year-olds. *Brit. J. educ. Psychol.*, 1958, **28**, 232–42. *254*

CATTELL, R. B. and GRUEN, W. Primary personality factors in the questionnaire medium for children 11–14 years old. *Educ. Psychol. Measmt.*, 1954, **14**, 50–76. *254*

CATTELL, R. B. and PETERSON, D. R. Personality structure in four and five-year-olds in terms of objective tests. *J. clin. Psychol.*, 1959, **15**, 355–69. *254*

CATTELL, R. B. and WHITE, P. O. The use of higher-order personality factors in relation to variables. Unpublished manuscript. 1962. *199*

CHILD, D. Personality and social status. *Brit. J. soc. clin. Psychol.*, 1966, **5**, 196–199. *259*

CHILD, D. The relationship between introversion, extraversion, neuroticism and performance in school exams. *Brit. J. educ. Psychol.*, 1964, **34**, 187–96. *90*

CHOPPY, M. and EYSENCK, H. J. In: *Experiments with drugs*. H. J. Eysenck (Ed.) Pergamon Press, Oxford, 1963. *95*

CHOYNOVSKI, M. Inwentarz Osobowości. Pracovnia Psychometrydzna, Warsaw, Pau, 1966. *95*

CLARIDGE, G. In: Eysenck, H. J. (Ed.) *Experiments in Personality*. Routledge & Kegan Paul, London. 1960. *131*

COHEN, J. I. Physique, size and proportions. *Brit. J. med. Psychol.*, 1939–41, **18**, 323–7. *340*

COLLIER, R. and EMCH, M. Introversion-extraversion: the concepts and their clinical use. *Amer. J. Psychiat.*, 1938, **94**, 1045–75. *26*

COPPEN, A. and METCALFE, M. Effect of a depressive illness on MPI scores. *Brit. J. Psychiat.*, 1965, **111**, 236–9. *57, 58*

CORAH, N. L. Neuroticism and extraversion in the MMPI.: empirical validation and exploration. *Brit. J. soc. clin. Psychol.*, 1964, **3**, 168–74. *45*

CORCORAN, D. W. J. The relation between introversion and salivation. *Amer. J. Psychol.*, 1964, **77**, 298–300. *151*

COSTELLO, C. G. The control of visual imagery in mental disorders. *J. ment. Sci.*, 1957, **103**, 840–9. *132*

COSTELLO, C. and BRACHMAN, H. Cultural and sex differences in extraversion and neuroticism. *Brit. J. educ. Psychol.*, 1962, **32**, 254–7. *262*

CRANDALL, Y. C. A child's social desirability questionnaire. *J. consult. Psychol.*, 1965, **29**, 27–36. *263*

CRANDALL, V., CRANDALL, V. J. and KATKOVSKY, W. A children's social desirability questionnaire. *J. consult. Psychol.*, 1965, **29**, 27–36. *263*

CRONBACH, L. J., RAJARATNAM, NAGESWARI and GLESER, GOLDINE, C. Theory of generalization: a liberalization of reliability theory. *Brit. J. stat. Psychol.*, 1963, **16**, 137–63. *198*

CROOKES, T. G. and HUTT, S. J. Scores of psychiatric patients on the Maudsley Personality Inventory. *J. consult. Psychol.*, 1963, **27**, 243–7. *84*

CROWNE, D. P. and MARLOWE, D. A new scale of social desirability independent of psychology. *J. Consult. Psychol.*, 1960, **24**, 349–54. *115*

CROWNE, D. P., and MARLOWE, D. The approval motive: studies in evaluative dependence. Wiley & Sons, New York, 1964. *115*

CRUPLEY, A. J. and D'AOUST, B. R. Performance of Canadian school children on the JMPI. *Brit. J. educ. Psychol.*, 1965, **35**, 378–9. *259*

DAS, GITA. Standardization of the Maudsley Personality Inventory (MPI) on an Indian population. *J. psychol. Res.*, Madras, 1961, **5**, 7–9. *95*

DAVIS, D. G. Pilot error—some laboratory experiments. HMSO, London, 1948. *131*

DICKMAN, K. W. The factorial validity of a rating instrument. Unpublished doctoral dissertation. University of Illinois, 1960. *196*

DUFFY, E. Activation and behavior. J. Wiley, London, 1962. *50*

DUMMER, W. Persönlichkeitsveranderungen bei Tuberkulösen. *Zeit. für ärztliche Fortbildung*, 1959, **23**, 1466–73. *95*

DUMMER, W. Die Starke der neurotischen Tendenzen bei Tuberkulosen. *Schweizerische Zeit. fur Psychologie*. 1960, **19**, 152–72. *95*

DUMMER, W. Psychodiagnostische Probleme in der Klinischen Psychologie. *Psychol. u. Praxis*, 1964, **8**, 123–38. *95*

EDWARDS, A. L. The social desirability variable in personality assessment and research. Dryden., New York, 1957. *115*

EMMERICK, W. Continuity and stability in early social development. *Child Development*, 1964, **35**, 311–32. *260, 261*

ERIKSEN, C. W. Psychological defences and 'ego strength' in the recall of completed and incompleted tasks. *J. abnorm. soc. Psychol.*, 1954, **49**, 45–50. *116, 131*

ESCALONA, S. and HEIDER, G. *Prediction and Outcome*. 1959, Basic Books: New York. *260*

ESTABROOK, M. and SUMMER, R. Study habits and introversion and extraversion. *Psychol. Rep.*, 1966, **19**, 750. *90*

EYSENCK, H. J. Dimensions of personality. 1947, Routledge & Kegan Paul, London. Praeger, New York. *22, 36, 37, 40, 131, 167, 169, 328*

EYSENCK, H. J. Cyclothymia and schizothymia as a dimension of personality. I. Historical Review. *J. Personality*, 1950a, **19**, 123–53. *22*

EYSENCK, H. J. Criterion analysis—an application of the hypothetico-deductive method of factor analysis. *Psychol. Rev.*, 1950b, **57**, 38–53. *17, 151, 169*

EYSENCK, H. J. *The scientific study of personality*. 1952a, Routledge & Kegan Paul, London. *63, 64*

EYSENCK, H. J. Schizothymia-cyclothymia as a dimension of personality. II. Experimental. *J. Person.*, 1952b, **30**, 345–84. *17, 151*

EYSENCK, H. J. Fragebogen als essmittel der Persönlichkeit. *Z.f. exp. u. angew. Psychologie*, 1953, **1**, 291–335. *128*

EYSENCK, H. J. The logical basis of factor analysis. *Amer. Psychologist*, 1953, **8**, 105–14. *150*

EYSENCK, H. J. *Psychology of politics*. 1954, Routledge & Kegan Paul, London. *115, 131*

EYSENCK, H. J. Cortical inhibition, figural after-effect and the theory of personality. *J. abnorm. soc. Psychol.*, 1955, 51, 94–106. *131*

EYSENCK, H. J. The inheritance of extraversion—introversion. *Acta psychol.*, 1956a, **12**, 95–110. *49, 131*

EYSENCK, H. J. The questionnaire measurement of neuroticism and extraversion. *Rivista di Psicologia*, 1956b, **50**, 113–40. *27, 37, 65, 71, 122, 123*

EYSENCK, H. J. *The dynamics of anxiety and hysteria*. 1957. Routledge & Kegan Paul, London. *42, 50, 52, 122, 131, 169, 257*

EYSENCK, H. J. A short questionnaire for the measurement of the dimensions of personality. *J. appl. Psychol.*, 1958, 92, 14–17. *82*

EYSENCK, H. J. *Manual for the Maudsley Personality Inventory*. 1959a. University of London Press, London. Educ. & Indust. Testing Service, San Diego. *37, 60, 127*

EYSENCK, H. J. Personality and the estimation of time. *Percept. mot. Skills*, 1959b, **9**, 405–6. *131*

EYSENCK, H. J. Personality and verbal conditioning. *Psychol. Reports*, 1959c, **5**, 520. *131*

EYSENCK, H. J. Personality and problem solving. *Psychol. Reports*, 1959d, **5**, 592. *131*

EYSENCK, H. J. Der Maudsley Personality Inventory als Bestimmer der neurotischen Tendenz und Extraversion. *Ztschr. exp. angew. Psychol.*, 1959e, **6**, 167–90. *95*

EYSENCK, H. J. Classification and the problem of diagnosis. In: Eysenck, H.J. (Ed.) *Handbook of Abnormal Psychology*. 1960a. Pitman, London. *85, 86*

EYSENCK, H. J. *Behaviour therapy and the neuroses*. 1960b, Pergamon Press, Oxford. *56*

EYSENCK, H. J. (Ed.) *Experiments in Personality*. 2 vols. 1960c, Routledge & Kegan Paul, London. *52, 133*

EYSENCK, H. J. Der MPI test auf Deutsch. 1960d, Gottingen: Hogrefe. *95*

EYSENCK, H. J. *The structure of human personality*. 1960e, Routledge & Kegan Paul, London; John Wiley, New York. *18, 24, 25, 28, 29, 30, 32, 42, 47, 50, 86, 155, 169, 256, 259, 317*

EYSENCK, H. J. (Ed.) *Handbook of abnormal psychology*. 1960f, Pitman, London. *135*

EYSENCK, H. J. Response set, authoritarianism and personality questionnaires. 1962a, *Brit. J. soc. clin. Psychol.*, 1, 20–4. *103*

EYSENCK, H. J. Reminiscence, drive and personality. *Brit. J. soc. clin. Psychol.*, 1962b, **1**, 127–40. *131*

EYSENCK, H. J. (Ed.) *Experiments with drugs*. 1963a, Oxford, Pergamon Press. *52, 54*

EYSENCK, H. J. Biological basis of personality. *Nature*, London, 1963b, **199**, 1031–4. *52, 169, 254*

EYSENCK, H. J. Smoking, personality and psychosomatic disorders. *J. psychosom. Res.*, 1963c, **7**, 107–30. *129*

EYSENCK, H. J. (Ed.) *Experiments in behaviour therapy*, 1964a, Pergamon Press, Oxford. *56*

EYSENCK, H. J. *Crime and personality*, 1964b, Routledge & Kegan Paul. *40, 56, 114, 308*

EYSENCK, H. J. Biological factors in neurosis and crime, 1965a, *Scientia*. Dec. 1964, 1–11. *51, 52*

EYSENCK, H.J. Extraversion and the acquisition of eyeblink and GSR conditional responses. *Psychol. Bull.*, 1965b, **63**, 258–70. *51, 52, 131*

EYSENCK, H. J. *Smoking, health and personality*, 1965c, Weidenfeld, London. *129*

EYSENCK, H. J. *The biological basis of personality*, 1967, C. C. Thomas, Springfield. *xi, 19, 20, 49, 50, 52, 53, 89, 90, 131, 169, 315, 324, 331*

EYSENCK, H. J. and BROADHURST, P. L. Introduction: Experiments with animals. In: Eysenck, H. J. (Ed.) *Experiments in motivation*, 1964, Pergamon Press, Oxford. *50*

EYSENCK, H. J. and CLARIDGE, G. The position of hysterics and dysthymics in a two-dimensional framework of personality description. *J. abnorm. soc. Psychol.*, 1962, **69**, 46–55. *39*

EYSENCK, H. J. and EYSENCK, S. B. G. *Manual of the Eysenck Personality Inventory*, 1964, London, University of London Press. San Diego: Educ. Test. Service. *37, 142, 155*

EYSENCK, H. J. and EYSENCK, S. B. G. On the unitary nature of extraversion. Acta Psychol., 1967, **26**, 383–90. *150, 151*

EYSENCK, H. J. and RACHMAN, S. *Causes and cures of neurosis*, 1965, London: Routledge & Kegan Paul; San Diego: R. Knapp. *56, 58, 131, 262*

EYSENCK, H. J. and PRELL, D. The inheritance of neuroticism: an experimental study. *J. ment. Sci.*, 1951, **97**, 441–65. *49*

EYSENCK, S. B. G. Personality and pain assessment in childbirth of married and unmarried mothers. *J. ment. Sci.*, 1961, **107**, 417–30. *115, 129*

EYSENCK, S. B. G. The validity of a personality questionnaire as determined by the method of nominated groups. *Life Sciences*, 1962, **4**, 13–16, *118, 124*

EYSENCK, S. B. G. *Manual of the Junior Eysenck Personality Inventory*, London: Univ. of London Press, 1965a; San Diego: Educ. & Indust. Test. Service, 1965. *262, 263, 265*

EYSENCK, S. B. G. A new scale for personality measurements in children. *Brit. J. educ. Psychol.*, 1965, **35**, 362–7. *265*

EYSENCK, S. B. G. *Manual of the Eysenck-Withers Personality Inventory for subnormal subjects*, London: Univ. of London Press, 1966; San Diego: Educ. & Indust. Testing Service, 1966. *317*

EYSENCK, S. B. G. and EYSENCK, H. J. The validity of questionnaire and rating assessments of extraversion and introversion and their factorial stability. *Brit. J. Psychol.*, 1963a, **54**, 51–62. *121*

EYSENCK, S. B. G. and EYSENCK, H. J. An experimental investigation of 'desirability' response set in a personality questionnaire. *Life Sciences*, 1963b, **2**, 343–55. *108, 111, 113*

EYSENCK, S. B. G. and EYSENCK, H. J. Acquiescence response set in personality questionnaires. *Life Sciences*, 1963c, **2**, 144–7. *105*

EYSENCK, S. B. G. and EYSENCK, H. J. On the dual nature of extraversion. *Brit. J. soc. clin. Psychol.*, 1963d, **2**, 46–55. *141, 167*

EYSENCK, S. B. G. and EYSENCK, H. J. 'Acquiescence' response set in Personality inventory items. *Psychol. Rep.*, 1964a, **14**, 513–14. *107*

EYSENCK, S. B. G. and EYSENCK, H. J. The personality of judges as a factor in the validity of their judgment of extraversion-introversion. *Brit. J. soc. clin. Psychol.*, 1966, **3**, 141–4. *124*

FAHRENBERG, J. Eine statistische Analyse functioneller Beschwerden. *Zeit. f. Psychosom. Med.*, 1966, **12**, 78–85. *95*

FARLEY, F. H. Social desirability, extraversion and neuroticism: a learning analysis. *J. Psychol.*, 1966, **64**, 113–18. *115*

FARLEY, F. H. On the independence of extraversion and neuroticism. *J. clin. Psychol.*, 1967, 23, 154–6. *155*

FENZ, W. and EPSTEIN, S. Manifest anxiety: unifactorial or multifactorial composition? *Percept. & Motor Skills*, 1965, **20**, 273–80. *135*

FINE, B. J. Introversion-extraversion and motor vehicle driver behavior. *Percept. & Motor Skills*, 1963, **16**, 95–100. *115*

FITCH, W. M. and MARGOLIASH, E. Construction of phylogenetic trees. *Science*, 1967, **155**, No. 3760, 279–84. *8*

FOULDS, G. A. The ratio of general intellectual ability to vocabulary among psychoneurotics. *Int. J. soc. Psychiat.*, 1956, **1**, 5–12. *131*

FRASER, R. The incidence of neurosis among factory workers, London, HMSO, 1947. *27*

FRIES, M. and WOLF, P. Some hypotheses on the role of congenital activity in personality development. *Psychoanal. study Children*, 1954, **8**, 48–62. *260*

FURNEAUX, W. The psychologist and the University. Univ. Quart., 1962, 17, 33–47. *61, 90*

FURNEAUX, W. and GIBSON, H. B. A children's personality inventory designed to measure neuroticism and extraversion. *Brit. J. educ. Psychol.*, 1961, **31**, 204–207. *259, 265*

GARNETT, J. C. M. General ability, cleverness and purpose. *Brit. J. Psychol.*, 1918, **9**, 345–66. *28*

GIBSON, H. B. The Lie Scale of the MPI. *Acta Psychol.*, 1962, **20**, 18–23. *264*

GIBSON, H. B. A lie scale for the Junior MPI. *Brit. J. educ. Psychol.*, 1964, **34**, 120–4. *262, 263*

GOTTESMAN, I. I. Heritability of personality: a demonstration. *Psychol. Mon.*, 1963, Vol. 77, **9**, 572. *49*

GOUGH, H. G. *Manual for the California Psychological Inventory*. Palo Alto: 1957, Consult. Psychol. Press. *47*

GRAY, J. Pavlov's typology. Oxford, Pergamon Press, 1964. *50*

GROSS, O. Die cerebrale Sekundärfunktion. Leipzig: 1902. *19*

GROSS, O. Ueber psychologische Minderweirtigkeiten. Leipzig: 1909. *19*

GUILFORD, J. P. and GUILFORD, R. B. An analysis of the factors in a typical test of introversion-extraversion. *J. abnorm. soc. Psychol.*, 1939, **28**, 377–99. *29, 142, 148*

GUILFORD, J. P. and GUILFORD, R. B. Personality factors S, E and M and their measurement. *J. Psychol.*, 1934, **2**, 109–27. *29*

GUILFORD, J. P. and GUILFORD, R. B. Personality factors N and GD. *J. abnorm. soc. Psychol.*, 1939a, **34**, 239–48. *29*

GUILFORD, J. P. and GUILFORD, R. B. Personality factors D, R, T and A. *J. abnorm. soc. Psychol.*, 1939b, **34**, 21–6. *29*

GUILFORD, J. P. and ZIMMERMAN, W. S. Fourteen dimensional temperament factors. *Psychol. Mon.*, 1956, **70**, No. 10, 1–26. *30*

GUTMAN, G. M. A note on the MPI: age and sex differences in extraversion and neuroticism in a Canadian sample. *Brit. J. soc. clin. Psychol.*, 1966, **5**, 128–9. *90*

GUTTMAN, L. Some necessary conditions for common-factor analysis. *Psychometrika*, 1954, **19**, 149–61. *159, 336*

GUTTMAN, L. Multiple group methods for common-factor analysis; their basis, computation, and interpretation. *Psychometrika*, 1952, **17**, 209–22. *336*

HALLWORTH, H. J. The dimensions of personality among children of school age. *Brit. J. Math. Stat. Psychol.*, 1965, **18**, 45–56. *257*

HAMMOND, W. H. An application of Burt's multiple general factor analysis to the delineation of physical types. *Man*, 1942, 4–11. *340*

HANNAH, F., STORM, T. and CAIRD, W. K. Sex differences and relationships among neuroticism, extraversion and expressed fears. *Percept. motor. Skills.*, 1965, **20**, 1214–16. *89*

HARBAUGH, J. W. and DEMIRMEN, F. American limestone. Kansas Geological Survey Special Dip. Pub. 15, 1964. *98*

HARMAN, H. *Modern Factor Aanlysis.* University of Chicago Press, Chicago. 1960. *197, 198, 337*

HARPER, R. and BARON, M. Factorial analysis of rheological measurements on cheese. *Nature*, 1948, **162**, 821. *97*

HARPER, R. and BARON, M. The application of factor analysis to tests on cheese. *Brit. J. appl. Physics.*, 1951, **2**, 35–41. *97*

HARPER, R., KENT, A. J. and SCOTT BLAIR, G.W. The application of multiple factor analysis to industrial test data. *Brit. J. appl. physics*, 1950, **1**, 1–6. *97*

HEILBRUNN, A. B. Social-learning theory, social desirability and the MMPI. *Psychol. Bull.*, 1964, **61**, 377–87. *115*

HENDRICKSON, A. E. and WHITE, P. O. Promax: a quick method for rotation to oblique simple structure. *Brit. J. stat. Psychol.*, 1964, **17**, 65–70. *152, 158, 196*

HENDRICKSON, A. E. and WHITE, P. O. A method for the rotation of higher order factors. *Brit. J. Math. Stat. Psychol.*, 1966, **19**, 97–103. *152, 158, 196, 197*

HENNIG, W. Gründzuge einer Theorie der phylogenetischen Systematik. Deutscher Zentralverlag, Berlin, 1957. *8*

HEWITT, L. and JENKINS, R. *Fundamental patterns of Maladjustment.* D. H. Green, Illinois, 1946. *255*

HEYMANS, G. and WIERSMA, E. Beiträge zur apeziellen Psychologie auf Grund. einer Massenuntersuchung. *Ztschr. f. Psych.*, 1909, **51**, 1–72. *25*

HILDEBRAND, H. P. A factorial study of introversion-extraversion. *Brit. J. Psychol.*, 1958, **49**, 1–11. *40*

HIMMELWEIT, H. T. The intelligence vocabulary ratio as a measure of temperament. *J. Person.*, 1945, 14, 93–105. *131*

HIMMELWEIT, H. T. Speed and accuracy of work as related to temperament. *Brit. J. Psychol.*, 1946, **36**, 132–44. *131*

HIMMELWEIT, H. T. A comparative study of the level of aspiration of normal and neurotic persons. *Brit. J. Psychol.*, 1947, **37**, 41–59. *131*

HIMMELWEIT, H. T. A factorial study of 'Children's Behaviour Problems'. Unpublished mss., 1952. *257, 262*

HOLIZINGER, K. J. and HARMAN, H. H. Factor Analysis. Chicago: Chicago Univ. Press, 1941. *334*

INGHAM, J. G. Changes in MPI scores in neurotic patients: a three-year follow up. *Brit. J. Psychiat.*, 1966, **112**, 931–9. *59*

INGHAM, J. G. and ROBINSON, J. D. Personality in the diagnosis of hysteria. *Brit. J. Psychol.*, 1964, **55**, 276–84. *39, 85*

IWAWAKI, S., SUJIYAMA, Y. and NANRI, R. Maudsley Personality Inventory. Japanese Manual, 1964. *91*

JACKSON, P. L. and MESSICK, S. A note on 'ethnocentrism' and acquiescent response set. *J. abnorm. soc. Psychol.*, 1957, **54**, 132–4. *103*

JALOTA, S. Some data on the Maudsley Personality Inventory in Punjabi. *Brit. J. soc. clin. Psychol.*, 1964, **3**, 148. *94*

JALOTA, S. A study of Maudsley Personality Inventory (in Hindi and Punjabi versions.) *Indian Psychol. Rev.*, 1965, **2**, 29–30. *94*

JANET, P. *L'etat mental des hysteriques*, Paris: Rueff, 1894. *22*

JANET, P. *Les obsessions et la psychasthenie*, Paris: Alcan, 1903. *22*

JENSEN, A. The Maudsley Personality Inventory. *Acta Psychol.*, 1958, **19**, 314–25. *84*

JENSEN, A. The Maudsley Personality Inventory. In: Buros Mental Measurement Yearbook, 6th Edition, New Jersey: Gryphon Press, 1965. *84*

JUNG, C. *Psychologische Typen*. Zurich: Rascher, 1921. *20, 24*

KAGAN, J. and MOSS, H. *Birth to Maturity*, Wiley, New York, 1962. *260*

KAISER, H. F. The varimax method of factor analysis. Unpublished doctoral dissertation. University of California, 1956. *196*

KAISER. H. F. The varimax criterion for analytic rotation in factor analysis. *Psychometrika*, 1958, **23**, 187–200. *158, 196*

KAISER, H. F. Relating factors between studies based upon different individuals. Unpublished manuscript, 1960. Printed with additions as Appendix. *270*

KAISER, H. F. Image analysis. In: *Problems in Measuring Change*. Ed. C. W. Harris, Wisconsin, University of Wisconsin Press, 1962. *196*

KAISER, H. F. Psychometric approaches to factor analysis. In: *Invitational Conference on Testing Problems*, Educational Testing Service, 1964. *195*

KAISER, H. F. The varimax criterion for analytic rotation in factor analysis. *Psychometrika*, 1958, 23, 187–200. *335*

KAISER, H. F. and CAFFREY, J. Alpha factor analysis. *Psychometrika*, 1965, 30, 1–14. *335*

KASSEBAUM, C. G., COUCH, A. S. and SLATER, P. The factorial dimensions of the MMPI. *J. consult. Psychol.*, 1959, **23**, 226–36. *42*

KATKIN, E. S. The Marlowe-Crowne social desirability scale: independent of psychopathology? *Psychol. Rep.*, 1964, **15**, 703--6. *115*

KEAR-COLWELL, J. J. Studies of the IPAT neuroticism scale (NSQ) *Brit. J. soc. clin. Psychol.*, 1965, **4**, 214–23. *135*

KELVIN, R. P., LUCAS, C. J. and OJHA, A. B. The relation between personality, mental health and academic performance in University students. *Brit. J. soc. clin. Psychol.*, 1965, **4**, 244–53. *61, 90*

KLINE, P. Extraversion, neuroticism and academic performance among Ghanian university students. *Brit. J. educ. Psychol.*, 1966, **36**, 91–2. *90*

KNAPP, R. R. *Manual of the Eysenck Personality Inventory*, San Diego: Educ. & Indust. Testing Service, 1960. *84, 89*

KNAPP, R. R. Relationship of a measure of self-actualization to neuroticism and extraversion. *J. consult. Psychol.*, 1965, **29**, 168–72. *133*

KNOWLES, J. B. The temporal stability of MPI scores in normal and psychiatric populations. *J. consult. Psychol.*, 1960, **24**, 278. *59*

KNOWLES, J. B. and KREITMAN, N. The Eysenck Personality Inventory: some considerations. *Brit. J. Psychiat*, 1965, **111**, 755–60. *59*

KOCH, H. L. A factor analysis of some measures of the behaviour of pre-school children, *J. genet. Psychol.*, 1942, **27**, 257–87. *257*

KREITMAN, N. The patient's spouse. *Brit. J. Psychiat.*, 1964, **110**, 159–73. *61, 62*

KRETSCHMER, E. *Körperbau und Charakter*, Springer, Berlin. 1948. *22*

LAWLEY, D. N. and MAXWELL, A. E. *Factor analysis as a statistical method*, Butterworth, London, 1963. *18*

LEVINSON, F. and MEYER, V. Personality changes in relation to psychiatric status following orbital cortex undercutting. *Brit. J. Psychiat.*, 1965, **111**, 207–18. *59*

LEVITT, E. Ecological differences in performance on the CMAS. *Psychol. Rep.*, 1957, **3**, 281–6. *263*

LIERNERT, G. A. and REISSE, H. Ein korrelations analytischer Beitrag zur genetischen Determination des Neurotizismus. *Psychol. Beitr.*, 1961, **7**, 121–130. *49*

LINN, R. L. Use of random normal deviates to determine the number of factors to extract in factor analysis. Unpublished Master's thesis. University of Illinois, 1964. Quoted by Peterson, 1965. *42*

LINDSLEY, D. B. The reticular system and perceptual discrimination. In: H. H. Jasper *et al.* (Eds.) *Reticular Formation of the brain*, London: Churchill, 1957. *54*

LOVELL, C. A study of the factor structure of thirteen personality variables. *Educ. psychol. Measmt.*, 1945, **5**, 335–50. *30*

LUCAS, C. J., KELVIN, R. P. and OJHA, A. B. The psychological health of the pre-medical student. *Brit. J. Psychiat.*, 1965, 111, 473–8. *61, 90*

LUNNEBORG, P. Relations among social desirability, achievement and anxiety measures. *Child Developm.*, 1964, **35**, 169–82. *263*

LUNNEBORG, P. and LUNNEBORG, C. The relationship of social desirability to other test-taking attitudes in children. *J. clin. Psychol.*, 1964, **20**, 473–7. *263*

LYNN, R. Personality changes with ageing. *Beh. Res. Ther.*, 1964, **1**, 343–9. *90*

MACCACARO, P. A. La misura delle informazione contennta nei criteria di classificazione. *Ann. Microbiol.*, 1958, **8**, 231–9. *7*

MCCLAY, C. N. A factor analysis of personality traits to underlie character education. *J. educ. Psychol.*, 1936, **27**, 375–87. *28*

MCEVEDY, C. P., GRIFFITHS, A. and HALL, T. Two school epidemics. *Brit. med. J.*, 1966, *26th Nov.*, 1300–2. *86*

MACFARLANE, J. W., ALLEN, L. and HONZIK, M. *A developmental study of the behaviour problems of normal children.* Berkeley: Univ. California Press, 1954. *260, 261, 263, 313*

MCGUIRE, P. J., MOWBRAY, R. M. and VALLANCE, R. C. The Maudsley Personality Inventory used with psychiatric inpatients. *Brit. J. Psychol.*, 1963, **54**, 157–66. *85*

MCNEMAR, Q. Lost our intelligence? Why? *Amer. Psychologist*, 1964, **19**, 871–882. *324*

MALMO, R. B. Activation: a neurophysiological dimension. *Psychol. Rev.*, 1959, **66**, 367–80. *52*

MANN, R. D. The relationship between personality characteristics and individual performance in small groups. Unpublished doctoral thesis. Univ. of Michigan. (Quoted by Carrigan, 1960). *142*

MARTIN, J. Acquiescence—measurement and theory. *Brit. J. soc. clin. Psychol.*, 1964, **3**, 216–25. *102*

MARTIN, J. and STANLEY, R. Social desirability and the Maudsley Personality Inventory. *Acta Psychol.*, 1963, **21**, 260–4. *115*

MASLOW, A. *Motivation and personality.* Harper, New York, 1954. *133*

MERRIAM, D. F. Geology and the computer. *New Scientist*, 1965, 513–15. *97*

MEYER, A. E. and GOLLE, R. Zur Validierung des Brengelmann—Fragebogens E—N—NR an klinischen Stichproben. *Diagnostica*, 1966, **12**, 93–105. *95*

MICHAEL, C. M., MORRIS, D. P., and SAROKER, E. Follow-up studies of shy withdrawn children. II: Relative incidence of schizophrenia. *Amer. J. Orthopsychiat.*, 1957, **27**, 331–7. *292*

MICHEL, L. Untersuchungen mit dem MMQ an normaler Erwachsenen. *Diagnostica*, 1960, **6**, 136–51. *95*

MILLER, D. R. Responses of psychiatric patients to threat of failure. *J. abnorm. soc. Psychol.*, 1951, **46**, 378–87. *131*

MITCHELL, K., and PIERCE-JONES, J. A factor analysis of Gaugh's California Personality Inventory. *J. consult. Psychol.*, 1960, **24**, 453–6. *257*

MOSS, P. D. and MCEVEDY, C. P. An epidemic of overbreathing among schoolgirls. *Brit. Med. J.*, 1966, 26th Nov. 1295–1300. *85, 86*

MOTT, B. W. Measuring 'hardness'. *New Scientist*, 1964, **386**, 103–105. *98, 100, 101*

MOWRER, O. H. *Learning theory and personality dynamics.* Ronald, New York, 1950. *56*

NAMECHE, G., WARING, M. and RICKS, D. Early indications of outcome in schizophrenia. *J. nerv. ment. Dis.*, 1964, **139**, 232–40. *292*

NICHOLS, R. C. and SCHNELL, R. R. Factor scales for the California Psychological Inventory. *J. consult. Psychol.*, 1963, **27**, 228–35. *47*

NORTH, R. D. An analysis of the personality dimensions of introversion-extraversion. *J. Person.*, 1949, **17**, 352–367. *30*

ORNE, M. T. On the social psychology of the psychological experiment. *Amer. Psychologist*, 1962, **17**, 776–83. *112*

ORTEGA, J. M. On Sturm sequences for tri-diagonal matrices. *J. Assn. Computing Machinery*, 1960, **7**, 260–3. *196*

PETERSON, D. R. Age generality of personality factors derived from ratings. *Educ. Psychol. Measurement*, 1960, **20**, 461–74. *168, 254*

PETERSON, D. R. Scope and generality of verbally defined personality factors. *Psychol. Rev.*, 1965, **72**, 48–59. *42*

PETRIE, A. Regression and suggestibility as related to temperament. *J. Person.*, 1958, **10**, 445–8. *132*

PORTER, R. B. and CATTELL, R. B. Handbook for the IPAT Children's Personality Questionnaire. Inst. Person. Ability Testing, 1960. *265*

QUAY, H. C. and QUAY, L. C. Behavior problems in early adolescence. *Child Developm.*, 1965, **36**, 215–20. *257*

RAFI, A. A. The Maudsley Personality Inventory: a cross-cultural study. *Brit. J. soc. clin. Psychol.*, 1965, **4**, 266–68. *95*

RAO, S. A note on the investigation of the MPI with different occupational groups in India. *Brit. J. soc. clin. Psychol.*, 1966, **5**, 274–5. *94*

REES, L. Constitutional factors and abnormal behaviour. In: Eysenck, H. J. (Ed.) *Handbook of Abnormal Psychology*, Pitman, London, 1960. *24*

REMANE, A. *Die Grundlagen des natürlichen Systems.* Leipzig: Akadem. Verlagsges, Geest & Portig, 1956. *8*

REYBURN, M. A. and TAYLOR, J. G. Some aspects of personality. *Brit. J. Psychol.*, 1939, **30**, 151–65. *28*

RICHARDS, T. W. and SIMONS, M. P. *The Fels Child Behavior Scales*, 1941. *Genet. Psychol. Monogr.*, **24**, 259–309. *253*

RIE, H. An exploratory study of the CMAS Lie Scale. *Child Develpm.*, 1963, **34**, 1003–17. *262*

ROBACK, H. *Psychology of character*, 1931. Kegan Paul, London. *11*

ROBINS, L. N. Deviant children grow up. Baltimore: Williams & Wilkins, 1966. *292*

ROHRACHER, H. *Kleine Charakterkunde*. Urban & Schwarzenberg, Wien, 1965. *15*

RORER, L. The great response-style myth. *Psychol. Bull.*, 1965, **63**, 129–56. *117*

SARASON, S. B. *et al. Anxiety in elementary school children*, 1960, Wiley, New York. *263*

SAVAGE, R. D. Personality factors and academic performance. *Brit. J. educ. Psychol.*, 1962, **32**, 251–3. *61, 90*

SAVAGE, R. D. Electro-cerebral activity, extraversion and neuroticism. *Brit. J. Psychiat.*, 1964, **110**, 98–100. *53*

SAVAGE, R. D. Personality factors and academic attainment in junior school children. *Brit. J. educ. Psychol.*, 1966, **36**, 91–2. *90*

SCHAEFFER, E. Converging conceptual models for maternal behavior and for child behavior. In *Parental Attitudes & Child Behavior*. (Ed. J. Glidewell.) 1961. Thomas Springfield. *253*

SCHAEFFER, E. and BAYLEY, N. Consistency of maternal behaviour from infancy to pre-adolescence, 1960. *J. abn. soc. Psychol.*, **61**, 1–6. *260*

SCHAEFFER, E. S., DROPPLEMAN, L. F. and KALVERBOER, A. F. Development of a classroom behaviour checklist. 1966. Unpublished MS. *258*

SCOTT BLAIR, G. W. Some aspects of the search for invariants. *Brit. J. Phil. Sci.*, 1951a, **1**, 1–16. *98*

SCOTT BLAIR, G. W. Possible industrial application of factor analysis. *Oil*, 1951b, **1**, 14–16. *97*

SHAGASS, C. A measurable neurophysiological factor of psychiatric significance. *EEG clin. Neurophysiol.*, 1957. **9**, 101–8. *131*

SHAGASS, C. and SCHWARTZ, M. Neurophysiological dysfunction associated with some psychiatric disorders. *Psychiat. Res. Rep.*, 1963, **17**, 130–52. *53, 55*

SHAGASS, C. and KERENYI, A. The 'sleep' threshold. A simple form of sedation threshold for clinical use. *Canad. Psychiat. J.*, 1958, **1**, 101–9. *23*

SHAW, G. K. and HARE, E. H. The Maudsley Personality Inventory (short form). Distribution of scores and test-retest reliability in an urban population. *Brit. J. Psychiat,*. 1965, **111**, 226–35. *89*

SHIELDS, J. *Monozygotic twins*. 1962. University Press, Oxford. *49*

SHOSTROM, E. L. A test for the measurement of self-actualization. *Educ. psychol. Measmt.*, 1964, **24**, 207–18. *133*

SHOSTROM, E. L. *The Personal Orientation Inventory*. San Diego: Educ. Indust. Testing Service, 1964. *133*

SIBOUR, F., AMERIO, P. and IONA, G. Adattamento italiano del MPI. *Bull. di Psychol. applic.*, 1963, 59–66, 11–22. *92*

SIMPSON, G. G. Principles of animal taxonomy, 1961. Columbia Univ. Press, New York. *8*

SINGER, C. *A history of biology*, 1959. Abelard-Schuman, London. *6*

SINGH, U. P. Another study of a Hindi version of the Maudsley Personality Inventory (MPI). *Indian Psychol. Rev.*, 1966, **3**, 57–8. *94*

SINHA, S. Occupational choice of extravert and introvert penal students. *Indian Psychol. Rev.*, 1966, **3**, 59–62. *94*

SLATER, P. E. Parent behaviour and the personality of the child, 1961. Unpublished MSS. referred to by Schaeffer. *257*

SLATER, E. and SLATER, P. A heuristic theory of neurosis. *J. Nurol. Neurosurg. Psychiat.*, 1944, **7**, 49–55, *61*

SNEATH, P. H. S. The constructional taxonomic groups. In: *Microbiol Classifications*, pp. 282–332. Cambridge University Press, 1962. *7*

SNEATH, P. H. S. Computers in bacterial classification. *Advancement of Science*, 1964, 572–82. *9, 10*

SOKAL, R. R. and SNEATH, P. H. S. *Principles of numerical taxonomy*. W. H. Freeman & Co., London, 1963. *7, 10, 18*

SOUEIF, M. I. Extreme response sets as a measure of intolerance of ambiguity. *Brit. J. Psychol.*, 1958, **49**, 329–34. *105*

SOUEIF, M. I. Response sets, neuroticism and extraversion: a factorial study. *Acta Psychol.*, 1965, **24**, 29–40. *105*

SPARROW, N. H. and ROSS, J. The dual nature of extraversion: a replication. *Austral J. Psychol.*, 1964, **16**, 214–18. *142*

SPEARMAN, C. *Abilities of man*. Macmillan, London, 1927. *28, 323*

SPRINGOB, H. K. and STREUNING, E. L. A factor analysis of the California Personality Inventory. *J. counsel. Psychol.*, 1964, **11**, 137–9. *257*

SUGIYAMA, Y. and NANRI, R. Maudsley Personality Inventory in Japan: a preliminary report. *J. Pre-med. Course, Sapporr Med. Coll.*, 1964, **5**, 1–26. *91*

SYMONDS, C. P. The human response to flying stress: neurosis in flying personnel. *Brit. med. J.*, 1943, **2**, 703–6. *60*

TAFT, R. and COVENTRY, J. Neuroticism, extraversion and the perception of the vertical. *J. abnorm. soc. Psychol.*, 1958, **56**, 139–41. *132*

TUSS, W. Maudsley Personality Inventory, neurosis and stress. *Psychol. Rep.*, 1964, **14**, 461–2. *60*

TERMAN, L. and TYLER, L. Psychological sex differences. In *Manual of Child Psychology* (Ed. Carmichael, L.). Wiley, New York, 1954. *262*

THOMAS, A., CHESS, S., BIRCH, H. and HERTZIG, M. A longitudinal study of primary reaction patterns in children. *Comp. Psychiatry*, 1960, **1**, 103–12. *260*

THOMAS, A. *et al.* Behavioural Individuality in Early Childhood. London: Univ. London Press, 1964. *260*

THURSTONE, L. L. Factor analysis of body types. *Psychometrika*, 1946, **11**, 15–21. *340*

THURSTONE, L. L. Multiple factor analysis. Chicago: Chicago Univ. Press, 1947. *337*

TUCKER, L. R. A method for synthesis of factor analysis studies. Dept. of the Army, A.G.O. Personnel Res. Sec., Rep. No. 984, 1951. *334*

TUDDENHAM, R. The constancy of personality ratings over two decades. *Genetic. Psychol. Monogr.*, 1959, **60**, 3–30. *261*

TURLAND, D. The measurement of anxiety in children. Unpublished Dissertation. Univ. London, 1965. *262*

VENABLES, P. H. Change in motor response with increase and decrease in task difficulty in normal, industrial, and psychiatric patient subjects. *Brit. J. Psychol.*, 1955, **46**, 101–10. *131*

VERNON, P. E. The assessment of psychological qualities by verbal methods. HMSO, London, 1938. *26*

VERNON, P. E. Ability factors and environmental influences. *Amer. Psychologist*, 1965, **20**, 723–33. *324*

VERSCHUER, O. Beitrage zum Konstitutions problem aus den Ergebnissen der Zwillingsforschung. *Z. menschl. Vererb.-u-Konstitutions Lehre*, 1952, **30**, 646–61. *24*

VINGOE, F. J. Validity of the Eysenck extraversion scale as determined by self-ratings in normals. *Brit. J. Soc. clin. Psychol.*, 1966, **5**, 89–91. *128*

VOGEL, F. and WENDT, G. G. Zwillings-untersuchung über die Erblichkeit einiger anthropologischer Masse and Konstitutions. indices. *Z. menschl. Vererb.-Konstit.-Lehre*, 1956, **33**, 425–46. *24*

WALTER, W. G., ALDRIDGE, V. J., COOPER, R., MCCALLUM, C. and COHEN, J. L'origine et la signification de l' d'expectative. *Rev. Neurol.*, 1964, **111**, 257–273. *54*

WARNCKE, P. and FAHRENBERG, J. Eine Item analyse am ENNR,—Fragebogen von Brengelmann und Brengelmann. *Diagnostica*, 1966, **12**, 105–15. *95*

WEBB, E. Character and intelligence. *Brit. J. Psychol. Monogr. 28*

WHITE, P. O., A Fortran program for relating factors (Abstract). *Brit. J. Math. Stat. Psychol.*, 1966, **19**, 282. *198*

WILDE, G. J. S. Inheritance of personality traits. *Acta Psychol.*, 1964, **22**, 37–51. *49*

WILKINSON, J. H. The calculation of eigenvectors for co-diagonal matrices. *Computer J.*, 1958, **1**, 90–6. *196*

WILKINSON, J. H. Householder's method for the solution of the Algebraic eigenproblem. *Computer J.*, 1960, **3**, 23–7. *196*

WILLIAMS, W. T. and LAMBERT, J. M. Multivariate methods in plant ecology. Association-analysis in plant communities. *J. Ecol.*, 1959, **47**, 83–101. *7*

WOLPE, J. *Psychotherapy by reciprocal inhibition.* Univ. Press, Stanford, 1958. *56*

WRETMARK, G., ÅSTRÖM, J. and OLANDER, F. MPI—resultat vid endogen depression fore och efter behandlig. *Nordisk Psychiatriker Tidsskrift*, 1961, **15**, 448–54. *59*

WRIGLEY, C. and NEUHAUS, J. O. The matching of two sets of factors. Paper presented to A.P.A., San Francisco, Sept. 1955. *166*

WUNDT, W. Frundzüge der physiologischen Psychologie, 5th Ed. Vol. 3. Leipzig, W. Engelmann, 1903. *14*

SUBJECT INDEX

www.ingramcontent.com/pod-product-compliance
Ingram Content Group UK Ltd.
Pitfield, Milton Keynes, MK11 3LW, UK
UKHW021955180926
475701UK00003B/33
* 9 7 8 0 4 1 5 8 4 0 9 1 0 *